THE HIDDEN WISDOM IN THE HOLY BIBLE

BY THE SAME AUTHOR

THE ANGELIC HIERARCHY

Fairies at Work and at Play.   English and French Editions.
The Kingdom of Faerie.
The Brotherhood of Angels and of Men.
Be Ye Perfect.
The Angelic Hosts.
Man, The Triune God.
The Supreme Splendour.
The Coming of the Angels.
The Kingdom of the Gods.   Illustrated.

THE SPIRITUAL LIFE

First Steps on the Path.
Thus Have I Heard.
Meditations on the Occult Life.   English and German Editions.
The Pathway to Perfection.
Destiny.
The Inner Side of Church Worship.

THE POWERS LATENT IN MAN

The Science of Seership.   English and French Editions.
Clairvoyance and the Serpent Fire.
Occult Powers in Nature and in Man.
Man's Supersensory and Spiritual Powers.
The Soul's Awakening.   American Edition.
A Yoga of Light.   English, Danish and Spanish Editions.
Some Experiments in Four-Dimensional Vision.
The Psychedelic and the Yogic Pathways to Reality.

THE THEOSOPHICAL PHILOSOPHY OF LIFE

Theosophy Answers Some Problems of Life.
Vital Questions Answered.
Reincarnation, Fact or Fallacy ?   Indian, American and Arabic Editions.
The Miracle of Birth.
The Spiritual Significance of Motherhood.   English and Spanish Editions.
Through the Gateway of Death.
The Seven Human Temperaments.
The School of the Wisdom Lecture Notes, Vol. I (Revised Edition).

INTERPRETATIONS OF SCRIPTURES AND MYTHS

The Hidden Wisdom in the Holy Bible, Vols. I and II. Indian and American Editions.
The Hidden Wisdom in the Christian Scriptures.   American Edition.
The Divine Wisdom in the Christian Scriptures.   New Zealand Edition.

HEALTH

Health and the Spiritual Life.
New Light on the Problem of Disease.
An Occult View of Health and Disease.
The Way to Perfect Health, Spiritual, Mental and Physical.
Radiant Health From a Meat-free Dietary.
Plant Foods, Their Nutrient Properties.
The Case for Vegetarianism.

ANIMAL WELFARE

An Animal's Bill of Rights.
The Humanitarian Cause, Its Extreme Urgency.
Animals and Men, The Ideal Relationship.
Authentic Stories of Intelligence in Animals.
Our Friends the Animals.

THE HIDDEN WISDOM IN THE HOLY BIBLE

BY

GEOFFREY HODSON

VOLUME III

THE GOLDEN GRAIN OF WISDOM IN THE BOOK OF GENESIS

(*Genesis*—Chapters Twenty-five to Fifty)

1971

THE THEOSOPHICAL PUBLISHING HOUSE

ADYAR,   MADRAS 20,   INDIA

Wheaton, Ill., 60187, U.S.A.   London, England

SBN 0— 7229—7493— 0

ISBN 0—8356— 7493—2

PRINTED IN INDIA

At Hoe & Co., 31, Stringers Street, Madras-1.

DEDICATION

This work is dedicated to Philo Judaeus,
the great Alexandrian Sage.

ACKNOWLEDGEMENTS

I acknowledge with gratitude the help in the production of this work received from my wife, Sandra, who at dictation wrote out all the original interpretations of Biblical passages, and is continuing to do so; my valued literary assistant, Myra G. Fraser; and my friend Nell K. Griffith, who for many years cared for my domestic needs and assisted in typing from the first draft of the manuscript. I also wish to express my heartfelt thanks to my valued friends, Roma and Brian Dunningham, for their unfailing support, their provision of stenographers, and their generous help throughout many years of collaboration.

All quotations and references in this work are taken from the King James version of the Holy Bible.

THE HIDDEN WISDOM AND WHY IT IS CONCEALED

THE greatest degree of power which occult science can bestow is to be derived from knowledge of the unity and interaction between the Macrocosm and the microcosm, the Universe and man. "The mystery of the earthly and mortal man is after the mystery of the supernal and immortal One", wrote Eliphas Levi. Lao Tzu also expresses this truth in his words: "The Universe is a man on a large scale."

The whole Universe with all its parts, from the highest plane down to physical Nature, is regarded as being interlocked, interwoven to make a single whole—one body, one organism, one power, one life, one consciousness, all cyclically evolving under one law. The "organs" or parts of the Macrocosm, though apparently separated in space and plane of manifestation, are in fact harmoniously interrelated, intercommunicative and continually interactive.

According to this revelation of occult philosophy the Zodiac, the Galaxies and their component Systems, and the planets with their kingdoms and planes of Nature, elements, Orders of Beings, radiating forces, colours and notes, are not only parts of a co-ordinated whole and in "correspondence" or mutual resonance with each other, but also—which is of profound significance—have their representations within man himself. This system of correspondences is in operation throughout the whole of the microcosm, from the Monad to the mortal flesh, including the parts of the mechanism of consciousness, or vehicles and their *chakras*,[1] by means of which the Spirit of man is manifested throughout his whole nature, varying in degree according to the stage of evolutionary development. *The human being who discovers this truth could enter the power aspect of the Universe and tap any one of these forces. He would then become endowed with almost irresistible influence over both Nature and his fellow men.*

H. P. Blavatsky writes:[2]

"The danger was that such doctrines as the Planetary Chain, or the seven Races, at once give a clue to the seven-fold nature of man, for each

---

[1] Chakra (sk.)—A vortex or "wheel" in the etheric and superphysical bodies of man. q.v. *The Chakras*, C. W. Leadbeater, and Glossary to this Vol.

[2] q.v. *The Secret Doctrine*, Vol. I (Adyar Ed.), pp. 57–58, H. P. Blavatsky.

principle is correlated to a plane, a planet, and a race, and the human principles are, on every plane, correlated to seven-fold occult forces, those of the higher planes being of tremendous power. So that any septenary division at once gives a clue to tremendous occult powers, the abuse of which would cause incalculable evil to humanity; a clue which is, perhaps, no clue to the present generation—especially to Westerns, protected as they are by their very blindness and ignorant materialistic disbelief in the occult—but a clue which would, nevertheless, have been very real in the early centuries of the Christian era to people fully convinced of the reality of Occultism, and entering a cycle of degradation which made them rife for abuse of occult powers and sorcery of the worst description.

" The documents were concealed, it is true, but the knowledge itself and its actual existence was never made a secret of by the Hierophants of the Temples, wherein the MYSTERIES have ever been made a discipline and stimulus to virtue. This is very old news, and was repeatedly made known by the great Adepts, from Pythagoras and Plato down to the Neo-Platonists. It was the new religion of the Nazarenes that wrought a change—for the worse—in the policy of centuries. "

In his *Yoga Aphorisms*, Patanjali writes:[1]

" The (successful) ascetic acquires complete control over the elements by concentrating his mind upon the five classes of properties in the manifested universe; as, first, those of gross or phenomenal character; second, those of form; third, those of subtle quality; fourth, those susceptible of distinction as to light, action, and inertia; fifth, those having influence in their various degrees for the production of fruits through their effects upon the mind.

" From the acquirement of such power over the elements there results to the ascetic various perfections, to wit, the power to project his inner-self into the smallest atom, to expand his inner-self to the size of the largest body, to render his material body light or heavy at will, to give indefinite extension to his astral body or its separate members, to exercise an irresist-ible will upon the minds of others, to obtain the highest excellence of the material body, and the ability to preserve such excellence when obtained.

" Excellence of the material body consists in colour, loveliness of form, strength, and density. "

This knowledge of the relationship between Universe and man is also part of the secret wisdom of Kabbalism, which teaches that in the chain of being everything is magically contained within everything else. Where one stands, there stand all the worlds; what is below is above, what is inside is outside and, in addition, ceaselessly acts upon all that exists. Kabbalism thus stresses the inter-relationship of all worlds and levels of being according to exact, though unfathomable, laws. All things, moreover, possess their infinite depths which from every point may be contemplated.

[1] q.v. *Yoga Aphorisms of Patanjali*, Book III, slokas 45–47.

Such is a portion of the wisdom which is said to be implicit—and, indeed, revealed under the veil of allegory—in the *Torah*.[1] This sacred book is for Kabbalists a revelation of the laws of the Cosmos and the intimate and active relationship between the parts of the Cosmos, the Spirit of man, and the vehicles in which that Spirit is incarnate. The history of the Jews forms a foundation upon which the edifice of this secret knowledge is erected. Modern Christian theology would seem to have fallen into the grievous error of regarding the sub-structure of metaphoricised history as a total and divinely inspired revelation of God's guidance to mankind.

The mission of the Jews and the purpose of the erudite and Initiated authors of the Bible was, I submit, to preserve, to enunciate and to deliver to humanity this wisdom of the Chaldeo-Hebrew Sanctuaries. It is for this and not for lordship over the Earth, I suggest, that the Jews were a chosen people, a nation or " kingdom of priests "[2] in very truth. May not their tribulations have partly arisen from their neglect of this mission, and may not their earthly wanderings and centuries of physical homelessness have followed upon and resulted from their departure from their true Sanctuary and the real purpose for which they were " chosen "? Happily the light still shines, however deeply veiled, in and through this marvellous record of the Scriptures of the Hebrew Race.

The task of unveiling the hidden truth demands some knowledge of Cosmogenesis, of the emanation of the Universe from the Absolute, the finite from the Infinite, and of the successive cycles, major and minor, of involution and evolution. In addition, both knowledge of the Symbolical Language, its purposes, methods and classical symbols, and the faculty of analysing and interpreting historical metaphors, are necessary to open the casket containing the treasures of concealed wisdom—the Holy Bible itself.

" Where the Word found that things done according to the history could be adapted to these mystical senses, he made use of them, concealing from the multitude the deeper meaning; but where in the narrative of the development of super-sensual things, there did not follow the performance of those certain events which were already indicated by the mystical meaning, the Scripture interwove in the history the account of some event that did not take place, sometimes what could not have happened; sometimes what could, but did not. "

> *De Principiis,* Origen, Christian philosopher and Biblical scholar, famed for his teaching at Alexandria and Caesarea (C. 185—C. 254 A.D.)

---

[1] *Torah* (Heb.): " Law ". The *Pentateuch* or Law of Moses.
[2] *Ex.* 19:16.

" What man of sense will agree with the statement that the first, second and third days in which the *evening* is named and the *morning*, were without sun, moon and stars, and the first day without a heaven ? What man is found such an idiot as to suppose that God planted trees in Paradise, in Eden, like a husbandman, and planted therein the tree of life, perceptible to the eyes and senses, which gave life to the eater thereof; and another tree which gave to the eater thereof a knowledge of good and evil ? I believe that every man must hold these things for images, under which the hidden sense lies concealed. "

> Origen: Huet., *Origeniana*, 167, Franck, p. 142.

" Every time that you find in our books a tale the reality of which seems impossible, a story which is repugnant to both reason and common sense, then be sure that the tale contains a profound allegory veiling a deeply mysterious truth; and the greater the absurdity of the letter, the deeper the wisdom of the spirit. "

> Moses Maimonedes, Jewish theologian, historian, Talmudist, philosopher and physician (1135-1205 A.D.).

" Woe....to the man who sees in the Thorah, i.e., Law, only simple recitals and ordinary words ! Because, if in truth it only contained these, we would even today be able to compose a Thorah much more worthy of admiration.... The recitals of the Thorah are the vestments of the Thorah. Woe to him who takes this garment for the Thorah itself !.... There are some foolish people who, seeing a man covered with a beautiful garment, carry their regard no further, and take the garment for the body, whilst there exists a still more precious thing, which is the soul.... The Wise, the servitors of the Supreme King, those who inhabit the heights of Sinai, are occupied only with the soul, which is the basis of all the rest, which is Thorah itself; and in the future time they will be prepared to contemplate the Soul of that soul (i.e., the Deity) which breathes in the Thorah. "

> *Zohar* III, 152b. (Soncino Ed. Vol. V, p. 211).

" Rabbi Simeon said: ' If a man looks upon the Torah as merely a book presenting narratives and everyday matters, alas for him ! Such a Torah, one treating with everyday concerns, and indeed a more excellent one, we too, even we, could compile. More than that, in the possession of the rulers of the world there are books of even greater merit, and these we could emulate if we wished to compile some such Torah. But the Torah, in all of its words, holds supernal truths and sublime secrets.' "

> *Zohar* III, 152a.

" Like unto a beautiful woman hidden in the interior of a palace who, when her friend and beloved passes by, opens for a moment a secret window, and is only seen by him: then again retires and disappears for a long time; so the doctrine shows herself only to the elect, but also not even to these always in the same manner. In the beginning, deeply veiled, she only beckons to the one passing, with her hand; it simply depends (on himself) if in his understanding he perceives this gentle hint. Later she approaches him somewhat nearer, and whispers to him a few words, but her countenance is still hidden in the thick veil, which his glances cannot penetrate. Still later she converses with him, her countenance covered with a thinner veil. After he has accustomed himself to her society, she finally shows herself to him face to face, and entrusts him with the innermost secrets of her heart (Sod). "

Zohar II, 99a (Soncino Ed. Vol. III, p. 301).

THE TORAH

" Jewish mystics are at one in giving a mystical interpretation to the Torah; the Torah is to them a living organism animated by a secret life which streams and pulsates below the crust of its literal meaning; every one of the innumerable strata of this hidden region corresponds to a new and profound meaning of the Torah. The Torah, in other words, does not consist merely of chapters, phrases and words; rather is it to be regarded as the living incarnation of the divine wisdom which eternally sends out new rays of light. It is not merely the historical law of the Chosen People, although it is that too; it is rather the cosmic law of the Universe, as God's wisdom conceived it. Each configuration of letters in it, whether it makes sense in human speech or not, symbolizes some aspect of God's creative power which is active in the Universe. "

Major Trends in Jewish Mysticism, Gershom G. Scholem.

A SYMBOL

" A symbol retains its original form and its original content. It does not become, so to speak, an empty shell into which another content is poured; in itself, through its own existence, it makes another reality transparent which cannot appear in any other form. A mystical symbol is an expressible representation of something which lies beyond the sphere of expression and communication, something which comes from a sphere whose face is, as it were, turned inward and away from us. A hidden and inexpressible reality finds its expression in the symbol. The symbol 'signifies' nothing and communicates nothing, but makes something transparent which is beyond all expression. Where deeper insight into the structure of the

allegory uncovers fresh layers of meaning, the symbol is intuitively understood all at once—or not at all. The symbol in which the life of the Creator
and that of creation become one, is—to use Creuzer's words—'a beam of
light which, from the dark and abysmal depths of existence and cognition,
falls into our eye and penetrates our whole being.' It is a 'momentary
totality' which is perceived intuitively in a mystical *now*—the dimension of
time proper to the symbol. "

Major Trends in Jewish Mysticism, Gershom G. Scholem.

" The shell, the white, and the yolk form the perfect egg. The shell
protects the white and the yolk, and the yolk feeds upon the white; and when
the white has vanished, the yolk, in the form of the fledged bird, breaks
through the shell and presently soars into the air. Thus does the static
become the dynamic, the material the spiritual.

" If the shell is the exoteric principle and the yolk the esoteric, what
then is the white ? The white is the food of the second, the accumulated
wisdom of the world centring round the mystery of growth, which each
single individual must absorb before he can break the shell. The transmutation of the white, by the yolk, into the fledgling is the secret of secrets of the entire Qabalistic philosophy. "

The Secret Wisdom of the Qabalah, J.F.C. Fuller.

" Having taken the Upanishad as the bow, as the great weapon, let
him place on it the arrow, sharpened by devotion ! Then having drawn it
with a thought directed to that which is, hit the mark, O Friend, namely,
that which is Indestructible ! Om[1] is the bow, the Self is the arrow,
Brahman[2] is called the aim. It is to be hit by a man who is not thought-
less, and then as the arrow becomes one with the target, he will become
one with Brahman. "

Mundaka Upanishad, II.

" Know the Self as the Lord of the chariot and the body as, verily, the
chariot; know the intellect as the charioteer and the mind as, verily, the
reins.

" The senses, they say, are the horses; the objects of sense the paths (they
range over); (the self) associated with the body, the senses and the mind—
wise men declare—is the enjoyer.

[1] OM or AUM: The name of the triple Deity. A syllable of affirmation, invocation
and divine benediction.

[2] Brahman (Sk.): The impersonal, supreme and incognisable Principle of the Universe,
from the Essence of which all emanates and into which all returns.

" He who has no understanding, whose mind is always unrestrained, his senses are out of control, as wicked horses are for a charioteer.

" He, however, who has understanding, whose mind is always restrained, his senses are under control, as good horses are for a charioteer.

" He, however, who has no understanding, who has no control over his mind (and is) ever impure, reaches not that goal but comes back into mundane life.

" He, however, who has understanding, who has control over his mind and (is) ever pure, reaches that goal from which he is not born again.

" He who has the understanding for the driver of the chariot and controls the rein of his mind, he reaches the end of the journey, that supreme abode of the all-pervading. "

> The *Kathopanishad* 1-3-3- to 1-3-9, Dr. Radhakrishnan's translation from *The Principal Upanishads*.

" And the disciples came, and said unto him, Why speakest thou unto them in parables ?

" He answered and said unto them, Because it is given unto you to know the mysteries of the kingdom of heaven, but to them it is not given....

" But blessed are your eyes, for they see: and your ears, for they hear."

> *Matt.* 13:10, 11 and 16.

" Whoso eateth my flesh, and drinketh my blood, hath eternal life; and I will raise him up at the last day.

" For my flesh is meat indeed, and my blood is drink indeed.

" He that eateth my flesh, and drinketh my blood, dwelleth in me, and I in him.

" As the living Father hath sent me, and I live by the Father: so he that eateth me, even he shall live by me. "

> *Jn.* 6:54-57.

" The early Genesis accounts of the creation, Adam and Eve and the Fall of man contain truths of a religious nature which do not depend for their validity upon historical or scientific confirmation. Such accounts expressed truths of a timeless nature. They were myths, teaching spiritual truths by allegories. "

> From a Sermon by The Most Reverend Dr. Frank Woods, Anglican Archbishop of Melbourne, speaking at St. Paul's Cathedral on the 18th February, 1961.

The same may well be said of the narratives of the temptation of Christ in the wilderness *Luke* 4:1-13 and His agony in the Garden of Gethsemane.

These do not include references to the presence of a third person. Under normal circumstances, however, this would be necessary if record were to be made, preserved and introduced into the Gospel narrative.

Support for a symbolical reading of the Bible also is gained by comparison of the promises of perpetual prosperity and divine protection[1] made by God to Abram and his successors with the subsequent defeats by invaders, exile under their commands in Babylon and Egypt, and the destruction of the Temples of King Solomon and King David. To these misfortunes may be added the later fate of the Hebrew people, including their miseries and homelessness since the *Diaspora* and the holocaust of German Jews under Nazi rule. This marked divergence between divine assurances and promises on the one hand and what actually happened on the other provides strong grounds for a non-literal reading of the Scriptures.

The alternative of a total rejection of the *Pentateuch* as being, on the surface, unworthy of serious consideration would, I suggest, involve the loss of invaluable treasures of wisdom which are revealed when the veil of allegory and symbol is removed.

GEOFFREY HODSON.

---

[1] *Gen.* 17: 2, 5–8; 26: 2–5; 28: 13–16.

AUTHOR'S PREFACE TO VOLUME III

My purpose in making a close examination of the *Book of Genesis* has been to seek for, and when found to reveal, the deeply hidden wisdom —the Theosophy of the Hebrews —known as Kabbalism, which teaches that ". ...The Torah[1] (law), in all of its words, holds supernal truths and sublime secrets. "[2] This wisdom is thought to have been concealed by the authors beneath the supposedly historical account of the founding and early life of the Hebrew nation. Mankind today is, I believe, in pressing need of this wisdom, and the Old Testament is by no means to be regarded as merely a collection of ancient writings but also, and far more, as a very important source of guidance to mankind.

" What kind of guidance ? ", it may here be asked. That which is applicable to almost every aspect of human life, I suggest. If, for example, diseases are rampant throughout the world, and many of them can at present be neither prevented nor eradicated, this is due to lack of knowledge of the way to perfect health. If, despite World Organisations for peace, wars continue to threaten the security of nations and to bring death and destruction to tens of thousands, again it is because of lack of knowledge of the true pathway to peace.

If the economic life of nations and individuals, and the conduct of their industries and trade, bring wealth to a restricted number and poverty and unemployment to many, with tendencies to warfare between them, then the cause of this inequity is lack of knowledge of the laws governing harmony between nations and individuals. If human morals are declining and the institutions of home life and marriage, with their special provision of loving care and wise training for children, are failing in the fulfilment of their functions, then again the fault is due to lack of knowledge, especially concerning the true nature of man and the purposes for which he exists.

This greatly needed information, I submit, is to be found in the Scriptures of mankind, and *notably* in those of the earlier Hebrew people who gave to the world such writings as the *Pentateuch*. What, then, may this important knowledge be ? It consists, I suggest, of the plan, the mode and the ultimate outworking of those procedures of Nature whereby Universes, Solar Systems,

---

[1] *Torah*—The *Pentateuch* or first five Books of the Bible.
[2] *Zohar* III, 152-a.

planets and their inhabitants, have come into existence. Such enlightenment, when possessed and applied to life, provides guidance for every individual human being, directing him in the conduct of his own life, in his relationships with his fellows, and in that willing and intelligent participation in Nature's grand design which is the true assurance of health and happiness.

This ancient wisdom is clearly more needed today than ever before throughout world history. Those who feel moved to seek such knowledge, both for their own illumination and happiness and in order to be effective servants of their fellows, may find themselves prepared to travel with me through portions of the allegorical and symbolical literature of the wise and well-informed authors of World Scriptures.

In the following pages I offer the fruits of my own attempts to delve into the Books of the Old Testament in search of truths that I believe to be timeless and which, if applied, could profoundly affect those living in this present war-threatened, and actually war-torn, age in which man possesses the power of self-extermination.

GEOFFREY HODSON

Auckland,
New Zealand.
1969.

CONTENTS

PART FOUR

THE LIFE OF JOSEPH AS A MYSTERY DRAMA

APPENDIX

Part One of this Volume consists mainly of extracts from Part One of Volume II of this work, with slight alterations and some additions. The extracts are here repeated and the additions included as an introduction to the subject of symbolism, a guide to the hidden meaning of the Scriptures of the world, and an exposition of the methods of interpretation employed.

PART ONE

THE LANGUAGE OF ALLEGORY AND SYMBOL

PROBLEMS ARISING FROM A LITERAL READING OF THE BIBLE, AND SOME SOLUTIONS

SINCE comprehension and appreciation of the esoteric teachings contained in the Bible depend upon a knowledge of the Sacred Language, a fuller and more detailed exposition of this particular category of literature must now be given. At the outset of this task it is recognised that to those who have hitherto regarded the Bible either as divinely inspired or solely as a record of historical events, the idea that it was written in allegory and symbol in order to transmit universal truths to mankind may seem strange and unacceptable.

As the subject is profound, impartial examination and progressive study are essential to its comprehension. Apart from the parables of Jesus, the language of analogy, dramatic allegory and symbol is for many people a little known art form. Vocabulary, grammar and composition must, in consequence, be mastered before the transmitted ideas can be perceived and wholly understood. Time, too, is always required in order to become accustomed to an unfamiliar method of presentation and hitherto unknown aspects of truth.

In the field of the Arts, for example, some training in appreciation is necessary in order to enjoy and understand a great picture and receive the artist's message. Preparation and experience are needed in order to open the eyes and prepare the mind. This is true also of music. With the exception of those passages—perhaps the slow Movements—which can be readily enjoyed, a Symphony can at first hearing be difficult to comprehend. As one begins to perceive its significance, however, the whole work takes on an added meaning and evokes a new delight. To a child a wonderful jewel is but a glittering toy. He will choose just as readily any shining thing, however tawdry and cheap. A connoisseur in precious stones, on the other hand, sees in them depths of beauty hidden from others, comprehends and appreciates both the stones themselves and, when they have been cut and set, the craftsmanship of the jeweller.

The Language of Allegory and Symbol may, in its turn, be regarded as an art form. One therefore similarly needs to acquire by practice the ability to appreciate the many and varied ways in which it is used and to discover the underlying meanings. Without such preparation allegories and symbols may be wrongly regarded as unnecessary obstructions and their interpretations as arbitrary, or at best far-fetched. Since profound truths are conveyed and spiritual experience, knowledge and power can be obtained by the successful unveiling of the symbolism of the Bible, the student's preparations must in their turn be not only intellectual, but to some extent spiritual as well. Indeed, such preparations almost assume the character of a vigil.[1]

THE VEIL OF ALLEGORY

Whilst many of the incidents in the Bible are doubtless founded upon fact, nevertheless great wisdom and light are also to be discovered within the Scriptural record of historical and pseudo-historical events. When, however, statements are made which could not possibly be true, three courses of action present themselves to the reader. He can accept such statements unthinkingly, in blind faith; he may discard them as unworthy of serious consideration; or he may study them carefully in search of possible under-meanings and revelations of hitherto hidden truths. Incidents such as the passage of three days and nights and the appearance on Earth of vegetation before creation of the sun,[2] and the action of Joshua in making the sun and moon stand still,[3] cannot possibly have occurred. Here, as in so many other places, the Bible piles the incredible upon the impossible. If, however, the intention was not to record supposed astronomical facts or historical events alone, but also to reveal abstract, universal and mystical truths and to give guidance in finding and treading " The way of holiness ",[4] and if night, sun and moon are but concrete symbols of abstract ideas, then the outwardly meaningless narrative may reveal inward truth and light. Before that truth and light can be perceived, the veil of allegory must be lifted and the symbols interpreted; for, as already stated, partly in order to render abstract ideas comprehensible by expressing them in concrete form and also to safeguard the truth and reveal it when the time should be ripe, the Teachers of ancient days deliberately concealed within allegory and symbol the deep, hidden wisdom of which they had become possessed.

TIME AS MIRROR OF ETERNITY

My own studies have led me to the conviction that the authors of the Scriptures saw eternal truths mirrored in events in time. For them, illumined as they were, every material happening was alight with spiritual

---

[1] Vigil—a devotional watching, as in the days of Chivalry for example.
[2] Gen. 1:13-16.
[3] Joshua 10:12-14. q.v. Vol. I of this work, Pt. I, Ch. V.
[4] Is. 35:8.

significance. They knew the outer world for what it is—the shadow of a great reality. They could say with Elizabeth Browning: " Earth's crammed with heaven, and every common bush afire with God ", and with her would add " but only he who sees, takes off his shoes. "[1] Their records of the history of the Universe and of the Earth—the Scriptures of the world—portray far more than events in time; they reveal in concrete and therefore more readily understandable form eternal truths, ultimate reality, universal occurrences. Sometimes the real was more visible to them than the shadow, whereupon history took second place. At other times the record of physical events predominated.

This concept of the purposes and the method of the ancient writers is advanced in this work as being the key to the mystical study of the Bible, the clue to the discovery of the inexhaustible treasures of wisdom and truth concealed within the casket of exoteric Scriptures. The spiritual Teachers of long ago, by using historical events as well as allegories and symbols, proved themselves able to overcome the limitations of time. They recorded history in such a way as to reveal to readers of their own and later times the deeper truths of life. Even thousands of years after their death such Teachers are able to give to mankind both guidance along the pathway of spiritual illumination and solutions of many human problems. Nevertheless a measure of concealment from the profane of truths which they desired to impart to the worthy, and to the worthy alone, was forced upon the ancient writers. The motive for such concealment, as earlier stated, was to safeguard both the individual and the race from the dangers of premature discovery and possible misuse of knowledge which could bestow theurgic and thaumaturgic powers. Thus, I believe, came into existence the inspired portions of the legends, Mythologies and Scriptures of the world, many of which are pregnant with spiritual and occult ideas, and therefore with power.

SOME DIFFICULTIES CREATED BY A DEAD-LETTER READING OF THE BIBLE

In addition to its value as a vehicle for hidden wisdom, the Sacred Language can prove helpful in solving otherwise insoluble Biblical problems. Whilst belief or faith in the possibility of super-natural intervention makes some Scriptural statements credible, nevertheless physical laws and astronomical facts cannot be changed. Indeed some " miracles "[2] do strain almost

---

[1] Poems of Elizabeth M. Browning, Bk. 7.

[2] *Miracle*. Occult science does not admit of the possibility of any action by any being, however lofty, which contravenes the laws of Nature. Whilst phenomena on the physical plane may appear to be miraculous, they are nevertheless the product of the action of the trained will applied according to the laws and processes of Nature appertaining to the superphysical as well as the physical worlds.

beyond reasonable limits one's power to believe in them. The hydrostatic pressure invisibly exerted in dividing and holding back on either side of a dry bed the waters of the Red Sea[1] and the river Jordan[2] would have involved the use of almost incalculable energy. Nevertheless, if direct theurgic action is presumed to have occurred then these "miracles" would not have been entirely impossible.

The heliocentric system, however, cannot be altered. The sun is at the centre of our Solar System, for which it is the source of light. Planets throughout their orbital motion round the sun revolve on their axes, and without that rotation there could be no alternation of day and night. In spite of this, in the First Chapter of *Genesis* it is plainly stated that, having brought light into existence and divided it from the darkness, "....God called the light Day, and the darkness he called Night. And the evening and the morning were the first day. "[3] An even greater anomaly is added by the further statement that three days and three nights had passed before the sun, moon and stars were created.[4] Such events would have been astronomical impossibilities. Indeed, they could not have happened in the sequence affirmed in *Genesis*.

" SUN, STAND THOU STILL UPON GIBEON "[5]

Since the rotation of the Earth causes night and day and the sun does not move round the Earth, Joshua could not by any means have lengthened the day by making the sun and the moon stand still. The prolongation of day or of night by the arrest of the motion of either sun or Earth (the moon would not be directly concerned in such a procedure) is a total impossibility; for if the Earth had suddenly stopped turning no human being would have lived to record the event. Every movable object on Earth, including the oceans and the atmosphere, would have continued the normally rotating movement and thus travelled towards the East faster than the speed of sound. Read literally, therefore, the narrative is totally unacceptable.

The story of the Tower of Babel—especially verses six, seven, eight and nine of the Eleventh Chapter of the *Book of Genesis*—would seem to imply that the Supreme Deity is deliberately and callously responsible for the major sufferings of mankind, rooted as they are in the human delusion of self-separated individuality and consequent egoism. According to verses six and seven many evil works by man upon man, including individual

---

[1] *Ex.* 14:21:31.
[2] *Joshua* 3:14-17.
[3] *Gen.* 1:5.
[4] *Gen.* 1:16.
[5] *Joshua* 10:12-14. q.v. Vol. I, Pt. I, Ch. V.

and organised crime and the waging of innumerable wars, arose and still arise from the two supposed actions of a personal Deity. The first of these was to confound human language so that men could no longer understand one another's speech, and the second to scatter humanity abroad upon the face of the Earth. Such supposed divine actions can, indeed, legitimately be regarded as having been major causes of those human errors which are born of individualism and self-separateness. The attribution to the Supreme Deity of motive and conduct so detrimental to humanity as to make difficult for long ages the attainment of harmonious human relationships between groups, nations and races of men upon earth, is totally unacceptable to the thoughtful and reverent mind. The study of the Bible less as literal history, and far more as a revelation of fundamental truths by means of historical metaphors and allegories, thus receives strong support from the passages concerning the building of the Tower of Babel.

" AND IT REPENTED THE LORD THAT HE HAD MADE MAN ON THE EARTH "[1]

The story of Noah and his Ark also presents many grave stumbling blocks. One of these consists of the ideas implicit in verses five, six and seven of the Sixth Chapter of *Genesis*—namely that an all-loving Father in Heaven could conceive of an imperfect plan which failed, experience wrath at that failure, and with insensate cruelty decide to destroy " both man, and beast, and the creeping thing, and the fowls of the air....[2] " In their literal reading these statements are an affront to reason. The assertion that God could be guilty of such actions and could later be moved to make the promises not to " again curse the ground any more for man's sake "[3] or " again smite any more every thing living "[3], is either an erroneous ascription to the Deity of conduct of which even man would not be guilty or else a deliberately constructed blind for the concealment of an underlying truth.

The concept is inconceivable, surely, that there could be in existence a single, extra-cosmic, personal God Who could Himself fail as a Creator of mankind and then be destructively wrathful at the wicked conduct of a human race which was solely and entirely the product of His own creation. Such a conclusion is strengthened by the divine proclamation that man was made in God's image.[4] It is similarly inconceivable that the conjoined

[1] *Gen.* 6:6.
[2] *Gen.* 6:7.
[3] *Gen.* 8:21.
[4] *Gen.* 1:26, 27.

Elohim [1] (wrongly translated as " God " in *Genesis*) could be capable either of imperfection in the planning and fulfilment of Their cosmic functions or of wrath at a failure which was solely attributable to Themselves. In the presence of such affronts to human reason, acceptance of the concept of the use of a special category of literature known as the Sacred Language is surely preferable to either blind faith or total unbelief in the Bible on account of the inconsistencies and errors which a literal reading of certain passages could bring about. Such rejection of the whole Bible with its inspiring message of the existence of a Supreme Being as the Directive Intelligence in Nature, on account of incredibilities and impossibilities found in certain passages, would indeed be a mistake. The great scientist, Dr. Albert Einstein, evidently felt himself to be under no necessity to make this rejection, for he wrote: " That deeply emotional conviction of the presence of a *superior reasoning power* (italics mine, G.H.) which is revealed in the incomprehensible Universe, forms my idea of God. " Nevertheless, the actions attributed to the Deity in the Biblical verses under review certainly do not present Him in the guise of a " superior reasoning power ".

To return to the Biblical account of the Flood; if, as is indicated in several places, the Flood covered the whole of the Earth and if all the water in the atmosphere had thus been added to all the water in the oceans, the mixture would have been indistinguishable from sea water. In such case no animal that lived on Earth would have been able to drink it and survive, whilst in addition all land plants would have died. In consequence the inhabitants of the Ark would have had neither food nor water to sustain them after they landed.

Furthermore, Noah would have found it extremely difficult, if not impossible, to collect animals and fowls from the four quarters of the Globe and persuade them to begin travelling towards the Middle East from many parts of the Earth—arctic, temperate, subtropical and tropical. In many cases this would have demanded the crossing of thousands of miles of ocean. Indeed, such incredibilities need hardly be mentioned save to underscore the absurdities into which a literal reading of the Bible can lead one, and to

---

[1] *Elohim* (Heb.)—" Gods ". A sevenfold power of Godhead; the male-female Hierarchies of creative Intelligences or Potencies through which the Divine produces the manifested Universe; the unity of the powers, the attributes and the creative activities of the Supreme Being. " Elohim " is a plural name, the singular form of the word being " Eloha ", i.e. a " god ". " Elohim ", therefore, literally means " gods ", personifications of divine attributes or the forces at work in Nature. Admittedly the " Elohim " are also conceived as a Unity in the sense that They all work together as One, expressing One Will, One Purpose, One Harmony. Thus Their activities are regarded as the manifestation of the Eternal One, the Absolute. " Elohim " might therefore be explained as " the Unity of gods " or " the Activities of the Eternal One ", namely God omnipresent and revealing Himself outwardly in creative activity. (Partly paraphrased from *The Unknown God*, P. J. Mayers).

provide support for the approach advanced in this work. The sloth, for instance, which travels with extreme slowness—hence its name, perhaps—would have needed to begin its journey long before the onset of the Flood in order to reach the Ark in time. This would also apply to other animals travelling from great distances. In addition, the task of housing and feeding so large a number of animals throughout forty days and forty nights would have presented grave, if not insurmountable, difficulties.

The Scriptural account (A.V.) distinctly states that the animals and fowls were so collected together as to ensure that on arrival at the Ark in readiness to enter it they could be arranged in a certain numerical order. Their classification into categories, and the number of each class to be selected, is indicated thus: " Of every clean beast thou shalt take to thee by sevens, the male and his female: and of beasts that are not clean by two, the male and his female. Of fowls also of the air by sevens, the male and the female...." [1]

The Revised Version, however, corrects the seeming anomalies by translating from the original as follows:

2. *Take with you seven pairs of all clean animals, the male and his mate; and a pair of the animals that are not clean, the male and his mate;*

3. *And seven pairs of the birds of the air also, male and female, to keep their kind alive upon the face of all the earth.* (R. V.)

The possible underlying significane of the story itself and of the numbers introduced into it will be considered at the appropriate place in the text.[2]

" NOW THE LORD HAD PREPARED A GREAT FISH TO SWALLOW UP JONAH " [3]

If the Prophet Jonah—to take another example—had actually spent three days and three nights in the stomach of a large mammal like a whale, digestive secretions and processes would have rendered it most unlikely that he could have remained alive and unaffected throughout such a period. This story in its literal reading must in its turn be regarded as extremely doubtful, if not totally false. The possibility of the existence of a recondite meaning (as, for example, a description of the procedures of Initiation or spiritual regeneration as suggested by the symbol of the fish[4]) will be considered in a later Volume of this work.

[1] *Gen. 7:2, 3.*
[2] See Pts. II and IV of this Volume.
[3] *Jonah 1:17.*
[4] q.v. *Lecture Notes of the School of the Wisdom,* Vol II pp. 11, 12,

" AND THEY (LOT'S DAUGHTERS) MADE THEIR FATHER DRINK WINE THAT NIGHT...." [1]

Incredibility apart, the obscenity—such as the drunkenness of Lot and the incest (admittedly unconscious on his part) with his two daughters[2]—and the attribution to the Supreme Deity of the human weakness of anger, jealousy and bloodthirstiness as evinced by " His " encouragement of the Israelites to attack and massacre the animals, men, women and children of other tribes[3]—these, with all the other Biblical incongruities, must in their turn be repellant to thoughtful and sensitive minds.

A great many other passages could be referred to, including verses seventeen and eighteen of the Nineteenth Chapter of *Revelation*, which read as follows:

> 17. *And I saw an angel standing in the sun; and he cried with a loud voice, saying to all the fowls that fly in the midst of heaven, Come and gather yourselves together unto the supper of the great God;*
> 18. *That ye may eat the flesh of kings, and the flesh of captains, and the flesh of mighty men, and the flesh of horses, and of them that sit on them, and the flesh of all men, both free and bond, both small and great.*

Such verses as these are so obviously unacceptable in their literal reading that they scarcely call for comment. The idea therefore receives support that, as already noted, the authors of certain passages in the Bible were spiritually instructed men writing for the following purposes, amongst others[4]: to present abstract ideas in concrete and so more readily comprehensible form; to describe phases of human evolution and their associated psychological and mystical experiences ; to evoke wonder and so initiate enquiry; to preserve for posterity profound spiritual, occult and potentially power-bestowing truths; to conceal from the profane knowledge which could be misused, even whilst revealing it to the trustworthy servant of humanity who possesses the keys of interpretation.

In the Sermon on the Mount Christ would seem to have given in allegorical form strict instructions that this last purpose more especially should be followed, for He is reported to have said:

> *Give not that which is holy unto the dogs, neither cast ye your pearls before swine, lest they trample them under their feet, and turn again and rend you.*[5]

In order to achieve these objectives—if further repetition be pardoned—the authors of the inspired portions of the world's Scriptures, allegories

---

[1] *Gen.* 19:35.

[2] *Gen.* 19:30-38.

[3] e.g. *Ex.* 23:23-33, *De.* 9:14; *Nu.* 31:1-17; *Ezk.* 25:16, 17 etc.

[4] Here repeated verbatim from Ch. I of this Volume because of their importance to the central theme of this work.

[5] *Matt.* 7:6.

and myths used the methods of the Symbolical Language, which include the occasional introduction of inconsistencies as part of the concealing veil.

BIOLOGY, NOMENCLATURE AND THE LIMITATIONS OF TIME

In the New Testament also, difficulties are met if a literal reading of certain passages be adopted.   Two of the Evangelists affirm the immaculate conception of Jesus and consequently a virgin birth[1]—medically regarded as a virtual impossibility—whilst the others do not.   The genealogies of Jesus as given in the Gospels of St. Matthew and St. Luke are totally different and could not apply to the same person.   St. Matthew traces His descent through Joseph, which is meaningless in the case of a virgin birth, and St. Luke through Mary.

Furthermore, the events said to have occurred during the night before the Crucifixion of Jesus are too numerous to have happened within the prescribed time.   Here is a list of them: the Last Supper (*Lu.* XXII: 15-20); the agony in the Garden (*Matt.* XXVI: 36-46); the betrayal by Judas (*Matt.* XXVI: 47-50) ; the questioning, firstly before Annas and Caiaphas (*Jn.* XVIII: 13-24), secondly before the Sanhedrin (*Matt.* XXVI: 59-66), thirdly before Pilate (*Matt.* XXVII: 11-14) and finally in the Hall of Judgment (*Jn.* XVIII: 28-38)—regardless of the fact that Courts to try malefactors did not usually sit in the middle of the night;[2] the visit to Herod (*Lk.* XXIII: 7-11), recorded only by St. Luke; the return to Pilate; Pilate's speeches and his washing of his hands (*Matt.* XXVII: 11-24); the scourging, the mocking and the arraying of Jesus in a purple robe (*Mk.* XV: 16-20); the long and painful bearing of the Cross to Golgotha, followed by the Crucifixion (*Jn.* XIX: 16-18)— all these events could not possibly have occurred in so short a time.   According to estimated chronology the arrest of Jesus occurred at midnight on a Thursday, and the Crucifixion at 9·00 A.M. on Good Friday.[3]   Biblical accounts of these and many other events present a completely insoluble problem, if only because of the unalterable demands and divisions of time itself; for time and space, or location are inflexible.   This list is repeated and a solution of the problems is advanced in the Chapter entitled " Four Major Keys of Interpretation ".

SOME ECCLESIASTICAL ADMISSIONS

Although a number of Christian denominations proclaim the Bible to be the verbally inspired word of God, some churchmen frankly recognise the above-mentioned difficulties.   Canon T. P. Stevens, Vicar of St.

---

[1] *Matt.* 1:18; *Lk.* 1:34, 35.

[2] The possibility that the urgency of the case could have made immediate action imperative has not been overlooked.

[3] q.v. *The Oxford Cyclopedic Concordance*, Oxford University Press.

Paul's Church, Wimbledon, when explaining his reasons for banning the teaching of certain Old Testament stories in his Sunday Schools, said :

> " No matter how many say the Bible should be taught in full, I am not going to do it.   Men like Bernard Shaw, Arnold Bennett and H. G. Wells all turned against the Church through wrongful teaching, when they could have been a powerful force to us...
>
> " It takes a man of considerable intelligence to understand the whole of the Bible.   Some of the stories are helpful, interesting and lovely, but quite often they deal with rape, murder, lies and brutality, exaggerated nationalism and war.   What purpose is to be served by teaching all these unpleasant stories to the young ?   If they are intelligent they will get the strangest ideas of God.
>
> " I believe the Christian religion is in a state of decline partly because so many people cannot make head or tail of it.   Unfortunately the whole (not entirely—G.H.) Christian Church is against me.   I am the odd man out over this question. "[1]

A new dark age was foreseen by Dean Inge, as reported in *The New Zealand Herald*, (8-6-'50) : " Dean Inge, 'The Gloomy Dean', is aged 90 today (June 6th).... On the eve of his birthday, the Dean declared: 'We seem to be on the threshold of another dark age...The first thing ought to be to get rid of a good deal of the Old Testament.   We are living in an age different from the days when I had a fashionable West End Church, where ladies dripping with pearls and furs would sing the Magnificat with more fervour than a Communist ever sang the Red Flag ".

The Most Reverend Dr. Frank Woods, Anglican Archbishop of Melbourne, speaking at St. Paul's Cathedral on the 18th February, 1961, on the early *Genesis* accounts of the creation, Adam and Eve and the Fall of man, said that Christians should not be dismayed if these were attacked on scientific or historical grounds.   They contain truths of a religious nature, he stated, which do not depend for their validity upon historical or scientific confirmation.   The *Genesis* accounts expressed truths of a timeless nature. They were myths, teaching spiritual truths by allegories.

In October, 1962, *The New Zealand Herald* published a statement by the Rev. Dr. Leslie Weatherhead, a former President of the Methodist Conference and Minister at the famous City Temple, London.   In the course of an interview with the Press the Reverend Doctor, who is also the author of a booklet entitled *The Case for Reincarnation*, said " he would like to go through the Bible being very free with a blue pencil ".

Still more recently *The Auckland Star* (23-3-'63) printed a news item concerning a recent book, *Honest to God*, written by the Bishop of Woolwich, Dr. John Robinson.   In this article it is stated that the Bishop makes it

---

[1] q.v. *The New Zealand Herald*, 2-5-50.

clear in his book that, amongst other dogmas, he does not believe in God as a separate Being and that he is agnostic about the Virgin Birth.

A SOLUTION OF THE PROBLEM

Most, if not all, of these difficulties disappear when once it is assumed that the authors' intention was less to record history alone than also to present cosmogonical, solar, planetary and racial ideas and to describe mystical and psychological conditions and experiences of man. An additional explanation of the otherwise inexplicable presence of these incongruities in the Bible as we know it today is that they were additions, and not part of the original writings. Later interpreters, editors and translators are, by some Biblical scholars, held responsible. My own studies have led me to the conclusion that deliberate interference with original texts, deletions, interpolations, or, successive editings and translations and some deletions, have been partly responsible for the confusion, rendering the literal reading of many portions of the Old Testament entirely unacceptable. Such offensive passages should, I think, be attributed to later writers, totally unillumined and still influenced by local supersitions and primitive moral standards. These crude ideas and evidences of ignorance were, I feel sure, not included in the original inspired revelations. Many of the resultant criticisms can successfully be met, however, and most of the problems solved once the existence of the Sacred Language is accepted and its symbolism applied to difficult passages of World Scriptures and Mythologies.

If this approach be regarded as both permissible and potentially valuable, then the choice of both subject-matter and language made by the *original* authors of the Scriptures suggests that a recondite meaning exists. Amongst these indications are: the direct intervention *in propria persona* of the Supreme Deity; the occurrence of miracles, whether credible or incredible; and the appropriate use of classical symbols such as physical objects and features of the landscape including, for example, mountains, rivers, deserts, gardens, trees, animals and birds.[1] Where these are included in the narrative in a manner and place which appear to suggest an allegorical intention on the part of the writer, then with due caution the method of interpretation herein described and employed may be helpfully applied, particularly to those portions of the Scriptures which are susceptible of such treatment.

As has heretofore been stated, impossibilities appearing in the Bible which bear the imprint of inspiration may, however, in conformity with the allegorical method of writing be part of a deliberately constructed cover or blind—a veil of incredibility, incongruity, absurdity, inconsequence,

---

[1] q.v. Vol. I of this work, Pt. III.

fantasy, and even horror.[1] The previously quoted words of Moses Maimonedes, the Jewish theologian and historian, may perhaps usefully be here repeated: " Every time you find in our books a tale the reality of which seems impossible, a story which is repugnant to both reason and common sense, then be sure that the tale contains a profound allegory veiling a deeply mysterious truth; and the greater the absurdity of the letter, the deeper the wisdom of the spirit. "

THE TESTIMONY OF EARLY AUTHORITIES [2]

Knowledge of the existence of a secret meaning contained within the Scriptures is openly confessed by Clement of Alexandria (A.D. 150-220 approximately) when he says that the Mysteries of the Faith are not to be divulged to all. " But ", he says, " since this tradition is not published alone for him who perceives the magnificence of the word; it is requisite, therefore, to hide in a Mystery the wisdom spoken, which the Son of God taught."[3]

Origen is no less explicit concerning the Bible and its symbolical fables. " If we hold to the letter", he exclaims, " and must understand what stands written in the law after the manner of the Jews and common people, then I should blush to confess aloud that it is God who has given these laws; then the laws of men appear more excellent and reasonable."[4]

" What man of sense ", he writes, " will agree with the statement that the first, second and third days in which the *evening* is named and the *morning*, were without sun, moon, and stars, and the first day without a heaven ? What man is found such an idiot as to suppose that God planted trees in Paradise, in Eden, like a husbandman, and planted therein the tree of life, perceptible to the eyes and senses, which gave life to the eater thereof; and another tree which gave to the eater thereof a knowledge of good and evil ? I believe that every man must hold these things for images, under which the hidden sense lies concealed. "[5] St. Paul's unequivocal statements that the story of Abraham and his two sons is " an allegory " and that " Agar is mount Sinai "[6] offer Biblical support for the acceptance of certain portions of the Bible as allegorical.

---

[1] Some of the reasons for such enveiling are also offered in Pt. I, Ch. I, of this Volume.

[2] Certain of the quotations which follow in this and other Chapters also appear at the beginning of this book.

[3] *Clement of Alexandria*, Vol. I, *Stromata*, Ch. XII, p. 388.

[4] See *Homilies* 7, in Levit., quoted in *The Source of Measures*, pp. 306-7, J. Ralston Skinner.

[5] Origen: Huet., *Origeniana*, 167; Franck, p. 142.

[6] *Gal.* 4:22-26.

H. P. Blavatsky writes:[1] " Rabbi Simeon Ben-'Jochai (sic), the compiler of the *Zohar*,[2] never imparted the most important points of his doctrine otherwise than orally, and to a very limited number of disciples.   Therefore, without the final initiation into the *Mercavah*,[3] the study of the *Kabbalah* will be ever incomplete, and the *Mercavah* can be taught only 'in darkness, in a deserted place, and after many and terrific trials' " (the preparation those days of Candidates for Initiation, G.H.).[4]   Since the death of that great Jewish Initiate this hidden doctrine has remained, for the outside world, an inviolate secret.

" Among the venerable sect of the Tanaim, or rather the Tananim, the wise men, there were those who taught the secrets practically and initiated some disciples into the grand and final Mystery.   But the *Mishna Hagiga*, 2nd Section, say that the table of contents of the Mercaba 'must only be delivered to wise old ones.'   The *Gemara* is still more dogmatic.   ' The more important secrets of the Mysteries[5] were not even revealed to all priests. Alone the initiates had them divulged.'   And so we find the same great secrecy prevalent in every ancient religion.

" What says the *Kabbalah* itself?   Its great Rabbis actually threaten him who accepts their saying *verbatim*.   We read in the *Zohar*: ' woe....to the man who sees in the Thorah,[6] i.e., Law, only simple recitals and ordinary words !   Because if in truth it only contained these, we would even to-day be able to compose a Thorah much more worthy of admiration.   For if we find only the simple words, we would only have to address ourselves to the legislators of the earth, to those in whom we most frequently meet with the most grandeur.   It would be sufficient to imitate them, and make a Thorah after their words and example.   But it is not so; each word of the Thorah contains an elevated meaning and a sublime mystery....The

---

[1] q.v. *The Secret Doctrine*, H. P. Blavatsky, Adyar Ed., Vol. V, pp. 67-68.

[2] *Zohar*.   *The Book of Splendour*, the basic work of Jewish mysticism, the greatest exposition of the *Kabbalah*.

[3] *Mercavah* or *Mercaba* (Heb.)—A " chariot ".   According to Kabbalists the Supreme Lord, after He had established the Ten Sephiroth, used Them as a chariot or throne of glory on which to descend upon the souls of men.   Also a hidden doctrine delivered only as a mystery orally, " face to face and mouth to ear ".   q.v. *Appendix, The Sephirothal Tree*.

[4] *Initiation*—see Glossary and Pt. VI of Vol. I of this work.

[5] *Muo* (Gr.)—" to close the mouth ", *Teletai* (Gr.)—" Celebrations of Initiation ". The Sacred Mysteries were enacted in the ancient Temples by the initiated Hierophants for the benefit and instruction of the Candidates.   They formed a series of secret dramatic performances, in which the mysteries of cosmogony and Nature were personified by the priests and neophytes.   These were explained in their hidden meaning to the Candidates for Initiation.   q.v. *Eleusis and the Eleusinian Mysteries*, George E. Mylonas; *The Eleusinian and Bacchic Mysteries*, Thomas Taylor; *The Mysteries of Eleusis*, George Meautis, Prof. at the University of Neuchâtel.

[6] *Thorah* (Heb.)—" The Law of Moses ".   *Pentateuch* (Gr.)—*Penta*, " five " and *teukhos*, " book ".   The first five books of the Old Testament.

recitals of the Thorah are the vestments of the Thorah. Woe to him who takes this garment for the Thorah itself.... The simple take notice only of the garments or recitals of the Thorah, they know no other thing, they see not that which is concealed under the vestment. The more instructed men do not pay attention to the vestment, but to the body which it envelops.' "

AN ILLUSTRATION

The story of the cursing of the fig tree[1] may here be taken as an example of an account of a somewhat unlikely event which, when interpreted as an allegory, becomes not only acceptable but also a source of illumination. It seems un-Christlike to curse the fig tree, and still more so since the act was performed in the early Spring before the Passover when, being out of season, the tree could not have had any figs upon it. Indeed, the story may rightly be regarded as self-contradictory, even absurd. In that very absurdity, however, is said to be both a clue to the meaning and an encouragement to look for the wisdom concealed within the supposed narrative of events.

The world's allegories are, in fact, less records of events in time and place than both descriptions of interior experiences and enunciations of universal laws. Simply put, the particular law here referred to is that if all living things and beings—including races, nations and men—do not share the fruits of their lives they will metaphorically wither away and die. Applied to the individual, the person who seeks to have, to hold and to hoard for himself alone the fruits of his life—his material possessions and his discovered wisdom, truth and power—giving nothing to others, will inevitably find that his own life, outer and inner, stagnates and then atrophies.

SELFLESS GIVING BRINGS SPIRITUAL ENRICHMENT

Attention is thus drawn to a further mysterious law—it might be called " the law of flow "—under which he who wisely and unselfishly gives of himself gains a more abundant life. Obedience to this law brings not loss but gain, not death but everlasting life. Inversely, disobedience of this law brings not gain but loss, not life but death. This has been repeatedly demonstrated throughout the history of both nations and individuals. The same principle is allegorically presented in the story of Abraham's attempted sacrifice of his son Isaac. The act was supposedly to be performed as a sign of complete submission to the will of the Lord; yet even whilst Abraham's arm was raised to strike, an angel stayed his hand and later

---

[1] *Matt.* 21:19; *Mk.* 11:14, 21.

he found a substituted sacrifice in the form of a ram.[1] The incident allegorically portrays the truth that once complete readiness is shown wisely to surrender self and treasured personal possessions in pursuance of an ideal way of life, or in the service of the Lord, then the sacrifice is not demanded.

This principle is fundamental for it is the law by which the Universe subsists. The Logos Himself nourishes and sustains the Solar System by the perpetual outpouring, self-giving, "self-emptying" (kenosis, Gr.) of His own life. This kenosis (the self-emptying attitude of mind and mode of life) is a key-note in the Christian religion. It is applied to the life of the disciple by Our Lord in His words :"….he that hateth his life in this world shall keep it unto life eternal ",[2] and "….Except a corn of wheat fall into the ground and die, it abideth alone: but if it die, it bringeth forth much fruit. "[3] The neophyte must become " the wheat of Christ ", as a Christian mystic has said.

The poverty of the Nativity of Jesus, the surrender to Pilate, to the Jews and to Crucifixion, the exposure of the Sacred Heart, the endurance of open wounds and the piercing of the skin, are all symbols of this attitude of uttermost selflessness towards life. Such self-emptying, such entirely self-forgetting love and such figurative death are necessary, it is said, for the attainment of a more abundant life. To " die " to the sense of separated individuality, to outgrow egoism and possessiveness—this is to live unto life eternal. Mysterious, and even contradictory, though such a statement appears, it is nevertheless thought by mystics to be one of the greatest truths ever uttered.

Apparently we are in the presence of a strange law. In order to live the larger life in imitation of the Great Exemplar, the Lord of Love, we must die to self-desire, pour ourselves out in selfless sacrifice and service and surrender self for love's sake. Universal love is the only true way to eternal life, because it involves " self-emptying " of self. Self-forgetfulness is the basis of all spirituality. Every sincere esotericist is faced with this truth and with necessity, and the renunciation so often seems to be of that which we hold most dear.

Applied to the Logos, these words " self-emptying " and " dying " are not to be taken as wholly expressing the truth; for, of course, the Logos does not ever become empty, nor does " He " ever really die. Indeed, the Logos is ever Self-renewed from a higher dimension. Similarly the sun, which in occult philosophy is regarded as His physical " heart ", does not exhaust itself despite its immeasurable outpouring, for proportionate

[1] Gen. 22:13.
[2] Jn. 12:25.
[3] Jn. 12:24.

2

inpouring or upwelling occurs. This is also true in every walk of life whether secular or spiritual.

REVELATION OF TRUTH BY MEANS OF ALLEGORY

In relating the incident of the withered fig tree, the author of the Gospel according to St. Matthew appears to have enunciated this principle in the form of an otherwise unacceptable story describing a supposed action of the Lord of Love which brought about the cessation of the life of a tree.[1] A profound spiritual truth of the greatest significance to every neophyte of every age who seeks to discover the " strait gate " and enter upon the narrow way [2] is thus portrayed by means of a miniature drama, an allegory concealing—to guard against unwise application of the law to necessary material possessions, for example—the all-important principle that life is not lost, but fulfilled, by renunciation. This interpretation is supported by the fact that after the incident Our Lord went on to refer to the nature and range of the tremendous powers attainable by those who enter upon the Path of Discipleship and Initiation, saying:

> *Jesus answered and said unto them, Verily I say unto you, If ye have faith, and doubt not, ye shall not only do this which is done to the fig tree, but also if ye shall say unto this mountain, Be thou removed, and be thou cast into the sea; it shall be done.*
>
> *And all things, whatsoever ye shall ask in prayer, believing, ye shall receive.*[3]

The entry of Jesus into Jerusalem and the acclamation by the crowd, commemorated by the Church as Palm Sunday, which immediately preceded the withering of the fig tree, indicated that a certain spiritual advance had been made, a triumph of Spirit over flesh, of the Christ-power within over mind, emotions, vitality and physical body—the lower quaternary (the docile ass)—and the multitude of habits, desires and appetites (the responsive crowd) inherent in the substance of the physical and super-physical bodies. Jerusalem is a symbol of the state of awareness of the Divine Self or Ego in the Causal Body, the universalised consciousness of an immortal, spiritual being. Entry into Jerusalem portrays realisation of the Self as divine, eternal, indestructible and universal. Absence, and especially exile, from a city may imply being temporarily or permanently cut off from a spiritual state of consciousness. The heavenly city, " the city of the living God"[4], is thus a symbol of the *Augoeides*[5], the *Kārana Sharīra*

---

[1] *Matt.* 21:19.

[2] q.v. *The Hidden Wisdom in the Holy Bible*, Vol. I, Pt. VI, Geoffrey Hodson.

[3] *Matt.* 21:21, 22.

[4] *Heb.* 12:22.

[5] *Augoeides* (Gr.)—" The self-radiant, divine fragment ", the Robe of Glory of the Gnostics and the *Kārana Sharīra*, " Causal Body ", of Hinduism.

(Sk.), the Robe of Glory of the Gnostics,[1] in which the self-radiant divine fragment, the Monad-Ego, abides and is self-manifest at the level of the spiritualised intelligence of man.

LITERAL OR SYMBOLICAL ?

If it be objected—as would be very natural—that too much is being deduced from so simple and so briefly described an incident as the withering of the fig tree, firstly it can be repeated that a literal reading presents one with an unacceptable attribute in the character of the Christ, Who described Himself as a life-giver and not a death-dealer; for He said: " I am come that they might have life, and that they might have it more abundantly ".[2] Secondly, in its literal meaning the incident introduces a meaningless and somewhat repellent exercise of thaumaturgic power such as was and still is displayed, for example, by the medicine men of primitive peoples and by some, though by no means all, of the *Tohungas* of the Maoris[3] of New Zealand.

Whilst it is admitted that the fact that one idea is preferable to another is no proof of its verity, the cumulative evidence obtained by this and similar interpretations of a very great number of Bible stories is so strong as almost to amount to proof.   When to this is added the avowed intention of ancient writers, as evidenced by the quotations which appear at the front of this Volume, and the strongly worded command of the Christ to conceal from the profane, and yet reveal to the worthy, power-bestowing knowledge and " the mystery of the Kingdom of God "[4] (pearls[5]) which could be dangerous in the wrong hands (swine[5]), then the case for the existence and use of the Sacred Language would seem to be unassailable.

---

[1] All these titles are names for the same principle of man—the vehicle of the reincarnating Ego at the formless levels of the mental plane.

[2] *Jn.* 10:10.

[3] q.v. *Lecture Notes of the School of the Wisdom*, Vol II, Ch. IX, *The Sacred Science of the Maori Tohunga*. Geoffrey Hodson.

[4] *Mk.* 4:11.

[5] *Matt.* 7:6.

CHAPTER II

SOME KEYS OF INTERPRETATION

WHILE the preceding chapter contains introductory examples of the use of the symbolical language and methods of interpretation, in this Chapter a fuller exposition is offered. This is very necessary, for those who would discover the truths concealed within the Scriptures of the world should first acquaint themselves with the various keys to the symbolical writings. Then, reading each story very carefully, giving special attention to the symbols employed, they should dwell in concentrated thought upon its various parts, meditatively seeking the reality behind the shadow, the eternal truth within the story in time; for successful interpretation is primarily an experience in consciousness.

Certain age-old symbols serve as signposts on the way, each with its meaning constant throughout all time, as the doctrine everywhere revealed is constant also. The Hierophants of Egypt, Chaldea, Assyria and Greece, the sages of the Eastern worlds and the inspired authors of the Bible all made use of these symbols as living, time-free ideographs which questing men of every age might comprehend. Nations, civilisations and religions rise and fall, but these earthly symbols of spiritual truths are ageless and unchanging. By their use an Egyptian Hierophant, a Jewish Prophet, an Essene monk, an Eastern sage, may speak direct from the remote past to the mind of modern man.

The authors who wrote in this allegorical manner wished to reveal Macrocosmic and microcosmic truths, to describe supersensuous conditions of consciousness. They used history only as weft and warp on which to weave a representation of everlasting verities, the esoteric wisdom of all ages, the deeply occult knowledge of the Initiates of the Mystery Schools of both ancient and more modern days. Time and the world of time were of far less importance to these inspired authors than eternity and the eternal truths of which they wrote.

When we open our Bible, then, we should remember that we are reading a special category of literature, foreign to us at first. In order to discover the intention of the authors we need to learn the meaning of the words, to understand the method of writing and to possess the keys of interpretation. We must, indeed, find a Rosetta stone. Then, as we learn to lift the veil of allegory, symbol, imagery, and even incongruity, the light of truth will illumine our minds.

FOUR KEYS OF INTERPRETATION

The foregoing enunciation of the principal theme of this work, namely that the inspired portions of World Scriptures and Myths are allegorical in character, may now be followed by a statement of four of the seven possible keys of interpretation and their Macrocosmic and microcosmic[1] applications to a number of such passages.

ALL HAPPENS WITHIN

The *first key* is that some narratives of supposedly historical events are also descriptive of subjective experiences of races, nations and individuals; in this sense, all happens within. When this key is " turned ", certain stories are found to have at least two possible underlying meanings. One of these refers to the experiences and attainments of those advancing by the normal evolutionary method, and the other to mystics who are treading the Way of Holiness or Path of Swift Unfoldment.

The need for the veiling of magical and occult knowledge in allegory and symbol is especially great in the latter of these two applications of the first key; for, quite early in the approach to and entry upon the Path, an enhancement of will-power and the mental and psychic faculties begins to be apparent. Premature awakening and development of these supernormal powers, and their employment for purely personal, and especially for destructive, purposes could prove extremely harmful both to those who misuse them and to their fellow men.

" CHRIST IN YOU, THE HOPE OF GLORY "[2]

The Apostle Paul would seem to have accepted this first key—the mystical interpretation. For him the Nativity of Christ, for example, is not only a particular event which occurred at a certain time in Bethlehem, but also refers to a universal human experience. The narratives of the Annunciation, the Immaculate Conception and the Nativity of Christ are so written as also to describe allegorically the gradual awakening of Christ-

---

[1] Macrocosm and Microcosm. All allegories and symbols are susceptible of a threefold interpretation—Macrocosmic or applying to Logoi and Universes, microcosmic or applying to man, and Initiatory or applying to mystical experiences and stages of unfoldment passed through by those treading the path of discipleship and Initiation. (See Glossary and Pt. VI of Vol. I of this work).

[2] Col. 1: 27.

like powers of perception within the Soul[1] of advanced man. For St. Paul, evidently, the birth and activities of the Lord Christ were descriptive of the interior awakening and perfecting of the inherent, redemptive Christ-power and nature *within* man. Thus he wrote: " ....I travail in birth again until Christ be formed in you "[2] and " To whom God would make known what is the riches of the glory of this mystery among the Gentiles; which is Christ in you, the hope of glory ".

As the student of the Bible reads the great narratives with this key in his hand, as it were, he may even himself share in the recorded experiences. He may ascend " the mount " with Abraham, Moses, Elijah and Jesus and, in however slight a measure at first, begin to participate in their exaltation. With the two dejected disciples he may walk the road to Emmaus,[3] and hear the wise words of their temporarily unknown Companion. At the description of the breaking of the bread he may then become illumined by that inner light which shone when " ....their eyes were opened, and they knew him....". Such indeed, I suggest, is part of the intention of the inspired authors. As one studies the Scriptures of the world, therefore, one must read intuitively, sensitively, with one's mind open and responsive to that vaster consciousness which so often seems waiting to burst through. Thus, the first key is that some recorded events also occur interiorly.

PEOPLE PERSONIFY HUMAN QUALITIES

The *second key* is that each of the *dramatis personae* introduced into the stories represents a condition of consciousness and a quality of character. All the actors are personifications of aspects of human nature, of attributes, principles, powers, faculties, limitations, weaknesses and errors of man. When purely human beings are the heroes, the life of a person evolving normally is being described. When the hero is semi-divine, however, the accent is upon the hastened progress of the spiritual Self of man, particularly after it has begun to assume preponderant power. When the central figure is an *Avatār*[4] or " descent " of an Aspect of Deity, the account of His experiences also describes those passed through during the later phases of human evolution to the stature of perfected manhood. Such, I suggest, is the general purpose and such the method of the ancient writers of the world's immortal allegories, parables and myths.

---

[1] SOUL. When spelt with a capital " S " this word refers to the unfolding, immortal, spiritual Self of man, the true individuality behind the bodily veil. When spelt with a small " s " it is used for the *psyche* or mental, emotional and vital parts of the mortal man Heb. *Nephesh chaiah*, " souls of life " or " living soul ". *Gen.* 2:7.

[2] *Gal.* 4:19.

[3] *Lk.* 24:13-31.

[4] *Avatār* (Sk.). The doctrine of Divine incarnation or " descent ". See Glossary.

The Deity or Father when introduced into a narrative generally refers to the highest spiritual Essence in man, the Divine Spark, the Monad,[1] as also to the Oversoul of the race. Those who are following the pathway of Initiation seek to hasten this realisation, first of their divine, immortal nature and thereafter of their unbroken unity with the Supreme Lord of All. This full recognition of man's unity with God, of the oneness of man-Spirit with God-Spirit, is the ultimate goal for all mankind. In Hinduism this state is called *Moksha* or Liberation; in Buddhism, *Nirvāna* or conscious absorption; in Christianity, Salvation, Ascension, Christhood.

In this method of Biblical study the characters—divine, semi-divine, patriarchal and human—are thus regarded as personifications of principles and powers of both Nature as the Macrocosm, and of man as the microcosm. Allowances must, however, be made for differing correspondences necessitated by the stories themselves. This reading is supported by St. Paul, who writes: "....all these things happened unto them for ensamples "[2] and "....it is written, that Abraham had two sons, the one by a bond-maid, the other by a freewoman....which things are an allegory...."[3] It is not unreasonable to assume that such a theory may also be true of many other portions of the Bible. One may even go further than this and assert that the practice of studying the Scriptures of the world in their literal meaning, and as records of actual historical events alone, can lead to grave error and serious confusion of mind.

Other errors in modern Christianity urgently need to be corrected, I submit. Amongst these are: the already mentioned degradation of the concept of the Divine Emanator of the Universe to the level of a tribal god;[4] reliance upon an external (instead of an interior) redemptive power; and the erection of a vast though changing theological edifice founded upon dogmas, some of which are based upon a literal reading of the Scriptures.[5]

These difficulties are all avoided, and profound inspiration consistent with reason is gained, by the recognition of a mystical intent and meaning underlying many portions of the Scriptures and Mythologies of the peoples of old. Thus the humility, the devotion and the selfless love of Mary, the

---

[1] Monad. (Gr.)—"Alone". Other terms are the Immortal Germ, the Logos of the Soul, the Dweller in the Innermost. See Glossary.

[2] *I Cor.* 10:11.

[3] *Gal.* 4:22-24.

[4] Exoteric Hebraism, and a literal reading of certain Books of the Old Testament, alone present this view of Jehovah. Kabbalism, the theosophy of the Hebrews, their esoteric wisdom, proclaims the unnamed Deity as the self-existent, impersonal Emanator of Cosmos and all that it contains. See Appendix, *The Sephirothal Tree.*

[5] Even as this work is in course of preparation, many of these dogmas are being subjected to critical re-examination by the clergy and laity of certain Christian denominations such as, for example, the Roman Catholic, notably at its Ecumenical Council of recent years.

Mother of Jesus; the human frailty and the inherent sainthood of a Magdalene and a Peter; the valuable busyness of Martha and, evidently in the
eyes of Jesus, the even more valuable, spiritual, contemplative aspects of
human nature and modes of life displayed by her sister Mary[1]—all these
attributes form part of the character of every individual, the conditions of
life drawing out now one and now another.   On the surface the remark to
Martha, which almost reads like a rebuke, might seem to be somewhat
unfair.   Apparently, however, Jesus was referring to the fact discovered and
taught by every mystic that only in complete quietude of body and mind may
the voice of the Master within be heard.   Elijah appears to have made
this discovery, for after the wind, the earthquake and the fire a silence fell
upon him and in that silence he heard the " still small voice ".[2]   The
Psalmist in his turn received similar guidance from the Lord, Who said to
him: " Be still, and know that I am God...."[3]

Applying the second key, which is that the *dramatis personae of* many
scriptural narratives represent human characteristics, the twelve disciples
of Jesus are found to personify attributes and potentialities of man.   For
example, a twelvefold classification of them as microcosmic manifestations
of the qualities given by astrologers to the Zodiacal Signs is discernible.
Discipleship, or nearness to the divine Teacher, indicates that the evolution
of the disciple has reached an advanced stage.   Ultimately all powers of
heart, mind and Spirit will be fully developed.   Only as the twelve zodiacal
qualities in man are " discipled "—or disciplined and refined—is he able
to respond to his own inner spiritual will and to comprehend pure wisdom,
both of which are personified by the Master.   The Christ Presence and
Power—whether asleep as in the ship on Galilee,[4] awakening or being
" born " as in the mystical Nativity,[5] or fully grown to " the measure of the
stature of the fulness of Christ "[6]—must, however, be added to all human
attributes in order to present by means of personification a description of the
fully " perfected " man.

The interaction between these various aspects of human nature, the
effects they produce upon one another, the waxing or waning of one or
more of them at different times and in different lives, and the gradual,
triumphant emergence and predominance of the royal spiritual Self, the
Immortal King within, personified by the Saviour and the hero of every
saga—all this is allegorically portrayed by the Initiated authors of the

---

[1] *Lk*. 10:38-42.
[2] 1 *Kings* 19:12.
[3] *Ps*. 46:10.
[4] *Mk*. 4:38.
[5] *Gal*. 4:19.
[6] *Eph*. 4:13.

inspired portions of the Scriptures of the world. The marriages in which many of these exploits culminate may be interpreted as symbolic references to the unification of the consciousness of the outer and the inner, the mortal and the immortal selves of men. In mystical literature they are not inaptly referred to as " heavenly marriages ". Thus the narratives themselves describe the experiences—particularly the tests, ordeals, defeats and victories—of one person, who is man himself. Successful exploits describe interior achievements, while partial and complete failures, defeats and surrenders are allegories of temporary victories of the purely human over the divine in man—conquests of matter over Spirit. Thus the second key is that each of the *dramatis personae* represents a condition of conciousness and a quality of character.

STORIES DRAMATISE PHASES OF HUMAN EVOLUTION

The *third key* is that each story may be regarded as a graphic description of the experiences of the human Soul as it passes through the stages, and their intermediate phases, of its evolutionary journey to the Promised Land (cosmic consciousness)—the summit of human attainment. Inspired allegories are always distinguishable from mere novels and biographies by several characteristics, such as the intrusion of the supernatural and the inclusion in the story of angelic and divine beings, even of Deity itself. When these are found the existence of a hidden revelation may always be suspected. The reader possessed of and applying the keys may then penetrate the veil of symbolism and find that hidden wisdom which it had concealed.

In the main the manifold experiences of the immortal Self of each man on its pathway towards perfection are, as stated above, narrated as the adventures of numbers of persons in any one story. The twelve labours of Hercules, each susceptible of association with one of the twelve Signs of the Zodiac, the voyage of the Argonauts, the experiences of the Israelites, and the lives of the Lord Shri Krishna, the Lord Buddha and the Lord Christ, amongst many others, are all descriptive in the symbolic manner of the journey of the Soul and the psychological, intellectual and spiritual unfoldments which occur on that pilgrimage.

In this third method of interpretation, each story may be studied from at least two points of view. The first of these refers to normal evolutionary progress and the accompanying mental and emotional states, whilst the second reveals the allegories as more especially descriptive of the experiences of those who enter in at the strait gate and pursue the narrow way.[1]

[1] *Matt.* 7:13-14

In the Parable of the Sower[1] the different conditions of the ground—as the Christ explained privately to His disciples[2]—represent various evolutionary phases and states of spiritual receptiveness of the race and the individual, from complete unresponsiveness (wayside and rocky ground) to full perception and ratification (fertile ground). In the Parable of the Ten Virgins,[3] the foolish maidens may be regarded as those who are not as yet sufficiently evolved to be able to respond to impulses descending from their Higher Self (the bridegroom), and therefore not really to be blamed. The wise virgins, on the other hand, may be interpreted as personifying all those in whom the spiritual Self has attained to a considerable degree of evolutionary unfoldment. The outer, physical nature has then become sufficiently developed to be aware of this fact and to give expression in the conduct of daily life to higher idealism and the fruits of spiritual experiences. This state is, in its turn, followed by the progressive illumination of the mind-brain by the Ego (betrothal), leading to the fusion of the immortal and mortal natures (marriage).

The incidents of the marriage feast of Cana[4] may thus be taken to refer to this interior union achieved by those who have awakened the power of the Christ Presence which is within every man, allegorically indicated by the physical presence of the Master. After this attainment the coarser desires of the emotional nature (water) are transmuted into wisdom and spiritual intuitiveness (wine). Marriages of heroes and heroines in Mythologies and Scriptures, as we have seen, indicate that the all-essential blending of the mortal personality with the immortal Ego, and the further merging of the human individuality with the divine Self and life of the Universe as a whole, " the Mystic Identity " or cosmic consciousness, have both been attained.[5] The presence of the Christ in this story, as in all narratives in which He appears, including those which describe the " miracles ", implies that the phase of the evolutionary journey of the Soul has been entered at which spiritual wisdom, spiritual intuitiveness and a Christlike love and compassion are already well developed and active throughout the personal nature. The changing of water into wine at such " marriages " is not a miracle, but rather a natural process which occurs when a steadfast aspirant finds and successfully treads the narrow way. The grape and the wine also

---

[1] *Matt.* 13:1-9.

[2] *Matt.* 13:18-23.

[3] *Matt.* 25:1-13.

[4] *Jn.* 2:1-11.

[5] The numerous, and in the literal sense scandalous, *amours* of Zeus, the Father of the Gods, are all susceptible of similar interpretation, namely of unions between the Divine and the mortal in human nature. Indeed, each *amour* with its specific symbology (cloud, swan, shower of gold and bull, for example) may be interpreted as descriptive of a descent of the inner spiritual Self into union with the less Divine and also purely mortal levels of human consciousness.

symbolise knowledge, wisdom and comprehension of the spirit of things. As fermentation gives a certain " strength " to wine, so the action of the intellect upon accumulated esoteric knowledge turns it into pure wisdom, implicit insight and deeply penetrative intuitiveness. Thus the third key is that many Scriptural stories allegorically describe phases of man's evolutionary journey and their accompanying mystical experiences.

THE SYMBOLISM OF LANGUAGE

The *fourth key* is that some physical objects, as also certain words, have each their own special symbolic meaning. In the cipher of the Bible such words are chiefly used to denote levels of human awareness. Those referring to earthy or physical objects are descriptive of states of consciousness and attributes of character pertaining to the waking state. Water and its associations refer Macrocosmically to universal Space and microcosmically to the emotions. With certain exceptions, air and fire refer to the intuition and the mind respectively. Fire, it should be added, also has reference to the manifested creative life-force of the Logos and that same force as the procreative power in man. This is referred to as the Serpent Fire or *Kundalini*[1] and frequently represented by dragons and serpents. Thus the fourth key is that some physical objects and certain words have each their own symbolic meaning.

SOME APPLICATIONS OF THE KEYS

The Sacred Language of the Initiates of the Mystery Schools of old is indeed formed of hierograms and symbols rather than of words alone, their interpretation being ever constant, as constant also is the doctrine which this Language everywhere reveals. Many such words might thus be regarded as the locks into which the appropriate keys must be fitted. These keys consist of knowledge of the secret meanings given to the words by the Initiated writers of old.

[1] *Kundalini* (Sk.)—" The coiled up, universal Life Principle ". A sevenfold, occult power in Universe (*Maha Kundali*) and man (*Kundalini*), functioning in the latter in a spiral or coiling action, mainly in the spinal cord but also throughout the nervous systems. It is represented in Greek symbology by the Caduceus. When supernormally aroused, this fiery force ascends into the brain by a serpentine path, hence its other name—the " Serpent Fire ". Thus *Kundalini* is the power of life, one of the forces of Nature, and the seven-layered power in the base of the spine of man. It has three currents which flow along three canals in the spinal cord, named *Ida* (negative), *Pingala* (positive) and *Sushumna* (neutral). These names are sometimes also applied—erroneously—to the currents of force which flow in these canals. This occult electricity is intimately associated with Azoth of the Alchemists the creative principle in Nature, and *Akasa* (Sk.), the subtle, supersensuous, spiritual essence which pervades all space. q.v. *The Hidden Wisdom in the Holy Bible*, Vol. I, Pt. III, Ch. I, under " Serpents " and *Lecture Notes of the School of the Wisdom*, Vol. II, Ch. I, Sec. III, Geoffrey Hodson; *The Serpent Power*, Arthur Avalon (Sir John Woodroffe).

The sacred wisdom consists of seven layers, and this fact is allegorically referred to on many occasions. The fiery furnace, for example, had to be heated " seven times more than it was wont to be heated "[1] before the three men—Shadrach, Meshach and Abednego—were joined by a fourth, who appeared " like the Son of God ".[2] Similarly, the walls of Jericho were circumambulated on the seventh day seven times before they fell down.[3]

The idea thus emerges that in order to discover the Sacred Wisdom of the Christian and other Scriptures we must divest ourselves of the notion that they were conceived and written entirely as chronologically and historically authentic accounts of actual events. Rather are they to be read as blends of history, metaphor and revelations of occult and mystic lore. The Gospel narrative, for example, in its Initiatory[4] interpretation describes the progress of an advanced and elevated Soul through the final ascending phases of evolution until the highest, the Ascension is attained. To be fully appreciated, the great drama must be transferred from purely material to psychological, intellectual and spiritual realms and levels of human experience. A commentary on the Gospel narrative from this point of view forms the subject-matter of Parts Five and Six of Volume I of this work.

The disciples are thus personifications of the noblest attributes of man (the second key). Though still imperfect, they are becoming increasingly spiritualised or brought into the presence of their Master, Who personates the Dweller in the Innermost, the God-Self of man, the Logos of the Soul. The disciples are not yet equal to the Christ, being younger in evolution and in consequence still under the delusion of self-separateness. This is shown by their question as to who will be greatest in the kingdom of heaven.[5] They are still tainted by grosser material attributes, hence the deeply symbolical washing of their feet by their Master.[6] A traitor (Judas, in one of several possible interpretations[7] personifying cupidity and treachery) still lurks in their midst. He must be self-revealed and self-slain before

---

[1] *Dan.* 3:19.

[2] *Dan.* 3:25.

[3] *Joshua* 6:1-20 (Interpretations of these passages will be offered at the appropriate places in successive Volumes).

[4] q.v. *The Hidden Wisdom in the Holy Bible.* Vol. I, Pt. VI, Geoffrey Hodson.

[5] *Matt.* 18:1.

[6] *Jn.* 13:3-17.

[7] Amongst these are that Judas created conditions in which he expected the Christ to display His divinity and escape His attackers, whilst another expectation was that the Lord would free Himself from the Cross and thus demonstrate before all men the truth of His affirmation—also proclaimed at the Baptism—that He was indeed the Son of God (*Gen.* X). The hope is also supposed to have been held by Judas that, in thus manifesting His divinity, the Lord would at the same time justify the disciples in their belief in Him as being one with the Father.

the great Ascension can occur. The Master admonishes, rebukes and warns them, indicating the spiritualising activity of the divine Presence within.

By the exercise of theurgic powers many of the recorded—and miscalled —miracles could have been performed by an Adept, or even by an Initiate of lesser degree. In possible mystical interpretations they also illustrate the processes of arousing into activity the faculty of responsiveness to spiritual vision (restoring sight) and to the still, small voice within (restoring hearing), the free exercise of the intellect liberated from rigid orthodoxy (curing those paralysed), and an awakening to full spiritual awareness and knowledge (raising from the dead). This approach will be used in those later Volumes of this work in which the life of Christ as related in the New Testament will be considered.

If this view be accepted, then the Gospel Story, and indeed all the inspired portions of the Bible, are addressed less to the reasoning mind than to the intuition, which can perceive in them references to the evolution of the spiritual Soul of both Universe and man; for, as we have seen, the processes of the development and active use of latent deific powers are portrayed in World Scriptures by means of symbols and dramatic allegories. This mystical view, it may be repeated, does not totally deny the presence of history. The kernel of tradition within the stories can still be a record of real events, however much the illumined authors may have lifted them out of time and space by the use of the Sacred Language.

INCONGRUITIES AS CLUES TO DEEPER MEANINGS

The student of the allegorical language is nearly always given a hint or clue—one, moreover, which at first sight might seem to be rather strange. This clue consists of an additional veil, cover or blind which tends to increase confusion and so to repel those who regard as purely literal those portions of Scripture in which potentially dangerous, because power-bestowing, knowledge is both revealed and concealed. Those who seek the hidden wisdom should guard carefully against this repulsion, whether it is aroused by statements which are incredible or impossible, or by stories which offend logic and one's sense of justice, decency and morality. Unfortunately many people *are* turned away from the Scriptures, and even from religion itself, by the discovery of these characteristics. The study and exposition of the Sacred Language are for this reason alone, I submit, of very great importance.

SOME INCREDIBILITIES AND THEIR POSSIBLE ELUCIDATION

An apparent digression is here made, therefore, briefly to examine certain incongruities in the Bible and to suggest solutions of the problems which they admittedly present. The statements concerning them given in Volume One of this work, Part One, Chapter Three, and in Part One, Chapter Two of this Volume, are here repeated in a somewhat revised form. They will also be further and more fully examined—together with many others—in their appropriate places in this and succeeding Volumes. These repetitions arise from a conviction of the great importance of the elucidation of the many incredible and incongruous accounts of supposed facts which occur in the Bible.

Certain admittedly difficult Biblical passages are:

(a) Three days and nights of creation pass before the sun is created.[1] Here universal creative epochs of activity and quiescence,[2] rather than alternations of day and night on a single planet, are implied.

(b) Deity enjoins massacre and extermination.[3]

In the Sacred Language enemies sometimes personify attributes which are hostile to the happiness and spiritual unfoldment of the individual or nation whose story is being told. If the enemies of the Israelites are so regarded, then Divine commands to massacre them lose their offensiveness, since extermination of undesirable characteristics is being enjoined. Whilst the normal history of an immigrant nation confronted by local adversaries has a rightful place in the national story, whenever the Lord God is introduced into a narrative and made responsible for events described, the authors may be presumed to be deliberately drawing attention to a mystical revelation. In such a reading the Lord God personifies the inner spiritual Self of the individual, the Monad, which is bringing its purifying and directive influences to bear upon mortal man.

(c) Noah collects pairs of every living creature from all parts of the Earth—arctic, temperate and tropical—and keeps them alive in the Ark for forty days.[4]

According to a universal principle, also operative throughout physical Nature, the seeds of all living things are preserved during the quiescence (" Night " and " Flood ") which intervenes between one period of activity or creative epoch and its successor. The fruits of each human rebirth are, for example, preserved between successive lives, the Ark being the symbol of the conserving vehicle—cosmic or human.

(d) The Lord declares Himself to be " a jealous God, visiting the iniquity of the fathers upon the children unto the third and fourth generation of them that hate me. "[5]

---

[1] *Gen.* 1:1-19.

[2] See Glossary—Brahmā's Day and Brahmā's night.

[3] *Gen.* 7:4 & 23; 19: 13, 24, 25; *Ex.* 22:20; *Joshua* 6: 21.

[4] *Gen.* 7:2-4.

[5] *Ex.* 20:5.

In the succession of reincarnations each human life is as the " father " of those which follow, they being referred to as its children. Read literally, the above quoted declaration makes of God a self-proclaimed monster of cruelty and injustice. Even a human father would not be guilty of such conduct. A more acceptable reading of this passage—depending upon the doctrine that the human Soul evolves to Christhood by means of successive lives on Earth—is that character developments are transferred from one life (the father) to its successors, (the children), whilst the effects of actions may either be received in the same life in which such actions are performed or else precipitated in succeeding incarnations.

(e) Jericho is brought down by the sound of trumpets, horns and shouting.[1]

The Logos Doctrine[2] of the formation and the dissolution of Universes by the occult potencies of sound, and their use in chanting to break down limitations of consciousness (walls) and to purify its vehicles, may well be implied. Archæologists have concluded that the destruction of the walls of Jericho was caused by an earthquake.[3]

(f) Joshua makes the sun and moon stand still to prolong the day.[4]

By the practice of contemplation the divine Will in man, his source of spiritual power and light (symbolically the sun), is brought to its maximum power (the midst of the heavens), enabling the mortal man to overcome the enemies of the Soul (Gibeonites) and attain serenity (victory and peace).

(g) The defeat of Samson by cutting off his hair, and his destruction of the temple by leaning his weight upon two of its pillars.[5]

Hair is the symbol of the effective relationship between the spiritual Soul and the mind-brain. When, symbolically, this contact is severed the power and the guidance of the inner Self are lost to the outer man, who becomes a slave to matter and the senses (Delilah). The spiritual relationship being restored, man attains to equilibrium between the pairs of opposites (the pillars), limitations (the walls of the temple) upon consciousness are dissipated and undesired qualities (the Philistines) are destroyed.

(h) Elijah goes to heaven in a chariot of fire.[6]

The sublimation of the fiery, creative force in man enables him to ascend to spiritual states of consciousness (heaven).

(i) Jonah enters the belly of a great fish and remains unharmed for three days and three nights.[7]

[1] *Joshua* 6:1-20.

[2] q.v. *Lecture Notes of the School of the Wisdom*, Vol. II, Pt. II, Ch. II, Sec. 2, Geoffrey Hodson.

[3] q.v. *The Bible as History*, pp. 156-157, Werner Keller.

[4] *Joshua* 10:12-14.

[5] *Judges* 16:17-30.

[6] *2 Kings* 2:11.

[7] *Jonah* 1:17

At Initiation the Candidate is withdrawn from his body (the ship), enters the Underworld (the sea), and is then elevated into full spiritual awareness or attains to Christ-consciousness (the fish).[1]   After the passage of sufficient time (generally three days and three nights), he returns to his body (is delivered to dry land).

(*j*) Tribute money is found inside a particular fish.[2] All the necessities (the tribute money) for spiritual, intellectual—and sometimes even physical—living are to be found in the divine aspects of human nature (the fish).   Man is encouraged to discover (catch) and draw upon the Christ power within him.

(*k*) A fig tree is withered for not bearing fruit in the early spring.[3] Unless a man gives freely of the fruits of his life, they will wither away and be lost.   The text may be regarded as the enunciation of a law as well as the description of an act.   A fuller interpretation of this incident appears in Volume One, Part One, Chapter Three of this work.

(*l*) Lazarus is raised after being dead for four days.[4] Death symbolises the total absence of spiritual awareness.   Miraculous restoration to life implies its attainment or recovery by virtue of the action of the interior divine Power and Presence (the Christ).   The period of death refers to the time during which the body of the Candidate is unconscious (figurative death) while Initiation is being conferred.   In the Ancient Mysteries death metaphorically described the condition of the uninitiated, whilst resurrection referred to passage through the Sacred Rite of Initiation.[5]

(*m*) The flesh of Christ is described as " meat " and the blood of Christ as " drink ", their consumption being declared essential to life.[6]
Our Lord insists that salvation depends upon partaking of His flesh and blood.   The " flesh " of a divine Being is a symbol for spiritual truth and law.   Eating such flesh implies intellectual absorption and full comprehension of eternal verities.   Blood symbolises the ever-outpoured divine life by which the Universe and man are spiritually sustained.   Drinking such blood refers to conscious coalescence with the one life of the Universe and realization of unity with its Source.   When read literally the passage is not only repellant and offensive to reason, but also closes the mind to the profound mystical import of the Lord's utterance.   Furthermore, being confronted with its total incredibility if so read, the pronouncement might

---

[1] q.v. *Lecture Notes of the School of the Wisdom*, Vol. II, Pt. I, Ch. I, Sec. 1, Geoffrey Hodson.

[2] *Matt.* 17:27.

[3] *Matt.* 21:19.

[4] *Jn.* 11:39-44.

[5] q.v. *The Mysteries of Eleusis*, p. 47, Prof. Georges Meautis.

[6] *Jn.* 6:47-58.

even prevent or delay an endeavour to attain by contemplation to the state
of illumination metaphorically described.   Hence the great importance of
mystical interpretation of such difficult passages.

      (*n*) The events of the night before the Crucifixion are too numerous
           for all of them to have occurred in the period allotted to them.[1]
Amongst these are:

    The Last Supper.

    The agony in the Garden.

    The betrayal by Judas.

    Appearance before Annas and then Caiaphas, and the questionings.

    Appearance before the Sanhedrin and the questioning.

    Appearance before Pilate and the trial in the Hall of Judgment.

      (Courts to try malefactors did not normally sit in the middle of
      the night).

    The visit to Herod, told of by St. Luke.

    The return to Pilate.

    Pilate's speeches and the washing of his hands, recorded by St.
      Matthew only.

    The scourging, mocking and arraying of Jesus in purple robes.

    The long and painful journey to Golgotha, followed by the nailing
      to the Cross.

The difficulty disappears, however, if the whole experience is regarded
as being descriptive of changes of consciousness as the state of human
perfection is approached.[2]

    A significant reference to this interpretation is found in the Apocryphal
Acts of John. This is the earliest of five books which were formed into a
corpus by the Manichaeans and substituted by them for the canonical *Acts.*
The book contains the following passages, which describe actions of the
Lord immediately before and during the Crucifixion.   These include both
singing an antiphonal hymn and ceremonial dancing, after which the Lord
said to John, who found himself on a mountain beside Him: " ' John, unto
the multitude below in Jerusalem I am being crucified and pierced with
lances and reeds, and gall and vinegar is given me to drink.   But unto thee
I speak, and what I speak hear thou.   I put it into thy mind to come up
into this mountain, that thou mightest hear those things which it behoveth a
disciple to learn from his teacher and a man from his God. '

    " And having thus spoken, he showed me a cross of light fixed (set
up), and about the cross a great multitude....And the Lord himself I beheld
above the cross, not having any shape, but only a voice: and a voice not

---

[1] *Lk.* 22 & 23.

[2] *Eph.* 4:13. See also *The Hidden Wisdom in the Holy Bible*, Vol. I, Pt. VI, Ch. II,
Geoffrey Hodson.

such as was familiar to us, but one sweet and kind and truly of God, saying unto me: 'John, it is needful that one should hear these things from me, for I have need of one that will hear....But this is not the cross of wood which thou wilt see when thou goest down hence: neither am I he that is on the cross, whom now thou seest not, but only hearest his (or a) voice....for know thou that I am wholly with the Father, and the Father with me. Nothing, therefore, of the things which they will say of me have I suffered: nay, that suffering also which I showed unto thee and the rest in the dance I will that it be called a mystery.' " *et seq.*[1]

Whilst interpretations of these and a great many other incongruous statements in the Bible will be offered in their due place in this and later Volumes, fuller explanations of two or three of the more perplexing texts may, perhaps, usefully be added here.

With regard to (*a*), applying the fourth key—that some physical objects, as also certain words, have each their own special Macrocosmic meaning—the days and nights of creation refer to alternations of creative activity or " day " and quiescence or " night ". These are referred to in the text of this work by their Sanskrit names of *Manvantara*[2] and *Pralaya*[2] respectively.

With reference to (*f*), Joshua personifies the Initiate who has brought his Monadic Will, symbolised by the sun, to its position of maximum power (the midst of the heavens or zenith). In consequence, he prevents the oncoming of night (in a microcosmic interpretation, mental darkness) and maintains his personal nature (the battlefield of Gibeon) in that condition of prolonged illumination (day) which ensures victory in the interior battle between Spirit (the Israelites) and matter (their enemies). This wonderful allegory has been more fully considered in Volume I, Part One, Chapter V of this work. Even from this brief interpretation, however, the element of impossibility may be regarded as both a hint or clue and an indication of a profound occult idea for which the reader is encouraged to search.

With regard to (*m*), quite clearly Our Lord was not exhorting mankind to consume human flesh and blood when He said: " Whoso eateth my flesh, and drinketh my blood, hath eternal life; and I will raise him up at the last day. For my flesh is meat indeed, and my blood is drink indeed. He that eateth my flesh, and drinketh my blood, dwelleth in me, and I in him. As the living Father hath sent me, and I live by the Father: so he that eateth me, even he shall live by me."[3] The words " flesh ", " blood ", " eateth " and " drinketh " are not to be read in the usual sense. They are

---

[1] *The Apocryphal New Testament*, newly translated by Montague Rhodes James, Litt. D., F.B.A., F.S.A., Oxford University Press, pp. 254-255.

[2] See Glossary—Chain.

[3] *Jn.* 6:54-57.

symbolical and metaphorical, and are so used in order to convey a hidden meaning.

What, then, could those four words—" flesh ", " blood ", " eateth " and " drinketh "—mean ? The flesh of Christ may be interpreted as divine truths, spiritual laws, or that in which He as Logos is clothed, by which He is covered and through which He is made manifest. The time comes—and is hastened as " The way of holiness "[1] is entered upon—when the human intellect absorbs divine knowledge, becomes illumined and inspired by the interior discovery and revelation of spiritual truths. This experience in consciousness is symbolised as eating the flesh of Christ. Bread is also used to describe knowledge of divine laws, processes and purposes. Eating consecrated bread is an allegory for the reception, absorption and application to life of that knowledge, *gnosis*, *sophia*, esoteric wisdom. Bread is also a symbol of the cyclic regeneration of life after each return to the seed state.

The blood of Christ is the ever-outpoured divine life by which the Universe is sustained and without which it could not live. The life-force does, indeed, perform a function for the Universe and all it contains which closely resembles the office which human blood performs for the physical body. Normally man is unaware either of the omnipresence of this divine outpouring or of the fact that it is the spiritually sustaining power within him.

At a certain stage of the evolution of the human intellect this fact is intuitively perceived. Such realisation by the neophyte can be hastened by means of certain spiritual practices, by meditation and prayer, and by the aid of his Master, of the Hierophant and of other Officiants in the Sacred Initiatory Rites of the Temples of the Greater Mysteries. Ultimately full knowledge may be gained of the outpouring of the Christ-life into the Universe and man, and also of man's identity with that life and its divine Source. This attainment is described symbolically as drinking Christ's blood. Our Lord may be assumed to have been referring to a state of consciousness of unity with the Cosmic Christ and His outpoured vital energy rather than to an act of physical nutrition.

Once this symbolical eating and drinking, this spiritual *agape*, has occurred, then the process can be initiated in others who in their turn, starving for truth, can be fed in vast multitudes. As the incident of feeding the five thousand[2] allegorically tells, in such ministration there is not, neither can there be, any loss. On the contrary there is more of spiritual wisdom, knowledge and upwelling vitality afterwards than before—even unto " twelve baskets full ".

[1] *Is.* 35: 8.
[2] *Matt.* 14:15-21.

Thus, in the fourth interpretation, all objects, as also many words, have each their own special meaning. The symbols employed of the Sacred Language are associated with one or more of the four elements of earth, water, air or fire.

PART TWO

INTERPRETATIONS OF TWO PASSAGES FROM
THE BOOK OF GENESIS

The following advance interpretations of portions of the *Book of Genesis* are here offered in the hope that they may fulfill at least three purposes. One of these is to prepare the reader for the more detailed study of the same passages which will follow later in this book. The second is to give typical instances of the concealment and revelation of truth by means of allegory and symbol, whilst the third is to provide examples of classical methods of interpretation.

CHAPTER I

THE STORY OF ESAU, JACOB AND THE BIRTHRIGHT; A MACROCOSMIC INTERPRETATION

COSMOGONICAL PROCEDURES

THE description of the birth and subsequent actions of the twins Esau and Jacob, as related in the Twenty-fifth Chapter of *Genesis*, is of especial interest to the student of symbology, whilst as an allegory of Cosmogenesis it is of added significance. Esau came forth first, was red and hairy, and became " a man of the field ".[1] Jacob followed, holding on to Esau's heel, and "was a plain man, dwelling in tents".[2] Esau, a skillful hunter—an often used symbol for divine power—represents the masculine potency in all creative processes, and Jacob the feminine. Esau is therefore rightly born first, since he personifies the primary activity in the cosmic creative process, the positive action of the Spirit of God or the Great Breath.[3] Red, as a primary colour, also represents masculinity and the positive pole. The hairs on the skin, like the feathers on the wings of goddesses as portrayed in Egyptian and other religious art, represent the outraying, forthshining powers, the superabundance of the creative energy of the Logos.

The feminine or negative pole is attracted into union with this power, and so at his birth Jacob, as personifying the receptive, conveying and re-expressing principle in Cosmos, reaches out towards the heel of Esau. The narrative thus symbolically describes electro-magnetic laws, as do later portions of the story which deal with incidents in the lives of the twins.

THE SEETHED POTTAGE

When the two boys have grown up Jacob, by means of deceit, receives the birthright of Esau, and in this also the analogy is exact; for the feminine matrix—pre-cosmic matter—receives the masculine, creative, birth-produ-

---

[1] *Gen.* 25:27.
[2] *Ibid.*
[3] *Purusha*—see Glossary.

cing power, pre-cosmic Spirit. This natural procedure is also referred to allegorically in the account of the exoterically reprehensible deception practised
by Rebekah and Jacob upon the blind and dying Isaac; for again it is
Jacob who receives the patriarchal blessing and a promise of fecundity and
multiplicity of seed.[1]   Esau, though chosen by his father as the recipient of
this inheritance, is tricked, receives but a secondary blessing, and is made
the servant of his more fortunate brother.

As in so many Biblical passages, a literal reading is here quite unacceptable, even repellant.[2]   The Bible, however, contains many such blinds.
The recorded deliberate deceits with which the pages of the *Pentateuch* are
disfigured are also susceptible of symbolic interpretation.   The actions of
both Abraham and Jacob in passing off their wives to Pharaoh as their
sisters are, in terms of modern morality, peculiarly unpleasant examples of
such deceitfulness for personal gain.   This may be a blind, however, and
these recorded experiences, events and human actions may similarly be
read not only in their literal sense, but also as vehicles for concealed truths.

In the particular story we are at present considering, an account of
wickedness being rewarded by favours may be read as a hint to look for an
intended inner meaning, full knowledge of which bestows theurgic powers.
Despite the unhappy ending of the allegory Esau remains the true heir,[3]
the creative Principle being ever unbound, ever free.   Symbolically, Esau is
" a man of the field ", or open country.   He thus personifies the masculine
current of the triple creative power, the positive pole of electro-magnetic
phenomena, Spirit in relation to matter and sperm in relation to ovum.
The great Passive (Jacob), the feminine, negative polarity—primordial substance or matter (*Mūlaprakriti*)[4]—is, however, the actual receptacle,
conserver and transmitter of the emitted creative power or Great Breath
(*Purusha*).

This triplicity or trinity of creative powers is thus clearly portrayed in
the remarkable imagery of the birth of the twins, which initiates the new
dispensation.   Esau portrays positive power, Jacob represents receptive,
differentiated substance and their mother, Rebekah, the original, pre-cosmic
matter, particularly that which had been employed in the preceding cycle
of activity.   The three are correctly linked together, for Jacob holds the
heel of Esau while he himself is still partly within Rebekah's womb.   With
the father, Isaac, they constitute a quaternary.   Isaac is the primordial
propulsive agent, the Breather, the Speaker of the " Word ", the Primary
Emitter of the creative power *in abscondito*.   When once the spiritual,

---

[1] *Gen.* 27:7-29.
[2] See Pt. One, Ch. I, of this Volume.
[3] *Gen.* 36.
[4] *Mūlaprakriti*—see Glossary.

creative energy is emanated, this primary agent is correctly represented by the *absent* Isaac.

RECURRENT CYCLES

After repeating Abraham's journeys, his experiences at wells and with the Philistines, Isaac grows old and becomes wealthy in his later years.[1] The story of his subterfuge in passing his wife off as his sister, for fear of death and in the hope of gain,[2] is another example of the use of a literary blind or cover. The narrative may be interpreted in precisely the same manner as was the similar conduct of his father, Abraham.[3] The universal law of ever-recurring cycles is indicated by such repetitions.

The fulfillment of the life, the old age and the death of central figures refer more especially to the culmination of the returning arc of a cycle and also those of successions of cycles. Evolving life, ascending by a spiral path, arrives *over* the same point reached in preceding rounds and then passes through similar experiences, performs the identical functions, resorts to the same apparent artifices, all with equally beneficent results.

Such is the method of teaching used by the ancient writers. All cycles of involution and evolution, major and minor, follow spiral paths and so are repetitions of their predecessors, but in a more advanced phase. The fundamental principles, allegorised in the Sacred Language as events, remain unchanged. In consequence the attainment of old age, riches and patriarchal power—meaning the creative impulse and the fruits of its exercise—must be followed by their transmission to the next cycle and its presiding genius.

The Parable of the Prodigal Son describes the process of the forthgoing of the outpoured, conscious life of the Logos, which bears with it into the field of evolution the Rays or radiations of the Monads of all beings (the " journey into a far country ").

At the beginning of each new manifestation these Monads are at varying stages of development and awareness, according to the degree of unfoldment reached in preceding cycles. At the farthest point of the path of forthgoing, represented in the Earth Scheme of our Solar System by the mineral kingdom of the physical plane, the power, the life and the consciousness of the Monad are most deeply encased in matter. In the parable this phase is portrayed by the deepest degradation of the prodigal son, who fain would have eaten " the husks that the swine did eat ".

The parable also describes in allegory the pathway of return, or evolution, at the close of which all the seed powers of the Monads have become

[1] *Gen.* 27:7-29.
[2] *Gen.* 26:7-11.
[3] *Gen.* 12:11-20. q.v. Vol. II of this work..p 310.

developed to the highest degree possible in any particular cycle.   The bliss
and the enrichment of the spiritual Soul are symbolised by the welcome,
the gifts and the feasting provided for the prodigal son on his return.   This
major cycle of involution and evolution is repeated in innumerable component sub-cycles of gradually diminishing degree and dimension.   Man as
Ego repeats it, for example, in each cycle of birth and death.   Throughout
this book the period of activity is called *Manvantara*, and the quiescence which
always follows is termed *Pralaya*.

THE DIVINE LIFE AS THE PRODIGAL SON

THE MACROCOSMIC CYCLE

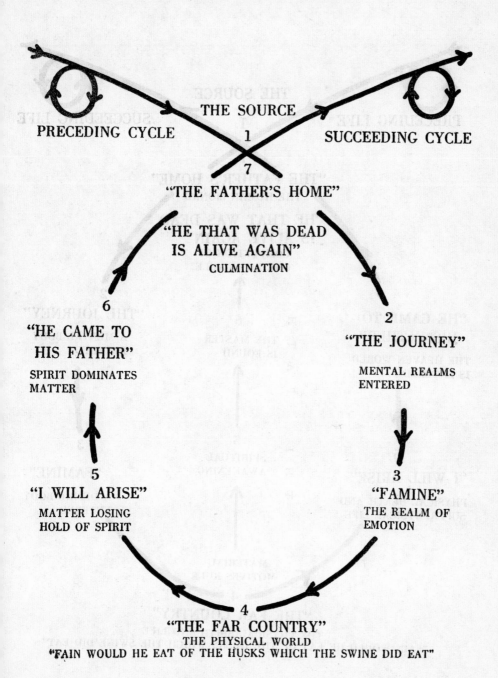

PRECEDING CYCLE

THE SOURCE
1

SUCCEEDING CYCLE

7

"THE FATHER'S HOME"

"HE THAT WAS DEAD
IS ALIVE AGAIN"
CULMINATION

6

"HE CAME TO
HIS FATHER"

SPIRIT DOMINATES
MATTER

2

"THE JOURNEY"

MENTAL REALMS
ENTERED

5

"I WILL ARISE"

MATTER LOSING
HOLD OF SPIRIT

3

"FAMINE"

THE REALM OF
EMOTION

4

"THE FAR COUNTRY"
THE PHYSICAL WORLD
"FAIN WOULD HE EAT OF THE HUSKS WHICH THE SWINE DID EAT"

THE HUMAN SPIRIT AS THE PRODIGAL SON

THE MICROCOSMIC CYCLE

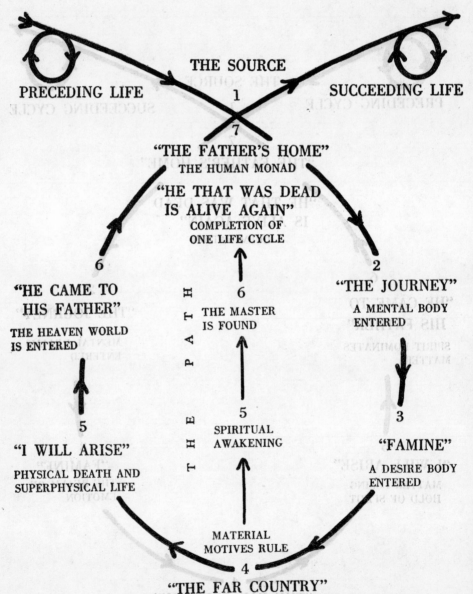

THE SOURCE
1

PRECEDING LIFE

SUCCEEDING LIFE

7

"THE FATHER'S HOME"
THE HUMAN MONAD

"HE THAT WAS DEAD
IS ALIVE AGAIN"
COMPLETION OF
ONE LIFE CYCLE

6

2

"HE CAME TO
HIS FATHER"

THE HEAVEN WORLD
IS ENTERED

6
THE MASTER
IS FOUND

"THE JOURNEY"

A MENTAL BODY
ENTERED

T H E   P A T H

5

3

5

"I WILL ARISE"

PHYSICAL DEATH AND
SUPERPHYSICAL LIFE

5
SPIRITUAL
AWAKENING

"FAMINE"

A DESIRE BODY
ENTERED

4
MATERIAL
MOTIVES RULE

"THE FAR COUNTRY"
THE PHYSICAL BIRTH AND LIFE
"FAIN WOULD HE EAT OF THE HUSKS WHICH THE SWINE DID EAT"

THE STORY OF JOSEPH, HIS COAT OF MANY COLOURS AND HIS DESCENT INTO THE PIT

Joseph himself may be interpreted from three points of view, namely, as a personification of: (*a*) the conscious life of a Universe (Macrocosm), (*b*) the highly evolved spiritual Soul or immortal Ego of man (microcosm), and (*c*) an Initiate of the Greater Mysteries.[1]

A MACROCOSMIC INTERPRETATION

JOSEPH AS THE INDWELLING LIFE

AT the formation of a new Universe its divine Architect first marks or circumscribes the area in the virginal, unparticled, precosmic space in which the Universe is to appear. He[2] then projects an atom-forming energy which differentiates the enclosed matter from undifferentiated Space. This process is carried out by the Holy Spirit, the third Aspect of the Trinity, the creative Mind, which is the Source and Director of the atom-forming electrical energies.

From the same divine Source—the threefold, active Deity—the all-preserving and vitalising life-force of the Second Aspect enters the prepared universal field. This outpoured life of God is personified by Joseph. It enters the newly projected Universe in its most spiritualised, tenuous condition (conception), gradually becomes more fully incarnate (Joseph's birth), and later is imprisoned (his adulthood) in matter of gradually deepening density (Joseph is lowered into the pit). This process of forthgoing thus culminates in incarnation in solid substance—earth and all that is of the earth, including the densest, hardest metals and jewels, an imprisonment indeed.

Joseph personifies the forthgoing life of God, and the authors of the *Pentateuch* recount the sending forth of Joseph by his father, Jacob, into the

---

[1] q.v. Vol. I of this work, Pt. Six.

[2] The masculine pronoun is used for convenience only, the Supreme Deity being regarded in occult philosophy as a-sexual.

field as an allegory of entry into a region of creative activity.   Out in the field Joseph is rightly wearing a coat of many colours; for when the one life becomes manifested in innumerable forms its white light is broken up into the many hues of the spectrum.   Shelley, in his poem " Adonais ", thus expresses this idea:

> " Life, like a dome of many-coloured glass,
>   Stains the white radiance of Eternity. "

Unity has become displaced by diversity.   As the path of forthgoing is entered upon, the one becomes the many, a fundamental fact which is allegorically portrayed by the action of Joseph's father, Jacob, in robing his son in a coat of many colours.[1]

JOSEPH'S BRETHREN SEE THE COAT AND ARE ENVIOUS

The descent of the life of the Logos from the highest spiritual level to the densest material encasement is typified by Joseph's departure from home. Its embodiment in the myriad forms of Nature, superphysical and physical, is assisted by Ministers of the Supreme Deity, first fruits of preceding Universes (Elohim),[2] who fulfil a major role during the forthgoing of the one life into matter (Joseph goes out into the field and later is lowered into the pit). The older brothers of Joseph personify these high Intelligences, Themselves manifesting in the superphysical realms of Nature and dwelling amidst the life of the Cosmos and its associated forces.   Appropriately, Joseph's brothers carry out their function from above the pit and so, Elohim-like, do not themselves go down into it.

These same procedures are allegorically described in the Parable of the Prodigal Son,[3] in which corresponding cosmogonical procedures are revealed.   In that story the elder son is stated to be jealous of his younger brother. Similarly the brothers of Joseph are presented as being envious of the youngest member of the family.   As already stated, this may legitimately be regarded as a deliberate blind used in order to conceal, and yet reveal, power-bestowing knowledge concerning the mystery of forth-going, of the descent of the divine life and of the Monads of men into the " tomb " of matter, as also of the divine Intelligences associated with that descent.   The action of the brothers in forcibly lowering Joseph into a pit after they had taken off his coat of many colours, does, however, aptly portray by allegory the function of the Order of Intelligences involved in the forthgoing or involution of life.   The revelation particularly applies to those members of that Order who bring about the manifestation of life at the densest physical

---

[1] Gen. 37:3.

[2] see Glossary and Vol. II of this work, Pt. Three, Ch. III.

[3] q.v. The two diagrams preceding this Chapter and Vol. I of this work, Pt. Four.

level (the pit). In one of his aspects Satan is a symbolic personification of these Beings who thus imprison life in matter, and are sometimes referred to as the Satanic Hierarchy.[1]

James Stephens, the Irish poet, expresses this profoundly occult idea in his poem, " Fullness of Time "[2]:—

" On a rustly iron throne,
　　Past the furthest star of space,
　　I saw Satan sit alone,
　　Old and haggard was his face;
　　For his work was done, and he
　　Rested in eternity.

" And to him from out the sun
　　Came his father and his friend,
　　Saying—Now the work is done
　　Enmity is at an end—
　　And He guided Satan to
　　Paradises that He knew.

" Gabriel, without a frown;
　　Uriel, without a spear;
　　Raphael, came singing down,
　　Welcoming their ancient peer;
　　And they seated him beside
　　One who had been crucified. "

Life incarnate in substance inevitably becomes stained with the taint of matter. In the animal and human kingdoms, sensation and sense-pleasure sully the pure spirituality of the emergent life. They also restrict it by materialising and thereby degrading it. This is portrayed by the brothers of Joseph dipping his coat in animal blood before sending it back to their father with the untrue story of his beloved son's death. If accepted literally, this is a very unpleasant episode. Thus interpreted, however, it proves to be a revelation of a spiritual law.

In the Sacred Language the final stage of the path of forthgoing is frequently described as the death and burial of a Saviour or a hero, just as entry upon the path of return is portrayed by a Resurrection and Ascension.

If the repetition be pardoned, upto this point the story of Joseph may be read as an allegory descriptive of the forthgoing of the divine life into a Universe in order that the substance and forms thereof might be vitalised, ensouled and preserved. God is said to die in order that His Universe may live. Christ, as the one life, is crucified and buried in the rock tomb, St.

[1] q.v. *The Kingdom of the Gods.* Pt. III. Ch. V, Geoffrey Hodson.
[2] *Collected Poems*, James Stephens. Macmillan & Co., London, 1931.

John the Divine referring to Him as " the Lamb slain from the foundation of the world ".[1]

THE RAISING, THE JOURNEY TO EGYPT AND THE HIGH ATTAINMENT OF JOSEPH

In the cosmic interpretation the Midianite merchants in their turn represent a group of spiritual Intelligences, members of which participate in and assist the evolution of life following its involution, thereby performing a spiritualising function. This is in opposition to that of their " Brothers " (*Pitris*)[2] who are concerned with the downward arc. These two Orders of Archangels and angels are sometimes portrayed as being at war[3] or as being Satanic and redemptive respectively. The truth, carefully veiled in the allegorical method of revelation, is that the function of each Order is equally important, just as people passing in and out of an enclosure through a turnstile, despite their opposite movements, cause it to rotate in the same direction.

A MICROCOSMIC INTERPRETATION

JOSEPH AS PERSONIFICATION OF THE DIVINE SPIRIT IN MAN

The Ageless Wisdom teaches that, in the innermost Essence of his being, man as Monad[4] is pure Spirit, indestructible, eternal, a spark within the one undying Fire which is God. This primordial seed of Deity contains in various degrees of latency all the powers of the parent God-head, which one day will become fully manifest.[5] In the Sacred Language the divine aspect of man's nature is generally personified by the Supreme Deity, the Lord Who inspires Saviours, Prophets and other central figures.

In order that the seed-like powers innate in the Monad may germinate and develop, a Ray is projected from it into evolutionary fields—Universes, superphysical and physical. This Ray in due course becomes expressed as an immortal, unfolding individuality, a spiritual Soul, a human Ego, which thereafter unfolds its Monadic powers to the degree of Adeptship or perfected manhood, " the measure of the stature of the fulness of Christ ".[6]

---

[1] *Rev.* 13:8.

[2] *Pitris*—see Glossary and *The Kingdom of the Gods*, Pt. III, Chs. IV and V, Geoffrey Hodson.

[3] One interpretation of the so-called War in Heaven.

[4] Monad—see Glossary.

[5] " Ye shall be perfect, even as your Father which is in heaven is perfect. " (*Matt.* 5:48, Rev. Version).

[6] *Eph.* 4:13.

In this microcosmic interpretation the Ego is personified by Joseph, the Monadic Ray by his father, Jacob, and the Monad itself by the Lord God, Who inspires both.   The forthshining of the Ray into the denser fields of matter is dramatically portrayed by Joseph's departure from home, the loss of his coat of many colours (his aura,[1] which becomes invisible at the physical level) and his imprisonment in the pit.   This action also symbolically describes the " descent " of the immortal Ego into human birth.

These procedures are variously represented in the Sacred Language as murders, dismemberments, entombments and burials.   Since, however, the inner Self of man is immortal, all such symbolical descents and deaths are followed by ascents and resurrections.   Major and minor cycles of manifestation—whether cosmic or human—are, as above stated, portrayed by these forthgoings and returns, descents and ascents, burials and resurrections.

In the human interpretation of great allegorical dramas, various people personify qualities of character, powers, faculties, weaknesses and defects, the two last-named sometimes being symbolised by sickness, blindness, sleep and death.   The twelve children of Jacob typify, for example, Zodiacal attributes present in man from the beginning and ultimately to be fully developed—their father himself having described them in such terms.[2]

When recovery from adversities is said to be miraculously brought about by an inspired Personage, an evolutionary phase is being described in which limitations are outgrown.   This is achieved by virtue of an awakened and active divine power *within* the hitherto unillumined personality.   The brothers of Joseph display these defects and are made to feel envy, and even hatred, towards Joseph.   They rob him of his coat, for example, and deceive their father by returning it to him blood-stained.   Later on they plot to bring about their brother's death.

In terms of the Sacred Language these brothers microsmically represent the material encasements of the Soul—the mental, emotional, vital and physical bodies with their limitations and shortcomings.   They also personify tendencies which materialise bodily consciousness and diminish the degree of the light, power and spirituality of the Monad-Ego manifesting in the personal nature.   They display undesirable qualities of character, and thus metaphorically imprison the Soul as in a tomb or pit.

[1] q.v. *Man Visible and Invisible*, C. W. Leadbeater.
[2] *Gen.* 49.

AN INITIATORY INTERPRETATION

JOSEPH AS CANDIDATE FOR INITIATION AND AS INITIATE

The unfoldment of the human Monad from man to Superman may be delayed, may proceed normally, or may be hastened. Delay arises from deliberate selfishness and self-materialisation in thought, motive and mode of life. Since the evolution of germinal Monadic powers from latency to increasing potency inevitably occurs throughout *Manvantara*, this process may be regarded as the normal procedure.. Hastening, however, is achieved by self-spiritualisation and by service to others. The impulse to embark upon self-quickening, or to tread the Path, arises within a Neophyte when the inner Self has reached a certain degree of development. This is evidenced by the responsiveness and ultimate surrender of the outer personality to purely spiritual influences. The decision to find and tread " The way of holiness "[1] is thus perfectly natural, because inwardly inspired.

As a youth Joseph typifies a spiritual Neophyte, whilst his adventures, including his disasters and triumphs, allegorically portray difficulties encountered and successes achieved by those who enter in at " the strait gate "[2] and tread the narrow way. The tests, ordeals, victories and rapid unfoldment of many faculties and powers are also described allegorically in the narrative. Progressive stages in the story of the life of a Saviour or hero portray expansions of consciousness associated with passage through the five great Initiations, culminating in Adeptship at the Fifth.[3]

This method of revelation of the inner life of those who tread " the Ancient Way " is also exemplified by the action of placing Joseph in a dark pit, or out of the sight of normal passers-by. Reference is thus made to Rites of Initiation in olden days in which, in secret Halls of Initiation, Candidates were deprived of physical consciousness and laid either upon a cross or in a sarcophagus within a Temple or crypt. This was dark to the Candidate because he was physically unconscious, having been plunged into an Initiatory trance. Three days and three nights then passed, and during this period the spiritual Self entered into full realisation of oneness with the divine life within all Nature, knowing itself to be identical with that life. At the end of this period the Ego re-entered the body, which then awakened to the light of day. Thus Joseph is raised from the dark pit and restored to the blessing of light. As a result of this experience the Initiate was as one reborn, renewed, and is sometimes referred to as being born again or

---

[1] *Is.* 35:8.
[2] *Matt.* 7:13.
[3] q.v. Vol. I of this work, Pt. six.

" twice born ". In allegorical literature all Nativities of Saviours and heroes are susceptible of similar interpretation.

The resistance of the substances of which man's mental, emotional and physical bodies are built, and of the involving[1] consciousness within those substances, the despiritualising effects of undesirable habits and the difficulties of adverse karma[2]—all these create obstacles and cause sufferings on the Path of Swift Unfoldment which, in consequence, is sometimes referred to as " the Way of the Cross ". In the Joseph story these adverse influences are portrayed by his attempted seduction by Potiphar's wife, and by the several misfortunes which followed. Joseph's interpretation of dreams, his rise to power as Grand Vizier of Egypt and his death in great honour—all these portray degrees of development, powers attained, and the Initiate's final triumph when he becomes an Adept.

Such are three possible readings of the life story of Joseph— Macrocosmic, microcosmic and Initiatory.

---

[1] Involving—a term applied to the divine life on the pathway of forthgoing deeper and deeper *into* matter.

[2] *Karma*—see Glossary.

4

PART THREE

ISAAC, REBEKAH, ESAU AND JACOB

COSMOGENESIS

Since some of the concepts of the cosmogony of occult philosophy are included in the interpretations of the life stories of Abraham's sons and grandsons which now follow, a brief statement of them may prove helpful, especially to those contacting these ideas for the first time.

Basic amongst such concepts is an idea with which a member of the Christian Faith and a reader of the Bible is likely to be completely unfamiliar. I therefore advance it at this point. This idea is that of the eternity of the Universe as a whole, within which numberless Universes incessantly manifest and disappear. Madame Blavatsky states this as follows:

" Our 'Universe' (the Solar System) is only one of an infinite number of Universes, all of them 'Sons of Necessity', because links in the great cosmic chain of Universes, each one standing in the relation of an effect as regards the predecessor and of a cause as regards its successor. "

If this be accepted then the Universe, the creation of which is described in the *Book of Genesis*, was not an entirely new and single production. Rather is it to be regarded in the terms of occult philosophy as one in a succession of such Universes, and not one created alone and for ever.

The first five verses of the *Book of Genesis* describe the opening phases of the process of creation[1] as follows:

1. In the beginning God created the heaven and the earth.
2. And the earth was without form, and void; and darkness was upon the face of the deep. And the Spirit of God moved upon the face of the waters.
3. And God said, Let there be light; and there was light.
4. And God saw the light, that it was good; and God divided the light from the darkness.
5. And God called the light Day, and the darkness he called Night. And the evening and the morning were the first day.

Thus originally there existed duality in unity, namely the Spirit of God (the masculine creative potency) on the one hand and the face of the deep (the feminine creative potency) on the other. Primarily there was a dual Principle, a positive and a negative, Spirit-matter. During the long creative " Night " which in Sanskrit is called *Pralaya*[2] (rest), there was dark-

---

[1] Creation—the emergence and subsequent development of a Universe and its contents is regarded in occult philosophy as being less the result of a single act of creation, followed by natural evolution, than a process of emanation guided by intelligent Forces under immutable law. The creation or emergence of Universes from nothing is not an acceptable concept, the Cosmos being regarded as emanating from an all-containing, sourceless Source the Absolute.

[2] *Pralaya*—see Glossary.

ness upon the face of the deep.   The whole of boundless Space was dark
and quiescent.   Then, it is stated, a change occurred.   The Spirit of God,
having emerged from Absolute Existence, moved upon the face of the waters.
The " Great Breath " breathed upon the " Great Deep ", whereupon
emanation began and *Manvantara*[1] (ordered manifestation) was initiated.

Thus, behind and beyond and within all is the Eternal and Infinite
Parent from within which the temporary and the finite emerge, or are born.
That Boundless Self-Existence is variously referred to as the Absolute, the
Changeless, the Eternal ALL, the Causeless Cause, the Rootless Root.
This is Non-Being, Negative Existence, No-Thing, *Ain* (as the Kabbalist
says), an impersonal Unity without attributes conceivable by man.

In occult philosophy the term " God " in its highest meaning refers
to a Supreme, Eternal and Indefinable Reality.   This Absolute is inconceivable, ineffable and unknowable.   Its revealed existence is postulated
in three terms: an absolute Existence, an absolute Consciousness and an
absolute Bliss.   Infinite Consciousness is regarded as inherent in the Supreme
Being as a dynamic Force that manifests the potentialities held in its own
infinitude, and calls into being forms out of its own formless depths.   From
THAT, the Absolute, emerged an active, creative Power and Intelligence
to become the formative Deity, the *Demiurgos*,[2] of the Universe-to-be.   The
illumined Sages thus taught that the Eternal One, which is potentially
twofold (Spirit-matter), is subject to cyclic, rhythmic Motion, a primordial
Third which is also eternal.   Under certain conditions the relationship of
the conjoined Spirit-matter changes from passive unity into active
duality—distinct positive and negative potencies.

Thus, when " interior " Motion causes hitherto unified, quiescent
Spirit-matter to become oppositely polarised or creatively active, then there
is activity, light, " Day "; for these two (universal Spirit and universal
Matter) produce a third, a " Son ", which becomes the presiding Deity,
the Logos, the Architect of the resultant Universe.   A finite Principle has
now emerged from the Infinite.   Universal Spirit-matter-motion have
become focused into a " Being ", Who is beyond normal human comprehension.   This is the One Alone, the " only-begotten Son "[3] (when correctly
translated, " alone begotten " or emanated from a unified, single Source),
being of " one substance with the Father ", which in this case is the Absolute,

---

[1] *Manvantara*—see Glossary.

[2] *Demiurgos* (Gr.)— the *Demiurge* or Artificer, the Supernal Power which built the Universe.   Freemasons derive from this word their phrase " Supreme Architect ".   With the
occultist it is the third manifested Logos, or Plato's second God, the second Logos being
represented by him as the " Father ", the only Deity that he, as an Initiate of the Mysteries,
dare mention.   The *demiurgic* Mind is the same as the Universal Mind, named *Mahat* (Sk.),
the first "product " of Brahmā.

[3] From *The Gloria in Excelsis*, a translation of an early Greek hymn.

the Uncreate. By this " Son ", the cosmic Christ, all worlds are fashioned. " He " being the Emanator, Architect, Sustainer and Regenerator of Universes and all that they will ever contain.

This formative Logos is the first objective Emanation of the Absolute. It is the Principle of divine Thought, now to be made manifest in an individual sense, firstly as the Logos of the whole Cosmos, secondly as the Solar Deity of a single Solar System, and thirdly as the Logos of the Soul of every human being—the Dweller in the Innermost. These Three are One, indivisible, identical, an integral part of each other, a whole. In the beginning, when newly formed, the First, the One Alone, is purely spiritual and intellectual. Ultimately, as we have seen, It becomes manifested as the presiding Power, Life and Intelligence transcendent beyond all that objectively exists, and also as the indwelling and transforming divine life immanent within all Nature, all beings and all things.

Such, in outline,[1] are some of the cosmogonical ideas to be found in occult philosophy. Further expositions of them will be found in the interpretations of the *Book of Genesis* which follow.

---

[1] For a fuller description and other Scriptural accounts of these and succeeding phases of Cosmogenesis, q.v. *Occult Powers in Nature and in Man* and *Lecture Notes of the School of the Wisdom*, Vol. II, Pt. II, Geoffrey Hodson. T.P.H., Adyar, Madras, India.

CHAPTER I

THE BIRTH OF ESAU AND JACOB

THE second Volume of this work brought the study of the *Book of Genesis* to the narrative of the death and burial of Abraham, as described in verses eight and nine of the Twenty-fifth Chapter:

> 8. *Then Abraham gave up the ghost, and died in a good old age, an old man, and full of years; and was gathered to his people.*
>
> 9. *And his sons Isaac and Ishmael buried him in the cave of Machpelah, in the field of Ephron the son of Zohar the Hittite, which is before Mamre.*

The life stories of Abraham's sons and grandsons now receive consideration, interpretations being offered in accordance with the principles expounded in Part One of this book.

The subject-matter of the present Volume includes divine and patriarchal successions; Cosmogenesis; the operation of the law of major and minor cycles with their component arcs of forthgoing and return;[1] immaculate conception; the law of correspondences; the four basic elements of earth, air, fire and water; famine and plenty; wells; members of families as personifications of laws, processes and successions in Nature, as also of qualities of human character; and " The way of holiness "[2] leading to discipleship, Initiation and Adeptship.[3] This last is more especially accentuated in the interpretations offered of the life of Joseph with which the Volume closes.

> *Gen.* 25: 20. *And Isaac was forty years old when he took Rebekah to wife, the daughter of Bethuel the Syrian of Padan-aram, the sister to Laban the Syrian.*
>
> 21. *And Isaac intreated the LORD for his wife, because she was barren: and the LORD was intreated of him, and Rebekah his wife conceived.*
>
> 22. *And the children struggled together within her; and she said, If it be so, why am I thus? And she went to enquire of the LORD.*

---

[1] q.v. Vol. I of this work, Pt. Four.
[2] *Is.* 35:8.
[3] q.v. Vol. I of this work, Pt. Six.

23. *And the LORD said unto her, Two nations are in thy womb, and two manner of people shall be separated from thy bowels; and the one people shall be stronger than the other people; and the elder shall serve the younger.*

24. *And when her days to be delivered were fulfilled, behold, there were twins in her womb.*

25. *And the first came out red, all over like an hairy garment; and they called his name Esau.*

26. *And after that came his brother out, and his hand took hold on Esau's heel; and his name was called Jacob: and Isaac was three score years old when she bare them.*

27. *And the boys grew and Esau was a cunning hunter, a man of the field; and Jacob was a plain man, dwelling in tents.*

28. *And Isaac loved Esau, because he did eat of his venison; but Rebekah loved Jacob.*

29. *And Jacob sod pottage: and Esau came from the field, and he was faint.*

30. *And Esau said to Jacob, Feed me, I pray thee, with that same red pottage; for I am faint: therefore was his name called Edom.*

31. *And Jacob said, Sell me this day thy birthright.*

32. *And Esau said, Behold, I am at the point to die: and what profit shall this birthright do to me?*

33. *And Jacob said, Swear to me this day; and he sware unto him: and he sold his birthright unto Jacob.*

34. *Then Jacob gave Esau bread and pottage of lentils: and he did eat and drink, and rose up, and went his way: thus Esau despised his birthright.*

JACOB BORN HOLDING ESAU'S HEEL

The symbology of human generation and maternity is, I suggest, here employed to portray cosmic creative processes. Conception by the parents corresponds to the first modification in pre-cosmic Ideation, the forming or arising in the Universal Mind of the concept of a Universe, and its primary effect as a differentiation of pre-cosmic Space. This is generally fore-shadowed by the first faint stirrings in hitherto quiescent, pre-cosmic Mind—the germ from which emanates thought-imbued creative impulses, after which the generative process continues according to eternal Law.

This emanation of the divine " Idea " is, in literature written in the Sacred Language symbolised severally by the " Voice " or " Word " of God (Logos), by visitations and promises of fertility made by God, or by Angelic Annunciations of coming conceptions. Before this extremely remote, highly spiritualised transition from creative quiescence to the first tremor of creative activity occurs, the matter side of Spirit, also quiescent and undifferentiated, is non-productive— "....darkness was upon the face of the deep. " This is indicated by the preceding barrenness or virginity of concubine or wife—in the present case Rebekah. Hitherto quiescent, non-manifested, equipolarised, utterly unified Spirit-matter continues to function as a unit, even after the first modification of the one (Spirit) and differentiation of the other (matter) have occurred. In consequence, creative activity is simultaneous and so continues in the first cycle, symbolised by the life of the embryo *in utero*.

This highly metaphysical truth is beautifully and skilfully portrayed in this part of the story of Isaac and Rebekah, first in the conception of twins by the hitherto barren Rebekah, and secondly by the carefully recorded phenomenon that they emerged still united, with Jacob's hand grasping Esau's heel. Nevertheless they emerge in the correct order. Spirit, as Esau, leads and matter, as Jacob, follows. The unity in duality and duality in unity of Spirit-matter is thus indicated by their joint masculinity. The functional separation of Spirit from matter which follows is indicated by the separated existence of the two infants, and by their markedly different appearance, character and mode of life.

That Jacob represents the productive side of Nature is at once indicated in the quaintly worded English sentence: " Jacob sod (seethed or cooked) pottage."[1] This implies the production of Nature's forms from natural elements. More precisely, there is indicated the production of the subsequent states of matter, or *tattvas*,[2] of the seven planes of Nature from protyle[3] or *Adi-tattva*. Thus the combined life of Esau and Jacob *in utero* and their contact at birth via heel and hand have constituted a creative union and interaction, the result of which is Nature herself, produced by the matter side of the duality and symbolised by the pottage which Jacob made.

Isaac's wedding occurred in his fortieth year and the birth of the twins, Esau and Jacob, when he was sixty years old. Indications are found in ancient literature of a development which gave to numbers their real significance, and employed them in a system of symbolism which referred to something more than enumeration alone. Each number is regarded as possessing a certain power not expressed by the figure or symbol, which is employed to denote quantity only. This power rests in an occult connection existing between the relations of things and the principles in Nature of which they are the expressions. According to this system of numerical symbology the number 4 refers to the personal nature, the lower quaternary—mind, emotion, vitality and flesh—as yet unmarried or not consciously united

---

[1] *Gen.* 25:29.

[2] *Tattvas*—see Glossary.

[3] Protyle (Gk.): Postulated by chemists as the first homogeneous, primordial substance

with the threefold Higher Self, in its turn indicated by the number 3. The resultant number 7 refers to the fusion of the Higher Triad and the lower quaternary in man, accompanied by the fully conscious experience of spiritual awareness—sometimes described as the " heavenly marriage ".

Esau and Jacob are the first twins whose birth is recorded in the Bible, and they and their subsequent history are of profound occult significance. Esau, as has already been noted, was born first and he was red and hairy. Jacob followed, holding on to Esau's heel.

THE HEEL IN SYMBOLISM

In the Sacred Language the heel symbolises the point of creative contact between Spirit and matter, just as in man it is the place on his body which first touches the earth when he stands erect and from which he acquires the necessary contact and the leverage when he walks. For this, as for all generative processes, a price must be paid. Spirit is inevitably stained by contact with matter, and life loses freedom when in contact with form. Consciousness, manifesting through concrete mind and brain, sacrifices a measure of its universality and its capacity for abstract realisation and generalisation. This loss (vulnerability) of immortality by Spirit is portrayed in the allegory of Achilles. In the story of Esau and Jacob, however, the closing of a circuit and the conveyance of the electrical, creative force from positive to negative is also indicated.

The winged heel of Mercury symbolises the regaining of all temporarily surrendered powers on the later stages of the upward arc. In man the recovery of Egoic consciousness attained at the First Initiation is implied by the possession of winged heels. A price must, however, be paid for fully self-conscious enjoyment of divine powers. This price is symbolised by the loss of one shoe, or the uncovered heel, which makes the body vulnerable but which also provides primary contact with Mother Earth. Thus Esau (Spirit) comes in contact with Jacob (matter) by the heel, and Jacob (matter) comes in contact with Esau (Spirit) through the hand. In these various ways the first phase of the creative process, Macrocosmic and microcosmic, is described in the *Book of Genesis*.

ESAU RED AND HAIRY

The statements in verses twenty-five and twenty-six that at the birth of the twins Esau came forth first and was red and hairy, and Jacob followed holding on to Esau's heel, are not without possible occult significance. Esau became a man of the country and Jacob a man of the town, or a dweller in tents. As already stated, Esau represents the masculine potency in all creative processes and Jacob the feminine. Esau is therefore born first, is first " breathed out " by the Great Breath. Red as a primary colour represents masculinity, power, the positive pole. The hairs on the skin, like the feathers on the wings of goddesses in Egypt, represent the outraying, forthshining powers, the superabundance of the creative energy. To this, when manifested, the feminine or negative pole is ever attracted into union. Thus at their birth Jacob, as the material receptacle conveying and re-expressing spiritual principles, reaches out towards and holds the heel of Esau. Jacob thus personifies the receptive and transmitting vehicle of the creative energy which receives and conveys to the physical world the *fohatic*[1] power, which is also symbolised by the birthright or birthing power which Jacob received from Esau.

ESAU'S BIRTHRIGHT AND JACOB'S POTTAGE

Whilst the possibility is not overlooked that the whole narrative was intended to record actual facts in the history of the people concerned, and that such items as Esau's faintness and the bargain between the brothers were included because they were part of that history, an esoteric inter-pretation of the whole story as an allegory concealing occult truths cannot in the author's opinion be wholly discounted, and is therefore now presented.

Just as sunlight is dependent upon a medium of transmission, such as the postulated ether, and electricity is dependent for its conveyance upon a conductor, so also both creative will-force and spiritual will are dependent for their physical expression upon the life principle in matter and the vehicles of wisdom and emotion in man. Since knowledge of these laws is of great importance in thaumaturgical and alchemical processes, it is concealed under the veil of a strange allegory, which is that of Esau's action, when faint, of selling his birthright for Jacob's pottage.

The whole story, with its suggestion of despicable surrender, (which is a blind), portrays the entry of the masculine potency (*Purusha-Fohat*[2])—the pottage—into the feminine creative potency (*Prakriti*[2])—Jacob. In man the microcosm, the fiery " descent " is portrayed of the pure Spirit-Essence *Atma*,[3] which is the core of existence. This power rays forth from the Monad (Esau) into the individuality, thence to the personality (Jacob). The faintness of Esau which supposedly led to the sale of his birthright, represents the interdependency of Spirit and matter, and partic-ularly the impotence of the former bereft of the latter. Microcosmically, the faintness of Esau indicates the dependence of *Atma* upon a vehicle (*Buddhi*[4]), for without that vehicle the Monad cannot be manifest as pure

---

[1] *Fohat*—see Glossary.
[2] *Purusha—Prakriti*—see Glossary.
[3] *Atma* (Sk.)—see Glossary.
[4] *Buddhi* (Sk.)—see Glossary.

wisdom. Symbolically it is " faint " for that which the vehicle alone can supply, namely a means of transition and self-expression (birthright). The intimate interchange (bargain) between the brothers indicates that an evolutionary phase had been reached at which the life principles in man, the emotional and intuitive natures, had become sufficiently developed to serve as a means for the transition of the fiery power of *Atma* throughout the whole man. Jacob's pottage may be interpreted as the inherent capacity of the *Buddhic* Principle to serve as vehicle for the *Atma*, which in this sense receives it and in consequence loses its hitherto separate, original, inherent capacity or " birthright ". Thus the underlying principles of the creative process are revealed in a skilfully composed allegory which contains the blind of an apparent surrender under the duress of exhaustion.

Jacob, as we have seen, receives the birthright of the fainting Esau. The material, femine matrix receives the spiritual, masculine, birth-producing power. Similarly, later in the exoterically reprehensible deception practised by Rebekah and Jacob upon the blind and dying father, Isaac, it is Jacob who receives the patriarchal blessing and promise of fecundity and multiplicity of seed. Esau, though first chosen by his father as the recipient of this inheritance, is tricked and receives but a secondary blessing and is made the servant of his more fortunate brother. The Bible in its literal reading is full of these blinds in which wickedness is rewarded by favours, each of them being—esoterically—a clue to an underlying meaning.

One possible interpretation is that, Macrocosmically, matter (Jacob) receives the creative power of Spirit (the birthright from Isaac) in order that Nature's forms (Jacob's family) may be produced. In the microcosm the full expression of spiritual will-force (the birthright) is dependent upon the availability of intuitive wisdom as a vehicle. Thereafter, and only then, can a power-endowed human being come into existence. When in the course of evolution, whether natural or hastened, Nature produces a mortal man thus illumined and thus equipped with a vehicle for his will-force, then the power of the Cosmos is at that man's disposal and can be used either beneficently or adversely—hence the necessity for a blind.

CHAPTER II

GOD'S PROMISE TO ISAAC

Gen. 26: *Isaac because of famine goeth to Gerar: God appeareth to him at Beer-sheba, and blesseth him. Abimelech's covenant within. Esau's wives.*

Gen. 26: 1. *And there was a famine in the land, beside the first famine that was in the days of Abraham. And Isaac went unto Abimelech king of the Philistines unto Gerar.*

2. *And the LORD appeared unto him, and said, Go not down into Egypt; dwell in the land which I shall tell thee of:*

3. *Sojourn in this land, and I will be with thee, and will bless thee; for unto thee, and unto thy seed, I will give all these countries, and I will perform the oath which I sware unto Abraham thy father;*

4. *And I will make thy seed to multiply as the stars of heaven, and will give unto thy seed all these countries; and in thy seed shall all the nations of the earth be blessed;*

5. *Because that Abraham obeyed my voice, and kept my charge, my commandments, my statutes, and my laws.*

6. *And Isaac dwelt in Gerar:*

7. *And the men of the place asked him of his wife; and he said, She is my sister: for he feared to say, She is my wife; lest, said he, the men of the place should kill me for Rebekah; because she was fair to look upon.*

8. *And it came to pass, when he had been there a long time, that Abimelech king of the Philistines looked out at a window, and saw, and, behold, Isaac was sporting with Rebekah his wife.*

9. *And Abimelech called Isaac, and said, Behold, of a surety she is thy wife: and how saidst thou, She is my sister? And Isaac said unto him, Because I said, Lest I die for her.*

10. *And Abimelech said, What is this thou hast done unto us? one of the people might lightly have lien with thy wife, and thou shouldest have brought guiltiness upon us.*

11. *And Abimelech charged all his people, saying, He that toucheth this man or his wife shall surely be put to death.*

12. *Then Isaac sowed in that land, and received in the same year an hundred fold: and the LORD blessed him.*

13. *And the man waxed great, and went forward, and grew until he became very great.*

14. *For he had possession of flocks, and possession of herds, and great store of servants: and the Philistiness envied him.*

Support for a symbolical reading of the Bible is gained by comparison of the promises of perpetual prosperity and divine protection[1] made by God to Abraham and his successors with the subsequent defeats by invaders, exile under their commands in Babylon and Egypt, and the destruction of the Temples of King Solomon and King David. To these misfortunes may be added the later fate of the Hebrew people, including their miseries and homelessness since the *Diaspora* and the holocaust of German Jews under Nazi rule. This marked divergence between divine assurances and promises on the one hand and what actually happened on the other provides strong grounds for a non-literal reading of the Scriptures. The alternative of a total rejection of the *Pentateuch* as being, on the surface, unworthy of serious consideration would, I suggest, involve the loss of invaluable treasures of wisdom which are revealed when the veil of allegory and symbol is removed.

Chapter Twenty-six of *Genesis* interrupts the story of Esau and Jacob by continuing that of Isaac, who is made to pass through experiences so similar to those at the corresponding phase of the life of his father, Abraham, that the same interpretations may be exactly applied. As already stated, these repetitions indicate the operation of the one Law under which all creative processes occur, and that this Law unfailingly rules all such activities of whatever degree from Cosmoi, Galaxies and Universes to cells, molecules, and atoms.

After repeating Abraham's journeys, his experiences with the Philistines concerning wells, and his subterfuge of passing off his wife as his sister for fear of death,[2] Isaac grows old and very wealthy in his old age. All this may be interpreted precisely as in his father's story, of which it is a repetition, and need not be further considered here.[3] Cyclic law is indicated and that ascent by a spiral path, travelling which evolving life arrives over the same point reached in preceding rounds. Thereat it passes through identical experiences, performs similar functions, and resorts to the same artifices: with similar but greater and more beneficent results, for evolution though cyclic is not an eddy, but a spiral ascent.

---

[1] *Gen.* 17:2, 5-8; 26:2-5, 28:13-16.

[2] The possibility is not discounted that the practice of the offering of one's wife by a visitor to his host was in those days considered normal—even a courtesy—amongst those wandering tribes to which the Israelites belonged.

[3] q.v. Vol. II of this work, p. 310.

THE PRINCIPLE OF PATRIARCHAL SUCCESSION

All cycles, major and minor, are repetitions of their predecessors but on a higher scale and in a more advanced phase, the fundamental principles, allegorised as successive events, remaining unchanged. In consequence there must always follow the attainment of old age and riches and the handing on of Patriarchal power, meaning the creative impulse and the fruits of its exercise, on to the next cycle through its presiding genius, of whatever degree.

The most enduring attribute of the impermanent aspects of Universes in which evolution through successive cycles of manifestation occurs consists of the passage of life and its products from one cycle of activity to the next. Seasons follow each other in seemingly interminable sequence. Throughout them all Nature conveys both her invisible life, and the refined essence of all which she produces, from one season to the next and from one age to another. The transmission of life and of harvested fruits continues throughout all ages as an unchanging and fundamental phenomenon. As long as Nature's processes continue, seed as a principle is immortal and indestructible. The seed which is the innermost Soul of man, the Monad, is similarly immortal and indestructible. From life on Earth to life after death, and on into succeeding lives, the Seed-Self (Monad) with its divine attributes, both inherent and developed, is transferred from cycle to cycle of existence throughout long ages.

This process continues until Adeptship is attained, bringing freedom from the " wheel of birth and death ". The Monad, whilst still obedient to the law of cyclic unfoldment, is no longer obliged to submit to the limitations of embodiment in physical matter. This principle of transference is revealed in the Old Testament by means of historical metaphors descriptive of Patriarchal succession. For example, Patriarchs, Prophets, Judges and Kings, superior in stature to those whose lives they direct, transmit their power and their wisdom to a chosen successor. A fundamental and universal principle is thus mirrored forth by the writers responsible for the allegorical portions of the Scriptures of the world.

In the Mystery Schools of ancient peoples, as in certain of their modern ceremonial survivals, this principle was revealed by means of symbolical dramas. One of these consisted of the ritual transmission of Hierophantship or Headship from one reigning Official to his successor. A ceremony which included physical contact, as by the clasp of a hand and a whispered Word of Power, brought this about. When Elijah was carried up to Heaven in a chariot of fire, for example, his mantle fell upon Elisha, his appointed and duly installed Successor.

Thus a universal principle is revealed. The Hierophant of a Mystery Temple, endowed with spiritual power and trained to wield it to help Initiates to resurrect themselves from the tomb of the flesh, eventually reaches the end of his period of Office. Thereupon another Officient, carefully prepared and trained, receives the Word of Power, is vested with the mantle of authority and is duly installed in that Chair or Throne from which, during his term of Office, he in turn will preside over the activities of Sanctuary and Temple.

ISAAC, ESAU AND JACOB PERSONIFY COSMIC GENERATIVE POWERS

This procedure was evidently followed in the transmission of the leadership of the Israelites from Isaac to Jacob. The narrative is, however, susceptible of interpretation as a description, under a pseudo-historical veil, of both the emanation of primordial will-thought into pre-cosmic matter and the manifestation of the self-same power in the human individual. Esau, despite the unhappy ending of the allegory, remains the true heir; for the positive, creative Principle is ever unbound, ever free or, symbolically, " a man of the field " (v:24). This Principle is *Purusha-Fohat* or Isaac-Esau, and especially the positive current of the triple *Fohat* and the positive pole of electro-magnetic phenomena, Spirit in relation to matter, sperm in relation to ovum.

The great Passive, the feminine, negative polarity which is known as substance or matter is, however, the actual receptacle of the emitted *purushic* Breath. Esau is the first emission or first-born (*Fohat*), which is the bridge or link between Spirit and matter, husband and wife, positive and negative. This triplicity is clearly portrayed in the remarkable imagery of the birth of the twins, which means the new dispensation; for Isaac is *Purusha*, Esau is *Fohat*, Jacob is the differentiated substance and recipient in the new cycle, whilst Rebekah is original *Prakriti*, and particularly that which was employed in the predecessor. Therefore, as has previously been suggested, the three are linked together, as Jacob is holding on to the heel of Esau while he himself is still partly within the womb of Rebekah.

The three make a unit with the father, Isaac, as the propulsive agent, the Breather, the Speaker of the " Word ", the primary Emitter of the creative power *in abscondito*; for when once the energy is emitted this primary Agent is correctly represented by the absent Isaac.

THE TRANSMISSION OF THE FRUITAGE OF THE PAST TO FUTURE HUMAN INCARNATIONS

Applied to man, Isaac is the Monad and Rebekah is the higher *manasic* Principle, the Causal Body, vehicle of the Triple Self at the level of the abstract intellect. Esau is the *Atmic* ray and Jacob is the *Buddhi*-to-be. In terms of successive physical incarnations Isaac is the Monad-Ego and

Rebekah is the life-ensouled matter of the concrete mental and the physical worlds. Esau is both the projected Egoic ray and the physical spermata-zoon, whilst Jacob is the life Principle of the whole personality.

In terms of cycles of physical incarnation Isaac is the Ego enriched by the fruits of a single life. Rebekah and Esau represent the sum total of one life cycle, whilst Jacob stands for its successor into which the fruits of the former—the patriarchal riches and blessing—are transmitted. Esau more especially personifies these fruits or products of one life which are handed on to the next. Thus Esau appears to lose both his birth-right and his inheritance in favour of his younger brother, Jacob. The complete revela-tion is that of eternal progression, conservation, re-transmission and reincarnation, which together constitute a universal law.

> *Gen.* 26: 15. *For all the wells which his father's servants had digged in the days of Abraham his father, the Philistines had stopped them, and filled them with earth.*
>
> 16. *And Abimelech said unto Isaac, Go from us; for thou art much mightier than we.*
>
> 17. *And Isaac departed thence, and pitched his tent in the valley of Gerar, and dwelt there.*
>
> 18. *And Isaac digged again the wells of water, which they had digged in the days of Abraham his father; for the Philistines had stopped them after the death of Abraham: and he called their names after the names by which his father had called them.*
>
> 19. *And Isaac's servants digged in the valley, and found there a well of springing water.*

WELLS AND THE DIGGING OF WELLS

In its primary interpretation, the digging of wells suggests the effect of the " Breath " of the Logos upon universal substance, which is to render it first atomic and then molecular. This process constitutes the essential preparation of matter for the production of forms. In this portion of the *Book of Genesis* it is therefore made to occur towards the end of one dispen-sation and at the beginning of its successor. Abraham digs wells and Isaac follows the same custom. The filling in of the wells by the Philistines[1] and their later re-opening by the Israelites may be taken to refer to the natural resistance of matter (the Philistines) to the work of Spirit on the one hand, and on the other to the fact that this work must perforce be repeated in all successive cycles, Macrocosmic and microcosmic.

In the universal sense water is a symbol for both the matter of space and the sustaining life by which all forms are preserved. As a well holds the

---

[1] *Gen.* 26:15-22.

supply of water which is essential to physical existence, it may aptly be regarded as a representation of the containing vehicle for the spiritual " waters of life ". The earth itself, and particularly the country or field where the well is dug, in its turn represents pre-cosmic matter in which, when once the process of emanation has begun, Spirit creatively " digs holes" or sets up whirlpools, which in occult philosophy are regarded as the first, the primordial, atoms.[1] The Source of the outpoured (well-digging) life-force is within the creative Logos, Who thus is Himself a well-spring of life.

> *Gen.* 26: 20. *And the herdmen of Gerar did strive with Isaac's herdmen, saying, The water is our's: and he called the name of the well Esek; because they strove with him.*
>
> 21. *And they digged another well, and strove for that also: and he called the name of it Sitnah.*
>
> 22. *And he removed from thence, and digged another well; and for that they strove not: and he called the name of it Rehoboth; and he said, For now the LORD hath made room for us, and we shall be fruitful in the land.*
>
> 23. *And he went up from thence to Beer-sheba.*
>
> 24. *And the LORD appeared unto him the same night, and said, I am the God of Abraham thy father: fear not, for I am with thee, and will bless thee, and multiply thy seed for my servant Abraham's sake.*
>
> 25. *And he builded an altar there, and called upon the name of the LORD, and pitched his tent there: and there Isaac's servants digged a well.*
>
> 26. *Then Abimelech went to him from Gerar, and Ahuzzath, one of his friends, and Phichol the chief captain of his army.*
>
> 27. *And Isaac said unto them, Wherefore come ye to me, seeing ye hate me, and have sent me away from you?*
>
> 28. *And they said, We saw certainly that the LORD was with thee: and we said, Let there be now an oath betwixt us, even betwixt us and thee, and let us make a covenant with thee.*
>
> 29. *That thou wilt do us no hurt, as we have not touched thee, and as we have done unto thee nothing but good, and have sent thee away in peace : thou art now the blessed of the LORD.*
>
> 30. *And he made them a feast, and they did eat and drink.*
>
> 31. *And they rose up betimes in the morning, and sware one to another : and Isaac sent them away, and they departed from him in peace.*

---

[1] q.v. *The Secret Doctrine* (Adyar Ed.), Vol. I, p. 203, H.P. Blavatsky.

32. *And it came to pass the same day, that Isaac's servants came, and told him concerning the well which they had digged, and said unto him, We have found water.*

33. *And he called it Shebah: therefore the name of the city is Beersheba unto this day.*

34. *And Esau was forty years old when he took to wife Judith the daughter of Beeri the Hittite, and Bashemath the daughter of Elon the Hittite.*

35. *Which were a grief of mind unto Isaac and to Rebekah.*

At first the herdsmen of Gerar and of Isaac were at enmity with each other, but eventually they became reconciled. In this apparently simple account of the experiences of small wandering tribes of long ago may be discerned references to the primordial conflict between form-producing and life-giving Spirit on the one hand, and on the other the relatively inert and resistant substance of which the forms are to be built. This applies both to Cosmogenesis and to the earlier relationship between the innermost Spirit of man and the resistant matter of which the vehicles of the human Monad are built.

Such warfare—as it appears to be on the outer plane—whilst incessant in the early periods of the emanation of Universes, and in people who are passing through primitive evolutionary phases, does not continue, however. As the allegory shows, peace is eventually established between the erstwhile combatants. One reason for this is hinted at in verse Twenty-eight, wherein the enemies of Isaac confess that they now recognise him as an agent of security, saying: "....We saw certainly that the LORD was with thee"[1]. Translated into terms descriptive of the results of the age-long evolutionary process, matter in general becomes obedient to Spirit, and the hitherto hostile tendencies in the mortal man become transformed and brought into mutual collaboration with—and eventual submission to—the Spirit-Self, the human Monad.

Thus read, a practical application of this knowledge emerges; for what may appear on the surface to be a simple story telling of the experiences of nomadic peoples is seen to be replete with knowledge.[2] Understood and applied, this knowledge explains those evil tendencies in man from which his sorrows arise, and the way of that sorrow's ending—namely, surrender by the mortal man (personified by the herdsman of Gerar) to his divine and immortal Self (the herdsmen of Isaac).

Whilst the feasting which followed upon reconciliation would be regarded as a natural sequence, especially in those days, the feast is also recognisable

---

[1] *Gen.* 26:28.

[2] see Quotations from the *Zohar* in the front of this Volume.

as a symbol of the inner harmony and refreshment which follow the realisation of spiritual oneness. The mutual pledges, the further digging of wells (deeper realisation of wisdom) and the naming of the place (level of consciousness) where harmony was established and unity experienced—particularly the last-named—refer to the permanence of the achievement. " Naming ", in the allegorical language, implies full recognition of the expansion of consciousness which has been attained; for naming indicates the bestowal of individuality throughout a particular phase of spiritual unfoldment.

Verses Thirty-four and Thirty-five, like so many others, may be purely historical. Nevertheless the number four obtained from Esau's age of forty[1] suggests the firm establishment, in the formal mind of the mortal man, of the power and knowledge attained in the higher consciousness. If the analogy be not over-stressed, then the two wives could represent the emotional and physcial parts of the personality, whilst marriage could indicate a fusion of these three principles—mind, emotion and body—with the incarnated spiritual Self.

---

[1] In the symbolism of numbers Zeros, according to the context, may either be dropped or else interpreted as bestowing an added value to the meaning to be derived from the prime number.

CHAPTER III

JACOB IS BLESSED BY ISAAC

Gen. 27:   *Isaac sendeth Esau for venison. Jacob, instructed by Rebekah, obtaineth the blessing: Esau's complaint; he threateneth Jacob's life. Rebekah sendeth Jacob to Laban.*

Gen. 27: 1. *And it came to pass, that when Isaac was old, and his eyes were dim, so that he could not see, he called Esau his eldest son, and said unto him, My son: and he said unto him, Behold, here am I.*

      2. *And he said, Behold now, I am old, I know not the day of my death.*

      3. *Now therefore take, I pray thee, thy weapons, thy quiver and thy bow, and go out to the field, and take me some venison;*

      4. *And make me savoury meat, such as I love, and bring it to me, that I may eat; that my soul may bless thee before I die.*

ISAAC AND REBEKAH, ESAU AND JACOB, PERSONIFY SPIRIT AND MATTER IN COSMOGENESIS

The particular creative impulse by which the given cycle was initiated and sustained has now found its full expression. The process of its withdrawal and the onset of *Pralaya* are indicated in the old age of Isaac and his growing blindness. Sublimation to spiritual levels occurs in the later phases of all cycles. The intellectual attention, symbolised by eyesight, is being withdrawn from the lower worlds and from objective manifestation and centred in the higher and subjective states. Symbolically, but in no sense actually, the spiritual impulse, personified by Isaac, becomes " aged and increasingly blind ".

Esau, representing the creative impulse and energy, is the first to be affected by this approach of the close of the cycle. Allegorically, he is sent for and informed by his father of the latter's imminent death. The instruction to go out into the field, kill a deer by means of archery, bring it back, make it into venison and deliver it as food to the Patriarch, describes the process of withdrawal of consciousness from the field of manifestation.

In a human interpretation, in which the old age of Isaac and his approaching death refer to the decease of the physical body, the deer as a quadruped represents the fruits harvested by the spiritual Self as a result of life in the four lower planes of the objective Universe and the four mortal bodies of man. These fruits are withdrawn in a sublimated condition in order that they may become transmuted into terms of consciousness and power, and so be assimilated. This sublimation is indicated by the death of the body of the deer, the passing of the flesh through fire in cooking, and its delivery to the original Source.

JACOB, INSTRUCTED BY REBEKAH, OBTAINETH THE BLESSING

Since this Chapter of the *Book of Genesis* is a long one, in order to save space the verses themselves are not here printed, but the following main incidents in the narrative receive consideration: Isaac's promise of a paternal blessing; Rebekah, having overheard, plots to replace Isaac's favourite son, Esau, with her own favourite, Jacob; the methods whereby the deception is successfully practised, including dressing Jacob in Esau's clothing, putting the skins of goats upon his hands and the smooth of his neck, and preparing and giving to Jacob savoury meat and bread; Jacob's presentation of this food to his father and his untruthful affirmation that he was, in fact, his brother Esau; the success of the deceit despite Isaac's doubts; the bestowal of the blessing and promise of leadership of the nations; and the exposure of the deceit, with its troubling effect upon both father and eldest son.

The love of Isaac for Esau and of Rebekah for Jacob, earlier referred to, also indicates electro-magnetic laws. The formative electrical energy (*Fohat*), personified by Esau, emanates from the Source (*Purusha*), personified by Isaac, and later returns to the Source—symbolically is loved by it. Isaac wishes to bless and bestow his wealth upon Esau. Jacob, representing matter, the receptacle and producer of a succeeding cycle, emanates from the substance of the preceding cycle (Rebekah), to which he will return. Symbolically, Rebekah loves Jacob and is prepared to go to any lengths, even to deception, on his behalf. The opposite polarities are thus thrown into sharp and clear distinction, and the various feelings and activities of their personifications are explained once the symbolical method of writing is accepted. The fact that the twins are boys indicates the essential unity of Spirit and matter at the dawn of Creation, symbolised by their dual birth, which is so intimately described.

THE DECEPTION OF ISAAC AND ESAU BY REBEKAH AND JACOB—HISTORY OR ALLEGORY ?

The story continues with a description of gross deception practised upon Isaac and Esau by Rebekah and Jacob. The conduct thus ascribed to the two latter is so repellant to the moral sense that the student of symbology is at once prompted to examine it with care, lest it should be susceptible of interpretation as a deliberately constructed blind concealing profound and power-bestowing Macrocosmic and microcosmic truths. Since both Rebekah and Jacob represent receptive substance which is in the process of passing from one dispensation to its successor, it is in conformity with the natural procedure that Jacob should be the recipient of this inheritance.

Trickery and deception are allegories universally used by writers in the Sacred Language as a direct intimation to the reader—a prompting indeed—to look below the surface of the narrative in search of a hidden wisdom; for such episodes are not infrequently included in order to conceal and at the same time reveal knowledge concerning the impress of Spirit on matter in the Macrocosm, and of the Monad-Ego upon the mortal mind in the microcosm. The fiery touch of Spirit emanated from the solar Source has the effect of changing the preceding inertia of matter into that activity which is essential to practical responsiveness. In man this produces a change in the motives for living so profound that it may well be named revolutionary. The whole outlook of the person who is thus aroused from the attitude of indifference to the higher life becomes drastically, even dangerously, altered unless the character is stable and the mind is discriminative. The danger is that, under a strong spiritual impulse, individuals may ill-advisedly proceed to such a drastic change in their mode and habits of life as to threaten their health, their sanity, and the happiness of those associated with them. Indeed, the difficulty can be so great that this enormously important development in the evolution of the Monad-Ego is nearly always referred to by means of allegory in the inspired portions of the world's Scriptures. The Annunciations of the forthcoming births—and the births themselves—of John the Baptist and of Jesus to their mothers, Elizabeth and Mary, and the warnings and portents surrounding the stories of the conceptions—generally described as being immaculate—of World Saviours, are examples of this form of revelation. All such Annunciations and Nativities can be read as foreshadowings and attainments of full spiritual awareness.[1]

If such an approach to Biblical study be unacceptable, then the only alternative is to read this Chapter of the *Book of Genesis* as an account of another deplorable deceit for gain practised by Patriarchs themselves, and also upon them by members of their families, as in the present case. Abraham, for example, as previously stated, presented his wife to the Pharaoh as his sister,[2] whilst Rebekah and Jacob obtained the blessing of Isaac by means of a similar kind of subterfuge.[3] Such morally unacceptable conduct, if really performed, presents some of the principal Biblical characters as

---

[1] q.v. Vol. I of this work, pp. 213-214 Adyar Ed. and pp. 204-205 Quest Book Ed.
[2] *Gen.* 12:13.
[3] *Gen.* 27.

despicable human beings and the Holy Bible itself as a book which contains accounts of reprehensible actions performed by people who nevertheless continued to enjoy Divine favours. Indeed, acts of fornication, and even incest, are recounted and these, in their turn, are susceptible of interpretation as being descriptive of mystical experiences sought and passed through by devotees when they realise the unity of the Divine and the mortal parts of human nature. The amorous pursuits of Zeus, Father of the Gods in Greek Mythology, as a result of which he had intercourse with many maidens, and the plurality of the wives of the Lord Shri Krishna—portraying the intimate association (marriage) of a Representative of the Divine Spirit of the Universe with the spiritual Souls of all mankind—are all susceptible of the above suggested interpretation, namely that the God in man ever seeks to become intimately unified with his material, mortal self.

If, as would not be unnatural, particularly in those for whom this approach to the study of the Scriptures is new, these interpretations appear to be too far-fetched and the author to be taking unwarrantable liberties with Holy Writ, then may I again draw attention to the view expressed by a learned Hebrew scholar by repeating here his words which appear at the front of this book:

" Jewish mystics are at one in giving a mystical interpretation to the Torah; the Torah is to them a living organism animated by a secret life which streams and pulsates below the crust of its literal meaning; every one of the innumerable strata of this hidden region corresponds to a new and profound meaning of the Torah. The Torah, in other words, does not consist merely of chapters, phrases and words; rather is it to be regarded as the living incarnation of the divine wisdom which eternally sends out new rays of light. It is not merely the historical law of the Chosen People, although it is that too; it is rather the cosmic law of the Universe, as God's wisdom conceived it. Each configuration of letters in it, whether it makes sense in human speech or not, symbolises some aspect of God's creative power which is active in the Universe. "[1]

The trick played upon Isaac and Esau by Rebekah and Jacob also symbolises in another form the so-called enmity between Spirit and matter— the apparently inevitable resistance of matter to the formative impulse of Spirit. The ultimate establishment of a covenant between these apparent adversaries, followed by the great fruitfulness of the Israelites under Jacob's leadership, allegorises the relationship between Spirit and matter when considered objectively as primordial electricity, with its harmoniously co-operative currents and foci of opposite polarity.

Wars between opponents, as also treaties and covenants agreed upon, represent the interaction between the primordial pair at all levels, whether

---

[1] q.v. *Major Trends in Jewish Mysticism*, Gershom G. Scholem.

in terms of life and form, creative electricity, or human consciousness and its vehicles. Thus viewed, the great allegorical wars are only apparent conflicts; for actually no conflict occurs, since these two are essentially one and under genetic law interact with a common result, Macrocosmic and microcosmic, which is the production of Universes and of self-illumined human beings. Through these, by descent and ascent, Spirit-life continues in eternal progression its cyclic evolution to greater fulness of self-manifestation. Such, in truth, is the major key to all Scriptures and all allegories emanating from world Sanctuaries, and especially to those concerned with creative processes.

Returning now to a consideration of the narrative, when a new cycle opens and the same levels of density in matter are again to be entered by Spirit, the " wells are once more dug out ", the supposed enmity of matter is overcome and a covenant is established, meaning that equipoise and balance of power are attained. The result—the rich productiveness of Nature—is symbolised by the great increase in herds, flocks, possessions, servants and offspring of the Patriarch.[1] If this account be thus read as historical metaphor, then a reference may be discerned to the doctrine that in endless succession, though ever in greater degree and with richer result, the cosmogenetical process of perpetual unfoldment[2] under eternal law is initiated, resisted, but eventually completed.

As already indicated, a new cycle opened with Abraham's search, by means of his servant, for a wife for his son Isaac. Its progress is allegorically described in the marriage of Isaac and Rebekah and the birth of the twins, Esau and Jacob, the Spirit-matter of the next dispensation. All the *femmes fatales* of the major Biblical allegories, including Eve who supposedly produced the " Fall " of Adam and of all mankind; Rebekah, who deceived Isaac; Jael, wife of Heber, who drove a nail through the temple of Sisera; Delilah, who seduced Sampson; Jezebel, wife of Ahab, who was a murderess and incited her husband to evil; Salome, daughter of Herodias, who demanded and obtained the head of John the Baptist; and Mary Magdalene, at first an adultress and later sanctified by the Christ (within)—all these personify the ensnaring attributes of matter in relation to Spirit, form in relation to life, and vehicles in relation to consciousness.

The stories of successful deceit or entrapment portray the phase at which Spirit becomes deeply embedded in matter, eventually to be absorbed by it. Figurative deaths and burials, bondage and darkness, descents into pits, entombments—all these are allegories of the arrival of Spirit at the densest plane of manifestation, the deepest point of incarnation in matter. Similarly successions through heirs, freedom from bondage, and arisings from pits

---

[1] *Gen.* 26:13, 14.

[2] q.v. *The Secret Doctrine,* Vol. I (Adyar Ed.), p. 115, H.P. Blavatsky.

and sepulchres, all portray in symbol and allegory both entry upon the returning arc of forthgoing and return and the development in Universe and man of inherent qualities and attributes from latency to potency.

THE PRINCIPLE OF THE TRANSMISSION OF POWER

All celebrations, feasts, victories and ascents in glory in their turn symbolise the culmination of these processes in uttermost fruition. Throughout all successive cycles, major and minor, the one eternal Spirit is the parent, even as the one boundless space is the material field. The parentage of all created things is, in consequence, ever the same. This is brought out in the Bible by the careful preservation of records of genealogical descent and by the stories of the handing on of power, divine protection, blessing and possessions from father to selected heir. Thus an important spiritual principle is portrayed by means of allegory. The product or son of the primordial pair in its turn becomes the parent on the masculine side of the next cycle in succession. The cosmic Christos or " Son " of universal Spirit-matter becomes, in the second phase, the Logos and Architect of the Universe—of whatever dimension and degree—which follows. Thus in both cases, cosmic and geneological, the son is always heir to the father and in his turn assumes patriarchal (paternal) functions.

The mother, or the matter side, is the producer and nurse of the Logos-to-be and it is she who allegorically suckles, cares for and protects the interests of the heir. Rebekah it is, therefore, who sees to it that her son Jacob receives the blessing, which means the official handing on of power from the father, Isaac. Esau, on the other hand, represents Spirit and so proceeds to self-expression in another land.

As Eve was to Adam and Sarah to Abraham, so Rebekah is to Isaac. All of them typify the fertile, feminine principle or substance in the Macrocosm, and the Higher *Manas*[1] in the microcosm. Since they are in the direct line of succession, it is they and their children who are made the heirs and successors and whose story is told. In the purely psychological sense the barrenness of both Sarah and Rebekah is personal, merely implying evolutionary immaturity. As yet the lower mind is unillumined by the Higher, or in their personalities they are " barren " of intuition and spiritual will. This is but temporary, for in due course intellect reaches the stage where the latent germ of pure wisdom can be fructified by the Dweller in the Innermost, the Monad, and later be " born " as the faculty of spiritual intuitiveness and " an instantaneous, implicit insight into every first truth".[2] Allegorically, barrenness is replaced by fruitfulness, each wife conceiving and giving birth to offspring.

---

[1] Higher *Manas*—see Glossary—Causal Body.
[2] q.v. *The Mahatma Letters to A.P. Sinnett*, Letter XXXI,

To receive his patrimony and make it manifest, Jacob must assume the powers and attributes of the positive side (Esau), as he is made to do in his life story. Therefore Jacob is given by Rebekah the hairy skin and fine raiment appropriate to Esau. Neither deception nor theft occur in reality. The deeply occult truth is revealed that the Hierophant of one dispensation must personally receive from the hands of his predecessor the Hierophantic and Initiatory power. Similarly, Benjamin must find the cup in his sack, put there at the orders of Joseph.[1] The mantle of Elijah must visibly and materially fall upon Elisha.[2] John the Baptist must baptise Jesus[3] and the dying Jesus must, in His turn, hand on His power to the disciple John.[4] The concept of succession, whether Apostolic, Hierophantic or Masonic, as conveyed by words—whispered or at " low breath "—spoken to a successor, is based upon this spiritual principle and is in harmony with it.

Esau, however, is not actually deprived of the paternal blessing,[5] as is made to appear. Since, however, in the new genetic process Matter will again entrap Spirit, Esau is ordained to be the servant of Jacob, who carries on the line. Such, in its main outlines, are the Macrocosmic and racial revelations of this Chapter.

THE FAMILY OF ABRAHAM PERSONIFY PRINCIPLES OF MAN

Since Sanskrit words are so valuable in the exposition of philosophic subjects because of their brevity, directness and completeness of meaning, pardon is here asked of the reader who may hitherto have been unfamiliar with them for their constant use in the immediately following passages, as also elsewhere throughout this work.

In the microcosmic—and particularly the Initiatory—interpretations Isaac is the Monad, Esau the *Atma* (Spirit), Jacob the *Buddhi* (Wisdom) and Rebekah the Higher *Manas* (Abstract Mind). The *Atma* is ever the product of the Monad, or symbolically it is Esau whom Isaac loves. *Buddhi*, on the other hand, as intuitive insight, arises out of the attainment of Egoic or Causal Consciousness. Therefore Rebekah, representing the latter, loves Jacob better than Esau.

Two pairs thus exist. Two polarities within the inner Self of man are personified, each in its turn being dual. Isaac and Esau both personify the positive pole, the spiritual principle, the fructifying power. Rebekah

---

[1] *Gen.* 44:12 and Pt. Four of this Vol.
[2] *II Kings* 2:13
[3] *Matt.* 3.
[4] *Jn.* 19:26.
[5] *Gen.* 27:39-40.

and Jacob represent the material encasement, the negative pole. These four together portray the true immortal, creative, perpetually unfolding, Self.

Buddhi is the vehicle in man of the universal life. It cannot be used by the Ego as an instrument of consciousness until it has become individualised, or symbolically " born " from within the Causal Body, which in this sense is its " mother ". Otherwise expressed, spiritual wisdom cannot be wholly developed from below. The Egoic centre of awareness cannot of itself move into and use a body composed of the universal life-force. A co-ordinating principle must first be supplied, and this can only come from the positive polarity, the Monad-*Atma*. The *Atmic*, fructifying power in man must first descend from its own level into that of the *Buddhic* plane, and touch and thereby awaken into life the central atoms of the germinal *Buddhic* body within the Causal vehicle.

This process is allegorically described in the story of the birth of the twins. Esau is born first. Unity is, however, indicated by the fact that Jacob grasps Esau's heel. Interpreted, this reveals that *Atma* in its deepest descent, its lowest point of contact (heel) with the worlds below, is brought into contact and relationship with the *Buddhic* world. As a result Jacob, representing the *Buddhic* consciousness in man, follows Esau in birth. The intuitive faculty then begins its development and use by consciousness. This fructifying action continues until the vehicle is full grown, as it were. Symbolically, Jacob as a young man receives in return for his offer of vehicleship the mess of pottage, the continued, positive, fructifying power and presence of the *Atma*, symbolised as the birthright of Esau.

The hairiness of Esau portrays the outraying quality characteristic of the positive polarity, whilst the colour red is also a primary colour. Jacob, on the other hand, is represented as of an opposite type, being the favourite not of the father but of the mother, whilst in the account of the supposed deception by which the paternal blessing is gained a reference is made to the " smooth of his neck ". Furthermore, he is a dweller in tents, whilst Esau is a man of the field.

Eventually the *Buddhic* principle (Jacob) reaches its full development and assumes the position and power of headship in the new evolutionary cycle which is then entered. In terms of Christian Mysticism the heretofore germinal Christ nature, " ....Christ in you, the hope of glory ",[1] is fructified by the power and words of the Archangel Gabriel, develops within its mother-to-be, Mary, and at the Nativity is born or reaches a stage of self-conscious, Christ-like wisdom, compassion and all-embracing love. Thus *Buddhi*, originally born of Higher *Manas*, becomes consciously the vehicle of

---

[1] *Col.* 1:27.

Atma, ascent into the positive polarity is attained and identity with the Monad-*Atma* is realised (Jacob succeeds his father as Patriarch).

In the Macrocosm the " Son " becomes the Logos and officiates as the fully conscious vehicle for the creative Power or " Word ".   As the Evangelists (particularly St. John)[1] made clear, the *Christos* becomes identified with the Logos.[2]   That which is born as wisdom-love develops into wisdom-will; that which itself is a product of its spiritual parents becomes in its turn a progenitor.   This is the solution of the confusion caused by the identification by St. John of the Christ as Son, or Second Aspect, with the Father or Logos as the First.   The *Christos*, which has become a Logos, then creates in its turn.   This function is also portrayed by the later story of Jacob laying his head upon a stone, sleeping, dreaming of the Angelic Hierarchy (the *Elohim*[3] or Hierarchy of creative Intelligences through which the Divine produces the manifested Universe), and thereafter setting up the stone as a pillar (*lingam*)[4]; for all the symbols thus employed are of the positive, creative order.

To return to the narative in this great story we have a second-born son who came forth from his mother's womb holding the heel of his twin brother, grew up into deepening antagonism towards him, by tricks deprived him of both his birthright and his paternal blessing and inheritance, and yet was blessed of the Lord.   In both its Macrocosmic and its microcosmic senses the story is of one individual, one unit of consciousness.   In the former case the creative Logoi are implied, and in the latter the human Monad. *Atma, Buddhi* and Higher *Manas* are referred to.   The major allegory is also a story of two creative cycles, an old one which passes (Abraham's) and a new one which begins (Jacob's).   The principles and laws governing the creative process are, as we have seen, all portrayed by a group of component allegories.   These processes are of three orders at least: first, the Cosmic— the birth of a Universe; second, the Monadic—the birth of *Buddhi*, or the Christ-consciousness in man; and third, the Egoic—the birth of the physical body, to which is added the gathering in and preservation of the faculties and capacities developed by the Ego—as the result of life therein.

THE REASON FOR SECRECY

Such, within the admitted limits of the author's understanding, is the profound revelation concerning Macrocosmic and microcosmic genetic

---

[1] *Jn.* 1·1-5.

[2] cf ". . *there is a logos in every mythos,* or a ground-work of truth in every fiction." *Isis Unveiled*, Vol. 1, P. 162, H.P Blavatsky.

[3] *Elohim*—see Glossary.

[4] *Lingam* (Sk.) Physically, the phallus.   A symbol of abstract creation and of the divine, masculine, procreative force.

procedures revealed under a symbolic veil which has been rendered more dense by means of a narrative of events repellant to one's sense of justice. If the need for such enveiling here be questioned, justifiably since the resultant knowledge appears to be harmless, the reply could be given that full comprehension of the whole truth would enable an unworthy member of society to use it for the domination of susceptible people by means of cleverly directed will-thought, thus reducing them to virtual slavery. The author admits that his interpretations themselves fall short of totality, since he also is under certain prohibitions in this respect.[1]

[1] The reader is also referred to the author's statement with which this Volume opens: "The Hidden Wisdom and Why It Is Concealed."

CHAPTER IV

JACOB EMBARKS UPON PATRIARCHAL RESPONSIBILITY

Gen. 28:   *Jacob is blessed, and sent to Padan-aram: his vision, and God's promise in a dream. The stone at Bethel. Jacob's vow.*

Gen. 28: 1. *And Isaac called Jacob, and blessed him, and charged him, and said unto him, Thou shalt not take a wife of the daughters of Canaan.*

2. *Arise, go to Padan-aram, to the house of Bethuel thy mother's father: and take thee a wife from thence of the daughters of Laban thy mother's brother.*

3. *And God Almighty bless thee, and make thee fruitful, and multiply thee, that thou mayest be a multitude of people;*

4. *And give thee the blessing of Abraham, to thee, and to thy seed with thee; that thou mayest inherit the land wherein thou art a stranger, which God gave unto Abraham.*

5. *And Isaac sent away Jacob; and he went to Padan-aram unto Laban, son of Bethuel the Syrian, the brother of Rebekah, Jacob's and Esau's mother.*

6. *When Esau saw that Isaac had blessed Jacob, and sent him away to Padan-aram, to take him a wife from thence; and that as he blessed him he gave him a charge, saying, Thou shalt not take a wife of the daughters of Canaan;*

7. *And that Jacob obeyed his father and his mother, and was gone to Padan-aram;*

8. *And Esau seeing that the daughters of Canaan pleased not Isaac his father;*

9. *Then went Esau unto Ishmael, and took unto the wives which he had Mahalath the daughter of Ishmael Abraham's son, the sister of Nebajoth, to be his wife.*

As Universe (*Manvantara*) follows Universe, so epochs and dispensations succeed each other on the planet Earth. Thus the story of the Israelites moves on from the dispensation of Isaac to that of Jacob. In the meta-phorical language in which the *Pentateuch* is assumed to have been written, the successive Patriarchs and their historical periods are in a certain sense reflections upon Earth of the successive Logoi of Solar Systems and their component cycles. As the same principles apply in all creative epochs, the stories of each of them have certain incidents in common. Thus in the present Chapter of *Genesis* Jacob, like his forefathers, must go back to the place of racial origins (Padan-aram) to find his wife, implying in the Macrocosm a return between each *Manvantara* to the state of undifferentiated matter or *Pralaya*, and also the beginning of new creative processes by the use of the same root substance (*Mulaprakriti*).

   Gen. 28: 10. *And Jacob went out from Beer-sheba, and went toward Haran.*

           11. *And he lighted upon a certain place, and tarried there all night, because the Sun was set; and he took of the stones of that place, and put them for his pillows, and lay down in that place to sleep.*

           12. *And he dreamed, and behold a ladder set up on the earth, and the top of it reached to heaven: and behold the angels of God ascending and descending on it.*

           13. *And, behold, the LORD stood above it, and said, I am the LORD God of Abraham thy father, and the God of Isaac: the land whereon thou liest, to thee will I give it, and to thy seed.*

           14. *And thy seed shall be as the dust of the earth, and thou shalt spread abroad to the west, and to the east, and to the north, and to the south: and in thee and in thy seed shall all the families of the earth be blessed.*

           15. *And, behold, I am with thee, and will keep thee in all places whither thou goest, and will bring thee again into this land; for I will not leave thee, until I have done that which I have spoken to thee of.*

           16. *And Jacob awaked out of his sleep, and he said, Surely the LORD is in this place; and I knew it not.*

           17. *And he was afraid, and said, How dreadful is this place ! this is none other but the house of God, and this is the gate of heaven.*

THE SYMBOLISM OF JACOB'S LADDER

The dream of Jacob at Bethel in which he saw a ladder set up " and the top of it reached to heaven: and behold the angels of God ascending and descending on it ",[1] portrays the ordered emergence of the *Elohim* or creative Intelligences associated with the Ten Sephiroth or Emanations of Deity, each on its " rung " according to its place in the Sephirothal Hierarchy.[2]

This dream portrays the action of cosmic Ideation, the preparatory activity of Universal Mind. The ladder itself, being triple with two

---

[1] *Gen.* 28:12.

[2] see Appendix—" The Sephirothal Tree. "

6

sides and connecting rungs, in one interpretation (others follow later) represents the emergence or emission of the three-fold creative " Breath " and its gradual penetration—level by level—from the most spiritual plane down to the deepest densities of substance.   The forthgoing of divine Intelligence on the downward arc, under the direction of the appropriate Sephira, followed by its similarly directed return, are portrayed by the various symbols in the dream.

The ladder symbol may also be interpreted as signifying the universal law of descent and ascent, or involution and evolution.   On the pathway of forthgoing the Monad-bearing life wave becomes embodied in vehicles of increasing degrees of density until the mineral kingdom is reached.   On the pathway of return ascent is achieved through the plant, animal, human and superhuman kingdoms (rungs), as elsewhere explained in this book. As a means of ascent the form of the ladder suggests regularity and order. Composed of safely secured rungs placed at an equal distance apart, symbolically it indicates that life in all the kingdoms of Nature ascends from its deepest encasement, stage by stage, to ever greater degrees of development and unfoldment (heights).   If this interpretation be applied to man, each rung represents an evolutionary phase, beginning with the most primitive savage and progressing upwards to civilised man, genius, Initiate and Adept.

In the Macrocosmic interpretation Jacob as the dreamer corresponds to the first Emanation from the Absolute, which is Universal Mind on its journey towards Universal Substance (Rachel and Leah), whilst the stone upon which Jacob rested his head is pre-cosmic, unified Spirit-matter thus brought into contact with creative thought (the head of the dreamer). In his ability thus to perceive cosmic procedures, even if only by means of a symbolic dream, Jacob displays the powers of an initiated Seer who can discern and commune with Beings of the superphysical and spiritual worlds.

Gen. 28: 18. *And Jacob rose up early in the morning, and took the stone that he had put for his pillows, and set it up for a pillar, and poured oil upon the top of it.*

19. *And he called the name of that place Beth-el: but the name of that city was called Luz at the first.*

20. *And Jacob vowed a vow, saying, If God will be with me, and will keep me in this way that I go, and will give me bread to eat, and raiment to put on.*

21. *So that I come again to my father's house in peace; then shall the LORD be my God:*

22. *And this stone, which I have set for a pillar, shall be God's house: and of all that thou shalt give me I will surely give the tenth unto thee.*

Rachel and Leah, the wives-to-be, represent that same matter duly prepared, modified or differentiated by the action of the creative " Breath ".

The pillar which Jacob, on awakening, erected from the stones on which his head had rested in sleep, represents the positive current, the male creative potency and activity, whilst the anointing of the pillar with oil and the action of naming the locality in which the event occurred represent the negative current in action.

Macrocosmically, oil represents the equi-polarised, linking or conjoining product of positive and negative activity. The ceremonial action of anointing allegorically portrays the process of linking the superphysical with the physical parts of inorganic substances and the inner self of man with his outer personality. The act of naming is negative, in the sense that it is but a ratification by sound and thought of the decree of the positive creative Agent. Naming also affirms the existing individuality and refers to the processes of marking out an area in universal space, establishing its boundary or " Ring-pass-not ", and imparting to the enclosed matter its specific frequencies of oscillation; or, in the language of music, choosing the keynote and sounding forth the theme of the Universe-to-be.

In a Monadic-*Atmic* interpretation, the oil would correspond to *Buddhi* and the naming action to the function of Higher *Manas*. When the Ego is in incarnation the oil represents the astral principle, the unifying life-force, and in physical consciousness the seat of personal love and desire for union.

THE CORONATION STONE

The Coronation Stone upon which British Monarchs are crowned is an essential ritual object in the Ceremony of enthronement; for, as in the story just interpreted, the new Ruler personifies the Logos of the dispensation then being inaugurated, and more especially the presiding Deity of a Solar System, Planetary Scheme, Chain or Round.[1] The stone, whether the one upon which Jacob laid his head (imbued it with mind), or a Coronation Stone, represents the Spirit—impregnated basic Substance of which all things will be made. The vows of the Monarch-to-be correspond to the dream. The Crown itself and the act of Coronation portray the emergence of the future creative Logos and His assumption of Office. In terms of the Kabbalistic Tree of Life,[2] the Crown is Kether and the stone in the Coronation Chair corresponds to Malkuth, " the Kingdom ", over which the newly crowned Monarch will rule.

[1] see Glossary—Chain.
[2] see Appendix—" The Sephirothal Tree ",

CHAPTER V

THE ISRAELITE NATION IS FOUNDED

Gen. 29:   *Jacob, coming to the well of Haran, meeteth Rachel, and is entertained by Laban: he covenanteth for her, but is deceived with Leah.   Rachel also given him to wife on a new agreement. Leah beareth Reuben, Simeon, Levi, and Judah.*

Gen. 29: 1. *Then Jacob went on his journey, and came into the land of the people of the east.*

          2. *And he looked, and behold a well in the field, and, lo, there were three flocks of sheep lying by it; for out of that well they watered the flocks: and a great stone was upon the well's mouth.*

In this Twenty-ninth Chapter of the *Book of Genesis* the opening of the third cycle in the story of the Hebrew nation is described by means of a blending of history and allegory. The first cycle opened with the departure of Abram from the City of Ur[1] of the Chaldees, and the second with the birth of Isaac.[2]

The East, when used in the allegorical language, is less a direction of space than a reference to a particular time in major and minor cycles of activity. In the Macrocosmic sense the East implies the beginning of a new cycle, and also describes the pre-cosmic or undisturbed state of root Substance (*Mūlaprakriti*).[3] This undifferentiated matter is symbolically indicated in three ways namely by the place of origin of the Patriarch and his family, by the principal female—and even sometimes male—characters, and by water—whether as the open sea or the contents of pitchers or wells. The presence of sheep by the well aptly represents the ordered (shepherded), potentially fruitful, time-space condition. If a development of this theme be acceptable, the sheep when watering and grazing on the pasture represent the future inhabitants (Monads) of the Macrocosmic field or Universe-to-be. The number three—in this case referring to three cycles in the history of the Hebrew nation—if symbolically intended, may be regarded as a reference to the three outpourings of Spirit, Life and Intelligence from the one divine

---

[1] *Gen.* 12:1, 4.

[2] *Gen.* 21:2, 3.

[3] *Mūlaprakriti*—see Glossary.

Source, as also to the triple manifestation of the triune Logoi of Universes as expressions of Will, Wisdom and Intelligence.

Gen. 29: 3. *And thither were all the flocks gathered: and they rolled the stone from the well's mouth, and watered the sheep, and put the stone again upon the well's mouth in his place.*

The presence of the stone upon the well's mouth before the watering of the sheep and its replacement afterwards is suceptible of interpretation as referring to the " covered " or inactive and unused condition of water (Space) before each new cycle of emanation, involution, evolution and reabsorption of Spirit, and the subsequent—and consequent—return of the matter of Space to that condition. Symbolically, a stone covered the mouth of the well before the epoch began and again covered it when that period of activity had reached its close.

Gen. 29: 4. *And Jacob said unto them, My brethren, whence be ye? And they said, Of Haran are we.*

5. *And he said unto them, Know ye Laban the son of Nahor? And they said, We know him.*

6. *And he said unto them, Is he well? And they said, He is well: and, behold, Rachel his daughter cometh with the sheep.*

LABAN AS FIRST LOGOS

Laban, in one possible interpretation, the Macrocosmic, is a personification of the First Emanation from the Absolute, the Root Logos, the primary cosmic Mind, the ever-existent " Father ". He is thus the Patriarch who stays at home, who remains in the East (the place of origin), and who produces the female line from which the wives of the Patriarchs in the new land, or field, are chosen. He and his daughters therefore represent primordial, pre-cosmic, Spirit-matter, a duality of origin being indicated. Through Laban contact is maintained with the place of origin, the natural home.

In the Mysteries Laban is the hidden Hierophant, the Initiate in whose Name and by whose powers the Initiations are conferred and the occult wisdom (personified by females in this story) infused into and united with the Initiate Mind.

All allegorical marriages represent the illumination of the Higher and the lower *Manas* by the receipt of the Eternal Wisdom, as for example during the Rite of Initiation in the Greater Mysteries. In the main the principal wives are pure Wisdom itself, the unalloyed truth. Therefore they are always described as beautiful, well-favoured, fair to see. The sisters of these wives, sometimes also married, represent the same Wisdom clothed in human thought, whilst the handmaids and concubines symbolise varied aspects and attributes of that Wisdom as perceived and expressed in and through mental, emotional and bodily life.

In stories of polygamous marriages and irregular associations, when thus married, there is no carnal intent whatever, whether they be interpreted in terms of Cosmogenesis, of the evolution of human consciousness, or of the stages and experiences of the Initiates of the Greater Mysteries. The barrenness, often of the first chosen wife, symbolises a limitation, not of the wife but of the husband who at first is unable intellectually to conceive of, and so make fruitful in himself, the pure Wisdom. Microcosmically, it must always be remembered, the two are principles, bodies and states of consciousness of one person. The older sister, such as Leah, more readily conceives, as do the handmaidens, because the Eternal Wisdom reduced to terms of the lower mind is often more readily comprehensible than in its pure state. When, however, Rachel (the *Gnosis*[1]) does conceive, her son is always in the direct line of descent. He it is who initiates and carries on the new cycle to the next stage, of whatever degree.

Returning to the story at Laban, wells containing water are symbols of the outpoured cosmic life by which Universes and all lesser creations are vivified and sustained, and in man they symbolise the illumined, wisdom-filled *Buddhi-Manas*. In the microcosmic sense, women at the well, whether Rebekah, Rachel or the woman of Samaria,[2] personify the original spiritual intelligence (*Buddhi-Manas*) in the Causal Body, the instrument of illumination, the organ of pure perception and direct, intuitive insight into first truths.

JACOB MISTAKES LEAH FOR RACHEL

Since, on perusal of this Chapter of *Genesis*, the attention is arrested by the account of the deception practised by Laban upon Jacob, an interpretation of this incident is here offered in advance of a verse-by-verse consideration of the whole Chapter. Like so many incidents recorded in the Old Testament, this strange story is worthy of examination as a possible description, by means of allegory, of both psychological limitations and the phases of man's natural progress towards full spiritual illumination. The substitution of the eldest daughter, Leah, for the younger one, Rachel, who was so greatly desired by Jacob, may be interpreted as being descriptive of the effects of the limitations imposed upon neophytes by their position in evolution. Jacob sought pure wisdom (Rachel), but at first was unable to attain to it and so was wedded to Leah, representing the above-mentioned limitations. Every Candidate for Initiation begins by becoming spiritually awakened and, in consequence, seeking illumination. Whilst a full response is not withheld and ultimately is granted, intermediate steps must needs

---

[1] *Gnosis*—see Glossary.
[2] *Jn.* 4.

be taken or, in other words, truth must primarily be presented under the veil of allegory and symbol, but eventually in its pure state.

The aspirant is not at first aware of his own immaturity and so, allegorically, is led to accept a substituted " wife " for the one of his choice. Symbolically, Jacob marries Leah in the belief that she is Rachel. In the morning, however, which means the light of day or illumination of mind by Spirit, he discovers the deception which had been practised upon him. Actually it was his own limitations, particularly those of the formal mind, which are ever deceptive if wholly relied upon, that caused him to mistake Leah for Rachel—a substitute for the reality. Jacob, personifying every neophyte, received all that he was capable of understanding at that stage of his evolution and the whole procedure, symbolically described, was in fact perfectly natural and inevitable.

In the allegory Laban expresses this principle as the custom of giving the eldest daughter first. The description of Leah as " tender eyed " draws attention to the development of compassion, pity and love as essential to interior illumination, but it was Rachel to whom his soul clave from the moment when he first saw her at the well, kissed her and wept.[1] Pure Wisdom is ever the source of the secret longing of the heart of the aspirant for illumination, and no labour is too great and no disappointment or delay too grievous to bedull the fire of his aspiration. This is beautifully expressed in the words: " And Jacob served seven years for Rachel; and they seemed unto him but a few days, for the love he had to her."[2]

In the microcosmic, occult interpretation, the return of the young scion-to-be to the Patriarchal home in the East refers to that mental and spiritual journey to the Sanctuary wherein the original Wisdom is preserved and where spiritual light may be received.

THE SYMBOLOGY OF THE ROLLING AWAY OF THE STONE

The removal and replacing of the stone at the well's mouth in a graphic way indicates the opening and closing of a *Manvantara*, whether, major or minor. So far as the watering of the sheep is concerned, this would be regularly performed at about the same time each day. The sheep, in this sense, are the Monads, the three flocks lying near the well representing the three basic types or Rays[3] and that member of the Sephiroth with which they are associated, their Shepherd as it were. The successive unveilings of the secret Wisdom (the water in the well) for the welfare of mankind (the sheep)

---

[1] *Gen.* 29:11.
[2] *Gen.* 29:20.
[3] q.v. *The Seven Human Temperaments*, Geofrey Hodson, T. P. H., Adyar.

is also symbolised, and the author of the *Pentateuch* is directly informing the reader that he (the author) is himself engaged in that unveiling and warns the reader to be prepared. The careful replacing of the stone is especially suggestive of the preservation of Wisdom from both loss and profanation.

Those who remove the stone are the Earth's Adepts, the true Teachers of mankind. The rolling away of the stone suggests its spherical or circular shape, and also refers to the underlying principle of recurrent cycles. Precisely the same interpretation is applicable to the rolling away of the stone of the sepulchre in which Jesus was buried.[1] In both accounts the opening of a new *Manvantara* is implied, also the unveiling of Wisdom and the giving of assistance to man in his search for truth.

" TRUTH IS FOUND AT THE BOTTOM OF A WELL "[2]

The depth and the darkness of the waters of a well aptly symbolise both the precosmic state and, proverbially, the mysterious depths in which the hidden Wisdom (truth) is concealed. The filling in of the wells belonging to members of the Patriarchal line by those at enmity with them represents the action both of the *guna*[3] of inertia and of the Powers of Darkness,[4] which ever seek to make muddy the living waters of truth and to choke up the source of their supply to mankind.

The well of water, therefore, is much used in the Sacred Language as a basic symbol, and since water represents both root Substance and root Wisdom the old adage of Heraclitus, quoted above, is true. To attain wisdom man must either dig, if no well exists for him, or if it does, let down his bucket and draw forth water. These two processes correspond cosmically to the action of the emitted, intelligence-imbued, formative electrical energy (Fohat) which " digs holes in Space " (produces primordial atoms), and microcosmically to the effects of study, research, experiment and meditation. The very atoms of the brain, as channels for knowledge and consciousness, are " widened " in terms of that function. Water in wells is drained from free sources. It is free water with which the soil is soaked as a result of rain and of underground rivers and pools. The well, therefore, is a localisation and a concentration for special purposes of that which in its nature and normal existence is unconfined. This aptly applies both to the creative life indwelling in all Substance, but focused and directed in a Universe, and also to the primordial Wisdom inherent in the nature of things

---

[1] q.v. Vol. I of this work, p. 224 Adyar Ed. and pp. 214-215, (Quest Book Ed.) and *Lecture Notes of the School of the Wisdom*, Vol. II, p. 354, Geoffrey Hodson.

[2] Heraclitus.

[3] *Guna*—see Glossary.

[4] q.v. *Lecture Notes of the School of the Wisdom*, Vol. I, Ch. XVI, Sec. 7,

and in its turn focused by intellect, so that it may be drawn upon and used by mind.

THE WOMEN STANDING AT THE WELL

The wives-to-be, the women who draw water from wells and minister to the thirsty, may be regarded macrocosmically as personifications of spiritually fructified, differentiated matter in the Cosmos. They also represent the *Gnosis* itself, whilst in this sense wells are the Temples and Sanctuaries wherein it is enshrined. In terms of principles, the free water is the universal life or *Buddhi*. The water in the well is the *Buddhic* principle within the *Manas*, and the woman personifies the action of Higher *Manas* in perceiving or " drawing " it. The woman is placed at the well in Samaria to show the necessity for this function of the Higher *Manas*. Even the awakened *Christos* needs a vehicle as intermediary between itself and the world or, interiorly, between pure Wisdom (*Buddhi*) and the mind-brain.

In allegories referring to the processes of creation and human illumination, a woman must always be present. She personifies the basic principle of vehicleship, whilst her pitcher is an emblem of the particular vehicle appropriate to the level of action and interpretation under consideration. This principle is also typified by the Cup or Holy Grail and by the Chalice, especially when elevated and being used to administer Holy Communion. All recipients, at whatever level, are represented by the human beings and animals who receive water from the well. In Biblical allegories the opening of new cycles is frequently indicated by a process of vehicleship performed by a woman, well-known examples being Eve, Rebekah, Rachel, the woman of Samaria, Mary the mother of Jesus[1] and Mary Magdalene.[2]

The fact is of interest that this subjective, feminine function is projected and exhibited objectively. Physically, the feminine throughout all Nature is the receiver, the vehicle, and the producer. This applies equally to *Cosmogenesis* and to the illumination of the human mind by the comprehension of basic principles. The highest function of woman, as personification of abstract intelligence, is to perceive intuitively the root principles upon which any manifestation or cycle of events is founded, and then to convey the resultant knowledge to the mind-brain. To perform this office effectively she must transfer her focus of awareness and activity from the outermost to the innermost, from personality to Ego, and there be still. Thus the woman of Samaria listened at the well,[3] thereby indicating that physical and mental

---

[1] *Jn.* 19:25-27.
[2] *Jn.* 20:11-18.
[3] *Jn.* 4:7-26.

stillness are essential to the attainment of interior illumination. This is beautifully portrayed in the incident of the visit of Jesus to the home of Martha and Mary at Bethany, and explains His commendation of the apparently idle Mary and His gentle rebuke of the hospitably active Martha.[1]

The woman standing at the well with a pitcher by her side is one of the most beautiful, spiritual and revealing of all symbols. In terms of occult philosophy she represents in man the Higher *Manasic* receptacle and ministrant of the *Atma*-charged *Buddhic* Wisdom and Life—the illumined Causal Body.

Jacob, like Isaac his father before him, came to a well. Cosmically, he is positively polarised Spirit approaching negatively polarised matter—the potential Logos of a Universe-to-be.

ALLEGORIES OF THE LOGOS DOCTRINE

The questions and answers which form the subject-matter of verses four, five and six of the Twenty-ninth Chapter of *Genesis* are worthy of further consideration. They are reminiscent of those repeated at the opening of Mystery Temples and Lodges. Though modified and changed in various Rites, they represent the essential vocal interchanges which pass between the Creator and the creative Intelligences at the beginning of the emanation and formation of Universes. Somewhat similarly the Master of a Lodge interrogates his Officers and receives their replies. As always, the medium of communication is the sound of the voice, will-charged and thought-charged: for, as previously stated, the Logos doctrine is implicit in all Cosmogonies.

Jacob first asks: " My brethren, whence be ye ? " The answer is well-known to him, since he himself is present at their place of origin and they are obviously at home. It is necessary, however, to evoke a response, to arouse creative activity, to awaken the hitherto quiescent consciousness and its embodiment in pre-cosmic matter from its *pralayic* slumber. They answered "Of Haran are we." Thus their first response consists of mere repetition, a statement of the obvious, and not a self-initiated conveyance of original information. Jacob represents the primordial " Idea ". The herdsmen, awakened by the sound of the divine " Voice ", represent the *instinctual* life in matter, which but repeats the fact of its own existence.

Then asks Jacob: " Know ye Laban the son of Nahor ? " Here is allegorically portrayed the process of naming, which means bestowing individuality, thereby causing differentiation within original root substance. Laban personifies conscious life in matter and refers to the Lord of the preceding cycle on the matter side of its manifestation. He is male because in terms of function the Essence, Soul, noumenon of matter, is triple and Laban

---

[1] *Luke* 10:38-42,

represents the masculine or positive current or power therein, the Patriarch as it were, the father of the celestial " virgins "[1] who become the " mothers " of new creations. The word " Haran " may be interpreted as the condition of consummation, and so as also referring to the preceding cycle, the fruits of which have all been summed up in its creative Logos, symbolically stationed in the East. Therefore it is to the East, to Haran, that Jacob goes as the Logos of the new cycle. The herdsmen can but answer in their quasi-automatic way, " We know him ", and the interchange back and forth between Spirit and matter, Idea and substance, Logos and field, continues.

Jacob then asks, " Is he (Laban) well ? " They answer, " He is well ". Here the Logos has confirmed the existence of creative responsiveness and the adequate functioning or " well-being " of the life in the new field. Thereupon the feminine or negative current comes directly into action The herdsmen indicate this by their comment: "....behold, Rachel his daughter cometh with the sheep. " Here again, as in other Biblical allegories of Cosmogenesis, the mutual approach of positive and negative is indicated, the invariable mutual attraction and creative interaction of opposite polarities being described.

Gen. 29: 7. *And he said, Lo, it is yet high day, neither is it time that the cattle should be gathered together: water ye the sheep, and go and feed them.*

8. *And they said, We cannot, until all the flocks be gathered together, and till they roll the stone from the well's mouth; then we water the sheep.*

9. *And while he yet spake with them, Rachel came with her father's sheep: for she kept them.*

At once, in further interrogation and reply, the pure passivity and compliance of the life in matter is displaced by the resistance essential to all manifestation. In consequence, objections are raised to the request which follows. Although the instinctual, elemental consciousness in matter, symbolised by the herdsmen and sheep (the three flocks are the three *gunas*),[2] acts only according to the established material rule, the life and consciousness therein overrides the characteristic inertia. In this the play of the three *gunas* is interestingly described. Jacob is *rajas* or activity. The herdsmen, their flocks, the custom of only watering sheep in the evening, and the great stone over the well, aptly represent *tamas* or inertia. Rachel in her turn, corresponds to *sattva* or rhythm. That Rachel is associated with matter is distinctly and deliberately indicated by making her a herdswoman and giving her a flock, which she brings to the well.

---

[1] see Appendix and also Glossary under *Elohim.*

[2] *Gunas*—see Glossary.

CHAPTER VI

JACOB AND RACHEL MEET AT THE WELL

Gen. 29: 10. *And it came to pass, when Jacob saw Rachel the daughter of Laban his mother's brother, and the sheep of Laban his mother's brother, that Jacob went near, and rolled the stone from the well's mouth, and watered the flock of Laban his mother's brother.*

SINCE in these verses the elements of water and earth—the stone—are introduced into the narrative, an interruption in the sequential interpretation of the narrative is at this point deliberately embarked upon. Fundamental principles governing the method of writing in the Sacred Language and the inter-relationship between natural elements, vehicles, states of consciousness, faculties and senses of man here need to be considered; for these are the bases upon which the structure of allegorical literature is founded. An interpretation of verse eleven will, however, follow this diversion, which it is hoped will prove to be helpful.

As has been suggested in preceding interpretations, eternal and fundamental laws are allegorically described in Biblical accounts of journeys, relationships between families, Patriarchs, parents and their offspring, and in the courtships and, later, marriages of their sons and daughters. This practice is also followed in the present Chapter of *Genesis*. The story centres round the element of water, ever a symbol of the life inherent in all substance. This becomes individualised when placed in a well, (limited to one universe), and fructified when the positive element (Jacob) rolls away the stone which covers the well and " kisses " the personification of the divine consciousness intimately associated with that life (Rachel), as is indicated in verse eleven.

WATER, FIRE, EARTH AND AIR AS UNIVERSAL SYMBOLS

In all Biblical allegories, from Eden onwards, the inspired authors are at pains to introduce the element of water. Examples are the four rivers associated with the Garden of Eden,[1] the rain and the floods of the Noachian era, and the various wells at which scions and daughters of Patriarchs meet and where pitchers are filled with the water which the feminine personifications draw from them. Fire is introduced by the setting up of various

[1] *Gen.* 2:10-14,

altars and the making of burnt offerings thereon. Earth is represented by the very ground which is the stage upon which the dramas are played, and by the different countries and districts in which these acts are performed. The element of air is symbolised by references to birds—in Eden, in the Ark, and liberated therefrom—as also by the air which all the actors breathe.

Water, fire, earth, air—these represent physically those four basic elements, types of universal substance or *tattvas*[1] with which the Universal Mind constructs, moulds, beautifies and ultimately perfects Cosmoi, their component Universes and all that they contain. Behind and within these four is their parent, their Father-Mother Source—*Ākāsa*[2]—the fifth in addition to water, fire, earth and air. It is also the first of the divine Builder's materials of which Universes are composed; for all substances and the potentiality of all possible combinations of substances are contained within it. As is so constantly portrayed in the varying relationships of the actors in the Hebrew allegories, every chemical element is there, as also is every active, creative power and law, including that of attraction and repulsion.

Ākāsa is all; all is *Ākāsa*. This is the truth implied in the words of the Lord: " I AM THAT I AM ",[3] and of the Christ: " Before Abraham was, I am."[4] *Ākāsa* is the " Soul " of the waters of first differentiated cosmic Space. It is an intelligent, creative, electric, all-containing and all-producing life force and substance, ever obedient to eternal law. Such are the five basic elements of which Universes are built. In the microcosm they are represented by the principles and powers of man, and find expression both within him and through his sensory capacities.

CORRESPONDENCES[5] BETWEEN ELEMENTS, PLANES, HUMAN SENSES AND LEVELS OF CONSCIOUSNESS

In one classification the correspondences between the principles of man, the elements and man's sensory powers are as follows:

Physical body	— Earth, smell.
Astral body	— Water, taste.

---

[1] *Tattva* (Sk.) " Thatness " or quiddity—see Glossary.

[2] *Ākāsa* (Sk.)—Literally Space, the element first manifested in the Cosmos. Its characteristic is the root of sound. See Glossary.

[3] *Ex.* 3:14.

[4] *Jn.* 8:58.

[5] A correspondence, in the occult sense, is a characteristic found repeating itself at another level; something on the plane which tallies with something on another plane, as for example the same note in all octaves; the sap in the plant and the blood in the animal. q.v. *Lecture Notes of the School of the Wisdom*, Vol. I, Ch. XIII, Geoffrey Hodson.

Lower mental body	—	Fire, sight.
Higher mental body	—	*Ākāsa*, hearing.
Intuitional body	—	Air, touch.

Man's power to speak, as well as to hear, corresponds to the *Ākāsa*, the fifth element, which is the synthesis of the other four elements. These are unified in the vehicle of the Higher Mind, the Causal Body, the Auric Envelope.[1] Whenever an element, whether earth, water, air or fire (to quote them in their more usual order) is mentioned in Biblical allegories, an intentional reference is presumably made to a plane of Nature in the Macrocosm and a body and physical sense in man, the microcosm.

The whole man is a unit and his physical body is the synthesis of all his seven vehicles in terms of vibrational potentiality. Different types of bodily tissue in their turn correspond to the substances of the superphysical bodies. The senses, on the other hand, represent the faculties and inherent attributes of consciousness when using those bodies and active at any particular level. This system of correspondences was well known to the Initiates of the Chaldean and Egyptian Sanctuaries, who are mainly responsible for the *Pentateuch*. It was, however, regarded as a deeply occult, even a sacred, revelation. Since without its inclusion the cosmo-genetic account would be incomplete, this knowledge and the law of correspondences itself were perforce introduced into the allegories, but very heavily veiled.

Two profound ideas contained within the arcane teachings are firstly that of the unity of the Macrocosm or Universe—with its transcendent and its immanent Deity—and the microcosm of man, material and spiritual; and secondly, that there is a close similarity between the processes by which the powers within both become manifest and evolve. Man, in very truth, is created in the image of God. Eliphas Levi wrote: " The mystery of the earthly and mortal man is after the mystery of the supernal and immortal One. " Thus the Logos and man are not only one in essence but all that is in the Logos, which includes the Solar System, is innate in man. Their constitution is precisely similar—that is to say, it is at least seven fold. Man as Monad, like the Deity and the Universe, is also immanent within and transcendent beyond his field of manifestation, his seven principles. The creative power and processes by which a Solar System comes into being also operate in human procreation.

Occult philosophy thus teaches that the whole Universe with all its parts, from the highest plane of *Adi* down to physical Nature, is interlocked or interwoven to make a single whole—one body, one organism, one life, one consciousness, one law. All the " organs " or parts of this Macrocosm, though apparently separated in space and plane of manifestation, are in fact harmoniously interrelated and interacting. Certain of them are,

---

[1] auric envelope—see Glossary.

however, more intimately grouped together than others. They resonate harmoniously with each other like the notes of a chord, sharing a common basic frequency of oscillation.   In Occultism they are said to " correspond ". " Let a note be struck on an instrument and the faintest sound produces an eternal echo."[1]   For instance, a Zodiacal Sign, a planet, an element, a colour, a principle of man, a *chakra*, a type of tissue and a part of the physical body of man will all be vibrating in harmony.   Knowledge of these correspondences provides a key to the understanding of the Universe, and of man's place therein and relationship therewith.   It also explains the process of human development and thereby helps to solve human problems, such as those of health and disease.   This knowledge is the basic science behind all life and the key to all magic.   It reveals the *rationale* of both Astrology and *Karma*.

PART OF THE TABLE OF CORRESPONDENCES

Man	Zodiac	Planet	Plane and Principle	Chakras	Physical Body	Faculty
Atma	Aquarius	Uranus	Atmic body & Plane	Crown Chakra	Skeleton	Will
Buddhi	Virgo	Neptune & Mercury	Buddhic Plane & Body	Crown Chakra	Pineal Gland	Intuition
Manas I	Libra Taurus	Venus	Causal Plane & Body	Ajna	Pituitary Body	Abstract Thought
Manas II	Capricorn	Saturn	Lower Mental Plane & Body	Throat & Heart	Cerebro Spinal System	Concrete Thought
Astral	Scorpio	Mars	Astral Plane & Body	Solar Plexus	Sympathetic Nervous System	Emotions
Etheric	Cancer	Moon	Etheric Plane & Body	Connecting principle & pranic Spleen reservoir		
Physical	A synthesis of all					

Thus a profound, fundamental truth concerning man is that in his spiritual, intellectual, psychical and physical nature he is a miniature replica or epitome of the whole order of created beings and things.   Man is a model of the totality of Nature.   He contains within himself the collective aggregate of all that ever has existed, does at any time exist and will ever

[1] q.v. *Isis Unveiled*, Vol. I, H. P. Blavatsky.

exist throughout the eternity of eternities. This doctrine is innate in Kabbalism, where it is stated somewhat as follows:

In the vast chain of cosmic being all created things are linked together, everything being magically contained in everything else. Where one stands, there stand all the worlds. Everything is connected with everything else, and interpenetrates everything else, according to exact if mysterious law. "Nothing is unimportant in nature....even so small a thing as the birth of one child upon our insignificant planet has its effect upon the universe;...".[1] Man himself may be seen as a symbolic transparency through which the secrets of the Cosmos could be discerned. Goethe echoes this in his words: "The eye could not see the sun if it did not contain the sun within itself, and how could Divine things enrapture us if we did not carry the Power of God within us?"

FIRE

If this underlying principle be acceptable, then the introduction of the element of fire into certain Biblical narratives may be regarded as referring to the Ākāsa-tattva, the higher mental vehicle (the Causal Body) and the sense of hearing. This tattava is of itself sound-producing or soniferous, in consequence giving birth in man to the sense of hearing. Physically it is the preponderating tattva in the aural nerves and brain centres, as well as in their counterparts in the etheric, emotional, mental and higher mental vehicles. Whilst all of these bodies have all the tattvic states represented within their substances, one preponderates in each of them. The Ākāsa itself and, microcosmically, the Ego in the Causal Body, are all creatively parental, the other tattvas emanating therefrom. The Causal Body is the synthesis and conjoined essence of all the powers and faculties of man. It is represented by the element of fire, from which all things proceed and to which they all return.

WATER

Water is the opposite of fire and represents the receptive, maternal, all-productive element. In the Sacred Language it is the symbol for the astral plane, and for the astral body so far as man is concerned. Both of these correspond to the sense of taste in the organs, nerves and brain centres in which the element of water predominates. Physically the sense of taste is dependent upon the presence of water for its operation.

EARTH

The earth, meaning all solid ground and substances, corresponds to the form vehicles, and especially to the physical body and the sense of smell.

---

[1] *Ibid.*, p. 314.

In symbology all solid objects refer to states or experiences of waking bodily consciousness. Mountains, for example, represent exalted states; valleys, degradation; fields and gardens, fruitfulness; whilst deserts and wildernesses designate conditions of spiritual aridity.[1]

AIR

Air in its turn, particularly still air, corresponds to the faculty of intuition. When consciousness is exalted to the level of pure wisdom, spiritual intuitiveness and full realisation of unity, sometimes symbolised by a white cloud, then the almost omnipotent power of the Will-Self of man may be discerned. Thus the author of the Book of *Revelation* wrote: " And I looked, and behold a white cloud, and upon the cloud one sat, like unto the Son of man, having on his head a golden crown, and in his hand a sharp sickle."[2]

Since, however, clouds shut out the light of the sun they are, as also suggested above, symbols of that obscurity with which the higher nature of man is regarded by the analytical mind-brain. Elemental storms generally refer to disturbed mental and emotional conditions. Still air represents both the higher emotions and the intuition, whilst rushing winds sometimes refer to disturbed mento-emotional states.

Four elements, four principles and four senses of men have now been correlated. There remains the fifth, the sense of touch, which involves the total life principle of the whole human organism from highest Spirit ($\bar{A}tma$) to the dense physical body. Thus a synthesis of the whole is involved, rather than a single element. If, in order to complete the correspondences, a superphysical vehicle is indicated, it would be the Auric Envelope.[3]

Such, then, are the elements, *tattvas* and senses and such are their uses and significations in the Sacred Language. The four elements especially always refer to levels of consciousness in man and to *tattvas* in Nature.

Gen. 29: 11. *And Jacob kissed Rachel, and lifted up his voice, and wept.*

Proffered interpretations of the Biblical verses and the narrative which they relate are now resumed. The action of positive Spirit upon inert matter is indicated by Jacob's action of rolling away the stone from the well, whilst the interfusion of Spirit and matter, positive and negative, is shown in the kiss with which Jacob greeted Rachel. A kiss involves the sense of touch, symbolises the creative contact of the positive agent upon the negative recipient, and portrays a phase in the creative process. In human superphysical experience the lover's kiss is an expression of emotion and of a sense

[1] See Pt. One of this Vol., Ch. III.
[2] *Rev.* 14:14.
[3] Auric Envelope—see Glossary.

7

of oneness. Although physically given by the lips, superphysically it is an expression of love and desire inspired by a realisation of unity, however fleeting and faint that realisation may be. Since, however, unity is an unalterable fact behind apparent diversity, and since the life in all people is one and the same despite the variety of form, the instinct for togetherness finds constant and continual expression in man. In a kiss on the lips, emotion predominates. By a kiss on the brow, over the pituitary gland and the *Ajna Chakram*, the spiritual is implied. The fact that paternal, maternal, filial, fraternal and sisterly kisses are hardly ever upon the lips is of interest, indicating that desire is absent from them.

The kiss which Jacob gives to Rachel includes the feeling of attraction aroused by the sight of her beauty and the attainment of contact by touch. It also indicates positive action by the male and acquiescence and response by the female, thereby perfectly symbolising the Macrocosmic creative process which begins with the " kiss " of Spirit upon matter. The kiss bestowed by Judas upon Jesus represents the reaction or response of matter to Spirit; for it was a betrayal leading to the imprisonment, the degradation, the suffering, the death and the entombment of the Christ. Spirit (personified by Jesus) on entering, moulding and ultimately perfecting material vehicles, is enfolded and so " betrayed " and imprisoned by matter, primordial freedom being temporarily restrained. As expounded in the first Volume of this work, the life story of Jesus—especially as related in the fourth Gospel—is susceptible of interpretation as an allegory of Cosmogenesis (the Nativity), involution to the deepest depths (burial in the rock tomb), and evolution to fullest attainment (Ascension to the right hand of God).[1]

Such are possible interpretations of the symbol of the kiss as used in the Sacred Language.

> *Gen.* 29: 12. *And Jacob told Rachel that he was her father's brother, and that he was Rebekah's son: and she ran and told her father.*
>
> 13. *And it came to pass, when Laban heard the tidings of Jacob his sister's son, that he ran to meet him, and embraced him, and kissed him, and brought him to his house. And he told Laban all these things.*

Interpreted in terms of Cosmogenesis, the purely passive nature of receptive matter (Rachel) in relation to the generating energy (Jacob) is indicated in these verses. Rachel speaks no words to Jacob; he it is who speaks to her—a reference to the emanation of creative energy as sound. In her own inherent nature, however, as substance already differentiated, Rachel acts positively in relation to her own original Source personified as Laban, her father, the spiritual Essence of the Root Substance (*Mula-*

---

[1] q.v. also *Lecture Notes of the School of the Wisdom,* Vol. II, Ch. VII Secs. 3 & 4, Geoffrey Hodson, and Vol. I of this work, Pt. **Five.**

SOLOMON'S SEAL

SOLOMON'S SEAL

prakriti). Although in the allegory these are presented as two separate principles, father and daughter, in reality they are one. Laban may be regarded as the positive and Rachel as the negative current of the triple creative force inherent in the matter-side of Root Substance. From the positive comes an active response; for Laban approaches Jacob, speaks to him and kisses him.

Gen. 29: 14. *And Laban said to him, Surely thou art my bone and my flesh. And he abode with him the space of a month.*

15. *And Laban said unto Jacob, Because thou art my brother, shouldest thou therefore serve me for nought ? tell me, what shall thy wages be ?*

16. *And Laban had two daughters: the name of the elder was Leah, and the name of the younger was Rachel.*

17. *Leah was tender eyed; but Rachel was beautiful and well favoured.*

18. *And Jacob loved Rachel; and said, I will serve thee seven years for Rachel thy younger daughter.*

19. *And Laban said, It is better that I give her to thee, than that I should give her to another man: abide with me.*

20. *And Jacob served seven years for Rachel; and they seemed unto him but a few days, for the love he had to her.*

SEPTENNIAL PERIODS IN THE HISTORIES OF UNIVERSES, NATIONS AND MEN

The seven-year periods through which Jacob serves Laban, for no other recompense than marriage to Rachel, represent all sevenfold cycles by which *Manvantaras* are completed and through which fruition occurs. In man, the Initiate, the seven-year periods represent the seven principles which must be awakened, and in each of which work (evolutionary development) must have been carried out before illumination and Initiations into the Greater Mysteries (personified by Rachel) can be attained.

The first seven years of Jacob's labour bring him only a substitute for the wife of his choice, her sister Leah. Thus is portrayed a first completed cycle in which conceptual knowledge alone is gained as a substitute for the intuitively perceived truth. The first cycle must be made fruitful, particularly in and through the personal principles, these fruits being represented by Reuben, Simeon, Levi and Judah, the children of Jacob and Leah.

Throughout the *Book of Genesis* the cosmic design, or divine geometry, is insisted upon. The Solomon's Seal[1] or six-pointed star, and the hexagon formed by joining their points, are presented allegorically as the numerical and geometrical basis of the Universe, itself the product of the interaction

---

[1] Solomon's Seal—the symbolical double triangle within a circle. See diagram on opposite page.

and to be enumerated as the seventh.   The two triplicities are continually presented by means of personifications.   These are the primary triple Spirit, or threefold current of the creative Breath—the upward pointing triangle—and the same triplicity reflected and actively present in matter— the downward pointing triangle.

Thus the triple Essence of both Spirit and matter is revealed in the allegories, the former by parents and a son (the hero) and the latter by parents and a daughter (the heroine).   The blending of the two families, culminating in the marriage of the son and daughter, is represented by the interlacing or intermingling of the upward and downward pointing triangles. The enclosing circle of the Seal represents both the resultant Universe and the seventh principle involved.   The two triplicities are, in fact, drawn from the same Source, which is the Absolute, the Kabbalistic *Ain-Soph*.[1]   They are therefore identical in their nature, the difference being only in the order of their appearance, and consequently of their function.   The primary triplicity, the cosmic spiritual Triad, emerges first and officiates as the positive agent in the creative process.   The secondary Triad instantly follows the emergence of the primary, of which it is a reflection in the vast mirror of cosmic Space.[2]

SYMBOL OF THE MIRROR

Just as a reflected image in a glass mirror appears simultaneously with that which it reflects and is wholly dependent upon it for existence, so the reflection of the primary creative Triad in the " Mirror of Space " is contemporaneous with, but dependent upon, the appearance or manifestation of the original before that Mirror.   Unlike the reflected image, however, which is purely illusory, the threefold reflection of the spiritual Triad in the " Mirror of Space " does have an actual existence and power to function. Admittedly that function is decided by, and dependent upon, the nature and activity of the primary Triad which is its cause.   Nevertheless, since it is only a reflection and not a prime cause, it is regarded in occult philosophy as an illusion, although quite real in appearance when viewed from the matter side of a manifested unit.

These views were interestingly expressed in the Grecian Mysteries, wherein the Initiated Ones were shown secret objects, the full nature of which is not actually known.   One suggestion is that they were the playthings of Dionysus, the Divine Child, as Creator and Fashioner of the Universe. These toys, it has been stated, were the five Platonic solids, indicating the

---

[1] See appendix—" The Sephirothal Tree ".

[2] The reader is referred to the statement entitled " Cosmogenesis " at the beginning of Pt. Three of this Volume.

axes for the growth of the chemical elements and crystals. Added to these were the top as model of the atom, and the ball as model of the Earth. The mirror upon which the young God (Bacchus as boy) is dancing and playing is to be regarded as a symbol of matter in which is reflected all that the Logos fashions on high.[1]

When, therefore, as stated in the fourteenth verse of this Chapter of *Genesis*, Laban so positively affirms to Jacob that he is his " bone " and his " flesh ", he is in reality professing a profound spiritual truth; for Laban, his wife and two daughters, who are really one, are personifications of the lower or reflected upper Triad, whilst Isaac, Rebekah and their two sons, who are also really one, represent the origin of the reflection, the upward pointing triangle itself, the triple creative Spirit. The triplicity is further indicated by the three symbols of bone for the First Aspect, flesh for the Second and the home in which Jacob abode for a month for the Third. Thus the great cosmic principle of creation by reflection is most skilfully portrayed in this one verse alone.

The symbol of the mirror, whilst useful, might not perhaps be regarded as a wholly accurate representation of the function of matter in the creative process. If the reflected image were endowed with life and given creative responsiveness and productivity, then the truth would be correctly portrayed. Nevertheless, since all creative products are first conceived in the consciousness of the First Logos, and it is this primary " Idea" which is the model, the resultant Universe is in that sense but its reflection. The analogy should not be pushed too far, therefore, and the mirror symbol, although helpful, is not perfect. In general, however, it may be said that the causative " Idea " is the threefold Spirit, whilst the image is Nature herself, a faithful reflection but also endowed with creative and productive powers.

In man the mirror is primarily where the abstract and concrete aspects of intellect are merged or, technically, where the Causal and mental bodies are united. At this level the triple Ego, in terms of both consciousness and action, is reflected into the lower mental, the emotional and the physical bodies. These two triplicities become conjoined with varying degrees of symmetry and intimacy in each physical incarnation. As evolution proceeds through successive lives, symmetry and intimacy increase and this culminates in the ultimate production of a perfect manifestation of the Higher Triad in the lower trilplicity. The final achievement is well symbolised by the interlacing of the equilateral triangles, the enclosing circle of Solomon's Seal representing in the Cosmos the Ring-pass-not and in man the Auric Envelope.

---

[1] One source of such information is *First Principles of Theosophy*, p. 237, by C. Jinarajadasa.

SYMBOLOGY OF THE NUMBERS THREE AND SEVEN

A month of thirty days, by reduction giving the number three, under-lines and points to an esoteric meaning.   The periods of seven years during which Jacob served Laban in return for the gift in marriage of each of the two daughters refer, as already suggested, first to the septenate which is formed by the two interlaced triangles with their synthesis as the seventh, and secondly to the sevenfold creative cycles.   A major cycle is composed of a succession of these combined triplicities.

The primary creative cycle, which is always a complete round of a spiral movement of forthgoing and return, carries the creative process on the first part of its cyclic development in the direction of the ultimate imprison-ment of highest Spirit in lowest matter.   The greatest density of substance, however, is not reached in the first cycle, and Leah represents that early stage at whatever level may have been reached according to the point and plane of departure.

Another and second sevenfold cycle of creative activity, or service by Jacob to Laban, follows to its completion, which is the " wedding " of creative Spirit with matter of deeper solidity.   This second cycle is allego-rised by the second seven years of service and the marriage of Jacob and Rachel.   Leah represents the psycho-spiritual planes of matter and con-sciousness and the bodies of man.   These planes (Leah) are the first to be formed and to become active in conjunction with the spiritual creative potency (Jacob).   The goal, however, is the production of matter of the deepest possible density and the creation and perfection of forms by the " marriage " of Spirit with it.   Rachel represents this ultimate goal and so is the real love of Jacob, Leah personifying a stage—or a preceding sevenfold cycle—on the way to that consummation.

Gen. 29: 21. *And Jacob said unto Laban, Give me my wife, for my days are fulfilled, that I may go in unto her.*

22. *And Laban gathered together all the men of the place, and made a feast.*

23. *And it came to pass in the evening, that he took Leah his daughter, and brought her to him; and he went in unto her.*

24. *And Laban gave unto his daughter Leah Zilpah his maid for handmaid.*

25. *And it came to pass, that in the morning, behold, it was Leah: and he said to Laban, What is this thou hast done unto me? did not I serve with thee for Rachel? wherefore then hast thou beguiled me?*

26. *And Laban said, It must not be so done in our country, to give the younger before the firstborn.*

27. *Fulfil her week, and we will give thee this also for the service which thou shalt serve with me yet seven other years,*

28. *And Jacob did so, and fulfilled her week: and he gave him Rachel his daughter to wife also.*

29. *And Laban gave to Rachel his daughter Bilhah his handmaid to be her maid.*

30. *And he went in also unto Rachel, and he loved also Rachel more than Leah, and served with him yet seven other years.*

31. *And when the LORD saw that Leah was hated, he opened her womb: but Rachel was barren.*

32. *And Leah conceived, and bare a son, and she called his name Reuben: for she said, Surely the LORD hath looked upon my affliction; now therefore my husband will love me.*

33. *And she conceived again, and bare a son; and said, Because the LORD hath heard that I was hated, he hath therefore given me this son also: and she called his name Simeon.*

34. *And she conceived again, and bare a son; and said, Now this time will my husband be joined unto me, because I have born him three sons : therefore was his name called Levi.*

35. *And she conceived again, and bare a son: and she said, Now will I praise the LORD: therefore she called his name Judah; and left bearing.*

NIGHT AND DAY—SYMBOLS OF STATES OF CONSCIOUSNESS

The apparent deceit implied by the substitution of Leah for Rachel is a blind, as has already been said, though the statement that discovery was made in the morning is also of occult significance. Just as night and blindness symbolise a darkened state of mind as regards spiritual " light ", so the coming of day and the restoration of sight may be interpreted as re-entry into spiritual illumination and the consequent discovery of truth.[1] In exemplification of this form of symbolism, Jacob is unaware during the night of the substitution of Leah for Rachel, but discovers the truth in the morning.

The further idea is indicated that Spirit pays a price for its " marriage " with matter, the cost being a loss of pre-marital purity, freedom and transcendence. These, however, are recovered on the returning arc when the centre of awareness, or focus of divine attention, is raised from the densest to higher levels of manifestation. Full spiritual realisation then follows; symbolically, it is day.

Applied to man, the darkness of night also represents the period of physical life from birth to death, whilst the light of day refers to the return after death to a more spiritual condition, with death itself as the dawn.

[1] see Pt. One of this Vol., Ch. III—Night,

In another possible interpretation, night symbolises psycho-spiritual conditions of consciousness in which form temporarily rules life, matter imprisoning and blinding the intellect so successfully that interior awareness is lost and, in consequence, conscience with its spiritual impulses is in eclipse. These materialistic phases pass, however, this being portrayed by the coming of day, the high noon of which represents the peak of exaltation and expansion. Thus Jacob discovers Leah in the morning, and Peter experiences remorse when the cock crows thrice at the break of day.[1]

The adventures and misadventures of Jacob in his early domestic life are all components of a great solar allegory which equally applies to man—and especially initiated man. The life history of Jacob, like that of other Patriarchs and heroes in Mythology, is susceptible of an Initiatory interpretation in which Jacob personifies every Initiate, whilst the events of his life are made to portray spiritual, psychological and physical experiences during successful passage through the Grades of the Lesser and the Greater Mysteries.

Every Initiate is as a microcosmic Sun God on Earth and his victories and temporary defeats, his obscurations and eclipses, are all reflections in him of solar events. His birth, for example, portrays the " birth " of the Solar Logos, meaning His so-called " new birth " at the commencement of the process of the emanation of a Universe. This method of presenting deeply occult truths was used by those who wrote the life stories of the Lord Shri Krishna, Horus of the Egyptians, the Lord Buddha and the Lord Christ. Identification of Jesus Christ with the creative Logos, or cosmic " Word ",[2] is made clear by the Evangelists, and especially by St. John in the first five verses of his Gospel, which read as follows:

1. In the beginning was the Word, and the Word was with God, and the Word was God.
2. The same was in the beginning with God.
3. All things were made by him; and without him was not anything made that was made.
4. In him was life; and the life was the light of men.
5. And the light shineth in darkness; and the darkness comprehended it not.

Part of the mystery of the Greater Initiations is that within the Initiate there is focused and manifested microcosmically, often through physical experiences, the interplay of forces between the sun and the planet on which the Initiation occurs. This mystery reaches its height during an *Avatara*[3]

---

[1] *Jn.* 18:27.

[2] For a fuller exposition of this view see *Lecture Notes of the School of the Wisdom*, Vol. II, Ch. VII, Secs. 5 and 6, Geoffrey Hodson.

[3] *Avatara* (Sk.)—The descent of an exalted, divine Being into the body of a mortal, A divine Incarnation,

or " descent " of a Deity, when the activities and experiences of the over-shadowing deific Presence partially reflect and portray certain procedures, relationships and phases of manifestation of the Solar Logos in His Universe.

The twelve children of Jacob, and later the twelve tribes of Judah,[1] like the twelve disciples of Jesus, typify the Signs of the Zodiac. Each Sign, in its turn, represents one of the deific attributes, powers and Orders of Beings or *Dhyan Chohans*.[2] These become successively preponderant in the spiritual influence radiated upon a planet throughout each of the Zodiacal epochs during which the sun passes through the Sign.

Arbitrary though these Signs in the heavens may seem, being made up as they are of groups of stars which apparently have no figurative connection with each other whatsoever, they do nevertheless both represent in them-selves, and focus upon the Earth, special types of cosmic and solar energies. Although, owing to the absence of any real direct connection between the component stars of a constellation, no physical astronomer could ever have originated the idea of the combination of certain stars to form twelve Signs, with animal and human configurations and names, they actually do repres-ent groups of such influences. These groupings could be known only to the highest Initiates and it was They, the very loftiest of the Adepts Who, first through the Ancient Mysteries and later through the Initiates thereof, gave to the humanity of this planet its knowledge both of the Zodiacal Signs and of the science of Astrology, which is based upon that knowledge.

---

[1] q.v. *Gen.* 49 *et. seq.* and pp. 386 *et. seq.* and pp. 404 *et. seq.* of this Volume.

[2] *Dhyan Chohans*—The Lords of Light; The Lords of Contemplation; the divine Intel-ligences charged with the supervision of Cosmos, see Glossary.

CHAPTER VII

THE BIRTH OF THE TWELVE TRIBES

Gen. 30: *Rachel's grief for her barrenness: Bilhah beareth Dan and Naphtali: Zilpah beareth Gad and Asher: Leah beareth Issachar, Zebulun, and Dinah: Rachel beareth Joseph. Jacob's new covenant with Laban: his policy to become rich.*

Gen. 30: 1. *And when Rachel saw that she bare Jacob no children, Rachel envied her sister; and said unto Jacob, Give me children, or else I die.*

2. *And Jacob's anger was kindled against Rachel: and he said, Am I in God's stead, who hath withheld from thee the fruit of the womb?*

3. *And she said, Behold my maid Bilhah, go in unto her; and she shall bear upon my knees, that I may also have children by her.*

4. *And she gave him Bilhah her handmaid to wife: and Jacob went in unto her.*

5. *And Bilhah conceived, and bare Jacob a son.*

6. *And Rachel said, God hath judged me, and hath also heard my voice, and hath given me a son: therefore called she his name Dan.*

7. *And Bilhah Rachel's maid conceived again, and bare Jacob a second son.*

8. *And Rachel said, With great wrestlings have I wrestled with my sister, and I have prevailed: and she called his name Naphtali.*

9. *When Leah saw that she had left bearing, she took Zilpah her maid, and gave her Jacob to wife.*

10. *And Zilpah, Leah's maid bare Jacob a son.*

11. *And Leah said, A troop cometh: and she called his name Gad.*

12. *And Zilpah Leah's maid bare Jacob a second son.*

13. *And Leah said, Happy am I, for the daughters will call me blessed: and she called his name Asher.*

14. *And Reuben went in the days of wheat harvest, and found mandrakes in the field, and brought them unto his mother Leah. Then Rachel said to Leah, Give me, I pray thee, of thy son's mandrakes.*

15. *And she said unto her, Is it a small matter that thou hast taken my husband? and wouldest thou take away my sons's mandrakes*

also?   And Rachel said, Therefore he shall lie with thee tonight for thy son's mandrakes.

16. *And Jacob came out of the field in the evening, and Leah went out to meet him, and said, Thou must come in unto me; for surely I have hired thee with my son's mandrakes.   And he lay with her that night.*

17. *And God hearkened unto Leah, and she conceived, and bare Jacob the fifth son.*

18. *And Leah said, God hath given me my hire, because I have given my maiden to my husband: and she called his name Issachar.*

19. *And Leah conceived again, and bare Jacob the sixth son.*

20. *And Leah said, God hath endued me with a good dowry; now will my husband dwell with me, because I have born him six sons; and she called his name Zebulun.*

21. *And afterwards she bare a daughter, and called her name Dinah.*

22. *And God remembered Rachel, and God hearkened to her, and opened her womb.*

23. *And she conceived, and bare a son; and said, God hath taken away my reproach:*

24. *And she called his name Joseph; and said, The LORD shall add to me another son.*

This Thirtieth Chapter of the *Book of Genesis* is a characteristic example of portions of the *Pentateuch* which even the most devout believer in the Bible as the inspired Word of God must find difficulty in accepting in the literal sense.   The great Patriarch is shown as engaging in both marital and extra-marital intercourse, having been encouraged by his wife in the latter, she up to that time being barren.   In addition, the life story of Jacob shows him to have been guilty of the following evil deeds: by a despicable deceit planned by his mother he received the blessing which his father Isaac had designed to bestow upon his other son, Esau (*Gen.* 27); by a further deception he obtained the most valuable cattle of his father-in-law, Laban, and ensured for himself possession of the stronger of these (Chapter Thirty of *Genesis*, verses thiry-seven to forty-three).

In spite of this conduct Jacob was visited by God in person in a dream (Chapter Thirty-one of *Genesis*, verse twenty-four), and was later met by the angels of God at Mahanaim (Chapter Thirty-two of *Genesis*, verses one and two).   Furthermore, he was personally instructed by God concerning his future travels and told to change his name to Israel, " for as a prince hast thou power with God and with men, and hast prevailed ".   (Chapter Thirty-two of *Genesis*, verse twenty-eight).   As if this were not enough, Jacob received both paternal and implied divine encouragement, as a result of which—by the production of eleven sons and one daughter—he was enabled to become the Patriarch of the twelve Tribes of Israel.   Being

commanded by God to "be fruitful and multiply; a nation and a company of
nations shall be of thee, and kings shall come out of thy loins. " (Chapter
Thirty-five of *Genesis*, verses one, nine, ten and eleven *et seq*.). Indeed, it must
be confessed that the greater part of this Chapter of *Genesis* contains subject-
matter which is repugnant to both the intellect and the modern sense of
morality. Readers might, in consequence, discard the Chapter as a whole,
and even have their faith in the Bible as the inspired Word of God greatly
shaken.

Fortunately, however, as the title and the themes of these Volumes
imply, an alternative exists. This is to regard the scientifically impossible
and morally offensive statements as delibarate blinds or covers for profound
philosophical ideas—a view which receives support from the authorities
quoted at the beginning of this book, and also from many other
authors writing upon the subject. I repeat here one such inspiring
statement:

" Every time that you find in our books a tale the reality of which
seems impossible, a story which is repugnant to both reason and
common sense, then be sure that the tale contains a profound allegory veiling a deeply mysterious truth; and the greater the absurdity of the letter, the deeper the wisdom of the spirit. "—Moses
Maimonedes, Jewish theologian, historian, Talmudist, philosopher
and physician (1135-1205 A.D.).

If this approach be adopted then the Thirtieth Chapter of *Genesis*,
like many others in the Old Testament, may be carefully re-read with an
eye to the presence of classical symbols and evidence of the use of the allegorical method of writing. At once some of such symbols are discovered,
including mandrakes, trees, rods, water, watering troughs and breeding of
cattle. Human procreative procedures are also frankly referred to and,
with the aforementioned, may be susceptible of interpretation as allegories
describing the emanation, involution and evolution of Universes and all that
they contain, including the Monads of men. I have myself examined the
Chapter from this point of view and now advance for consideration the
results of its interpretation as an example of the particular category of
literature known as the Sacred Language.

At this point, however, should it be considered that insults to the
intelligence, descriptions of concubinage, and the affirmation that the
Supreme Deity of the Universe performed an obstetrical operation upon
Rachel, are objectionable means of concealing wisdom, it may possibly
be replied that what is offensive to modern morality and custom may not
have been so amongst the tribes whose history is being recounted. Polygamy
and intercourse with servants may have been regarded by them as permissible
and natural, particularly—as was the case in this story—if the wife, because
of her barrenness and the necessity for ensuring the family succession,

actually instructed her husband (Chapter Thirty of *Genesis*, verses three to five) thus to engage in extra-marital intercourse.

Polygamy seems to have been a well-established institution in primitive Jewish society. The law regulated and limited the practice, whilst the Prophets and scribes looked upon it with disfavour. The first instance of bigamy occurred in the family of Cain (Chapter Four of *Genesis*, verse nineteen). Abraham had only one wife, but was persuaded to marry Hager (Chapter Sixteen of *Genesis*, verses two and three). Jacob married two sisters because he was deceived by his father-in-law, Laban (Chapter Twenty-nine of *Genesis*, verses twenty-three to thirty), and married his wives' slaves at the request of his wives (Chapter Thirty of *Genesis*, verses four and nine). Polygamy was practised amongst the rich and the nobility (Chapter Eight of *Judges*, verse thirty; Chapter Two of I *Chron*, verse twenty-six; Chapter Four of I *Chron*, verse five; Chapter Eight of I *Chron.*, verse eight). The tribe of Issachar practised polygamy (Chapter Seven of I *Chron.*, verse four). David and Solomon had many wives (Chapter Five of II *Sam.*, verse thirteen; Chapter Two of I *Kings*, verse one to three). The Mosaic law, while permitting polygamy, introduced many provisions which tended to confine it. A woman slave taken as a wife by the son of her master was entitled to all the rights of matrimony (Chapter Twenty-one of *Ex.*, verses nine to eleven).[1]

Furthermore, primitive peoples were inclined to attribute to divine intervention such unusual occurrences as the fruitfulness of a wife after many years of barrenness, although this may simply have been the result of natural physiological changes.

Occult philosophy contains the view, as partly indicated in the second Chart entitled " The Human Spirit as the Prodigal Son ", facing page 55 of Volume II of this work, that in their evolutionary pilgrimage the Monads of men achieve the unfoldment of germinal powers by means of the embodiment of their projected Rays in the mineral, plant, animal, human and superhuman kingdoms of Nature successively. As will be seen, the interpretation of the Chapters under consideration is largely based upon this view, which is implicit in both Hinduism and Islam, being stated in the latter as follows:

" I died from the mineral, and became a plant.
I died from the plant, and reappeared in an animal.
I died from the animal, and became a man.
Wherefore then should I fear ? When did I grow less by dying ?
Next time I shall die from the man,
That I may grow the wings of the angel.
From the angel, too, must I seek advance;

---

[1] q.v. *The Jewish Encyclopædia.*

'All things shall perish save His Face.'
Once more shall I wing my way above the angels;
I shall become that which entereth not the imagination.
Then let me become naught, naught; for the harpstring
crieth unto me: 'Verily, unto Him shall we return.'"

Mesnavi (Thirteenth Century).

In the interpretations now offered I advance the view that the same doctrine is discernible in Hebraism, admittedly being presented under a heavy veil of allegory in the life story of Jacob. A quotation from the *Zohar* may permissibly be included at this point, for there one reads:

"Rabbi Simeon said: 'If a man looks upon the Torah as merely a book presenting narratives and everyday matters, alas for him! Such a Torah, one treating with everyday concerns, and indeed a more excellent one, we too, even we, could compile. More than that, in the possession of the rulers of the world there are books of even greater merit, and these we could emulate if we wished to compile some such Torah. But the Torah, in all of its words, holds supernal truths and sublime secrets.'" Zohar III, 152a.

If the reader cares to examine with me this possible approach, then I offer suggested interpretations of the Thirtieth Chapter of *Genesis*, in studying which it has seemed to me that profoundly philosophic and occult ideas concerning Cosmogenesis are allegorically presented. It will be noted that later I refer to the Chaldean Mysteries, a deliberate choice since those Institutions were active at the period of the founding of the Hebrew nation.[1] Their Hierophants and Initiates would therefore have been aware firstly of the danger of a direct revelation of power-bestowing Mystery teaching, secondly of the law that knowledge gained must be shared with humanity, and thirdly of the existence of the Sacred Language as a vehicle through which such knowledge might with reasonable safety be shared with their fellow men. The Sages of old knew that the whole Universe, spiritual, super-physical and physical, is composed of the continually interactive parts of one vast organism. Man, being a microcosm or miniature reproduction of all that the Macrocosm contains, possesses within himself, in however germinal a form as yet, the same powers as those which bring a Universe into being. Whoever becomes aware of this fact as an experience in consciousness, and awakens cosmic powers into activity within himself, could employ them for purely personal benefit, having become endowed with an almost irresistible capacity to control and oppress other human beings. This, I believe, is the reason why the teachers of old were under the necessity of both concealing and revealing their knowledge beneath a veil of allegory and symbol. Of the two alternatives—completely discarding these

---

[1] For a fuller exposition of this subject See Vol. II of this work, pp. 240 et. seq.

and similar Chapters of the Bible, or systematically applying to them the classical keys[1] by which the allegories and symbols of the Sacred Language may be interpreted—I personally have found the latter to be the more acceptable.

JACOB AND HIS FAMILY AS PERSONIFICATIONS OF SOLAR GENERATIVE FORCES AND INTELLIGENCES

The Chaldean Mysteries[2] were appointed as the especial recipients, guardians and deliverers of this deeply occult knowledge as far as the Aryan Race[3] is concerned. True, all the other Mysteries—especially those of Egypt,—shared in this knowledge, but the Chaldeans were the specialists amongst the Initiates of the planet in the twin sciences of Astronomy and Astrology, the latter being regarded as the " soul " of the former. Since the Hebrew Patriarchs derived their esoteric wisdom largely from the Chaldean Mysteries, the authors of the *Pentateuch* were informed of, but dare not directly reveal, the essential elements of the two sciences, as well as their mutual relationship. In their allegories, however, they disclose a great deal of information and in the strange and apparently repugnant stories of Jacob's polygamy and concubinage, resulting in the birth of twelve children, certain elements of both Astronomy and Astrology are indirectly indicated.

In this sense Jacob is the sun itself, Leah is the psycho-spiritual Solar System, and Rachel is its etheric-physical aspect. Their handmaidens are merely attributes and aspects of themselves, being personifications of *gunas*,[4] planes and sub-planes. The products of the effect of fructifying solar rays upon the different types of matter are symbolised by the offspring, their natures being portrayed kabbalistically by their names and their Zodiacal correspondences by their characters and ways of life.[5]

In this reading Jacob represents the sun, physical and superphysical,[6] source of the *fohatic* energy of the Solar System. The women with whom he associates stand for the planes of Nature with their subdivisions and attributes. The children, in their turn, are the products of the interplay

---

[1] q.v. Pt. One of this Volume, Ch. II.

[2] Chaldean Mysteries—see Glossary.

[3] Aryan Race—the fifth in Theosophical ethnology. See Glossary— Chain.

[4] *Gunas*—see Glossary; as also for the other Sanskrit terms here used.

[5] q.v. *Gen.* 49 and Pt. Four, Ch. X of this Volume.

[6] In occult philosophy the physical sun is regarded as the densest of the seven vehicles of the Solar Logos, the mighty Being in Whom and by Whom the Solar System exists. The other six vehicles are said to be constructed of superphysical matter of decreasing degrees of density, and to be sheaths and centres for the radiation of the power, life and consciousness of the Solar Logos.

between solar energy or *Fohat* and the *tattvas* and sub-*tattvas* of which, in both its superphysical and physical aspects, *Prakriti* consists.

In another possible interpretation Leah represents the combined *Dhyan Chohans* of the formless or *arupa* and Rachel those of the form or *rupa* planes, whilst their handmaidens represent the *shaktis*[1] thereof, the auric forces and substances or free matter of the planes; for during Cosmogenesis and throughout cosmic evolution—in this case applying especially to our Solar System—the primary *Dhyan Chohans* are in the highest spiritual sense " married " to the First Logos and fructified by its outpoured *fohatic* energy.

Jacob, who became the Patriarch of Israel, and his eleven sons and one daughter whose names were applied to the twelve Tribes, macrocosmicale represent the whole of creation. This includes the totality of all beings resulting from all possible combinations of the One, the Three and the Seven *Cosmocratores*,[2] the *Dhyan Chohanic* creative principles, Rays, Powers and Intelligences.

Twelve, in the deepest occult sense, is the true whole number, the totality of the Orders of creative " seeds " or potential powers and attributes resident in the First Emanation from *Parabrahman*.[3] Ten is the number of evolutionary culmination and indicates the about-to-be-reborn Crown or *Kether*[4] at the close of the cycle when all sinks back into the primary Pair, primordial Spirit and Matter, making in all twelve Principles.

THE MANDRAKE

Reuben and Joseph were related by their shared sonship of Jacob. Their mothers were different, however, Reuben being born of Leah and Joseph of Rachel. The incident of the mandrakes[5] is introduced in verses fourteen to seventeen, where we read that Reuben discovered mandrakes in the field and brought them to his mother, Leah.   Rachel

---

[1] *Shakti* (Sk.)—Expression or Power—see Glossary.

[2] *Cosmocratores* (Gr.)—" Builders of the Universe ", the " World Architects " or the creative Forces personified.

[3] *Parabrahman* (Sk.)—" Beyond Brahman ". The Supreme, Infinite Brahma. The Absolute. See Glossary.

[4] *Kether*—see Glossary and Appendix.

[5] Mandrake—a stemless plant of the potato family, with a large tap root, dark green flowers and yellow, pulpy fruit of the size of a large plum. H. P. Blavatsky writes: ". . . The roots of the plant are fleshy, hairy, and forked, representing roughly the limbs, the body, and even head of a man. Its magical and mysterious properties have been proclaimed in fable and play from the most archaic ages. . . . They are also worn by women as a charm against sterility, and for other purposes. . . ." (*The Secret Doctrine*, Adyar Ed., Vol. 3, p. 40, footnote 2). It is supposed to cry when pulled out of the ground.

asked for some of these, and when taunted by Leah with having already taken her husband, and now also wanting some of her son's mandrakes, Rachel agreed to permit Jacob to cohabit with Leah on the understanding that she, Rachel, should receive some of the mandrakes. This agreement was kept, and as a result Issachar was born to Leah, whether or not because of her possession of mandrakes. On the other hand Rachel, who also received a portion of them, did not at that time conceive. Later, however, as recounted in verses twenty-two to twenty-four, Joseph was born of her.

The wrongly implied capacity of the root of the mandrake to cure sterility, as stated in verses fourteen *et seq.*, of the Thirtieth Chapter of *Genesis*, is obviously unacceptable in its literary meaning. It must be assumed, therefore, that it is either a deliberate blind to conceal an occult truth or a complete mis-statement of scientific possibility; for the root of the mandrake possesses no capacity to induce conception in a hitherto sterile person. In verses Twenty-two and Twenty-three of the same Chapter it is recorded that God served Rachel in the capacity of a physical, personal gynaecologist, having successfully " opened her womb ".

Legendary occult properties apart, the mandrake is here supposedly used to represent the active creative energy and potentiality inherent in matter, which is symbolised by the earth in which the plant grows. Firstly, the mandrakes exist as a property and produce of Nature and are growing in a field, meaning the material field of evolution. Secondly, when Reuben digs up the mandrakes it is harvest time, meaning the fruition of a cycle and a period at which the creative life force has reached its culminating state of productivity. Not only has corn been grown, but new seeds also, ready for planting in their turn in the succeeding cycle. In this state and in this period of hyper-productivity Reuben, as the Logos of that cycle, " digs up " or extracts from Nature the essence of the creative power symbolised by the mandrake. Through his mother, the primordial substance of his cycle, he passes it on to the matter of the next cycle (Rachel), whose barrenness (quiescent condition) thereafter gives place to fertility (conception), the child being Joseph who is to be the Logos of the next dispensation.

If this view be accepted, the mandrake is being used as a symbol of *Fohat*, the inherent (growing) creative power and potentiality of all Nature, and it is this power which must be handed on by the Logos of one System to the Logos of its successor.[1] The intermediaries, or conveying *media*, are the substance of the preceding System (Leah) and that of the new System, as yet unfertilised (Rachel, hitherto barren). This essential

[1] q.v. Vol. II of this work, Pt. Six, Ch. XI, " The Principle of the Succession of Logoi and Patriarchs ".

transmission of the innate and completely expressed creative energy and faculty, and the handing on of Office from one dispensation to the next, are most faithfully and carefully described by various skilfully invented allegories and symbols in the *Pentateuch* and throughout the Bible.

In the purely occult meaning, in which Mystery Rites are revealed, the preservation of the succession of Hierophants is also indicated. Reuben is the Initiator of one epoch or period who, having completed (harvest time) and brought to fulfilment his " year " of Office, hands on his " Word " or creative and Hierophantic power and position. Leah, his mother, represents the Mysteries as a whole, and especially the Temple and its Officers and Brethren of the Reuben cycle. Rachel, in her turn, personifies the Mysteries for the new cycle in which Joseph is to be Reuben's successor.

The other ten Tribes typify the totality of the creative Powers in manifestation and the essential Officers in the Temples of the Mysteries. According to occult philosophy these Powers are inherent in man, who is the synthesis[1] of all Universes and of every Mystery Temple and Rite. The so-called " cry " which the mandrake is said to utter when pulled from the earth may possibly have been given an occult significance in reference to both the creative " Word " by which Cosmogenesis is initiated and the Word which a Hierophant speaks at the installation of his successor.

Microcosmically, the mandrake represents the Monadic Ray, the *Atmic* fire, which is projected into the Causal Body after individualisation. From this union *Buddhic* or Christ consciousness is " born ". Reuben personifies the Monad, Leah the Causal Body and Rachel the personal vehicles, particularly the physical in this interpretation.

> *Gen.* 30: 25. *And it came to pass, when Rachel had born Joseph, that Jacob said unto Laban, Send me away, that I may go unto mine own place, and to my country.*
>
> 26. *Give me my wives and my children, for whom I have served thee, and let me go: for thou knowest my service which I have done thee.*
>
> 27. *And Laban said unto him, I pray thee, if I have found favour in thine eyes, tarry: for I have learned by experience that the LORD hath blessed me for thy sake.*
>
> 28. *And he said, Appoint me thy wages, and I will give it.*
>
> 29. *And he said unto him, Thou knowest how I have served thee, and how thy cattle was with me.*
>
> 30. *For it was little which thou hadst before I came, and it is now increased unto a multitude; and the LORD hath blessed thee*

---

[1] See Glossary—Law of Correspondences.

since my coming; and now when shall I provide for mine own house also ?

31. *And he said, What shall I give thee ? And Jacob said, Thou shalt not give me any thing: if thou wilt do this thing for me, I will again feed and keep thy flock.*

32. *I will pass through all thy flock to day, removing from thence all the speckled and spotted cattle, and all the brown cattle among the sheep, and the spotted and speckled among the goats: and of such shall be my hire.*

33. *So shall my righteousness answer for me in time to come, when it shall come for my hire before thy face: every one that is not speckled and spotted among the goats, and brown among the sheep, that shall be counted stolen with me.*

34. *And Laban said, Behold, I would it might be according to thy word.*

35. *And he removed that day the he goats that were ringstraked and spotted, and all the she goats that were speckled and spotted, and every one that had some white in it, and all the brown among the sheep, and gave them into the hand of his sons.*

36. *And he set three days' journey betwixt himself and Jacob: and Jacob fed the rest of Laban's flocks.*

37. *And Jacob took him rods of green poplar, and of the hazel and chestnut tree; and pilled white strakes in them, and made the white appear which was in the rods.*

38. *And he set the rods which he had pilled before the flocks in the gutters in the watering troughs when the flocks came to drink, that they should conceive when they came to drink.*

39. *And the flocks conceived before the rods, and brought forth cattle ringstraked, speckled, and spotted.*

40. *And Jacob did separate the lambs, and set the faces of the flocks toward the ringstraked, and all the brown in the flock of Laban; and he put his own flocks by themselves, and put them not unto Laban's cattle.*

41. *And it came to pass, whensoever the stronger cattle did conceive, that Jacob laid the rods before the eyes of the cattle in the gutters, that they might conceive among the rods.*

42. *But when the cattle were feeble, he put them not in: so the feebler were Laban's, and the stronger Jacob's.*

43. *And the man increased exceedingly, and had much cattle, and maidservants, and menservants, and camels, and asses.*

Although the incidents accompanying Jacob's departure are admittedly questionable in their morality, it is possible that they veil a deep esoteric revelation. The story is therefore now examined as being an allegory descriptive of laws and processes operative in the emanation of both Universes and the Monads of men. The choice and combination of both subject-matter and objects support this possibility. Amongst these are: ringstraked rods of three different woods placed in the gutters in the watering troughs; drinking cattle conceiving, their offspring being coloured by the parental sight of the pilled rods, green, brown and white; goats, rams and ewes of the sheep; the teraphim;[1] the marital customs of Jewish women at that time; Jacob himself and his two wives and family; Jacob's dream of ladder with angels ascending and descending; the pillar; and the covenant between Laban and Jacob—all of these are susceptible of interpretation in the terms of the Sacred Language as Macrocosmic and microcosmic generative procedures.

Studying the story from this point of view, the narrative tells that a new dispensation, that of Jacob, is about to succeed its predecessor, that of Isaac his father. Jacob has been sent to Padan-aram—the original family home—there to choose his wives and consorts. Eleven sons and one daughter are born to him. Herds of cattle and flocks of sheep and goats are obtained by means of selective breeding, Jacob marking them with his own distinguishing brand. Interpreting these actions as allegories of procedures in the emanation of Universes, Macrocosmically Jacob may be regarded as personifying the Logos of a new dispensation. In the capacity of the positive creative potency the Logos (Jacob) unites with the negative potency or root substance in both its noumenal (Leah) and phenomenal (Rachel) aspects. Jacob thus represents the creative Logos Who brings forth " Sons of God " and " Morning Stars " (his children), the *Cosmocratores*-to-be, the Sephiroth or *Dhyan Chohans*.

Thus interpreted, the otherwise strange story may be seen as a typical symbolic description of the processes followed in the earliest phases of the emergence and manifestation of the active Logos of a new Universe. The Monads of the Universe-to-be (Jacob's flocks) are given into the charge of the Logos, Who at once imprints upon them His own chosen characteristics by which they are differentiated from the hosts of " pure ", undifferentiated Monads of the pre-cosmic phase. All Logoi, of whatever degree, produce this effect upon both the evolutionary field and the evolving units. Having thus established the *tattvic*[2] qualities according to

---

[1] Teraphim—the idol-oracles of the ancient Jews, used for divinatory purposes, which Rachel stole from her father, Laban (*Gen.* 31: 19, 34). " The *Teraphim* of Abram's father, *Terah*, the ' maker of images ', were the Kabeiri gods, and we see them worshipped by Micah, by the Danites, and others (Judges XVII–XVIII, etc.). Teraphim were identical with the seraphim, and these were serpent-images, the origin of which is in the Sanskrit *sarpa* (the serpent), a symbol sacred to all the deities as a symbol of immortality." *Isis Unveiled*, Vol. I, p. 570, H. P. Blavatsky.

[2] *Tattva*—see Glossary.

His design, which is drawn from universal Ideation, the Logos proceeds to project the whole mentally conceived and " created " Cosmos into the realm of matter with its evolving forms (the land of Canaan). The Padan-aram period is that of Ideation or Archetypal thought. The Canaanite period is that of projection and evolution.

THE SYMBOLISM OF TREES

The tree is the central symbol in this remarkable allegory. Through-out the Bible it is employed to represent the omnipresent, ever active, prolific, creative life-force inherent in all substance, whether superphysical or physical—meaning Nature herself. The symbol is well chosen, for the tree draws its sustenance from the earth (*Prakriti*)[1], the roots being the means by which it is drawn up, collected and individualised into a single localised area of activity. The extracted nutriment and natural energy become concentrated therein, later to flow along the vertical trunk. Withdrawn from the earth, the element of air is entered and at a certain height from the ground the general shape of the root system is partially reproduced in the pattern of the branches.

Trees, whether deciduous or evergreen, are obedient to the law of cycles, successive, regularly spaced, seasonal periods of creative activity and of quiescence constituting their life. The principle of growth from a potential or seed-like condition, characteristic of spiritual as well as of physical evolution, is also displayed. Each phase culminates in the pro-duction of new seeds, and in this may be discerned that universal principle under which minor cycles contribute to the fulfilment of a major cycle. Leaves, by their inbreathing and outbreathing, also represent the phases of alternation through which all objective manifestations pass.

The beauty and the symmetry of the whole tree exemplify the harmony and unity upon which Creation is founded. These attributes are further portrayed by the colour and form of branch, leaf, flower, seed-vessel and seed. Intelligence is also plainly manifest in the methods of acquiring life needs, even if only as the mysterious, instinctual self-help observable when studying the plant kingdom of Nature. Seed distribution is a further example of this dawning mentality. The seeds of many trees are broad-cast by the wind which, playing upon their perfectly curved, propeller-like wings or, as in the case of the dandelion, wafting along its filmy, gossamer, seed-carrying " parachutes ", carries them far and wide so that deposit in suitable ground is ensured for at least a proportion of them.

Lastly, the tree provides shade for animals and men, shelter for birds and, more especially, secure nesting places in which they, in their turn,

---

[1] *Prakriti*—see Glossary.

may reproduce their kind in seasonal succession. Food for man and beast—fruit and seed which nourish them—are also produced by the tree, which may justly be regarded as a perfect symbol of the protean, creative life principle of the Universe. For these reasons, doubtless, it was chosen by those ancient Scriptural writers who, by allegory and symbol, sought to reveal the operation of universal laws.[1]

POPLAR, HAZEL AND CHESTNUT TREES

In the story of Jacob and the production of specially marked cattle, three kinds of trees are mentioned—the green poplar, the hazel and the chestnut. This choice may be of deep significance, for an occult tradition suggests that each of those trees has its own especial properties, one of the currents, and so qualities, of the creative life-force preponderating. In general terms, and allowing for exceptions in different species of the same genus, the poplar could be regarded as representing the positive polarity, the chestnut the negative, and the hazel being expressive of the combined, harmonised, equi-polarised and so relatively neutral currents. This may be the reason for Jacob's choice of these three trees for his experiment in cattle breeding, the description of which is hardly acceptable in its literal reading.

THE SYMBOLISM OF RODS

In man, in terms of the Sacred Language, rods refer to the human spine, as also to the currents of the creative life-force which play along the spinal cord. This triple Serpent Fire is indicated by the rods of the three types of trees.[2] The removal of the bark may possibly have been performed spirally to produce a spiral design along the rod, further suggesting the Serpent Fire. The revealing or uncovering of the white wood beneath the bark symbolises the bringing of the white fire of the divine will out of quiescence and pre-cosmic concealment into activity. The suggestion that Jacob's action in taking these rods, stripping them in a certain way and placing them in the gutters in the watering troughs, so producing specially marked cattle, is in its literal sense an affront to the intelligence and therefore a clear sign that an undermeaning of importance exists. The troughs themselves are vehicles for water, symbol of universal substance which has been rendered active and specialised, differentiated and employed for cosmogenetic purposes. The coition of the male and female cattle indicates clearly that creative processes in general are being described.

---

[1] See Appendix to this Volume—" The Sephirothal Tree ".
[2] See Ch. III of Pt. One of this Vol. under heading: " Serpents ",

The intrusion of the incredible into a supposedly historical record, and the description as a fact of that which is extremely improable,[1] are clear indications that in this phase of the narrative the authors were writing in the language of symbols. When this occurs, as it often does in scriptural literature, the hidden wisdom of the Sanctuary is generally being revealed. If this approach be accepted, then as if by magic that which has hitherto been incredible becomes credible, is indeed perceived as a revelation of divine truth. The actors become representatives of deific powers and the events descriptive of fundamental laws, whilst natural objects are alight with spiritual significance. So is it in this remarkable story of Jacob's cattle breeding. Whilst the outer story insults the intelligence, an esoteric interpretation reveals the deepest truths.

Trees are the central symbols employed and, as has been said, each of those chosen has particular occult properties according to the preponderance in its substance of one or other of the basic triple qualities or attributes of matter—the *gunas*[2] and the electric energies and polarities associated with them. The chestnut, for example, whether its fruit be edible or not, as already stated, represents the negative polarity (*tamas*), the feminine principle and the matter aspect of the creative triplicity. The hazel possesses positive and negative qualities (*sattva*), and so is responsive to both influences whilst in the poplar the positive is accentuated (*rajas*). The atomic structure of its wood makes it a particularly good conductor of certain occult forces. In the hands of one gifted with the faculty of water divination, a hazel twig is especially responsive to the electro-magnetic radiations from that element, in Sanskrit named *apas*— that *tattva* forming the manifestation of the Third Logos on the astral plane with which water is in correspondence. Diviners are those people in whose constitution, superphysical and physical, water[3] preponderates. The hazel twig, Y-shaped and therefore formed with a central stem and right and left hand branches, provides such people with an organic detector, the substance of which is endowed with the same properties as those existing within themselves. The combination makes possible the activity upon which divination depends and by which it is produced.

JACOB AS PERSONIFICATION OF THE LOGOS OF A NEW UNIVERSE

In general the allegory of Jacob and the cattle, whilst referring to these and other semi-occult ideas, in reality reveals fundamental creative

---

[1] See Ch. I of Pt. One of this Vol. and the quotations from the writings of Moses Maimonedes and others appearing at the front of this book.

[2] *Gunas*—see Glossary.

[3] Not so much the material fluid, but the so-called "invisible water" of the Alchemists and other Occultists.

processes. As has been said, the Logos of a new dispensation (Jacob) is receiving from the great granary of the Cosmos (Laban and his flocks) those " seeds " or Monads (sheep, cattle and goats) which through His agency, and under His direction, will be sent forth upon a new round of the evolutionary spiral.

Interpreted from this point of view, Jacob himself represents fructifying Spirit directed by Universal Mind, which then becomes a creative Logos of a Universe or the Director of the evolution of any component sub-cycle. Through his creative activity as husband he represents the masculine potency.   In his directive activity (cattle breeding) he represents Universal Mind, which shapes substance according to the Archetype delivered to and perceived by him as model.

Jacob's wives represent universal substance—Leah the superphysical and Rachel the physical, or Leah the life planes and Rachel the form planes of Nature. The two handmaids, Zilpah and Bilhah, typify subsidiary creative attributes of those planes, sub-*tattvas*, and as personifications they are inseparable from their mistresses. The twelve children each represent one of the creative Powers, Intelligences, Rays and Zodiacal attributes in the Universe. Each is thus one of the Sephiroth,[1] and it is noteworthy that all were born before the cattle breeding experiment begins. This was necessary as they personify the Directive Intelligences, the " firstfruits "[2] to Whom the Logos delivers the creative impulse, the creative Archetype and the creative power. These " Beings " are mirrored in the heavens—physically as the Signs of the Zodiac and in man, the Monad-Ego, as the twelve Zodiacal attributes which ultimately are to be developed to a " perfected " state.

To sum up, the first twenty-four verses of this Chapter recount allegorically the preparations for the production of the vast arena—the Universe—in which the drama of involution and evolution was to be enacted. The formative Agencies (the Sephiroth) had all emerged and each had been given his or her individual character and name. It is of interest to note that the names of the *dramatis personae* are of occult significance, their Kabbalistic, numerical and *mantric*[3] values being expressive of their characteristics and their functions. Nevertheless all proceed from the One Alone, personified by Jacob, whose life story is thus susceptible of interpretation as being descriptive of divine creative principles and processes, however heavily veiled in allegory and symbol. If this view be acceptable, then certain portions of the *Pentateuch* may be

---

[1] See Appendix to this Vol.—" The Sephirothal Tree ".

[2] *Rev.* 14: 4.

[3] *Mantras* (Sk.)— Verses from the *Vedas* rhythmically arranged so that, when sounded, certain vibrations are generated, producing desired effects upon the physical and superphysical bodies of *Mantra Yogis* and the atmosphere surrounding them.

regarded as revelations of occult wisdom delivered to mankind by Initiates of the Sanctuaries of the Mysteries of old.

From verse twenty-five onwards the processes of the preparation of matter and of the projection of the Archetype to the end of the production of forms is described in outline. These forms and the seeds of consciousness and life which will inhabit them, being drawn as it were from the universal supply (Laban), must all be stamped with the individuality or group of vibratory frequencies of the Logos of the new dispensation. Thus ultimately they produce a distinctive variation on the original and further developments throughout the Universe, great or small, and all that it will contain.

As stated, the changing by Jacob of the appearance of the rods of the three trees refers allegorically to the production of this imprint. It, in its turn, is threefold, namely ringstraked, speckled and spotted. This fact of differentiation naturally separates both substance and seeds from those within the original cosmic supply, symbolised by Laban and his estate. Thereafter a gradual and increasing separation occurs between the two Patriarchs. In the allegory Jacob is made to take his household, his herds and his possessions into another land (Canaan), symbolical of the next cycle, its evolutionary field and its future attainments.

A suggested microcosmic interpretation of these verses will be found near the end of Chapter VIII of this Part.

CHAPTER VIII

JACOB BECOMES THE SECOND PATRIARCH OF ISRAEL

Gen. 31.   *Jacob departeth secretly from Laban: Rachel stealeth away her father's images. Laban pursueth Jacob: their covenant at Galeed.*

Gen. 31:

1. *And he heard the words of Laban's sons, saying, Jacob hath taken away all that was our father's; and of that which was our father's hath he gotten all this glory.*

2. *And Jacob beheld the countenance of Laban, and, behold, it was not toward him as before.*

3. *And the LORD said unto Jacob, Return unto the land of thy fathers, and to thy kindred; and I will be with thee.*

4. *And Jacob sent and called Rachel and Leah to the field unto his flock,*

5. *And said unto them, I see your father's countenance, that it is not toward me as before; but the God of my father hath been with me.*

6. *And ye know that with all my power I have served your father.*

7. *And your father hath deceived me, and changed my wages ten times; but God suffered him not to hurt me.*

8. *If he said thus, The speckled shall be thy wages; then all the cattle bare speckled: and if he said thus, The ringstraked shall be thy hire; then bare all the cattle ringstraked.*

9. *Thus God hath taken away the cattle of your father, and given them to me.*

10. *And it came to pass at the time that the cattle conceived, that I lifted up mine eyes, and saw in a dream, and, behold, the rams which leaped upon the cattle were ringstraked, speckled, and grisled.*

11. *And the angel of God spake unto me in a dream, saying, Jacob: And I said, Here am I.*

12. *And he said, Lift up now thine eyes, and see, all the rams which leap upon the cattle are ringstraked, speckled, and grisled: for I have seen all that Laban doeth unto thee,*

13. *I am the God of Bethel, where thou anointedst the pillar, and where thou vowedst a vow unto me: now arise, get thee out from this land, and return unto the land of thy kindred.*

14. *And Rachel and Leah answered and said unto him, Is there yet any portion or inheritance for us in our father's house?*

15. *Are we not counted of him strangers? for he hath sold us, and hath quite devoured also our money.*

16. *For all the riches which God hath taken from our father, that is our's, and our children's: now then, whatsoever God hath said unto thee, do.*

17. *Then Jacob rose up, and set his sons and his wives upon camels;*

18. *And he carried away all his cattle, and all his goods which he had gotten, the cattle of his getting, which he had gotten in Padan-aram, for to go to Isaac his father in the land of Canaan.*

In advance of a more detailed interpretation, it may here be stated that an allegorical description of a cycle of forthgoing and return is given by means of the story of Jacob's departure, Laban's pursuit, his reunion with Jacob and the making of a covenant between them. Three days passed before the absence of Jacob was discovered, this being followed by a seven-day successful pursuit, recriminations, and the ultimate restoration of harmonious relationships between the two main characters. A pillar was erected as a witness of mutual agreement and as a promise that neither would ever pass over it in order to harm the other.

The story bears a distinct resemblance to the Parable of the Prodigal Son, with Jacob portraying the main character and his departure from Laban's house corresponding to the departure of the younger son from the family home. The stealing of the teraphim has a possible parallelism to the hunger of the Prodigal Son, who " would fain have filled his belly with the husks that the swine did eat " [1]—the deepest level of descent. The reunion and covenant between Jacob and Laban may be correlated to the joyously celebrated return of the Prodigal Son to the father's home.[2]

The pursuit of Jacob by Laban is an allegory of the responsiveness of matter to Spirit and of their mutual attractiveness, while the supposed complaint describes, perhaps, the innate resistance of matter to Spirit. No region of Cosmos is without the full presence of creative thought, universal Intelligence being omnipresent. Ideation rules all, creates all, designs all, produces and perfects all. The One Mind is the One God, all-inclusive, all-powerful, all-productive, according to eternal law. This deific Mind, inherent in *Prakriti*, present and active within all differentiated regions of space, is the Logos, the cosmic Christos, the masculine element

[1] *Lk.* 15: 16.
[2] *Lk.* 15: 20–24.

in Creation, as Space itself is the feminine. These two—Logos and Space —are not to be regarded as separate entities or powers, but a complementary and supplementary pair, each essential to the other's existence as also to their creative and evolutionary activity. The third or product —the Universe—is the result of this interaction. It includes equipolarised life currents, inter-harmonised life principles, states of human and divine consciousness, and all objective creations such as Universes with their suns, planets and everything that lives and evolves upon them.

The occult cosmogonies of the Ancients separate the positive and negative agencies, presenting them as male and female Deities, or heroes and heroines, according to the customs of the Sanctuaries from which such allegories emanated. In India, Egypt and Greece gods and goddesses fulfilled these roles. In Chaldea and Syria, Patriarchs and their wives and offspring also played leading parts. In these Biblical verses Laban and his estates represent *Prakriti*, the Eternal Source of all. His daughters and handmaids are the negatively polarised currents, whilst after his birth in the preceding cycle Jacob assumes in the emergent cycle the positively polarised Office of creative Logos. The whole drama is enacted in Padanaram, the land of Laban, a topographical symbol for the *prakritic* source— Laban's original stock. Jacob only takes the existent possessions of Laban, meaning the inherent powers and attributes of *Prakriti*, and from them produces the new Universe which is typified by the Israelite nation with its twelve (Zodiacal) tribes established in the land of Canaan.

Whilst the account given in these verses of the relationship between Jacob and Laban, his father-in-law, may be accepted as providing an example of human foibles, the direct intervention by the Lord affirmed in the third verse of the Twenty-first Chapter of the *Book of Genesis* can hardly be regarded as part of the history of a tribe and certain of its members. Human beings do practise deceptions upon each other, as did Laban upon Jacob concerning his wages. Not unnatural, also, was the counter action by Jacob and Rachel of stealing Laban's images. Nevertheless the supreme Deity of the Universe, the Lord of the Sun, of the planets and of all kingdoms of Nature, is surely not likely to participate in the minor affairs of members of wandering tribes.

The employment of deceptions and trickery has already received explanatory comments, which apply in this case also, giving to them profound significance as allegories of creative procedures in Universe and man. Since, as above stated, divine intervention is so extremely unlikely, an intention on the part of the authors to reveal secret wisdom under a veil may reasonably be assumed. In such an approach the story would be lifted out of the limitations of time, place and personalities into a realm of ideas which possess timeless and universal significance. The eleventh verse of this Chapter, in which an angel of God is made to speak to Jacob in a dream, may be similarly read as underlining the indication of the presence of a divine wisdom in a human story.

> Gen. 31: 19. *And Laban went to shear his sheep: and Rachel had stolen the images[1] that were her father's.*
>
> 20. *And Jacob stole away unawares to Laban the Syrian, in that he told him not that he fled.*
>
> 21. *So he fled with all that he had; and he rose up, and passed over the river, and set his face toward the mount Gilead.*
>
> 22. *And it was told Laban on the third day that Jacob was fled.*

JACOB FLED FROM LABAN, WHO PURSUED AND OVERTOOK HIM

The first half of the cycle of forthgoing and return [2] is indicated in these verses. The Monadic life emanates from the original source (the Solar Logos) into the new field. When once the furthest point of the outward journey is reached, actually after passage through three and a half minor cycles, the pathway of return is entered upon. The spiritual influence from the divine source thereafter begins increasingly to be felt, Spirit and matter drawing closer together. Symbolically, the Lord stretches out His hand to draw back the life and consciousness which had departed. Allegorically, Laban sets forth in pursuit of Jacob " on the third day that Jacob was fled " (v. 22).

> Gen. 31: 23. *And he took his brethren with him, and pursued after him seven days' journey; and they overtook him in the mount Gilead.*
>
> 24. *And God came to Laban the Syrian in a dream by night, and said unto him, Take heed that thou speak not to Jacob either good or bad.*
>
> 25. *Then Laban overtook Jacob. Now Jacob had pitched his tent in the mount: and Laban with his brethren pitched in the mount of Gilead.*

The reunion on Mount Gilead symbolises the meeting of the descending spiritual power of the Logos with the life and consciousness which had gone forth, and on its return journey was now spiritually elevated to its greatest possible height (the mount). On the arc of return in every cycle there is a point at which the indwelling life and consciousness become sufficiently evolved and self-consciously aware to be responsive again to pure Spirit. Symbolically, Jacob and Laban meet on Mount Gilead.

> Gen. 31: 26. *And Laban said to Jacob, What hast thou done, that thou hast stolen away unawares to me, and carried away my daughters, as captives taken with the sword?*

---

[1] Images—the idol-oracles of the ancient Jews. See Glossary—Teraphim.
[2] See diagrams facing p. 43.

27. *Wherefore didst thou flee away secretly, and steal away from me; and didst not tell me, that I might have sent thee away with mirth, and with songs, with tabret, and with harp?*

28. *And hast not suffered me to kiss my sons and my daughters? thou hast now done foolishly in so doing.*

29. *It is in the power of my hand to do you hurt: but the God of your father spake unto me yesternight, saying, Take thou heed that thou speak not to Jacob either good or bad.*

30. *And now, though thou wouldst needs be gone, because thou sore longedst after thy father's house, yet wherefore hast thou stolen my gods?*

31. *And Jacob answered and said to Laban, Because I was afraid: for I said, Peradventure thou wouldest take by force thy daughters from me.*

32. *With whomsoever thou findest thy gods, let him not live: before our brethren discern thou what is thine with me, and take it to thee. For Jacob knew not that Rachel had stolen them.*

33. *And Laban went into Jacob's tent, and into Leah's tent, and into the two maidservants' tents; but he found them not. Then went he out of Leah's tent, and entered into Rachel's tent.*

34. *Now Rachel had taken the images, and put them in the camel's furniture, and sat upon them. And Laban searched all the tent, but found them not.*

35. *And she said to her father, Let it not displease my lord that I cannot rise up before thee; for the custom of women is upon me. And he searched, but found not the images.*

The reproach symbolically uttered by Spirit (Laban) to matter (Jacob) signifies the awareness by consciousness of the limitations of form, for these two have not yet been unified. Furthermore, Spirit itself is caught, imprisoned, concealed within matter, and made subject to the pairs of opposites and to alternation between freedom and restriction of consciousness. This is revealed in the theft of the images or gods and their concealment by Rachel, representing densest substance, whilst subjection to alternation is referred to by the monthly "custom of women". In the Macrocosm the teraphim represent the Monads themselves, made as they are in the image of their Creator.

The flocks of sheep and herds of cattle, the offspring and the wives, all represent Monadic Rays projected into the new Universe and manifested there in varying stages of evolution. The teraphim, on the other hand, typify the Spirit-Essence, the Monads, the *Jivatmas*,[1] sent forth on

---

[1] *Jivatma* (Sk.)—Macrocosmically, the one universal Spirit; microcosmically, that Spirit in man as Monad.

their pilgrimage through matter and for a time hidden and lost to full spiritual awareness. The concealment in the " camel's furniture " (v. 34) refers to descent into the sub-human kingdoms of Nature, whilst Rachel's seated posture thereon suggests the completeness of the descent, the concealment in matter, or the loss of spiritual awareness on the path of forthgoing.

A profound psycho-spiritual significance in both the Macrocosmic and microcosmic interpretations may thus be seen in the theft of the teraphim, the method of concealment, and the fruitless search by Laban in Rachel's tent.

If it be presumed that Jacob represents creative Spirit, and that Laban and his household possessions and gods personify creative substance, then this difficult Chapter and these conversations become comprehensible. Laban and his daughters represent *Prakriti*; his goods the already awakened potentialities of this root substance; and his people, herds and flocks the seeds or potentialities of all the possible forms and beings which the new cycle will produce.

EGYPTIAN COSMOGENESIS

PICTURE OF THE GODDESS NUT AND THE GODS SEB AND SHU

The Egyptian system of Cosmogony included the Hindu concept that in *Parabrahman* Spirit and matter are united in absolute equilibrium during *Pralaya*, and separated during *Manvantara* to become the creatively active, masculine and feminine parents of the first Universe. The Egyptians in the Sanctuary evidently knew this, and composed an allegory for the populace. In illustration of this, Heaven and Earth are personified as the goddess Nut and the god Seb respectively, from whose marriage came forth all that has been, is, and shall be. These two deities were invested with human forms, and the Earth god Seb was said to be extended beneath the goddess Nut, named the " Starry One " because her body was studded with stars. The oncoming of *Manvantara* is allegorised as the separation of Seb and Nut by Shu, the god of the air, who lifted up Nut from the prostrate Seb and sustained her there, thus providing the essential third in this pre-cosmic trinity. This act is represented in many beautiful pictures which show the goddess stretching out her arms and her slender legs, with her body arched and her head drooping down so that she envelops the recumbent Seb.

THE SYMBOLIC SIGNIFICANCE OF THE TERAPHIM

Whilst the teraphim were household images used as idol-oracles, they may also be regarded as symbols of the sparks of the primordial flame, the highest essence of the creative power of conjoined *Purusha-Prakriti*, the Monads of *Devas* [1] and men. These may be thought of as single spiritual entities which in the course of their evolution successfully become men, Initiates, Supermen and *Dhyan Chohans*. Each Monad is thus a miniature creative Logos, with the potentialities of all beings in all kingdoms innate within it. Monads are therefore to be regarded as seeds of Cosmoi in both the masculine and feminine potencies. At the consummation of a major cycle they emerge as fully unfolded, creative Logoi.

The presence of these " seeds " in an awakened state is the essential factor in cosmic reproduction. The teraphim represent these God-like creative potencies without which the Logos of each new cycle could not become manifest. Hence in the allegory Rachel, as the feminine potency of *Prakriti*, " steals " the teraphim from the masculine potency of *Prakriti* (Laban), and presumably eventually delivers them to the " new " Logos (Jacob, her husband). Jacob is said to be unaware of the theft, whilst Laban has discovered it and at once institutes the fruitless search. If the incident be regarded, however, as an allegorical account of the transference of creative powers from one dispensation to its successor, then Rachel's action would be a legitimate, even preordained and necessary, expropriation of the elements necessary to the fulfilment of her husband's cosmogenetic task. As Jacob later implies (verses 38–42), everything that he removes to his new field of activity is his due by virtue of his years of service. In truth, the whole suggestion of detection, recrimination, wrath and ultimate " covenant ", is hardly acceptable literally and so points to concealed truths, as here partly outlined.

To make Rachel conceal the images and prevent a complete search by pretending to be in a state of creative rest (" the custom of women is upon me ") is a most skilful use of the allegorical method of writing. The opposite is the truth since, as Nature, she is at that time in a state of extreme creative and evolutionary activity, as is indicated by her posture, or the relative physical positions of the teraphim and herself. Here we are reminded of the superior posture, or position, of the goddess Nut reclining upon the God Seb in the Egyptian Cosmogony, the purpose being to indicate the enclosing, the enfolding and the covering relationship of *Prakriti*, as the eternal Fount, to *Purusha*, as the eternal Breath. The reader is here referred to the diagram and accompanying explanatory statement facing this page. Laban's search is unsuccessful because, in truth, no illegal theft had occurred and what had to pass must and did pass.

Gen. 31: 36. *And Jacob was wroth, and chode with Laban: and Jacob answered and said to Laban, What is my trespass ? what is my sin, that thou hast so hotly pursued after me ?*

---

[1] *Devas*—see Glossary.

SHÛ FORCIBLY SEPARATING SEB AND NUT

The Dawn of Civilisation

The Dawn of Civilisation

37. *Whereas thou hast searched all my stuff, what hast thou found of all thy household stuff? set it here before my brethren and thy brethren, that they may judge betwixt us both.*

38. *This twenty years have I been with thee; thy ewes and thy she goats have not cast their young, and the rams of thy flock have I not eaten.*

39. *That which was torn of beasts I brought not unto thee; I bare the loss of it; of my hand didst thou require it, whether stolen by day, or stolen by night.*

40. *Thus I was; in the day the drought consumed me, and the frost by night; and my sleep departed from mine eyes.*

41. *Thus have I been twenty years in thy house; I served thee fourteen years for thy two daughters, and six years for thy cattle; and thou hast changed my wages ten times.*

42. *Except the God of my father, the God of Abraham, and the fear of Isaac, had been with me, surely thou hadst sent me away now empty. God hath seen mine affliction and the labour of my hands, and rebuked thee yesternight.*

" THE WORLD IS BUILT UPON THE POWER OF NUMBERS "—PYTHAGORAS

The several numbers such as 7, 6, 10 and 20 which are introduced into the narrative may admittedly be merely historical. Since, however, they possess distinct symbolical meanings, I here offer an attempted interpretation of the passages in which they occur—particularly those concerning the involution and evolution of life, first from spiritual levels into the mineral and later through the plant, animal and human kingdoms and thence on to superhumanity, ". . . the measure of the stature of the fulness of Christ".[1]

The number 7, for example, represents not final perfection but the completion of a phase of development, followed by temporary cessation. The number 6, thus regarded, refers to a stage in which a cycle is not yet completed, but nearly so. The number 10 is a combination of the vertical line of self-consciousness and the ellipse or circle of super-consciousness. It is the number of perfection and suggests the completion of the outpouring of the life-forces through a directive Logos. The number 20, or 2, stands for the dualism of manifested life, the Divine on the one hand and Nature on the other, Spirit and matter and their inter-relationships.[2]

If this system of numerical symbology be applied to the bargainings between Laban and Jacob, then the numbers offer a clue enabling one

---

[1] *Eph.* 4: 13.

[2] See Ch. V of Pt. One of this Vol.—" The Symbolism of Numbers ".

9

to interpret the story as an allegory of the emanation and evolution of a Universe. Mathematical law governs the production of Universes, and the basic numbers are guardedly given.[1] As stated below, the 20 years of service by Jacob to Laban in return for Leah (7 years), Rachel (7 years) and the cattle (6 years), and the 10 changes in his wages, signify the successful productiveness of a pair (20). The time period for and successful phases of the completion of a single cycle (7), the approaching cessation or close of a third cycle (6) in which the animal kingdom is launched on its evolutionary journey, and the culmination of the productive processes (10), are all indicated.

Examining this law and these mathematical procedures, the number 2 —however many the ciphers which are placed after it—is the number of creatively inter-active Spirit-matter, positive-negative, mind-substance, or of every other generative pair. Universal generation and both potential and actual fruitfulness are implied by the number 2, which states the presence of the eternal pair. The ciphers or noughts after a number may indicate—and do so in very precise Cosmogonies and allegories—the particular cycle in a seven-fold major cycle the opening of which is being described.

JACOB SERVES LABAN SEVEN YEARS EACH FOR LEAH AND RACHEL

The statement concerning Jacob's two seven-year periods of service for each of Laban's daughters, Leah and Rachel, may refer to the evolution of life through the superphysical planes of Nature on the downward arc and embodiment at the deepest physical level (mineral), followed by a gradual return to the Source on the upward arc *via* the plant, animal and human kingdoms. This is partly illustrated in the diagrams facing page 42, to which attention is here drawn.

The number 7 is that of the total constituent phases of which a complete period of activity is composed. The third 7 years is not wholly completed in this allegory, only 6 phases in the third cycle having been passed through as indicated by the 6 years during which Jacob served Laban for the cattle. If the successive evolutionary advances of life and consciousness through the kingdoms of Nature from mineral to man are indicated by these numbers, then the third cycle will be that in which consciousness is established at the mobile, vocal, animal level with the plant stage intervening. This idea is supported by Jacob's statement that the 6 years of the third period of his service to Laban was " for thy cattle " [2]—a possible reference to the mineral kingdom of Nature.

[1] *Gen.* 31: 41.
[2] *Gen.* 31: 41.

The fact that two daughters have previously been received by Jacob as wages does not necessarily imply that evolution has as yet reached the human phase; for Leah and Rachel, in this sense, represent Nature herself at the superphysical (Leah) and physical (Rachel) levels. Leah is the Soul of Nature, its noumenon.[1] Rachel is the substance of Nature, its phenomenon.[2] The progress of life and consciousness from noumenon, through phenomenon and back again to the Source, passing—as said above—through mobile, sound-making, animal forms, may be referred to in this part of the allegory.

The Logos-to-be (Jacob) labours in the material fields (of Laban) for the wages or reward of evolutionary progress through the physical and superphysical kingdoms of Nature and levels of awareness. As stated, the third cycle is still incomplete, having passed through only six phases (years of service for the cattle), though nearing the fulfilment indicated in Jacob's reference to the ten times changed rate of payment; for 10 is a whole number implying the completion of one cycle and readiness for entry into its successor.

Further progress demands departure from the limitations of partially modified root substance. This will make possible advance into a more highly individualised field and state of consciousness. Thus, in the allegory Jacob and his estate must be moved to Canaan, where he will continue the work of his patriarchal predecessors (the Logoi of preceding Universes). A creative link with the original Source must, however, be maintained. This is recognised as a principle and is allegorically described in verses forty-three *et seq.*, which are now considered.

> Gen. 31:43. *And Laban answered and said unto Jacob, These daughters are my daughters, and these children are my children, and these cattle are my cattle, and all that thou seest is mine: and what can I do this day unto these my daughters, or unto their children which they have born ?*
>
> 44. *Now therefore come thou, let us make a covenant, I and thou; and let it be for a witness between me and thee.*
>
> 45. *And Jacob took a stone, and set it up for a pillar.*
>
> 46. *And Jacob said unto his brethren, Gather stones; and they took stones, and made an heap: and they did eat there upon the heap.*
>
> 47. *And Laban called it Jegarsahadutha: but Jacob called it Galeed.*

---

[1] Noumenon (Gr.)—The true, essential, superphysical nature of being as distinguished from the illusive objects of physical sense.

[2] Phenomenon (Gr.)—" An appearance ", a physical fact, occurrence or circumstance observed or observable, but philosophically regarded as illusive in comparison with its noumenon or real existence.

48. *And Laban said, This heap is a witness between me and thee this day.   Therefore was the name of it called Galeed;*

49. *And Mizpah; for he said, The LORD watch between me and thee, when we are absent one from another.*

50. *If thou shalt afflict my daughters, or if thou shalt take other wives beside my daughters, no man is with us; God is witness betwixt me and thee.*

51. *And Laban said to Jacob, Behold this heap, and behold this pillar, which I have cast betwixt me and thee;*

52. *This heap be witness, and this pillar be witness, that I will not pass over this heap to thee, and that thou shalt not pass over this heap and this pillar unto me, for harm.*

53. *The God of Abraham, and the God of Nahor, the God of their father, judge betwixt us.   And Jacob sware by the fear of his father Isaac.*

54. *Then Jacob offered sacrifice upon the mount, and called his brethren to eat bread: and they did eat bread, and tarried all night in the mount.*

55. *And early in the morning Laban rose up, and kissed his sons and his daughters, and blessed them: and Laban departed, and returned unto his place.*

COVENANT AT GALEED

In the foregoing verses Laban affirms the family unity and identity and proposes a covenant, whereupon Jacob " took a stone, and set it up for a pillar.   And Jacob said unto his brethren, Gather stones; and they took stones, and made an heap: and they did eat there upon the heap". The symbol of the pillar here employed is phallic, indicating that the link or covenant between the eternal and the temporal, the root substance and the Universes and forms created out of it, consists of the creative fire, process and act.

Spirit penetrates vertically the horizontal recipient—productive matter.   A right angle or square is thus formed by the upright pillar and the horizontal earth on and in which it stands.   The substance of the pillar called Galeed is stone, the solid rock representing root substance. Separated stones typify differentiated areas in it, whilst erected pillars are emblems of that substance shaped and " set up " in the image of the Creator or of the creative potency, also symbolised by the *lingam*.[1]

The food partaken of conjointly as part of the ceremony of the covenant indicates that intimate interplay which, at the close of the third

---

[1] *Lingam* (Sk.)—Physically, the phallus.   A symbol of abstract creation and of the divine, masculine, procreative force.

cycle, has been achieved between Spirit and matter, life and form, creative power and recipient substance. This is the basic significance of every symbolical feast, agape,[1] communion. The principle of transmission of original virtue and power, so continually insisted upon in the Biblical narratives, is also here indicated both in the ceremony of erection and feasting and in the naming of the pillar. [2] The interplay of words suggest a portion of a Mystery Ritual, as well as the permanent establishment of certain attainments and vibratory frequencies. In this story each protagonist makes a different choice, Jacob from the side of Spirit and Laban from the side of matter. Jacob's choice of " Galeed " (witness-heap) indicates the close of a cycle and entry into its successor, or the transference of the archetypal idea or pattern, as also of the life and the creative power, from one cycle to the next. Apart from the literal translation, " Galeed " indicates the formative process from the point of view of Spirit, life, consciousness, Universal Mind.

" Jegarsahadutha " (mound of testimony) means the same as Galeed but from the point of view of matter, form, vehicles, or the matrix from which a birth has occurred. " Mizpah " (a look-out) as Laban's second choice of name refers to the new Universe about to be emanated. " Jegarsahadutha ", with its six syllables, is a deeply occult word. " Jegar " thus used implies, in addition to its literal translation, a universal reservoir or Mulaprakriti, the conjoined yet quiescent Spirit-matter of Parabrahman. " Saha " represents manifested life, breath, being, whilst " dutha " indicates the progression of the creative function as an active process.

The apparent or exoteric meaning given by Laban to the foregoing words, and especially to " Mizpah ", correctly expresses the covenantal ceremonial and its purposes. Since the lesser follows the greater and the exoteric contains the esoteric, however deeply hidden, the human meaning[3] given to the word " Mizpah " is acceptable. The name is potent also as a charm or a verbal talisman, the degree of its power depending upon the level of consciousness and interpretation at which the user employs the symbol.

---

[1] Agape (Gr.)—Love Feast; festival in token of sympathy, love and benevolence.

[2] The interpretations, based on the construction and the meaning of their separate syllables, may be of interest to some of my readers. The word " Mizpah " offers an example. The initial " M " is the sound of gathering, concentrating and formulating (in this case the requisite Spirit-matter), whilst the " z " and " pah " represent expulsion, or expression of that power. The word " Galeed ", with its initial closed guttural and its final dental sound, suggests the completed creative procedure.

[3] Mizpah (Heb.)—" May the Lord watch between thee and me whilst we are apart one from the other, "

The Chapter concludes with mutual promises, the eating of bread and the introduction of the symbols of " mount ", " night ", " morning ", " the kiss " and " the return ", these having already been interpreted. In the Macrocosmic sense these denote the culmination of a cycle (the mount), *Pralaya* (night) which follows, the opening of *Manvantara* (morning), the resumption of creative activity (the kiss), and entry into the evolutionary field or a new path of forthgoing (the Jacob cycle).

MAN, A UNIVERSE ON A SMALL SCALE [1]

In their microcosmic meanings also, Chapters Thirty and Thirty-one of *Genesis* are of deep significance.   In this interpretation Laban personifies the primordial Light, the *Daivi-prakriti*,[2] the substance, source and abiding place of the human Monad, which is represented by Jacob and his wives and their handmaidens.   Jacob is married to them all because, within the Monad, when awkened to a new cycle of evolutionary progress, the masculine and feminine both inhere and become creatively interactive. The seven principles, sub-principles, and successive physical incarnations and their attributes then produced are typified by the children, the herds and the possessions.   Preceding Chapters describe this creative life and action of the Monad and the transmission to the new individuality of the threefold Monadic attributes.   These are symbolised by the markings on the cattle, which represent the three Aspects of the Deity within the Monad.   The awakening of the creative currents into activity is allegorised in the marriages, the concubinages and the cattle-breeding.

All that has been said of the Macrocosmic process applies equally to the Monad, which is a Cosmos in miniature, although as yet only at its embryonic state and phase.   First the interior creative forces, three in number, awaken into activity.   Caduceus-like, the Monadic currents flow and intertwine, as symbolised by the rods of the three trees.   Such triplicity is the protype, or model, for all subsequent activity which occurs and operates according to this pattern.   All Monadic manifestations, in whatever kingdom of Nature, must follow this design of two oppositely polarised, inter-active forces spirally intertwined round a central current, usually symbolised by a rod, a staff or a pillar.

Throughout the whole aeonic pilgrimage from heights to depths and back to heights again, the Caduceus is the pattern or inevitable " form " as well as symbol of all creative—as also redemptive—activity.   All products are stamped, as it were, with this design.   All forces and creative

---

[1] A reversal of the dictum of the Chinese philosopher, Lao-Tzu: " The Universe is a man on a large scale. "

[2] *Daivi* (Sk.)—Primordial, homogeneous light. *Prakriti* (Sk.)—Original, primary essence.

and growth processes follow this model. The spiral ascent of consciousness, sustained by the Monadic *sushumna*, *sūtrātma*[1] or "life-ray", is also thus portrayed. The pillar erected on Gilead and called Galeed represents the central column of the Caduceus, as Laban and his family and herds personify one serpentine force and Jacob and his whole estate the other. The covenant between them made at the pillar, the feast eaten on the heap of stones, and the kiss of departure all describe in allegory the activity of forces following and playing round the central column of the Caduceus, the everlasting pillar, *lingam* or obelisk.

Applied to the Macrocosm, the Thirty-first Chapter of the *Book of Genesis* thus describes in allegory the nature of the three basic creative Powers, Intelligences and forces and their interactions to produce the "forms" of Universes and all that they will contain. The whole is preparatory to the opening of a new phase of divine creative activity, a new *Manvantara*, of whatever degree. As has been said, Laban is the eternal Source of all Powers and all "seeds", whilst his daughters and their handmaidens represent the feminine or matter side of the one, triply polarised, creative Agency. Jacob and his servants personify the masculine potency and Joseph, the son of Rachel, typifies the product or third, the true heir and successor, who will later carry the creative and evolutionary procedure into the next—the post-Jacob—field.[2] First, however, the post-Isaac era must be entered. As will be seen in the next Chapter, Jacob is about to become a Logos and Patriarch of his particular manifestation in the everlasting succession of *Manvantaras* and *Pralayas*. Having fulfilled their share of the task, Laban and Rebekah retire in favour of newly differentiated substance (Jacob-Rachel), from which the immediate successor is to be "born".

Whilst the three constituent powers are essentially a trinity in unity, three aspects of a functional unit, so all the associates of the positive and negative personifications are, in their turn, components of a unit. Jacob (positive) and all his house, and Leah, Rachel and their handmaidens (negative) represent the two component streams and undulations, the attributes and potential powers and products, of the one creative Source (Laban).

At the end of Chapter Thirty-one of *Genesis* Laban as the one Producer, the eternal Monad, having given the primordial creative impulse, withdraws into silence and darkness (disappears from the story). Allegorically Laban, after making a covenant with the Logos of the new Universe (Jacob) in the presence and over the symbol of creative power (the pillar), returns to his own place, the *Mulaprakriti* of *Parabrahman*.

---

[1] *Sūtrātma*—see Glossary.

[2] The Joseph epoch is studied and interpreted in Pt. Four of this Volume.

The pillar is thus regarded as representing the active, positive, creative potency in Cosmogenesis—the emanated, formative power which, as does the phallus in human procreation, penetrates matter (*Yoni*). The inclusion of the symbol of the pillar in the accounts in *Genesis* of the adventures and actions of the members of the first Hebrew patriarchal family, indicates an intention on the part of the authors both to reveal certain principles underlying genetic processes at the cosmic and the human levels, and to advise the student thus to examine the narrative.

Perpendicular objects such as tree-trunks, obelisks, the vertical arms of crosses, staffs and rods held in the hand, and the elevated portion of the symbol of the *lingam*, are all susceptible of interpretation as symbols of the positive, masculine potency in generative acts.

CHAPTER IX

JACOB SEEKS REUNION WITH ESAU

Gen. 32 :   *Jacob's vision at Mahanaim: his message to Esau. He is afraid of Esau's coming; and prayeth for deliverance: he sendeth a present to Esau: he wrestleth with an angel at Peniel, and is called Israel. He halteth.*

Gen. 32 : 1. *And Jacob went on his way, and the angels of God met him.*

2. *And when Jacob saw them, he said, This is God's host: and he called the name of that place Mahanaim.*

By means of allegory, the creative process is again described. The Logos-to-be summons his creative Powers and Intelligences, evokes and specialises them to his own individuality and to the frequencies or " Name " of the Universe-to-be. " Mahanaim " (two camps) may be interpreted as " great circle " or enclosing boundary, the automatic appearance and establishment of which is the first phenomenon of the preliminaries to creation or new production. Next must follow the differentiation of the one creative Power into a pair in preparation for the interplay of *Fohat* between Spirit and matter. This is described in the splitting of Jacob's forces into two bands and their movement forward to meet Esau. Again it must be stressed that the whole process is interior and occurs within the area and being of a single Emanation.

HISTORY MAY VEIL TIMELESS TRUTHS

The interpreter of allegories which have a historical foundation must both recognise history when he reads it and discern the skilful use of historical narrative to conceal and reveal spiritual truths. Be it repeated, therefore, that history—and in many places exact history—is present in the *Pentateuch*. The supersensual is, however, continually introduced into the mundane and it is these constant interventions by the Lord God, by angels and by an unnamed man, and the relation of the dreams of heroes or heroines, that indicate to the interpreter the presence of a spiritual instruction. When introduced into narratives of events of long preceding eras, unlawful cohabitations are rarely—if ever—historical alone. They are sometimes used by allegorists as references to procreative unions of a perfectly natural character, an almost infinite variety of creative self-expressions by the first Emanation occurring when once the primary impulse has been imparted.

In the Chaldean Sanctuaries the cosmic, the solar and the individual or Monadic emanations, forthgoings and returns were all known and taught to Initiates.   Moses, an Initiate of the Egyptian Mysteries, also derived his wisdom from this source.   The interblending, identity and interaction of the cosmic, solar and Monadic emanations were also known and stressed in the very exact and highly scientific School of Cosmogony in Ancient Mesopotamia.   Biblical authors were ordered to give this teaching to humanity, under the law that nothing must be withheld which could be safely revealed, and that no genuine seeker must ever be bereft of a source of knowledge.   A Sanctuary is a misnomer from one point of view, for it is a place of concealment of that which must never be completely concealed.   As heretofore explained, the Adept Guardians of knowledge, " the Keepers of the Sacred Light ", are bound under the most stringent laws to ensure that spiritual knowledge shall always be available to every worthy student capable of receiving and rightly using it.

In the then prevailing " dark age " (*Kali Yuga*[1]) unworthy students abounded amongst mankind, and the Adepts had therefore both to conceal and reveal the Sacred Light.   The establishment of the Sanctuary System[2]

---

[1] *Yuga* (Sk.)—An age of the world.   The *Kali* or dark *Yuga* is the turning or balancing point of materiality in a series of seven cycles or racial epochs, each with its four ages. According to Hindu philosophy as expounded in the *Purānas*, *Kali Yuga* began in the year 3,102 B.C. at the moment of Shri Krishna's death, and extended for 5,000 years, thus ending in the year 1,898 A.D.   Each *Yuga* is, however, preceded by an epoch called in the *Purānas Sandhyā*, " twilight " or " transition " period, and is followed by another age of like duration called *Sandhyānsa*, " portion of twilight ".   Each of these is equal to one-tenth of the *Yuga* and in consequence, in accordance with this ancient system of chronology, the Earth is now in the " portion of twilight " of *Kali Yuga*, the dark or iron age.   Hence, presumably, the difficulties to which the human Race has been and still is subject.

[2] Reference to the establishment of a special School for the training of those deemed to be fit is to be found in *Daniel* 1: 3–8, where it is stated:

3. And the king spake unto Ashpenaz the master of his eunuchs, that he should bring certain of the children of Israel, and of the king's seed, and of the princes;

4. Children in whom was no blemish, but well favoured, and skilful in all wisdom, and cunning in knowledge, and understanding science, and such as had ability in them to stand in the king's palace, and whom they might teach the learning and the tongue of the Chaldeans.

5. And the king appointed them a daily provision of the king's meat, and of the wine which he drank: so nourishing them three years, that at the end thereof they might stand before the king.

6. Now among these were of the children of Judah, Daniel, Hananiah, Mishael, and Azariah;

and the invention of the Sacred Language of Symbols constitute Their solution of this problem. In the former the truth is taught direct to those whose evolutionary position, karma[1] and ardour for knowledge bring them thereto. In the latter the wisdom, veiled it is true, is also made available to all the world. Despite the darkness (selfishness, sensuality and materialism) of the present age, a reversal of this procedure—the unveiling of truth hitherto concealed in allegory and symbol—is encouraged by the Teachers of the Race. In the author's view one of Their representatives, H. P. Blavatsky, initiated this process amongst Western humanity in her two works, *Isis Unveiled* and *The Secret Doctrine*.

Gen. 32: 3. And Jacob sent messengers before him to Esau his brother unto the land of Seir, the country of Edom.

4. And he commanded them, saying, Thus shall ye speak unto my lord Esau; Thy servant Jacob saith thus, I have sojourned with Laban, and stayed there until now:

5. And I have oxen, and asses, flocks, and menservants, and women-servants; and I have sent to tell my lord, that I may find grace in thy sight.

6. And the messengers returned to Jacob, saying, We came to thy brother Esau, and also he cometh to meet thee, and four hundred men with him.

7. Then Jacob was greatly afraid and distressed: and he divided the people that was with him, and the flocks, and herds, and the camels, into two bands;

Esau, as the active creative potency, has been ceaselessly at work in his own, the Isaachian, Cosmos. Long before its culmination, preparations for its successor had begun. Jacob, as the Logos-to-be, had gone to the one Source and begun those preparations. Now he is ready to continue the succession. For this purpose triplicity is demanded. The One (Jacob) must become functionally a pair (Jacob and Esau) and a third (messengers) must pass, or interplay, between them. This is the

7. Unto whom the prince of the eunuchs gave names: for he gave unto Daniel the name of Belteshazzar; and to Hananiah, of Shadrach; and to Mishael, of Meshach; and to Azariah, of Abednego.

8. But Daniel purposed in his heart that he would not defile himself with the portion of the king's meat, nor with the wine which he drank: therefore he requested of the prince of the eunuchs that he might not defile himself.

Indeed, the whole of this First Chapter of the *Book of Daniel* may be read as describing, the rules to be followed by those who were to be instructed in the higher learning.

[1] *Karma* (Sk.)—" Action ", connoting both the law of action and re-action, cause and effect, and the result of its operation upon nations and individuals. q.v. *Reincarnation, Fact or Fallacy*: Geoffrey Hodson.

key to the verses in which the Logos " becomes " an active Trinity in Unity, as symbolised both by Esau's and Jacob's two apparently opposed groups and by the division of Jacob's people into two bands.

In the Symbolical Language subterfuge, fear and tortuousness are sometimes, and possibly in this instance, employed as blinds to cover up the profound cosmological verities here revealed. Human attributes are imposed upon the Patriarch to accentuate the human and the historical story, and so distract undue attention from the divine and the occult revelations, with their bestowal of thaumaturgical power. Actually, as subsequent events disclosed, all the strategy and diplomacy are quite unnecessary. Esau as the creative fire, the embodied *Fohat*, is irresistibly impelled to the fulfilment of the creative function or, as the story has it, to come into intimate relationship with Jacob and to embrace and kiss him (Chapter Thirty-three of *Genesis*, Verse Four).

The statement that four hundred men accompanied Esau may be read as a reference to the matter side of the cosmogonical process. The implied number four, together with the ternary—Jacob, Esau and the messengers—provides the septenate,[1] which at this stage constitutes the creative totality. A fourth *Manvantara* since that of Noah is also indicated, whether this be Chain,[2] Round, Planet or Root Race.

Gen. 32: 8. *And said, If Esau come to the one company, and smite it, then the other company which is left shall escape.*

9. *And Jacob said, O God of my father Abraham, and God of my father Isaac, the LORD which saidst unto me, Return unto thy country, and to thy kindred, and I will deal well with thee:*

10. *I am not worthy of the least of all the mercies, and of all the truth, which thou hast shewed unto thy servant; for with my staff I passed over this Jordan; and now I am become two bands.*

11. *Deliver me, I pray thee, from the hand of my brother, from the hand of Esau: for I fear him, lest he will come and smite me, and the mother with the children.*

12. *And thou saidst, I will surely do thee good, and make thy seed as the sand of the sea, which cannot be numbered for multitude.*

This prayer of Jacob represents an invocation individually to the Monad, racially to the tribal Deity and cosmically to the creative Source, whilst ethically it constitutes a dedication to the Most High. Such a prayer is both a renewal of the original dedication and a surrender to the original Power.

[1] See Pt. One of this Volume, Ch. V, " The Symbolism of Numbers ", with special reference to the numbers 3, 4 and 7. As previously stated, additional zeros may on occasion be ignored, leaving the prime number alone to be considered,

[2] See Glossary—Chain,

Cosmologically considered, the prayer by the Logos of a "new" *Manvantara* (Jacob) is an affirmation of unity with the primordial Source and of the continuity of creative power and Office. As the incoming Hierophant of a Mystery Temple invokes the aid of his predecessors and of the One Power behind all Hierophants and all Mysteries, so the racial Patriarch invokes the aid of the God of his predecessors and of his Race.

The terms of the prayer are worthy of note. The "Lord" Who gave both the verbal order to return to "thy kindred" and the promise of multiplicity of seed is none other than the primeval "Voice" (Logos) from on high. Through a Hierarchy of the Angelic Hosts the Logos issued the first creative command, liberated and directed the first creative impulse, and enunciated the first "Word". This "Word" is expressive of the foundation forces, their frequencies and modulations, by which the Universe is brought into being under law, is shaped, and is ultimately perfected.[1] This is the "God of my fathers", the Lord to Whom Jacob appeals at the outset of the period of Office and creative activity. The title is accurate, since Jacob as Logos is both a manifestation and an heir of the preceding Logos (his "father").

Verse ten makes reference to the primordial, creative pair in the form of the dual symbol of the staff and the River Jordan. These two combined form a square or angle of ninety degrees, the vertical staff (of wood) representing the masculine potency and the horizontal river (of water) the feminine, as always in the Sacred Language.

Jacob crosses Jordan twice. First, he journeys eastwards from the land of his birth and second, as bidden, he returns westward to the land of his kindred. The eastward journey was in search of a wife. The westward journey was undertaken in obedience to a Divine command and the promise of multiplicity of "seed". On the eastward journey Jordan represents matter creatively quiescent in relation to that particular Logos (Jacob, as yet unmarried and uncreative). On the westward journey Jordan represents matter rendered creatively active (Jacob is married), as symbolised by the use of the vertical staff to "cross over Jordan".

AN INITIATORY INTERPRETATION

Search for, discovery of and acceptance into the Sanctuary of the Mysteries, Initiation therein, and forthgoing in its service, are also implied in the great allegory. In this sense Padan-aram typifies the Greater Mysteries, fount of Earth's primeval wisdom. Laban and his family are its Hierophant and Officers respectively. Leah, Rachel and their women represent the wisdom thence delivered to the Initiate, *Buddhi* united with

---

[1] The reader is referred to the statement entitled "Cosmogenesis" which appears at the beginning of Pt. Three of this Volume.

Manas to produce the offspring and develop the herds and flocks, these being symbolical of the interior " fruit " of the power, wisdom and knowledge of the sacred Sanctuary.

Thereafter the new Initiate must go forth to carry his treasures to his " kindred ", who are his fellow human beings. As ever his symbol is the square, the swastika or the cross, all of which represent in this occult, microcosmic sense the fact that the *Atmic* fire of the One Initiator and of the Initiate's own Monad (the two are one) has vertically descended into the fourfold personality[1] (" four hundred men ") of the Initiate. It is this interior power on which he relies and to which he " prays " as he sets forth on his great mission to carry the seeds of wisdom, the " Word of God ", which he will sow in the ground, or the field to which he has been appointed.

THE PREPARATION FOR SEERSHIP

All of the above interpretations—Macrocosmic, microcosmic and Initiatory—are likewise applicable to the Parable of the Prodigal Son.[2] Similar interpretations are also applicable to the Parable of the Sower[3] and the many Biblical references to the " seed " of the Patriarchs and their successors. If this Initiatory interpretation be both acceptable and applied, then the *Pentateuch* may be read as an allegorical account of the illumination of the Soul of man, and of his forthgoing as an Initiated seer and light-bringer to the world. The Sanctuaries of India, Chaldea and Egypt initiated and sent out many such inspired messengers and the cosmogonies, religious history and art of contemporary nations, especially the Jewish and the Egyptian, contain references to them. Some of the greatest were deified and are known to us as gods. In addition, the Logoi of Planets, Rounds and Chains were represented by Superhuman Beings who moved for a time amongst primitive peoples, and were enthroned as deities by them, as also by later generations of men. This is the origin of certain of the Men-gods and God-men of remotest times. In Hinduism these are referred to as *Avatāras*, a Sanskrit word implying a Divine incarnation, generally the descent of a God or some exalted Being who has progressed beyond the necessity of rebirths into the body of a mortal man. The Lord Shri Krishna is regarded as an *Avatār*[4] of Vishnu, for example.

Verse eleven is of interest in that, in the relationship with Esau, Jacob—although the father of the family—regards himself as being in

---

[1] Personality—Mind, emotion, vitality and physical body. q.v. Vol. I of this work, Pt. One, Ch. VI.

[2] q.v. Vol. I of this work, Pt. Four.

[3] *Matt.* 13:1–23 (especially v. 23).

[4] *Avatār*—see Glossary.

the same danger as "the mother with the children". At their birth, it may be remembered, the twins Esau and Jacob typify positive and negative creative potencies respectively. Thus, in the present allegory of their reunion the martial attributes of the former are symbolically feared and awaited with apprehension by the latter, even whilst "she" (Jacob) is depicted as being drawn towards "him" (Esau).

> Gen. 32: 13. *And he lodged there that same night; and took of that which came to his hand a present for Esau his brother;*
>
> 14. *Two hundred she goats, and twenty he goats, two hundred ewes, and twenty rams,*
>
> 15. *Thirty milch camels with their colts, forty kine, and ten bulls, twenty she asses, and ten foals.*

The preponderatingly feminine gifts may also indicate that Jacob *vis-a-vis* Esau represents the female or negative potency. The presence of the males indicates that the masculine potency is present in each major feminine power, just as the feminine potency is also present in each major masculine power. The number " two hundred " twice repeated, referring to the she animals, and the number " twenty " also twice stated, referring to the males, allegorically again indicate the division of the primordial Unit into a primary pair as an essential preliminary to the new creative activity for which preparations are being made.

Similarly, the next numerical advance leads into triplicity and thence to the number four, as is indicated correctly in verse fifteen; for therein occult numerical sequences and powers are revealed in the guise of numbers relating to the constituents of herds and their separate classifications. If the numbering of the gifts which Jacob offers to Esau may permissibly be regarded as conveying a cosmogonical principle, then each of the numbers connotes the degree of Self-manifestation in which the Logos is to become incarnate in His Universe. The concept that the Deity of a Universe is both transcendent beyond and immanent within it may possibly here be discerned, as is also found in the Hindu Scripture, *The Bhagavad Gita,* where the divine Incarnation as the Lord Shri Krishna says: " Having pervaded this Universe with one fragment of Myself, I remain." If this idea be pursued, then the numbers of the varying gifts offered to Esau by Jacob may convey both a certain generosity and a reservation. Jacob does not give the whole of his various flocks and herds, but a specific portion thereof and this, moreover, is numerically defined. It is noteworthy that this portion is symbolised by herds and herdsmen or servants only, the other members of this household and he himself having remained behind to follow later.

Herein evolutionary necessities and sequences are indicated, for the sub-human (in this case animal) forms precede the human on to the stage of the new Cosmos. Mineral and plant have already been evolved in

preceding dispensations (Chains [1]).   Animals have followed, and in this
fourth divine Incarnation animal evolution leads directly to the production
of those human bodies in which the Monads who by a projection of a ray
have made the long pilgrimage, will shortly become embodied.

> Gen. 32: 16. *And he delivered them into the hand of his servants, every drove
> by themselves; and said unto his servants, Pass over before me,
> and put a space betwixt drove and drove.*
>
> 17. *And he commanded the foremost, saying, When Esau my brother
> meeteth thee, and asketh thee, saying, Whose art thou ? and
> whither goest thou ? and whose are these before thee ?*
>
> 18. *Then thou shalt say, They be thy servant Jacob's; it is a present
> sent unto my Lord Esau: and, behold, also he is behind us.*
>
> 19. *And so commanded he the second, and the third, and all that
> followed the droves, saying, On this manner shall ye speak unto
> Esau, when ye find him.*
>
> 20. *And say ye moreover, Behold, thy servant Jacob is behind us.
> For he said, I will appease him with the present that goeth
> before me, and afterward I will see his face; peradventure he
> will accept of me.*
>
> 21. *So went the present over before him: and himself lodged that
> night in the company.*

Five species of animals[2] were selected (vs. 14 and 15) and the servants
commanded to keep each apart, drove by drove.   They were the five
types of domesticated quadrupeds available to the nomadic peoples of the
country, and Jacob offered a measure of all of these which he possessed.
Each of them is, in fact, a distinct product of Nature and each evolves
into its own highest representative, which becomes the head of its type or
" Ray "[3] of animal evolution.   These must be kept distinct in order that
the ultimate attainment and product (a domestic animal) may conform
precisely to the separate types of each species of the animal kingdom.
Whilst no authoritative association of a genus of animal with a particular
Ray is to be found in the available literature of occult philosophy, a tradition exists which places them as follows: First Ray, extinct; Second Ray,
elephant; Third Ray, uncertain; Fourth Ray; cat; Fifth Ray, monkey;
Sixth Ray, dog; and Seventh Ray, horse.

Nature is indeed extremely precise in the production of her types
and classifications, being herself but the product of the major Archetype,
which is the ideation of the Universe and all its products or fruits as held

---

[1] See Glossary—Chain—where the doctrine of this sequence of evolution, Chain by
Chain from mineral to man, is expounded.

[2] Goats, sheep, camels, kine and asses.

[3] q.v. *The Seven Human Temperaments*, Geoffrey Hodson, T.P.H., Adyar, Madras, India.

within the divine Mind. Jacob's verbal instructions to the servants may
be regarded as a reference to " Creation " by the sound of the " Voice "
and as statements of numerical, chronological and natural law, and it is
this which the Kabbalist Doctors affirm to be the chief subject of revelation
throughout the allegories of the *Pentateuch*—hence, doubtless, the name
given to it, *The Torah* or " Law ".[1]

" IN THE BEGINNING WAS THE WORD "[2]

According to this view the Universe is emanated and fashioned by
the divine action of sending forth spiritual energy of the quality of sound
—the Logos Doctrine.[3] From within the all-productive root substance
(*Mulaprakriti*)—the sea of pre-universal space in a state, *during Pralaya*,
of creative rest and equipoise, and so silence—a " sound " arises. This
so-called sound, which is no audible noise, is the result of motion within
THAT which hitherto was relatively motionless. A ripple caused in still
water by movement below has its limits of influence causing a circular
ring which, widening, finally reaches the full extent of its range and
expansion. So, also, at the dawn of " Creation " the first motion in
matter differentiates from the boundless Sea of Space a spherical area
within which its frequencies obtain and rule. Since the resultant, altered
matter possesses the property of soniferousness, the movement produces
a phenomenon of the order or quality of sound. At this stage it is so
transcendently spiritual or primordial as to bear little or no relation to
any sound conceivable or cognisable by the human intellect. Nevertheless
the first active Cause is correctly described as sound, and since the sound
is limited to an area according to its power, and so its range, that Cause
is not inappropriately described as the sound of a " Voice " or as a
" Word " and the formative process as consisting of the enunciation of
" words " or commands.

THE THEURGICAL POWER OF SOUND

Thus, as in almost all cosmogonies emanating from the world's
Sanctuaries, sound is made the creative agency. Since words express
thought, so behind the " Word " is divine thought or archetypal ideation,
of which the Logos is an expression in Time, Space and Motion—the
everlasting, Trinity in unity. Again, therefore, in the verses of the Chapter
under consideration sound is introduced. A series of questions and answers

---

[1] q.v. *Zohar* III, 152-b (Soncino Ed., Vol. V, p. 211)—as partly quoted at the
beginning of this Volume, p. xii.

[2] *Jn.* 1: 1.

[3] The subject of " Creation " by " Word of God " is more fully dealt with in *Occult
Powers in Nature and in Man*, Geoffrey Hodson, and in Vol. II of this work. Also
see Glossary.

10

are initiated by the Logos (Jacob) and uttered by the *Elohim* (the servants) on entry into the evolutionary field (Esau's land).

The energy which in an appropriate medium (air) produces the effect of sound is released and expressed in every physical sound. Vocal self-expression is the mark of man, and did he but realise that fact he would be infinitely careful of his speech. The rituals of the Sanctuaries of old and the words uttered in such ceremonial Rites as have their origin therein, are all based upon recognition of the power in the human voice. When a man discovers the mystery of the soniferous Ākāsa he becomes an Adept, a Theurgist, a Magician—hence the practice of enveilment. All Nature obeys the " Voice " of the Divine, whether as Logos or illumined man. The ancient sages knew this and revealed it solely by allegory in the form of the creative utterances which their cosmogonies relate.

In Kabbalism, the theosophy or hidden wisdom of Hebraism, creative procedures are indicated by means of a diagram known as " The Sephirothal Tree of Life ". The ten Sephiroth of which this diagram consists are regarded as ten spheres of divine manifestation in which God emerges from His hidden abode in order to produce the Universe. This is accomplished with the aid of ten Hierarchies of spiritual Intelligences, or Archangels and angels. The action and development of the mysterious force which is the " seed " of all " Creation " is speech-force expressive of archetypal thought. The human faculty of speech is said to have been anticipated in God; for according to the *Zohar* the successive phases of the emanation of the Universe include the primeval Will, formative thought, inner and inaudible " Word ", audible voice and ultimately man's utterance of words. Malkuth (the Kingdom) occupies the lowest point in the diagram and represents the " sounding-board " of physical Nature. Kether (the Crown) at the top of the Tree is regarded as the Source of the creative sound. The Sephiroth are but chords in the creative " Word ", component characteristics of the One Sound or " Song Divine ". Thus the Lord challenged Job concerning the time when He laid the foundations of the Earth, asking him ". . . who laid the corner stone thereof; When the morning stars sang together, and all the sons of God shouted for joy? "[1]

If an apparent digression be here permitted, then it may be conceived and stated that all Nature is sound, all life a song, save when marred by individualistic, sadistic and primitive man. Harmony is the one law, and its true servants are ever harmonious. Wise is that man who, learning this truth, lives in obedience to the one law. Thus the Adept lives and such is the mark of Adeptship. The Adept Brotherhood itself[2] is a

---

[1] *Job*. 38: 6, 7.
[2] ". . . the spirits of just men made perfect " (*Heb.* 12: 23).

harmonious blending of self-harmonised and perfected individuals. Its consciousness is serene, undisturbed and undisturbable, the stable centre of immovable poise which serves as planetary fulcrum for the forces of the Solar Logos apportioned to the planet Earth. He who would fully share in Adept activity, participate in Adept knowledge and assist Adept work, must first achieve self-harmony. The Sanskrit word " *Aum* "[1] constitutes the harmonising and attuning sound and the Yogi chanting this word becomes consciously at one with the Logos.

Gen. 32: 22. *And he rose up that night, and took his two wives, and his two women-servants, and his eleven sons, and passed over the ford Jabbok.*

23. *And he took them, and sent them over the brook, and sent over that he had.*

24. *And Jacob was left alone; and there wrestled a man with him until the breaking of the day.*

25. *And when he saw that he prevailed not against him, he touched the hollow of his thigh; and the hollow of Jacob's thigh was out of joint, as he wrestled with him.*

26. *And he said, Let me go, for the day breaketh. And he said, I will not let thee go, except thou bless me.*

27. *And he said unto him, What is thy name? And he said, Jacob.*

28. *And he said, Thy name shall be called no more Jacob, but Israel; for as a prince hast thou power with God and with men, and hast prevailed.*

29. *And Jacob asked him, and said, Tell me, I pray thee, thy name. And he said, Wherefore is it that thou dost ask after my name? And he blessed him there.*

30. *And Jacob called the name of the place Peniel: for I have seen God face to face, and my life is preserved.*

31. *And as he passed over Penuel the sun rose upon him, and he halted upon his thigh.*

32. *Therefore the children of Isreal eat not of the sinew which shrank, which is upon the hollow of the thigh, unto this day: because he touched the hollow of Jacob's thigh in the sinew that shrank.*

A MACROCOSMIC INTERPRETATION

These are eleven of the most deeply occult verses of the whole Bible and they will now be considered in their possible Macrocosmic, microcosmic and Initiatory interpretations. In the Macrocosmic sense Jacob

---

[1] *Aum* (Sk.): The sacred syllable; the triple-lettered unit; hence the Trinity in one.

is regarded as the Logos of a new *Manvantara* Who has been long prepared in the fields (Universes) of His Predecessors and now, provided with all necessary powers and potentialities—actually evolved from within Himself —moves forward in time to His new Office. Padan-aram is used as a topographical symbol for the Mother Source (*Mulaprakriti*) of all Universes, whilst Laban personifies the masculine creative potency therein and his daughters and their handmaidens the *shaktis* [1] or feminine creative powers. The Isaachian Cosmos represents the existing cycle out of which Jacob has developed, and Joseph in his turn will develop out of that of his father Jacob. Isaac was the Logos of his era, Rebekah its substance and Esau its active *fohatic* energy. As Logos-to-be of the succeeding *Manvantara* Jacob leaves home in search of a wife, or journeys to the primordial Source. There he " labours for wages ", carries out creative and cattle breeding functions, and so " learns his craft ". Then with his wives (*shaktis* or powers) his flocks and his servants, meaning his developed and controlled creative powers and his potential and active faculties—particularly the conjoined power of thought and sound—he moves with his whole estate, including the Teraphim, across the ford " Jabbok " into the new field of activity. Such, Macrocosmically, is the great story thus far.

Verse Twenty-two indicates that a new phase is to begin. Verses Twenty-one and Twenty-two state that night had fallen, and verse Twenty-three that the company had approached " the brook " and that Jacob sent his womenfolk, servants, eleven sons and all " that he had " over the ford. Herein is described the assembly of creative powers and agencies at the threshold of a period and a region of renewed creative activity. The sun of the new " day " (*Manvantara*) had not yet risen. At the highest levels of divine thought (Mt. Gilead[2]) the first preparations had been made, and thence the creative " Word " had been conceived and uttered (the plan and the messages to Esau). The Archetype was thereby projected into the highest levels of the Soul of the Universe-to-be. Below, night still reigned and " darkness was upon the face of the deep ".[3]

THE FORD JABBOK

The brook to be crossed is here a symbol of both a period of time and a condition of space. It represents the conjoined time-space separating two *Manvantaras* within a *Maha-Manvantara*. It is a flowing stream and thus aptly portrays the passage of time in contradistinction to the timelessness of the pre-*Manvantaric* state. The condition across the brook must be

---

[1] *Shakti*—see Glossary.
[2] *Gen.* 31: 21.
[3] *Gen.* 1: 2.

entered, inhabited, and forced to submit to projected divine thought and its potencies. These are typified by the women and servants who are sent forward, and later followed by Jacob himself, personifying the action and operation of creative Will. The ford Jabbok also represents the potent yet clearly defined, concentrated projection of Logoic thought. Night still encloses the new field in a mantle of darkness, for the creative Will has not yet manifested its productive and reproductive potency.

JACOB WRESTLES WITH AN " ANGEL "

The Logos-to-be must still obtain from His Predecessor the Word of Power—His Name—before He can be installed, consecrated, and receive His official meed of power. These, symbolically, He must win as in a tournament, the suggestion of a conflict of enemies being a blind. The apparent separateness of Spirit and matter and the occurrence of conflict between them are purely allegorical, since the procedure of the emanation and fashioning of a Universe is to be conceived of as being either effortless on the part of the Logos or the product of creative dance (Shiva) or play (Bacchus). The necessity for intense effort, by which alone the highest powers are attained and expressed, is nevertheless truly conveyed by the account of the wrestling match. The processes of creation at all levels, from highest Macrocosm to physical microcosm, are symbolised in this contest. The achievement of illumination and its expression in man as genius are also implied. Jacob, the Creator-to-be, wrestles with the angel or " man " and must not be defeated. The two apparent enemies must stand on equal terms, otherwise the " name "[1] or nature of the new creation cannot be revealed.

The stress and strain of all preceding involutionary and evolutionary cycles and attainments are here concentrated in, and represented by, one intense creative effort, the successful result of which will be entry into a new kingdom of consciousness and power, a new Office and a new and patriarchal state of existence or " name " (Israel). The everlasting " battle " between Spirit and matter is also revealed in allegory in these pregnant verses. The eventual specialisation and moulding or " naming " of matter by Spirit is also portrayed.

Every creator, whether Logos or human genius, and its vehicle of expression for a time pays a price for the exercise of the power to create. Not only must resistant matter itself, as also all vehicles and forms, be moulded by effort, but in addition a limitation of freedom of action must be accepted and submitted to. The thigh out of joint symbolises this penalty, this temporary loss both of procreative power and of freedom, which must

[1] Vs. 27–29.

be suffered by every active fashioner of forms. In the process of Self-manifestation the Logos of a Universe must have sacrificed untainted spirituality, undivided wholeness and total unity with boundless cosmic life. Symbolically His thigh, or region of creative expression, is " out of joint ",[1] becomes the source of limitation and weakness.

All such penalties and limitations described in World Scriptures and Mythologies have a similar significance. Instances of these are: Achilles mortally wounded in the heel, Hercules poisoned by the shirt of Nessus, Balder wounded by an arrow made of mistletoe, Siegfried vulnerable because of a leaf, both Bacchus and Osiris slain, their bodies dismembered and the pieces later reassembled, and the " divine " Pelican with its self-torn and bleeding breast. These may be regarded as allegories descriptive of the limitations of primordial freedom, wholeness and integrity voluntarily assumed by all creative agents of whatever degree.

THE OCCULT SIGNIFICANCE OF A NAME

The name, whether of Logos, Universe, plane of Nature, principle of man or of man himself, signifies in the Sacred Language both distinguishing characteristics and the quality of individuality and power. To bestow a name is to single out that which is named from its surroundings. Since sound is involved in the concept of a name and the process of naming, a Scriptural reference to creation by sound is clearly intended. In the Biblical narratives the names of the patriarchal representatives of cosmic, creative Powers are either changed altogether, as in Jacob's case, or modified by the addition of syllables, as in the case of Abraham. Jacob, on the threshold of *Manvantara*, is given the distinctive set of frequencies which represent the Archetype, plan, power and future products of the new cycle. This name, however, is only as a syllable in the full name of the *Maha-Manvantara*, which latter represents the total power and products, actual and potential, of the larger Cosmos.

The emanation of the minor from the Major or, to reverse the statement, the condensation of the universal into the particular, is never achieved without effort, and this also is expressed in the wrestling conflict between Jacob and the unnamed " man ". To the particular the universal is formless, and so many of the " men " met in the evolutionary field by Patriarchs and others are frequently unnamed. Consciousness, however, desires to bring the universal increasingly within its grasp, and this is revealed allegorically when heroes and heroines are made to demand the names of the sources of power, protection or deliverance. These names cannot be given, however, without irretrievable loss, and so are often withheld.

[1] V. 25.

Descent from the universal to the particular is a constriction and a distortion for that which, in its essential nature, is ever free and unconfinable. Even when the feat is temporarily performed, nevertheless the universality of the power and the full significance of the implicit idea are lost. In an allegory from the Teutonic Mysteries, for example, Lohengrin departs when under duress he reveals his name. The process of creation is dependent upon the descent of power from a higher dimension. The Logos brings about that descent and so, appropriately, Jacob " prevailed " over the " man " and, on demand, received his blessing. A change of name followed,[1] signifying attainment of a new level of consciousness and official entry upon relevant activities.

THE DIVINE SURRENDER OF FREEDOM

Renunciation, or that which at first is felt to be renunciation and a limitation, is always demanded as the price of advancement. Agreeable to the symbolical method of revelation and portrayal, Jacob is injured in the thigh. Spiritual power at any level below that of its origin demands for its manifestation both particularisation of the power and the limitation of the freedom and faculty of the intelligent agent. Such are some possible interpretations of the story of the association of Jacob with the unnamed " man ".

THE DESCENT OF THE HUMAN MONAD

The shrinking of Jacob's thigh, in its microcosmic interpretation, represents the final renunciation of—evolution beyond—physical procreative activity. In this sense the " man " is the Monad, Jacob is the Ego and the " thigh " is the physical procreative power and experience. When the evolutionary phase is entered at which Monad and Ego are in conscious relationship (together) and the Ego is expressing Monadic attributes (has prevailed), then procreative activity is sublimated. Symbolically the organ of creation " shrinks ". Jacob is thus seen as the high Initiate who has attained *Atmic* Consciousness, whose physical body has lost all power to limit him, and whose creative activity is henceforth entirely mental and spiritual.

The microcosmic significance of Chapter Thirty-two of *Genesis* is also indicated in the twinship and differing characteristics of Jacob and Esau. Both are products and expressions of the Monad, Isaac. Both are personifications of creative power, since both are Patriarchs. Esau represents, microcosmically, the fiery, passionate and more physical expression of

---

[1] This instruction was not acted upon at this time, but only later when so commanded by the Lord God (*Gen.* 35: 10),

Fohat, whilst Jacob personifies the more subjective, intellectual and spiritual, creativeness. Esau is the personality, Jacob the Ego and Isaac, their father, is the Monad.

At the opening of a new descent into physical life the Ego projects its powers, human and animal, from the level of creative thought into the physical world (the land of Canaan). To reach that level the realm of emotion must be entered and crossed (the brook and the ford Jabbok). The Monadic, creative power personified by the " man " must be focused by thought-will into the limitations of a single, material expression. Allegorically, Jacob wrestles with a " man ", prevails, but suffers injury to his thigh or organ of creative faculty. All happens within and to a single individual, personified by Jacob, whose universality as an Ego must be limited but not destroyed by the process of incarnation in the flesh and subservience to the laws of creation and procreation.

HUMAN PROGRESSION THROUGH SUCCESSIVE LIVES

In this approach the incidents in the narrative become applicable to each human individual, in this case personified by Jacob, whose story as it has come down to us reveals phases in the evolution and experience of man. In a further interpretation Chapter Thirty-two of *Genesis* describes the process of descent into a new physical birth and so becoming a new individual, or receiving a new name. In this process knowledge and memory of the creative Source are obscured, forgotten, if not wholly lost. Symbolically, despite the request the " man " does not reveal his name. On the contrary, he himself bestows a different name upon Jacob, one implying disciplined command or kingship by the Ego over the personality.

Reincarnation, or birth in another family, may also be inferred, since each successive rebirth provides an extension of the Egoic domain by the attainment of a new personality (and so name) through which added powers and faculties will be developed. Eventually the twain—Inner Self and outer man—become mutually inter-related to form one consciousness. Deeply though this knowledge of Egoic unfoldment through successive lives was hidden from the profane, veiled for all outside of the ancient Sanctuaries, it was thoroughly well known within them. The later reunion of Esau and Jacob, who then embrace and kiss, as also the succession of Patriarchs, may also be regarded as revelations of the sequence of earthly lives. These culminate in perfection or the mystical birth of the Messiah, as later promised, and His Ascension on the attainment of Christhood. Indeed, many Books of the Bible may be read as allegorical portrayals of the origin, nature and evolution of the human Soul to " a perfect man, unto the measure of the stature of the fulness of Christ." [1]

[1] *Eph.* 4: 13.

Such, indeed, is a microcosmic key to the interpretation of those parts of the Bible which are Sanctuary-inspired. Admittedly all is not thus spiritually and occultly meaningful. Some parts of the Bible are simple history, others depict tribal superstition and egoism, whilst allowance must be made for outright error. Nevertheless much also is indeed truly inspired.

JACOB TREADS "THE WAY OF HOLINESS"[1]

In many significant passages of the Bible the life of the Sanctuary itself is mirrored. The pathway to supreme illumination, the conferring of Initiations after tests and ordeals, the reception of spiritual wisdom by Candidates after profound Soul-stirring, as well as the final triumphs of Initiates, are all indicated beneath the veil of allegory and symbol. For example, Jacob at a certain stage in his history becomes the Initiate triumphant, one who " crosses the stream "[2] (of the spiritual life) and reaches the further shore of Adeptship. The ford over the River Jabbok stands for the Sanctuary, by the aid of which the " stream " is crossed and a new and far wider sphere of creative activity is entered upon.

In such an interpretation the transference of power from a retiring Hierophant of a Temple of the Mysteries to his successor, and also of faculties developed by the Higher Self during preceding incarnations, is implied. Microcosmically, Jacob's original name signifies Monadic consciousness and power (*Ātma*), whilst the change to Israel indicates the influence of the Higher Mind or Egoic individuality (*Manas*).[3] From the union of these two (*Ātma* and *Manas*) Buddhic consciousness will be born to that individuality. Thereafter instinct and emotion give place to self-inspired mentality. All of these progressions are indicated in the change of name from Jacob to Israel.

In the wider sense the formative processes of Nature are allegorically described, Spirit being the positive and matter the negative agencies. Continually throughout *Manvantara* these two interact, their activity and unfoldment in the evolutionary field being generative in character and at the same time obedient to electrical laws of polarity and interchange. The Monad in man, consisting of focused creative fire and light, is positive, whilst the *Manas* or spiritual Intelligence is negative. The generative interaction of these two within man is productive of the " birth " of *Buddhi* or Christ Consciousness.

---

[1] *Is.* 35: 8.

[2] Stream—of which, in the Bible, the River Jordan is a topographical symbol, as also at this point is its tributory, Jabbok.

[3] q.v. Vol. I of this work, Pt. Five, Ch. I—" The Annunciation "—wherein the Monad is personified by Gabriel, *Manas* by Mary and *Buddhi* by the Christ-child.

In the world's allegories the numerous accounts of physical creative intercourse and its products, legitimate when within marriage and illegitimate when without, may be read as descriptive of natural Monadic, Egoic and physical laws of reproduction. This applies to both states of human consciousness and the vehicles through which they are expressed. The Logos is as a Patriarch at an exceedingly lofty level, and the sun is the physical agent of His spiritual creative power. Universes, Monads, Egos, physical bodies, and levels and attributes of human power and consciousness, are all personified in the great Biblical narrative by the Patriarchs, their wives, sons, daughters, tribes, cattle and possessions.

CHAPTER X

THE RECONCILIATION OF JACOB AND ESAU

Gen. 33:   *The kindness of Jacob and Esau at their meeting. Jacob cometh to Succoth. He buyeth a field, and buildeth an altar.*

Although this Chapter may well be read as an account of the reunion of the two brothers, Jacob and Esau, and no under-meanings be sought, nevertheless details are given and phrases used which are susceptible of interpretation as allegories of Cosmogenesis and human reincarnation. The separations and reunions of groups, relatives and male and female characters, for example, are suggestive of periods of quiescence and activity, as also of creative interactions and their fruits, in both the Macrocosmic and microcosmic senses. A general commentary in these terms is therefore offered, but with no intention of introducing complicated interpretations into what may be merely a simple narration of facts.

Gen. 33: 1. *And Jacob lifted up his eyes, and looked, and, behold, Esau came, and with him four hundred men. And he divided the children unto Leah, and unto Rachel, and unto the two handmaids.*

      2. *And he put the handmaids and their children foremost, and Leah and her children after, and Rachel and Joseph hindermost.*

      3. *And he passed over before them, and bowed himself to the ground seven times, until he came near to his brother.*

      4. *And Esau ran to meet him, and embraced him, and fell on his neck, and kissed him; and they wept.*

In this Thirty-third Chapter of *Genesis* the reconciliation of Jacob and Esau is described. The universal, electric, positive creative power, ceaselessly active throughout the Universe (Esau), now becomes an accepted " brother ", ally and friend of the negative creative potency (Jacob). In this, the pre-Canaan epoch, no further physical procreation occurs. In these verses people are brought together in two sets of five—Esau and his four hundred men, or four companies each of one hundred, and Jacob with his four women. Jacob advances and bows seven times to Esau, who comes to meet him. Thereafter they embrace, kiss and weep. Later Esau accepts the cattle of Jacob as a present and precedes him to Canaan. One cycle of manifestation is closing (that of Jacob) and a new one is about to open (that of Joseph). At this pre-creative stage the Logos-to-be is still in intimate association with root substance, and so Joseph is here still associated with his mother Rachel (substance).

The two leaders who will initiate the succeeding epoch represent the positive (Esau) and the negative (Jacob) creative potencies.   Their embrace refers to mutual unification, their kiss to interior creative activity, and their tears to the *fohatic* life fluid, the spiritual, seed-carrying or Monad-bearing one life.   The Jacob cycle thus draws to a close.   He withdraws, but does not die until later.   The focus of interest is now changed to the children, more especially Dinah at first, and then to Joseph as Logos of the new cycle.

> Gen. 33: 5. *And he lifted up his eyes, and saw the women and the children; and said, Who are those with thee?   And he said, The children which God hath graciously given thy servant.*
>
> 6. *Then the handmaidens came near, they and their children, and they bowed themselves.*
>
> 7. *And Leah also with her children came near, and bowed themselves: and after came Joseph near and Rachel, and they bowed themselves.*

At the opening of a new epoch of divine manifestation (*Manvantara*) the juxta-position of the universal positive and negative occurs.   This is here allegorically described with the implication that preceding eras, whether Planetary Schemes, Chains, Rounds, Races or individual incarnations, have heretofore been fruitful.   The bowing of the personifications of the feminine to the masculine potency is indicative of polarity and of the more receptive contribution which the former makes in the creative process. The active part played by the positive is indicated by the phrase: " Esau ran to meet him. "

THE SYMBOL OF RECONCILIATION

Just as disputes, accusations of dishonesty, enmity and quarrels between hitherto united nations, families and individuals have possible occult significance,[1] so also reconciliations may be read as ultimate re-harmonisations of the erstwhile antagonists.   Such incidents are numerous in the Bible and refer to the ultimate overcoming by Spirit of the inertia and resistance of matter, and to the voluntary surrender of the personality of an evolved human being to the spiritualising influence of the Higher Self.

> Gen. 33: 8. *And he said, What meanest thou by all this drove which I met?   And he said, These are to find grace in the sight of my lord.*
>
> 9. *And Esau said, I have enough, my brother; keep that thou hast unto thyself.*

---

[1] For example, apparent conflicts between Spirit and matter in the Universe and between Ego and personality in man.

10. *And Jacob said, Nay, I pray thee, if now I have found grace in thy sight, then receive my present at my hand; for therefore I have seen thy face, as though I had seen the face of God, and thou wast pleased with me.*

11. *Take, I pray thee, my blessing that is brought to thee; because God hath dealt graciously with me, and because I have enough. And he urged him, and he took it.*

12. *And he said, Let us take our journey, and let us go, and I will go before thee.*

13. *And he said unto him, My lord knoweth that the children are tender, and the flocks and herds with young are with me: and if men should overdrive them one day, all the flock will die.*

14. *Let my lord, I pray thee, pass over before his servant; and I will lead on softly, according as the cattle that goeth before me and the children be able to endure, until I come unto my lord unto* **Seir.**

15. *And Esau said, Let me now leave with thee some of the folk that are with me. And he said, What needeth it? let me find grace in the sight of my lord.*

16. *So Esau returned that day on his way unto Seir.*

17. *And Jacob journeyed to Succoth, and built him an house, and made booths for his cattle: therefore the name of the place is called Succoth.*

18. *And Jacob came to Shalem, a city of Shechem, which is in the land of Canaan, when he came from Padan-aram; and pitched his tent before the city.*

19. *And he bought a parcel of a field, where he had spread his tent, at the hand of the children of Hamor, Shechem's father, for an hundred pieces of money.*

20. *And he erected there an altar, and called it El-elohe-Israel.*

The very personal and the tribal details included in the narrative of the reconciliation between Jacob and Esau may be taken at their face value as being descriptive of not unnatural procedures under the circumstances. Nevertheless the statement by Jacob concerning his brother Esau—that he had seen his face " as though I had seen the face of God "—suggests something more than a fraternal reunion. If one is to accept the Kabbalistic view of the *Pentateuch*,[1] that it is in reality a vehicle for occult revelation under the veil of allegory and symbol, then references to creative processes of both the Cosmic and the human order may possibly be discerned. Whilst in general the method of the ancient writers has been to use masculine and feminine personifications, men and women, as representing Spirit and matter, in

[1] see the introductory quotations from Kabbalistic literature.

the story of Jacob and Esau the two brothers respectively are thus chosen. Their reunion, the recognition by Jacob that God is with Esau, the extremely generous gifts offered and their onward travel together, all describe allegorically the intimate interfusion of the two opposite polarities in preparation for the later opening of the new cycle—that of Joseph—which is to follow.

The ancient writers, it must be assumed, were deeply preoccupied with and versed in the profound mystery of generation, cosmic and microcosmic. As Initiates of the Mystery Schools of Chaldea—in their turn essential parts of the Ancient Mysteries by which occult learning and spiritual modes of living were communicated to man and kept alive in ancient days—secrecy had been enjoined upon them, so that revelations of their learning and their occult lore had to be most heavily veiled. This, however, is not the only reason for the intrusion into Hebrew history of revelations which also concerned laws and processes of a divine order; for the authors were men of vision, Initiates in whom the inner sight had been awakened. In consequence, they actually saw on occasion the manifestation of the divine in Nature and of the Spirit of man in certain people. Earth, for them, was indeed alight with heaven and this vision, together with their secretly avowed objective of teaching mankind, may be regarded as an added factor influencing them to write the history of their people in metaphorical form, rather than as a record of natural events alone.

With a request to the reader for pardon on account of repetitions, the above ideas are here offered as commentaries upon the Thirty-third Chapter of the *Book of Genesis*.

If readers should, not unnaturally, question the view that occult revelations are being made by means of allegorised history, and should they consider that the indications[1] are too few to justify this approach, then it must not be forgotten that the *Torah* has undergone many revisions and elisions, some of them it has been stated for theological and even personal motives, and some out of sheer ignorance.

Astrologically[2] and esoterically Joseph represents the next Zodiacal Sign to become dominant as the basic qualities and attributes of the new *Manvantara*, of which Joseph is to be the forthgoing and returning life and consciousness, or Logos.

---

[1] For example, divine interventions, appearances of angels, and spiritual visions by *dramatis personae*.

[2] The choice of twelve as designating the number of children born of Jacob and, in consequence the number of the Tribes of Israel, suggests a Zodiacal, and so astrological, intention in the minds of the authors of the story of the founding of the Israelite nation. A fuller consideration of this subject and a complete classification of the twelve Tribes are given on pp. 273 *et seq.* and pp. 287 *et seq.* of this Volume and in Volume II, Pt. Five, Ch. II of this work.

Microcosmically, the human Soul has entered fully upon the path of hastened evolution, has " crossed the stream " (Jabbok), and in consequence its creative powers are exercised solely at the spiritual level.   The story of the meeting and actions of the two brothers, who are twins, and of the women and children is full of interest from this interior, occult point of view.[1] Esau represents the Monadic *Atma*, the positive creative power and light which " runs to meet " Jacob, his women and his children.   Jacob is the triple reincarnating Self or Ego and his wives typify the Causal Body,[2] whilst the children personify the fruits, or capacities and powers, developed in preceding incarnations.

Embraces, kisses and tears all symbolise the creative interplay between Monad and Ego, the latter being receptive in relation to the former but positive in relation to successive physical personalities.   Thus viewed, the preparations or creative activities which occur within the Higher Self of man at the opening of a new physical incarnation are allegorically described in these opening verses of Chapter Thirty-three of *Genesis*.

[1] For a further exposition of the microcosmic or human significance of the Nativities and later experiences of Saviours, the reader is referred to the first Volume of this work, Pt. Five, Ch. I, and more especially to the opening paragraphs which deal with the mystical view of the Gospel narrative.

[2] Causal Body—see Glossary.

CHAPTER XI

PROCREATIVE UNIONS, LEGITIMATE AND ILLICIT, AS ALLEGORIES OF THE EMANATION OF UNIVERSES

Gen. 34: *Dinah defiled. The Shechemites are circumcised. The sons
of Jacob taking advantage thereof slay them, and spoil their
city. Jacob reproveth Simeon and Levi.*

Gen. 34: 1. *And Dinah the daughter of Leah, which she bare unto Jacob, went
out to see the daughters of the land.*

2. *And when Shechem the son of Hamor the Hivite, prince of the
country, saw her, he took her, and lay with her, and defiled
her.*

3. *And his soul clave unto Dinah the daughter of Jacob, and he
loved the damsel, and spake kindly unto the damsel.*

4. *And Shechem spake unto his father Hamor, saying, Get me this
damsel to wife.*

This Chapter deals with the defilement of Dinah, the quarrel between
the sons of Jacob and the Shechemites, the slaughter of all the males by
Simeon and Levi, the despoiling of the city, and Jacob's reproof of his two
sons for their actions. Whilst these incidents may have a purely historical
basis and therefore do not call for interpretation, they are nevertheless so
much out of character as to suggest an allegorical intent in the minds of
the authors. Jacob, the father of Simeon and Levi, has been portrayed as
an upright, kindly and God-guided man. The mothers of the two murderers
were members of Laban's household, and he is given a similar character.
The story of the outburst of brutality and the exaction of so terrible a penalty
upon a whole people for the crime of one of its members is, in consequence,
difficult to accept in a purely historical sense. In such cases it is justifiable,
indeed advisable, at least to examine the narrative in search of possible
under-meanings.

Further support for such an approach is provided by the strange fact
that the masculine and feminine participants in a creative act, after its
fulfilment are made completely to disappear. Dinah plays no further part
in the story of Israel whilst the Shechemites are obliterated. This occurs,

moreover, at the beginning of a narrative of the opening of a new Biblical cycle—that of Joseph—suggesting that Dinah and Shechem may thus be regarded as personifications of the primordial pair from whom the Logos-to-be is born. That pair, having performed their office in Cosmogenesis, having set in motion the cyclic processes, no longer participate in the drama.

Dinah was the only daughter or feminine product of Jacob, now named Israel. Eleven sons and one daughter completed his progeny before he entered into the land of Canaan, where he died. The Zodiacal powers and attributes in the Cosmos and the corresponding temperaments and qualities of man are indicated by these twelve children. Amongst these Dinah represents the sign Virgo, and also personifies both pre-cosmic matter and pre-pubertal and pre-Initiate man.

Israel and his children represent, therefore, a Logos Who has completed one cycle of creative and evolutionary activity, during which the qualities and attributes of each of twelve Signs of the Zodiac were accentuated and the relevant divine powers (children) were further developed. This fruitage must, in its turn, pass onwards into the succeeding *Manvantara*, and the journey from Padan-aram is allegorically descriptive of that procedure. In consequence the virgin feminine principle, represented by Dinah, must lose its virginity (Dinah is defiled). The creative process is later re-initiated by and in the offspring.

Shechem, son of Hamor the Hivite, illicitly procures Dinah and thereafter both of them disappear from the cosmogonical allegory. Israel, his wives and their handmaidens, his sons of the Padan-aram phase and one daughter, his herds, servants and possessions, all represent one individuality, whether interpreted Macrocosmically or microcosmically. The Logos of any Universe and the Monad-Ego of every man are both accurately personified by the Patriarch and his estate. Macrocosmically, Dinah is the virginal substance and state from which the succession will arise. Shechem is the creative agency, the kingly power, by which the virgin is made fruitful. The absence of mention of either her motherhood or her offspring indicates the intention of the authors of the Mosaic books to portray Dinah as the feminine principle essential to the succession of *Manvantaras* of whatever degree, and Shechem as the principle of positive generation. These, having played their parts, disappear in the sense that the centre of the stage is occupied by the chief actor in the next phase of the creative drama.[1]

---

[1] Readers unaccustomed to the idea that our Solar System is but one in both a number and a succession of such may find strange the affirmation in occult philosophy that the present Solar System was preceded by an unknown number of precursors, and in its turn will be followed by an irfinite number of successors. As in the past, each of these will in the future progress along an evolutionary spiral towards ever greater degrees of the development of its indwelling life and consciousness, and its individual intelligences. See Glossary—*Pralaya.*

Gen. 34: 5. *And Jacob heard that he had defiled Dinah his daughter: now his sons were with his cattle in the field: and Jacob held his peace until they were come.*

6. *And Hamor the father of Shechem went out unto Jacob to commune with him.*

7. *And the sons of Jacob came out of the field when they heard it: and the men were grieved, and they were very wroth, because he had wrought folly in Israel in lying with Jacob's daughter; which thing ought not to be done.*

8. *And Hamor communed with them, saying, The soul of my son Shechem longeth for your daughter; I pray you give her him to wife.*

9. *And make ye marriages with us, and give your daughters unto us, and take our daughters unto you.*

10. *And ye shall dwell with us: and the land shall be before you; dwell and trade ye therein, and get you possessions therein.*

11. *And Shechem said unto her father and unto her brethren, Let me find grace in your eyes, and what ye shall say unto me I will give.*

12. *Ask me never so much dowry and gift, and I will give according as ye shall say unto me: but give me the damsel to wife;*

13. *And the sons of Jacob answered Shechem and Hamor his father deceitfully, and said, because he had defiled Dinah their sister.*

14. *And they said unto them, We cannot do this thing, to give our sister to one that is uncircumcised; for that were a reproach unto us:*

15. *But in this will we consent unto you: If ye will be as we be, that every male of you be circumcised;*

16. *Then will we give our daughters unto you, and we will take your daughters to us, and we will dwell with you, and we will become one people.*

17. *But if ye will not hearken unto us, to be circumcised; then will we take our daughter, and we will be gone.*

18. *And their words pleased Hamor, and Shechem Hamor's son.*

19. *And the young man deferred not to do the thing, because he had delight in Jacob's daughter: and he was more honourable than all the house of his father.*

20. *And Hamor and Shechem his son came unto the gate of their city, and communed with the men of their city, saying,*

21. *These men are peaceable with us; therefore let them dwell in the land, and trade therein; for the land, behold, it is large enough for them; let us take their daughters to us for wives, and let us give them our daughters.*

22. *Only herein will the men consent unto us for to dwell with us, to be one people, if every male among us be circumcised, as they are circumcised.*

23. *Shall not their cattle and their substance and every beast of their's be our's? only let us consent unto them, and they will dwell with us.*

24. *And unto Hamor and unto Shechem his son hearkened all that went out of the gate of his city; and every male was circumcised, all that went out of the gate of his city.*

25. *And it came to pass on the third day, when they were sore, that two of the sons of Jacob, Simeon and Levi, Dinah's brethren, took each man his sword, and came upon the city boldly, and slew all the males.*

26. *And they slew Hamor and Shechem his son with the edge of the sword, and took Dinah out of Shechem's house, and went out.*

27. *The sons of Jacob came upon the slain, and spoiled the city, because they had defiled their sister.*

28. *They took their sheep, and their oxen, and their asses, and that which was in the city, and that which was in the field.*

29. *And all their wealth, and all their little ones, and their wives took they captive, and spoiled even all that was in the house.*

30. *And Jacob said to Simeon and Levi, Ye have troubled me to make me to stink among the inhabitants of the land, among the Canaanites and the Perizzites: and I being few in number, they shall gather themselves together against me, and slay me; and I shall be destroyed, I and my house.*

31. *And they said, Should he deal with our sister as with an harlot?*

The conduct of Simeon and Levi towards the Shechemites is so reprehensible as to be both repulsive and difficult of acceptance in its literal form. Admittedly the Israelites were at this time in their history still but a small and primitive tribe, and the enactment of such a revenge because of the defilement of a sister is not entirely beyond belief. Nevertheless, the *Pentateuch* is presented exoterically as an account of the creation of a Universe and its inhabitants, and of the rise of the Israelite nation as a God-chosen people destined to bring about on Earth a reign of obedience to the law of God (*Torah*) which was to culminate in a Messianic age. To sully the pages of its history with accounts of such ungodly and inhuman conduct is surely a strange way to narrate the saga of a nation. Since great Hebrew scholars from before the pre-Christian era have affirmed that the *Torah* is but an allegorical veil concealing profound truths,[1] then the student

---

[1] q.v. *Zohar* III, 152-b (Soncino Ed. Vol. V, p. 211) and similar statements as quoted at the beginning of this Volume.

seeking those truths finds justification for applying to the story the classical rules of interpretation.   Such being the theme of this work, the fruits of that endeavour are here—as elsewhere—offered to the reader.

The apparent duplicity and ruthless cruelty of Israel's sons, and especially of Simeon and Levi, and their plundering of the Hivite family of all their women, cattle and possessions, may thus be read as allegorically portraying the withdrawal of the primordial creative Monad from active participation in *Mavantara*, and also the absorption of the products of its activity and of its creative attributes into the new field.   The original Agent, the creative Initiator of *Manvantara* (Logos), having impregnated virgin Space and imparted the involutory and evolutionary impulses, plays no further part in the creative process.   Apart from His transmitted power and attributes, the first Logos is thereafter non-existent or symbolically, dies.

This strange, natural fact or law is represented in Nature by certain of her varied forms and processes.   The impregnating male bee dies after consummation of the hymeneal function.   Fertilising spermatozoa die and disappear after the completion of their task.   The Greeks revealed this truth by means of allegories describing the loss of the creative power, and even of the generative organs, after fulfilment of the process of impregnation. Thus Kronos mutilates Uranus, implying that manifestation in time temporarily robs the Eternal of its eternity.   This is part of the hidden meaning of all allegorical emasculations.   In the Hebrew epic Shechem and all his tribe are removed from the face of the Earth.[1]

The feminine principle (original Space) also disappears as such, being replaced by or becoming the active, productive mother substance (*Mahā-tattva*)[2] from which the seven principles and subtle elements (*tattvas*) are later evolved by the action of divine Thought, universal Intelligence (*Mahat*). *Mulaprakriti* as virgin " loses its virginity ", and in that sense disappears. So also in man.   The Monad, an imperishable Spark, having projected its Ray into the evolutionary field, takes no further deliberative part in the development of that Ray in the immediately succeeding cycles.   Ultimately after individualisation and when the Ego has attained to a certain stature, the Monad projects an additional power into the Ego and a new creative drama is enacted, a new being—an Adept—is conceived and born.   This secondary creative act is represented in the inspired allegories of the lives of Saviours and heroes by Annunciations, immaculate conceptions and births.[3]

The illegality of the union of Shechem and Dinah, in that it occurred outside of marriage, also portrays the principle that wherever positive and

---

[1] See author's statement concerning the blend of history and allegory in the Bible.

[2] See Glossary—*Tattva*.

[3] q.v. Vol. I of this work, Pt. Five, Ch. I, particularly pp. 212 *et seq*.

negative come into juxtaposition, interaction occurs; for these two represent the eternal poles and the incident of defilement, which may have an historical foundation, is made to reveal an esoteric truth. In addition the principle of causation, acting as retribution or *Nemesis,* is also indicated in the story. Shechem sinned according to convention, so he and his tribe are destroyed in their positive, creative capacity—in verse Twenty-five all the males are slain.

Dinah was the virginal principle inherent in Rachel, despite the latter's maternal office, and so was properly placed amongst her offspring, each of which is descriptive of the nature and the qualities (Zodiacal) inherent in their mother. Rachel, Dinah, Rebekah and Leah are one in reality, all of them personifying the feminine principle of Deity, the negative current of the triple creative Agency and Power. Rachel, as the universal maternal principle, gives birth to the two post-Israel Logoi—Joseph conceived in Padan-aram and Benjamin in Canaan.

A MYSTICAL SIGNIFICANCE OF CIRCUMCISION

The craft employed to ensnare the Shechemites may perhaps be regarded as a blind concealing an under-meaning. The rite of circumcision is, however, susceptible of interpretation as referring to the sublimation of the creative energy, after which it is no longer used for physical procreation. Although the rite was not peculiar to the Hebrew people, it became interpreted as a special sign of their covenant with Jehovah.[1] Various views are held concerning the original purpose of circumcision such as, for example: that it was intended as an offering of part of the body as a sacrifice to the Deity; that it evidenced consecration of the organs of reproduction and of the procreative function; that it was practised in the hope that it might secure a blessing from the Goddess of Fertility; that it was begun and practised as a mere physical convenience—hygienic purposes, for example. Eventually it became the symbol of the choice of the Hebrew peoples by the Deity. It was also regarded as the outward and visible sign of an inward and spiritual grace, the sixth verse of the Thirtieth Chapter of Deuteronomy referring to " circumcision of the heart "—an attitude of mind which enabled the people of Israel to love God with all their hearts. St. Paul discarded the outward rite and advanced the view that he who had interior spiritual experience did not need the outward sign.[2]

The statement that all the male Shechemites were slain may also be regarded as descriptive of a state of consciousness, for death in the Sacred Language always refers to cessation of awareness at the level at which it

---

[1] *Gen.* 17: 9–14.
[2] *Rom.* 2: 28 *et seq.*

supposedly occurs and the attainment of consciousness at a certain higher level. Decapitation, for example, as in the case of Goliath and John the Baptist, is susceptible of interpretation as the restriction of the power of the higher analytical and critical tendencies of the formal mind which limit facility for intuitive perception, and in consequence make possible a greater ability to be aware at the level of the abstract and intuitive intelligence.

Whilst a possible historical reading is not discounted, mystically no individuals necessarily passed through these extraordinary experiences related in the Old Testament. Each participant is made to personify a power and a principle in Nature, and the whole story of their actions to portray universal laws and processes. The post-circumcision soreness of the Shechemites, which exoterically produced their downfall, symbolises the temporary pain inseparable from the complete renunciation of physical sex life. When complete this renunciation leads to the exclusively spiritual and intellectual exercise of the creative power, allegorically described as the establishment of a covenant with God. This is symbolised as physical death, for in that sense also the Shechemites " die " or no longer exercise a particular physical function.

CHAPTER XII

JACOB OBEYS THE COMMAND OF GOD

Gen. 35:   *God sendeth Jacob to Beth-el: he purgeth his house of idols, and buildeth an altar; God blesseth him there. Rachel beareth Benjamin, and dies. The sons of Jacob. Isaac's death.*

Gen. 35: 1. *And God said unto Jacob, Arise, go up to Beth-el, and dwell there: and make there an altar unto God, that appeared unto thee when thou fleddest from the face of Esau thy brother.*

The journey from Padan-aram is further described in this Chapter. Whilst the narration of purely physical and objective events may be so read, and even accepted as true, direct personal intervention in the life of an individual or a family by the Supreme Deity of the Universe can less easily be so regarded. Fear of vengeance[1] may well have hastened the travellers on their way, but the words of God to Jacob at once draw attention to a possible occult interpretation of the narrative and may even provide a key to its deeper significance. If that view be accepted and applied, then the story of this journey may be read as allegorically portraying the transference of His potentialities and powers by the Logos of one period of divine manifestation to the Logos or Lord of the immediately succeeding dispensation. If such be the intention of the authors of the *Pentateuch*, as is suggested by erudite commentators—especially the learned Kabbalists earlier quoted—then Hebrew Patriarchs are made to personify the ensouling power, life and Intelligence (Logos) of a Universe within the larger divine manifestation, which is the Cosmos as a whole. Thus read, the inclusion of direct intervention by the Logos of this Solar System in a supposed history of a primitive Semitic tribe would, as suggested above, be understandable.

As is so often found in the Bible, cyclic recurrence is again indicated. Instructions are given by God that key points and places of earlier cycles are to be revisited and actions previously performed at those places are to be repeated, as in fact they were. In particular, a surrender and the setting up of an altar and pillar are described and verbal instructions given and

---

[1] Arising from the deceit successfully practised by Jacob and his mother, Rebekah, upon Isaac, by means of which Jacob obtained the birthright and blessing which properly belonged to Easu as the elder brother (*Gen.* 25 and 27).

obeyed.   Progression along a spiral path is apparently being described; for such progression inevitably brings the traveller to positions in his journey which are directly over corresponding positions on preceding rounds.[1]   At each of these points certain events will tend to recur, this fact accounting for the similarities, both general and particular, which are to be found in so many Biblical allegories of forthgoing and return.

The place called Beth-el is thus made to represent a key phase upon the spirally ascending path followed by the evolving life (the Patriarchs and other leaders) as described in allegory in the Old Testament.   Beth-el, formerly Luz, was so named by Jacob,[2] who built an altar there.[3]   The Bible relates also that Beth-el was occupied by " the house of Joseph "[4] and by " the sons of the prophets.[5] "   It is described as " the king's (Jeroboam's) chapel " and " the king's court ",[6] Jeroboam having set up a calf of gold to be worshipped there.[7]   This idolatry was destroyed by Josiah.[8]   Exoterically Beth-el means " the house of God " and esoterically, when applied to the Macrocosm, it refers to the plane and state of consciousness of the creative *Elohim*,[9] the gods, or in their synthesis and summation the one God.   Beth-el therefore refers to entry upon a " new ", yet repetitive, creative cycle.

The opening verse provides the key to this whole Chapter of *Genesis*, for in it Jacob is ordered to return to a starting point.   How different is his condition on the second occasion from that of the first !   At the opening of one of his creative cycles—for this is the nature of the revelation—he was alone and without possessions apart from his father's blessing, which had been obtained by a subterfuge.   At the close of the cycle his household is large and his possessions, the fruits of his labours, are great.   All was within him potentially when he journeyed forth.   All is made manifest objectively, and perfectly controlled, now that he returns.   He, Jacob, the Logos of a cycle, has completed one round of his spiral ascent.   A new round is to be entered upon, new heights essayed, new greatness achieved, a new " name " assumed and a new manifestation begun.   The close of each round of the spiral evolutionary journey brings the ascending life back to its highest spiritual condition.   Therefore, in a Macrocosmic interpretation, it is to Beth-el—the spiritual state—that Jacob is bidden to return.

[1] see **Charts** facing pp. (42).
[2] *Gen.* 28: 19 and 31: 13.
[3] *Gen.* 35: 1.
[4] *Judges* 1: 22.
[5] *II Kings* 2: 3.
[6] *Amos* 7: 13.
[7] *I Kings* 12: 28–33 and 13: 1.
[8] *II Kings* 23: 15.
[9] *Elohim*—see Glossary.

Gen. 35: 2. *Then Jacob said unto his household, and to all that were with him, Put away the strange gods that are among you, and be clean, and change your garments;*

3. *And let us arise, and go up to Bethel; and I will make there an altar unto God, who answered me in the day of my distress, and was with me in the way which I went.*

4. *And they gave unto Jacob all the strange gods which were in their hand, and all their earrings which were in their ears; and Jacob hid them under the oak which was by Shechem.*

THE LAW OF SACRIFICE OBEYED BY UNIVERSE AND MAN

The command to put away strange gods, to be clean and to change garments, is descriptive of the shedding of material accretions by life in the process of its ascent. Positive creative agencies and negative responses may also be implied; for gods are potencies and their power is of the order of sound, which is heard by the ear. Adornments of the ears—earrings—not unfittingly indicate the material products of creative sound. Together " the strange gods " and the " earrings " thus refer to the preceding creative process, cycle and fruitage, now in the past and so in this sense outgrown, renounced. They must be given back to life or Nature before the new cycle can open. The suggestion of compulsion is, however, inapplicable in the Macrocosmic sense; for the whole process of gradual ascent beyond existing material limitations is inevitable and natural.

Microcosmically effort, sacrifice and renunciation are demanded of those men who, treading the Way of Holiness, would penetrate to higher levels of awareness in advance of the Race. As each plane of consciousness is entered, each cycle and sub-cycle left behind, a certain renunciation of the past is demanded. The standards of the new stage are so much higher than those of the old that the inner attitude represented by the outer habiliments must be changed accordingly. These standards, adornments and material encasements of the past are symbolised in the fourth verse by " strange gods " and " earrings ". A fundamental law is thus enunciated in the opening verses of this Chapter of *Genesis*. It is the law of sacrifice, surrender, self-denudation, which must be " obeyed ", or rather fulfilled, at every advance by those who stand on the threshold of a new and higher level of consciousness and phase of evolution.

The proffered sacrifice of Isaac by Abraham,[1] the poverty of Christ's Nativity,[2] His metaphor of the corn of wheat which must die,[3] His instruction

[1] *Gen.* 22.
[2] *Luke* 2: 12 *et seq*
[3] *Jn.* 12: 24, 25.

to the rich young ruler[1] and His voluntary surrender, crucifixion and death,[2] all exemplify this law which individuals, nations and Cosmoi must obey. The power behind the evolving life is irresistible. If the surrender be not voluntary, it is enforced. " Strange gods " and " earrings " may be either put away or taken away, hence the idolatry of Jeroboam at Beth-el was stamped out by Josiah.[3] Wise is the man who, like the household of Jacob, voluntarily lays aside the attributes appropriate to the past and in consequence peacefully and naturally assumes those of the immediate future. The putting on of clean raiment and of new robes is another symbol of obedience to this law of life.

Burial of the gods and the earrings under an oak tree may thus be regarded as describing allegorically the return of cast-off principles or vestures of both Cosmos and man to their precreative condition within the bosom of Nature, the earth (*Prakriti*). The reabsorption of all forms and vehicles within the ever virgin, yet ever productive, substance of Space is thus indicated. The fact that the place of burial bore the same name as the male fructifying agent which supposedly violated Dinah is noteworthy. Thus the essential elements of both creation and procreation are denoted, namely the male agent (Shechem), the female agent (Dinah), the creative power and life-force (the oak tree), and the fruitage of the past upon which the future is founded. In addition, the laws of cyclic forthgoing and return to the same Source, of surrender and reabsorption, are here revealed.

> Gen. 35: 5. *And they journeyed: and the terror of God was upon the cities that were round about them, and they did not pursue after the sons of Jacob.*
>
> 6. *So Jacob came to Luz, which is in the land of Canaan, that is, Beth-el, he, and all the people that were with him.*
>
> 7. *And he built there an altar, and called the place El-beth-el: because there God appeared unto him, when he fled from the face of his brother.*

The final arc of the circle of forthgoing and return is traversed. The last sub-cycle is completed and the primogenitors of the Jewish Race under their new leader Jacob—personifying a Logos (the *Elohim* and Their abundant powers) and the products of a closing cycle—arrive at the point of the completion of one era of manifestation (*Manvantara*) and the opening of its successor. Insulation of a sphere of influence (Ring-pass-not)[4] is suggested

---

[1] *Lk.* 18: 20–22.
[2] *Lk.* 22 and 23.
[3] *II Kings* 23: 15.
[4] Ring-pass-not—see Glossary.

by the absence of any pursuit by the citizens of surrounding cities, the family of Jacob being thereby granted the desired seclusion. The terror of God which was said to be upon them may refer to dissimilarity of vibrational frequency from other involutionary and evolutionary fields and cycles which prevents mutual infringement.

Luz means light and Beth-el the house of God. Thus Jacob and his people arrive at " the light of the house of God ". In cosmogony light is frequently referred to as the first manifestation of the newly active Logos, the first objective product of resumed creative activity. Again, therefore, the opening of a new cycle and the emergence of new power, life and consciousness in the form of light are indicated. The building of an altar at that place, which thereafter is specifically named, describes in allegory the establishment of divine power and rule endowed with, or specially characterised by, the particular aspects, attributes and potentialities which will be the mark or " name " (*tattva*) of the cycle about to begin.

The so-called " flight " from Esau, the twin brother who was red and hairy, portrays the withdrawal—especially the feminine from the masculine— of the creative pair from each other after fructification is complete. The consequent and subsequent production of a new Universe from the feminine or relatively negative fructified field, ovum or cell then follows. The initial Esau-Jacob creative impulse is carried on and conveyed from Jacob to the females of his household. They, in their turn, continue the process through the children and grandchildren, all of whom allegorically portray profound cosmogonical truths.

Reunited, Esau and Jacob embraced and wept. Again they parted, Esau to go to Mount Seir and Jacob to journey on to his new field of productivity. It should be remembered, however, that all cosmogonical processes are subjective in the beginning and occur *within* the triune creative Agency under eternal law. Expositions, allegories and personifications are false if and when they indicate separate forces external to each other. All happens within the One, which only seemingly becomes the many after initial self-fructification and the symbolic enunciation of the " Word ", followed by self-manifestation as light. It should ever be remembered that One is All and All is One, this being the key to the comprehension of spiritual truths. The student should therefore not be misled by the supposed journeyings of the principal characters in allegorical accounts of Cosmogenesis. In the Sacred Language a journey implies only an interior change and nearly always the " birth ", development and perfecting of " new " powers. As all happens to one individual, whether the Logos of a Universe or the Monad, Ego or personality of a man, so all happens in the same place, which is the involutionary and evolutionary field, and even this is less a location than a state of being.

THE SIGNIFICANCE OF THE CHANGE IN JACOB'S NAME

Gen. 35: 8. *But Deborah Rebekah's nurse died, and she was buried beneath Beth-el under an oak: and the name of it was called Allon-bachuth.*

9. *And God appeared unto Jacob again, when he came out of Padan-aram, and blessed him.*

10. *And God said unto him, Thy name is Jacob: thy name shall not be called any more Jacob, but Israel shall be thy name: and he called his name Israel.*

11. *And God said unto him, I am God Almighty: be fruitful and multiply; a nation and a company of nations shall be of thee, and kings shall come out of thy loins;*

12. *And the land which I gave Abraham and Isaac, to thee I will give it, and to thy seed after thee will I give the land.*

13. *And God went up from him in the place where he talked with him.*

A MACROCOSMIC INTERPRETATION

Cosmic symbolism is here reintroduced. Whilst Rebekah represented the root substance of the Isaachian Universe, Deborah, her nurse, personifies its outermost and densest manifestation. The two together may be taken to typify the noumenon and the phenomenon of the preceding era. The cycle of its successor, that of Jacob, having been initiated, any limiting impress of the preceding *Manvantara* is now outgrown. Metaphorically Deborah, as the physical nature of the Isaac-Rebekah epoch, dies. The substance of that epoch goes back to the primordial state, to be used anew. Deborah is thus placed in the earth under an oak tree, the symbolism being the same as that applying to the buried earrings and gods.[1]

Allon-bachuth (oak of weeping) might be interpreted as mourning for the death of the old, even though it also implies the birth of the new. The name constitutes a password from one state to the next, a secret communion between Hierophant and successor, the justifying and proving " Word ". The past outgrown, the present established and the future prepared for, the creative impulse is again released. God appears unto Jacob, blesses (empowers) him and " speaks " to him, once more telling him to change his name to Israel.[2] This latter procedure has already been partially interpreted, as has the promise of extreme fertility. Another group of frequencies of oscillation is enunciated—or named—and the inevitable fruits of it are anticipated.

[1] Gen. 35: 4.
[2] Gen. 32: 28.

In terms of creative potencies, Jacob has hitherto been presented as receptive, passive, even feminine.   In this guise he participates in the production of a Universe with his twin brother Esau who, being red and hairy, clearly personifies the active, positive, masculine potency.   When, however, Jacob is himself to emerge as a succeeding Creator and Patriarch, he is ordered to change his name, and so also his entire character, from negative as before to positive from now on.   A new triplicity arises from the One into which the preceding cycle had been merged.   Israel becomes the First Aspect (*Purusha*), Rachel the Third (*Prakriti*) and their child, Benjamin, the Second (the *Christos*).   Thus the new dispensation is initiated, the close of its predecessor having been described by means of historical allegory.

Gen. 36: 14.   *And Jacob set up a pillar in the place where he talked with him, even a pillar of stone: and he poured a drink offering thereon, and he poured oil thereon.*

15.   *And Jacob called the name of the place where God spake with him, Beth-el.*

The symbol of the pillar is again—as so often—used to denote the active potency.   In order to indicate the opening of that phase at which the creative energy enters the new field, the ceremony of setting up a pillar of stone, anointing and consecrating it and naming its location " Beth-el ", is now introduced into the Biblical narrative.   Successive creative epochs within the period of major cosmic manifestation (*Maha-Manvantara*)[1] are here indicated.   Preceding pre-pillar periods are concerned with the reception of the Archetype and the production and selection of spiritual powers and material attributes.

Transferred potencies are generally described in allegory by naming a location and renaming a Logos-to-be.   Thereupon the " new " field is approached, this being, of course, the " old " or preceding field or area within which manifestation is to occur.   The divine impulse is then received and transmitted, as is allegorically portrayed by speech with the Lord God or the primal " Word ".   The promise is made of extreme productivity and the command is given to go forth into the new field, or country, and exercise patriarchal functions.   Thereupon the tribe and their cattle— symbols of " seeds " and potencies to be developed in the new epoch—are made to journey onwards to the new home, the path of forthgoing being thus described.   All of these episodes are of profound cosmogonical significance.   Each place-name, altar, person and event typifies both a power and a principle involved in the Macrocosmic creative process.   All repetitions of these patriarchal actions constitute minor books of genesis, or allegories of processes of universal generation.

[1] *Maha-Manvantara*—see Glossary.

ISRAEL AS THE SPIRITUAL SELF OF MAN

Since man is a microcosm, persons, actions and events are equally applicable to the emanation of a Ray of the human Monad into the evolutionary field. There it becomes clothed in bodies of increasing density, eventually outgrows their limitations, and develops to full potency the hitherto latent powers. Similarly the descent of the spiritual Soul, the Ego, into each successive incarnation[1] and the genetic principles involved, are symbolically described. The pillars, therefore, are signs that the masculine potency (Israel) is active and is entering the feminine (Rachel), as a result of which a new Universe and new generations of men are to appear. The setting up of the pillars and their anointing are spirituo-phallic and indicate the consecrated, divine nature of the cosmogonical and human genetic processes.

THE MYSTIC BIRTH

In a possible Initiatory interpretation of these verses the Candidate for Initiation, and for re-Initiation at a higher level, is represented by Jacob-Israel. Preparations for a further Rite and for passage through a higher Degree or Grade in the Greater Mysteries are also indicated. During the Initiatory Rite the Monad of the Candidate and his spiritual Self, or Ego, are brought into intimate relationship. Thus in verses ten, eleven and twelve God instructs Israel, who willingly obeys. The creative fire in the body and especially in the cerebro-spinal system, which is represented by the pillar, is further sublimated or " set up ", meaning directed upwards, its energy being consecrated to purely intellectual and spiritual creativity. Thereafter a new level of consciousness is entered and a " new " being is born from the " old ", as symbolised by the fact that the dying Rachel gave birth to Benjamin. Ever must the old, meaning the preceding, be displaced by the new, and this obtains on both the Spirit and the matter sides of the Cosmos as a whole, and applies equally to the successive incarnations and Initiations of man.

> Gen. 35: 16. *And they journeyed from Beth-el; and there was but a little way to come to Ephrath: and Rachel travailed, and she had hard labour.*
>
> 17. *And it came to pass, when she was in hard labour, that the midwife said unto her, Fear not; thou shalt have this son also.*

---

[1] As described in Pt. Two, Ch. II of this Volume, the doctrine of the evolution to ultimate perfection of the spiritual Self of man by means of successive lives on Earth—or reincarnation—is accepted and applied throughout this work. q.v. also: *Reincarnation, Fact or Fallacy ?*, Geoffrey Hodson.

18. *And it came to pass, as her Soul was in departing, (for she died) that she called his name Ben-oni: but his father called him Benjamin.*

19. *And Rachel died, and was buried in the way to Ephrath, which is Beth-lehem.*

20. *And Jacob set a pillar upon her grave: that is the pillar of Rachel's grave unto this day.*

Rachel's travail and death further portray both the intensity of effort and the self-surrender demanded of all, whether Logoi or men, who would and do advance from one dispensation or state of existence to its natural successor.

The double naming of the offspring, first by the mother and then by the father, indicates that both matter (Rachel) and Spirit (Jacob) transmit their powers and attributes to each " new " creation. The order of the naming correctly shows that the attributes of matter predominate in the early phases of manifestation and evolution and those of Spirit in the later stages. Furthermore, the fact that the name given by Israel is the one adopted indicates the preponderance and eventual triumph of Spirit over matter.

Those students and readers of the Bible who prefer a literal rather than an interpretative reading are reminded that a strictly historical narrative would hardly be likely to include direct, objective conversation with the Lord God and the receipt of instructions and promises from Him. Neither would it contain the repeated accounts of actions and events which so accurately, if allegorically, describe Macrocosmic, microcosmic, natural and Initiatory genetical principles, laws and processes. As these descriptions constantly appear and re-appear in many Books of the Bible, strong support is given to the view that the authors were inspired Initiates who had acquired cosmogonical, occult and mystical knowledge at their Initiations into the Greater Mysteries and thereafter sought to share it with humanity. This they did by revealing their acquired wisdom by means of allegorical stories of the primeval creation of the Universe and of events presumed to have occurred on this planet, including the appearance of the first man and woman, a global flood and the preservation by Noah of his family and certain animals in an ark, and pseudo-historical references to the birth and development, under divine direction, of the Israelite nation. This view is further supported by the constant use of the universal system of symbolism which is employed in the Scriptures and religious art of other ancient nations, and is always readily susceptible of the same interpretation.

Gen. 35: 21. *And Israel journeyed, and spread his tent beyond the tower of Edar.*

22. *And it came to pass, when Israel dwelt in that land, that Reuben went and lay with Bilhah his father's concubine: and Israel heard it. Now the sons of Jacob were twelve:*

23. *The sons of Leah; Reuben, Jacob's firstborn, and Simeon, and Levi, and Judah, and Issachar, and Zebulun:*

24. *The sons of Rachel; Joseph, and Benjamin:*

25. *And the sons of Bilhah, Rachel's handmaid; Dan, and Naphtali:*

26. *And the sons of Zilpah, Leah's handmaid; Gad, and Asher: these are the sons of Jacob, which were born to him in Padan-aram.*

27. *And Jacob came unto Isaac his father unto Mamre, unto the city of Arbah, which is Hebron, where Abraham and Isaac sojourned.*

28. *And the days of Isaac were an hundred and fourscore years.*

29. *And Isaac gave up the ghost, and died, and was gathered unto his people, being old and full of days: and his sons Esau and Jacob buried him.*

With the death of Rachel—and shortly afterwards of Israel—a dispensation comes to a close and the new or Joseph *Manvantara* is about to begin. The transition is indicated by the continued but brief journeying of the household, creative activity within it, and the enumeration of the progeny of Israel.

Certain occult numbers are introduced into these verses which deserve consideration. The number 1 is indicated by the tower of Edar, as also by the pillar at Rachel's tomb. This number, which is conceptive, Initiatory and phallic, refers to primary creative activity and the inception of that which is new. Reuben and Bilhah constitute a dyad and their intercourse portrays the generative activity and productivity characteristic of a pair, or the number 2.

The next mentioned number is 12, which by reduction is 3 and so indicates natural, numerical and creative progression. 3 is always indicative of completion of a phase of primordial creative activity consisting of the positive (father), the negative (mother) and their united offspring. 12 as a number also indicates totality, completion, a statement of the cosmic whole. All possible products are included in this number and, in consequence, at the close of the Israel dispensation the whole twelve children are named, indicating full attainment and the perfected expression of all potentialities. The twelve Signs of the Zodiac, with which the twelve sons of Israel are in correspondence and of which they are personifications, represent astrologically,[1] astronomically and numerically the total possibilities and powers of a *Manvantara*. The twelve offspring of Israel thus epitomise the complete fruit of his cycle.

[1] q.v. pp. 386 and 387.

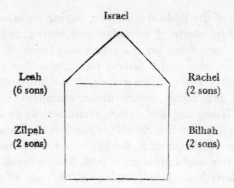

Dinah is universal and symbolises virginal Space which, when fructified, brings forth offspring.   Thereafter she, being emblematic of the condition of virginity, disappears from the scene, to be replaced by Benjamin.   The four mothers, with Israel as father, portray the fivefold Cosmos within which the whole process occurs.   They may be conceived of as a square with the point as apex of an equilateral triangle above.   The point, Israel, is over the square and is in direct relationsip—*via* the sides of the *triangle*—with the wives and in indirect relationship—*via* the sides of the *square*—with their handmaids.   This may be diagrammatically portrayed as above.

THE SEVENFOLD MAN

According to the teachings of the Ancient Wisdom man is a threefold, immortal, spiritual being incarnated in four mortal, material bodies.   The three parts of his spiritual nature are reproductions or reflections in him of the Will, the Wisdom and the Intelligence of the Supreme Deity.   These three together, in their vesture of light, are called the individuality, the Ego in the Causal Body.   The pertinent teaching concerning both the Deity and man is that they are threefold.   God the Trinity reproduces Himself as the threefold spiritual Self or Soul of every human being, each being made in God's image.   In this aspect of his nature man, sometimes called the microcosm, is one with the Divine or the Macrocosm, and therefore is immune from death.   This triple Self is aptly symbolised by an equilateral triangle.

Man's four material bodies in the order of their deepening density are: his mental body, vehicle of thought, the most tenuous of the four; his emotional body, vehicle of feeling and desire, finer than the physical ether; his vital or etheric body, the conserving principle of his vital forces and the link between the superphysical and physical bodies; his physical body, vehicle of awareness and action in the material world.   These four bodies —symbolised by a square—are subject to death and disintegration.

12

The authors of the Biblical narrative, having revealed these numerical laws to mankind by means of metaphor and history, bring the progenitor (Israel) back to one of the great starting and finishing places in *Genesis*, namely to Mamre, and to his father, Isaac, who dies at the age of one hundred and eighty years. This return to the home of Abraham,[1] from which the great pilgrimage began, draws attention to those major and minor cycles of forthgoing and return characteristic of all manifestation, allegorically referred to in the Parable of the Prodigal Son.[2]

By reduction 180 becomes 9, the last of the whole numbers, and indicates the completion and fulfilment of both Macrocosmic and microcosmic periods of manifestation. Isaac, dying at the age of one hundred and eighty, also represents the Monad-Ego dying to the human kingdom and its limitations and entering into Adeptship, with all powers developed and expressed and all duties fulfilled. The death of a Patriarch in Biblical allegories portrays symbolically the profound truth that every advance into a new evolutionary phase depends upon sacrifice, that—as heretofore indicated—all progress demands renunciation, and that every birth produces a death. Jesus enunciated this law in His references to losing life for His sake,[3] meaning in general the sacrifice and surrender of the particular for the universal, and in His description of the germination and growth processes of a corn of wheat.[4]

> *Gen.* 36:   *Esau's family in Canaan. He removeth to mount Seir. His sons. The dukes which descended of his sons. The sons and dukes of Seir. The kings of Edom.*

The Biblical narrative is very far from being a continuous and connected revelation of occult wisdom. The original documents were lost and the oral tradition has in all probability been inaccurately remembered.[5] The

---

[1] *Gen.* 13: 18.

[2] q.v. Vol. I of this work, Pt. Four.

[3] *Matt.* 10: 39. "He that findeth his life shall lose it: and he that loseth his life for my sake shall find it."

[4] *Jn.* 12: 24. "Verily, verily, I say unto you, Except a corn of wheat fall into the ground and die, it abideth alone: but if it die, it bringeth forth much fruit."

[5] One of the four scrolls bought from the Syrian Metropolitan, Mar Athanasius Samuel, at the Monastery of St. Mark in the Old City of Jerusalem, proved to be an Aramaic document related to the *Book of Genesis*, interwoven with various stories, most of them based on those in *Genesis* but with additional details and hitherto unknown names. Passages dealing with *Genesis* 12, 13, 14 and 15 describe how Sarai was taken by the King of Egypt, but Sarai—not Abram—is made to tell the Pharaoh that Abram was her brother. In this scroll Abram himself is apparently the author, for he describes how he was rebuked by the Pharaoh for the deceit and sent away from Egypt with many gifts, "exceedingly rich in cattle and also in silver and in gold. . . ." Reading the portions of the scroll which have been deciphered, it would seem that there are marked differences between *Genesis*

supposed historical records were written with a view to the revelation of occult truths rather than as temporal events.   These were delivered to the esoterically instructed and initiated compilers, with solemn warnings that no power-bestowing secrets were to be directly revealed.

This Thirty-sixth Chapter of *Genesis* constitutes a break in the continuity of occult revelation.   Patriarchal genealogy was interpolated, largely in order that the record might be preserved.   Thus, whilst names and numbers and the succession of the generations are here susceptible of kabbalistic interpretations, it is the next Chapter which provides the more readily discerned revelation.

as we know it and *Genesis* as Abram apparently wrote it.   This supports the ideas both that the originals were lost and that the *Torah* contains amended accounts in which occult revelations are made in the Language of Allegory and Symbol.   q.v. *The Message of the Scrolls*, Yigael Yadin—Grosset and Dunlap, New York.

PART FOUR

THE LIFE OF JOSEPH AS A MYSTERY DRAMA

CHAPTER I

JOSEPH PERSONIFIES THE LOGOS AND ITS MANIFESTATIONS

Gen. 37. Joseph hated [1] *of his brethren: his two dreams: his brethren conspire his death. He is cast into a pit. They sell him to the Ishmaelites, who sell him to Potiphar in Egypt.*

The centre of interest will now be transferred from the Patriarch Jacob to the life history of his son, Joseph. The succession of power and Office is indicated, and it is worthy of note that Joseph's rise to fame occurs not in the land of Canaan, but in Egypt. The story of Joseph, who is presented as a historical character, is also—as are other narratives in the *Pentateuch*—an allegory descriptive of the law of cycles, one major cycle being composed of almost innumerable minor ones. [2] The major cycle of the outpouring of creative life, the emergence of creative Officials, the building of the Cosmos, its densification and the entry of the indwelling life into the deepest depths, are all revealed in that part of the story which states that joseph was out in the field with his brethren, and culminates in the supposedly enforced descent of Joseph into the pit. Incarceration in a pit which had been dug down into the earth—as also the entombment of the Christ " in a sepulchre which was hewn out of a rock " [3]—may be taken as indicating that in the process of involution the emanated Monad-bearing life wave had reached the deepest level of embodiment in solid physical substance, the mineral kingdom of the Earth itself.

The ultimate victory of Spirit over matter, of life over form, is allegorically described in the account of Joseph's rescue from the pit and his later high attainment. The phenomena accompanying both interior unfoldment and outer development of Cosmoi and men leading to the close of a cycle are also portrayed in the closing portion of the story. In conformity with the unchanging rule, plans are made at the close of one

---

[1] An interpretation of the brothers' hate is offered later in this Chapter.

[2] The rotation of a planet on its axis whilst itself circling round the sun partially illustrates this idea, although the number of such related cycles and sub-cycles is far greater than two. The general principle involved is presented in the two diagrams facing pages 42 and 43 of this Volume and in the accompanying descriptive matter.

[3] *Mk.* 15: 46.

cycle for the opening of its successor, the Officients for which are also chosen. Such is a major interpretation of the life of Joseph. It is applicable to Cosmoi, Solar Systems, planets, kingdoms of Nature and the Monads of men, as also to the cycles of the successive reincarnations of the individual spiritual Soul. This remarkable allegory is conceived and related with such skill that it is equally applicable to, and a revelation of the principles governing the processes of involution and evolution in all degrees of magnitude. Experiences and attainments of those Initiates who tread the path of deliberately hastened evolution to perfected manhood, their passage through the Grades of the Lesser and the Greater Mysteries, and the temptations, tests and ordeals to which Aspirants are submitted, are also described in the story of Joseph, which is thus susceptible of Macrocosmic, microcosmic and Initiatory interpretations.

DRAMATIS PERSONAE AS LOGOI AND AS MONADS OF MEN

An elucidation of the story from these points of view demands a preliminary examination of each of the characters. Jacob, the Patriarch, for example, represents both the creative Intelligence or Logoi of a larger cycle and also the human Monad. In the former sense his cycle is drawing to a close and his successor, Joseph, has been produced, equipped (with a coat of many colours [1]) and introduced into the evolutionary field. His marriage to Asenath, the daughter of Potipherah,[2] is interpreted as an indication that he was an Initiate of the Egyptian Mysteries.[3] In some Jewish allegories the Logos is personified by a husbandman, and frequently he was a keeper of flocks. This choice was doubtless influenced by the fact that many of the Patriarchs were indeed wandering herdsmen and sheep breeders, the wealth of the tribes consisting for the most part of their herds and flocks. If this temporal fact be given a spiritual significance, then the symbology is remarkably apt. A Hebrew Patriarch is invested with the powers received from his predecessor, whilst the places and fields in the allegories represent the material Universe. The various kinds of flocks are the Monads of angels and of men which have to be sent out into the field, shepherded, and brought to maturity. The human members of the family of the Patriarch and those of the tribe, namely the shepherds and their wives and children, are seen as the directive spiritual Intelligences, the Sephiroth and Their subordinates.

Creative and evolutionary laws are revealed by means of minor allegories supposedly descriptive of the activities, experiences and adventures

---

[1] *Gen.* 37: 23.
[2] *Gen.* 41: 45.
[3] q.v. *The Secret Doctrine*, Vol. V, p. 266, H. P. Blavatsky.

of these people. In the stories one particular boy is generally chosen as the favourite son who, despite the enmity of jealous brothers, proves to be the lawful successor. At the death of the father this son inherits the flocks, riches and tribal responsibilities, and his life history continues the revelation. Each of the Patriarchs, therefore, personifies the Logos of a System of whatever magnitude, whilst he also represents the Monad of a man. In the former case—as Logos—His inherited possessions are the seeds of life delivered to Him by His predecessor, whilst the additions which He is able to make represent the fruits of His own evolutionary Scheme.

Applied to the Monad, the inheritance [1] is descriptive of innate powers, and the additions represent the gradual evolution of faculties which are the harvest of the successive lives as a reincarnating Ego. The elders of the family may be regarded as those *Dhyan Chohans* or Monads which reached the greatest evolutionary heights in the preceding Scheme and, in consequence, undertake creative responsibilities and Offices in its successor. In the Monadic interpretation these elders and workers in the fields are those Egoic qualities developed in earlier cycles which form the powers and the characteristics of the individuality. Wives, universally interpreted, represent the ensouling, creatively responsive life which is the Soul of matter, and also matter itself. The female members of the Patriarchs' families typify the vehicles of the Monad, especially the Causal Body and the Auric Envelope.[2] In the Initiatory reading women generally personify both the wisdom of the Sanctuaries, the *Gnosis, Theoscphia*, and the Sanctuaries themselves.

JOSEPH AS PERSONIFICATION OF LOGOI

In the narrative of his life Joseph may be regarded as representing both the divine Principle in a Universe and the Spirit-essence or Monad of man. Since he follows his father, Jacob, as the principal character in the story, he may be interpreted as the personification of the Logos of a new Solar System or of any sub-cycle thereof.[3] His story, thus read, is that of the transference of the centre of creative activity from one *Manvantara* to the next within the *Maha-Manvantara* partly described in the *Pentateuch*. Joseph—as Logos—is also the involving and evolving one life itself, and his story is an allegory of the experiences of that life from its initial manifestation in matter and form (birth and descent into the pit—

---

[1] " Inheritance " is the correct word, because the Monad is a seed of its parent (the Logos), and therefore contains all parental characteristics and all the divine powers in a latent state. q.v. *Reincarnation, Fact or Fallacy*, Geoffrey Hodson.

[2] see Glossary.

[3] see Glossary—Chain.

involution), through periods of increasing importance (rescue and Vice-Regency—evolution), to full expression (feeding the nations), followed by his death (end of *Manvantara*). Joseph is also the sun from dawn (birth) to meridian (Rulership in Egypt), and on to setting (death). Uniting these into a single concept, Joseph typifies the Solar Logos Whose involution culminates in entombment in the mineral kingdom (descent into the pit). This is followed by evolution (deliverance, slavery, and later success in Egypt), all this being allegorically described with great skill. Ultimate full self-manifestation throughout the Solar System and full fruition at *Manvantara's* close are indicated by the wealth and power to which Joseph attains.

Whilst esoteric philosophy does not admit of a personal God, it is nevertheless based upon the concept of the ubiquitous presence of an Absolute Deity.[1] As a unit, the Absolute is incomprehensible to the finite intellect, but Its emanated divine powers are regarded as the Source of all that breathes, lives and has objective existence. The One Supreme, Unknowable and Unnameable, the One without a Second, dwelt in the personified symbols or collections of divine Personalities [2] which were the gods, Patriarchs and semi-divine heroes of the Scriptures and Myths of ancient peoples.

JOSEPH AS MONAD OF MAN

Jacob, father of Joseph, represents—as earlier stated—the Logos of the preceding Solar System, whilst Joseph himself portrays the Monad of man which comes forth from the parent Source endowed with the parental qualities (brothers and one sister). The involution and evolution of the Monadic Ray through the seven planes and kingdoms of Nature to individual Egohood is described in the narrative of the early period of Joseph's life. The coat of many colours provided by his father is the aura as a whole, with special reference to the *Augoeides*.[3] In this microcosmic view physical incarnation is represented by the descent into the pit and the time spent there. Death is portrayed by elevation from the pit. Passage through the Underworld,[4] the region of desire, is indicated by the period of slavery, the imprisonment, and the enticements of the wife of Potiphar.

Ascension beyond the realm of desire and the casting off of the desire body, followed by entry into the Heaven World (Mental and Higher

---

[1] see Glossary—The Absolute.

[2] q. v. *The Secret Doctrine*, Vol. V, p. 462, H. P. Blavatsky.

[3] *Augoeides*—see Glossary.

[4] Underworld—the Astral Plane entered after death. q. v. *Through the Gateway of Death*, Geoffrey Hodson.

Mental Planes), are portrayed both by favours received by Joseph from Pharaoh and by his continually increasing prestige and power. The withdrawal of all the fruits of the life cycle into the Higher Self, and the inception of a new incarnation, are allegorically described by the events of the closing years, particularly the feeding of Joseph's family. The new Incarnation itself is represented by Benjamin, in whose sack of corn is placed a silver cup, symbol of Egoic power, life and consciousness.

JOSEPH AS INITIATE

The entry of the Monad-Ego upon the Path of Holiness is also portrayed in the life story of Joseph. The tests and trials of an Initiate (false accusation and imprisonment), the growing wisdom, the advancement, the favours of the land of Egypt and its Pharaoh—these indicate the procedures of Initiation into and through the Lesser and Greater Mysteries. The services rendered by Joseph and his death refer to "Ascension" or Adeptship.[1] Every Initiate enacts—at first figuratively only (in the Lesser Mysteries) and eventually fully (in the Greater Mysteries) the cycle of manifestation of the Solar Logos and of the human Monad, with both of which he is self-identified, even to the extent of adopting the name of the Deity. Thus the wonderful story of Joseph, one of the most remarkable allegories ever written, is also the story of the one life in both its universal and its individual or Monadic self-manifestations.

Despite its richness of content, the revelation of hidden wisdom is achieved with remarkable economy. Only the bare essentials survive the pruning process to which the narrative would seem to have been submitted. Councils of Initiates were, one assumes, responsible for the original documents, which contained the best of the Biblical allegories. Very close supervision was evidently given, with results which even the maltreatment and distortion of successions of translators and editors have not been able wholly to destroy. Joseph, then, is " the Word " made flesh,[2] the manifested Deity, the Ruler of the Universe in all its manifestations, as the dreams (obviously Zodiacal) of the sheaves and of the heavenly bodies [3] clearly indicate.

Biblical narratives into which the miscalled supernatural intrudes and, without explanation, is blended with natural or physical events, are to be regarded by students of symbolism as of special significance; for in them, it is to be presumed, revelation by allegory is associated with

[1] q.v. Vol. I of this work, Pt. Five, Ch. II, especially p. 224.
[2] Jn. 1: 14.
[3] Gen. 37: 5-11.

historical events. When such intrusions are absent, history is for the most part being related. Occult wisdom is, however, not very far away. For example, the seven-branched candlestick [1] of the Holy of Holies in the Jewish Temple—the Menorah—partly represents this sevenfold esoteric wisdom which, like its symbol, is also a unity. All septenates in Nature, including the seven Chains, Rounds, Globes, Root Races and sub-Races of a single Globe in one Planetary Scheme, the seven Sephiroth and the seven sacred Planets with their presiding Regents, are symbolised by the shape, the knops, the decorations and the lights of the seven-branched candlestick.[2] As these seven lights shone in the darkness to illumine the altar, so the Secret Wisdom shines through this Sanctuary-inspired Jewish history to illumine responsive minds. The mission of the Jews and the purpose of the erudite and Initiated authors of the Bible were, I submit, to preserve, to enunciate and to deliver to humanity this Wisdom of the Chaldeo-Hebrew Sanctuaries. It was for these reasons and not for lordship over the Earth, I suggest, that the Jews were a chosen people, a nation or " kingdom of priests " [3] in very truth. May not their tribulations have partly arisen from their neglect of this mission, and may not their earthly wanderings and centuries of physical homelessness have followed upon and resulted from their departure from their true Sanctuary and the real purpose for which they were " chosen "? Happily the light still shines, however deeply veiled, in and through this marvellous record of the Scriptures of the Hebrew Race.

---

[1] *Ex.* 25: 31–40.

[2] For a fuller interpretation see the inside of the back page of the jacket of this work, and the inside back page of the Quest Editions.

[3] *Ex.* 19: 6.

than all his children.

CHAPTER II

JOSEPH'S COAT OF MANY COLOURS

Gen. 37: 1. *And Jacob dwelt in the land wherein his father was a stranger,
in the land of Canaan.*

In this statement the authors of the *Book of Genesis* make it clear that
a new cycle opened with the birth of Joseph, that of Jacob thus drawing
to a close. Jacob's successor had been born and was later to be taken
into the new field, of which Egypt is the topographical symbol, there to
continue the great succession. In the same way Jacob himself had moved
from Mamre to Canaan, a land in which his father had been a stranger.

Gen. 37: 2. *These are the generations of Jacob. Joseph being seventeen
years old, was feeding the flock with his brethren; and the
lad was with the sons of Bilhah, and with the sons of Zilpah,
his father's wives; and Joseph brought unto his father their
evil report.*

3. *Now Israel loved Joseph more than all his children, because
he was the son of his old age: and he made him a coat of many
colours.*

4. *And when his brethren saw that their father loved him more
than all his brethren, they hated him, and could not speak
peaceably unto him.*

The age of Joseph—seventeen—is here deliberately introduced. The
numbers 7 and 1 each refer to generative activity, for 7 indicates the close
of a minor cycle and 1 the opening of its successor. By reduction the
number 8 is gained, representing the cancellation or equalisation of debts,
the balancing of *karma*. The action of destiny and its agents, as well as
the summation into unity and the absorption by the inner Self of the fruits
of preceding cycles, are also denoted by the number 8.

Jacob, the father, who loved ten of his sons less than the eleventh,
Joseph, and who had yet another and still younger son named Benjamin,
may here be discerned as a symbol of the Logos or incarnate Intelligence
of a Universe. As earlier suggested, the twelve sons each represent one
of the Signs of the Zodiac, meaning powers, attributes and capacities
present within the incarnate Deity and gradually to be developed in man.
Whilst elder sons represent those attributes of earlier times and cycles
already well unfolded but not completely developed, in the younger sons

these powers are as yet but partially awakened. They are therefore temporarily of greater importance or more loved, in the sense of being in receipt of especial care. Thus interpreted, the story of Joseph is an allegory of the development from within the Logos (Jacob) of the Joseph-like powers. Since this was the immediate task, the greatest attention was being bestowed upon it. In this sense " Israel loved Joseph more than all his children ".

THE RADIANT AURAS OF THE IMMORTAL AND THE MORTAL MAN

Since under the Law of Correspondences [1] a correlation exists between numbers and colours, Joseph's coat received from his father (previous lives) may be a symbolical representation of the possession of faculties (fruits of preceding cycles). In the *Augoiedes*, the body of light, in which these faculties are established and upon which they are impressed as vibratory capabilities, each developed capacity is indicated in terms of colour. Hence the true coat of many colours is the shining *Augoiedes* of man. Every human being is also thus enrobed, in the sense that it is the parent Monad whose light shines through both the inner and the outer man. Further-more, it is Monadic power which makes possible the response of the human Ego to the experiences of life as a result of which faculties are developed. The personal, mortal nature is similarly lighted and coloured, the various hues representing temperament, qualities, capacities and faculties of both the immortal Self and the mortal vehicles. The mental and emotional bodies of adult man thus shine with many Egoic and personal hues, but these are physically invisible save to those whose inner eyes are opened. The Ego is personified by Jacob, who gave the coat to his son (the new personality).

In addition to the interpretation already given, the provision of a coat of many colours for Joseph indicates that this special attention caused the associated attributes to shine out, each in its own particular hue, in the aura of the unfolding Logos, and therefore in the auras of those repre-sentative existences in the evolutionary field in whom the powers were being expressed. This verse, then, refers to the temporary accentuation of a special group of qualities by an evolving being, whether Logos or *Manu* [2] of a major Cycle or Monad or Ego of man; for upon these qualities, for the time being, attention is being specially concentrated.

---

[1] Law of Correspondences—see Glossary.

[2] *Manu* (Sk.). A generic term applied to Creators, Preservers and Fashioners. *Manvantara* means literally the period presided over by a *Manu*. According to their function and Office they are called Race *Manus*, Round *Manus* and Chain *Manus*, and so on up to the Solar Logos Himself. See Glossary.

In all interpretations the septenary principle is also indicated by the presence of the seven colours of the spectrum. The Monad, or Father, is the source of the light, and the faculties developed from life's experiences are represented by the colours. Some of the colouration in the *Augoiedes*, however, also portrays certain potential and active qualities in the Monad, as well as the fundamental temperament or Ray.[1] In the mystical sense Joseph is the Monad-Ego bringing illumination and grace to the personality. Every human being is, I repeat, Joseph-like, robed in a coat of many colours. This is the human aura with its many hues, each expressive of a developed power and a quality of character.

JOSEPH IS STRIPT OF HIS COAT OF MANY COLOURS

The symbolism is carried further, in that the coloured auric forces are only visible superphysically, these becoming lost to view when the Soul becomes incarnate in a physical body. Symbolically, Joseph as the conjoined mind, emotions and body of one human incarnation is " robbed " of his coat of many colours. Their frequencies of scintillation are too rapid for physical perception, but not for the clairvoyant. Allegorically, Joseph loses his coat (visible aura) when he is lowered into the pit (incarnated and as seen in the physical body).

Microcosmically, the field in which Joseph was feeding his father's flock represents those planes of Nature in which the Higher Self is to be born (lowered) and to become increasingly active. The descent into a physical body is thus described, and the brothers who bring it about are those *Pitris* [2] and *Devas* responsible for the furthering of progress on the downward arc of an Ego going " down " into incarnation.[3] These exalted Beings are, of course, not really enemies of the pilgrim Soul, though the descent into the depths of matter does for the time being bring about a serious deprivation and limitation of Egoic freedom.

JOSEPH AS THE DIVINE LIFE BECOMES
INCARNATE IN MATTER

Macrocosmically interpreted, Joseph is the Logos of the new cycle to Whom has been handed—by his Predecessor, and in the occult sense Progenitor or Father—the powers and the seeds of living beings, which are the fruits of the previous cycle, also symbolised by the coat of many colours. In the aura of the Logos-to-be all these shine as the solar spectrum at the physical level, and superphysically as the typical colours

---

[1] q.v. *The Seven Human Temperaments*, Geoffrey Hodson.

[2] *Pitris*—see Glossary.

[3] q.v. *The Miracle of Birth*, Geoffrey Hodson.

of the various fundamental forces, frequencies of vibration, planes of Nature and their indwelling Major Intelligences. They constitute the ineffable radiance, the shining aura or, Biblically, the " coat of many colours " of the Logos of a Universe. As Shelley wrote: [1]

" Life like a dome of many coloured glass
Stains the white radiance of eternity."

The story of the supposed antagonism of the elder brothers, their hostility, their actions in stealing Joseph's coat (v. 23) and in lowering him into the pit and all that followed (vs. 24-33) may be regarded as a veil concealing a deeply occult revelation. This concerns the process of the descent of the divine life into the depths of matter, which process is assisted by certain more highly evolved (elder) Intelligences, personified by Joseph's brothers, who were made responsible for lowering him into the pit. Just as such incarceration would be a severe restriction upon Joseph's movements, and the elder brothers who bring it about are in the allegory thus presented as enemies, in like manner matter appears to restrict—to be hostile to—Spirit.[2]

The previously mentioned Intelligences, variously named the Satanic Hierarchies and the Inverse Sephiras,[3] participate and assist in the penetration of the Abyss of Space by the creative Spirit, which means the entry of cosmic electricity—which is life itself—into the limitations of the vast electrical machine which is a Universe. Indirectly Their actions bring about the partial limitation of the normally universal awareness of the First Logos to the locally focused state. This materialising action is as essential to the full and complete manifestation of Spirit in matter as is the apparently opposite assistance given on the Pathway of Return when the embodied Spirit gradually frees itself from the imprisonment temporarily imposed upon it by matter. These seemingly adverse and beneficent functions are not regarded by the philosopher as either evil or good, since both are but parts of an inevadable, impersonal procedure of forthgoing and return.

In order to bring this profoundly metaphysical and power-bestowing knowledge within reach of the uninstructed, and to conceal it against premature discovery and misuse, the two processes have always been represented in the priestly language of all nations as being Satanic and redemptive, evil and good, respectively. Typhon, Ahriman, the Asuras, the Titans and Satan are all allegorically presented in world Scriptures and Mythologies as monstrous embodiments of evil, or the Devil, and so the opposite of good, or God. The " Dark Beings " are no more evil than the fulcrum which offers the necessary resistance to the lever; for,

[1] q.v. The poem, *Adonais*, by Percy Bysshe Shelley.
[2] q.v. *The Kingdom of the Gods*, Pt. Three, Ch. V, Geoffrey Hodson.
[3] *Ibid.*

not unlike the fulcrum, they perform a function essential to the material expression of energy.

Joseph's hostile elder brothers personify these supposedly evil agencies, being in fact none other than certain of the Sephiroth (Inverse Sephiras). In occult philosophy these are referred to as the " first fruits " of preceding cycles, and therefore as elders from the point of view of the present cycle (of return). Such Officials undertake the task of assisting the descent into matter of the triune Spirit-Life-Consciousness, as a result of which this triplicity becomes self-manifest in the field, which is the area between the centre and the circumference of a Universe.

At this point readers who in the course of their studies have learned of the existence of divine Powers of Darkness may wish to enquire concerning these. The Powers of Darkness are those human beings who turn and distort the Forces of Nature, who resist evolutionary progress, who seek the will of the individual self against the will of the Universe. These are the true enemies of man and they definitely exist on Earth. There are certain hallmarks by which evil men, their Movements, Organisations and actions may unfailingly be known. Amongst these are monstrous selfishness, egotism, pride, demoniacal ruthlessness, cruelty, ugliness and intolerance. Behind and within all this exists a continuing egotistical desire to dominate the mind and the life of others; for, the unfailing mark of these enemies of human happiness is fanatical egotism and the denial to man of the all-essential freedom of thought and life. These Powers of Darkness have their human agents. They vary in evolutionary stature from the cruel, lustful, selfish savage (whether called civilised or not) up to the highly intellectual man who works for self, either openly or secretly behind a veil.

In the world's allegorical dramas, when interpreted according to accepted rules, a revelation may be discerned of the powers, processes and events of the first half of the great Cycle, that of forthgoing, during which a Universe is produced and all that it contains is brought to the highest degree of development. The pre-natal period of each human birth is a repetition in miniature of this major procedure. Man, the microcosm, re-enacts continually major Macrocosmic processes. By so doing he, in his turn, brings his own innate powers into expression, and finally to perfection.

Additionally, as we have already seen, Joseph is a symbol of the Logos of the succeeding cycle. He is preparing for the activities of his Office during the period when his predecessor, Jacob, is approaching the end of his cycle. The suggestion of jealousy [1] in the fourth verse is, of course, a blind though not without significance, as has been shown.

[1] As also in the case of the elder brother of the Prodigal Son. q.v. Vol. I of this work, Pt. Four, Ch. II, p. 205 Adyar Ed. and p. 159, Quest Book Ed.

13

Gen. 37: 5. *And Joseph dreamed a dream, and he told it his brethren: and they hated him yet the more.*

6. *And he said unto them, Hear, I pray you, this dream which I have dreamed:*

7. *For, behold, we were binding sheaves in the field, and, lo, my sheaf arose, and also stood upright; and, behold, your sheaves stood round about, and made obeisance to my sheaf.*

8. *And his brethren said to him, Shalt thou indeed reign over us? or shalt thou indeed have dominion over us? And they hated him yet the more for his dreams, and for his words.*

THE LOGOS AS DIVINE HUSBANDMAN

Although doubts may be felt concerning Joseph's wisdom in relating his two dreams to his brethren, they both offer opportunities for interpretation in accordance with the view now being presented, namely that Joseph personifies the successor to his father, Jacob. The increasing importance and ascendancy of the Lord of the new cycle and the Representative of Zodiacal powers are perfectly portrayed in this allegorical dream. The period in the life cycle of forthgoing and return, indicated in the dream, is that of the harvesting of the fruits thereof, the close of the preceding cycle being also clearly implied. The analogy of husbandry is particularly appropriate; for involution may aptly be likened to planting, and evolution to growth and ripening. The process of storing the fruits of the dual process and using them as food and as seed for later cycles corresponds to the harvesting and the preserving of the ripened corn. This, together with the bound sheaves in the field, refers to that closing phase or arc in the cycle at which form, symbolised by root and straw, was being disintegrated. The indwelling life had unfolded further capacities (the grain) through experience in form, and these were being garnered. The ripened seed of the corn plant thus represents acquired characteristics and powers sublimated to their finest essence, thereafter to be retained partly as food (acquired knowledge) and partly as seed for new plantings and harvestings (innate faculties to be manifested and further developed in later incarnations). This is equally applicable to the Macrocosm, where ripened and harvested corn is a symbol of the powers developed by the Logos in the Universe. In their turn these are similarly retained and used (planted) in the succeeding cycle.

Ripened grain is thus a very interesting emblem of those powers which the Monad-Ego has developed in a single life cycle or incarnation and has stored in the Causal Body. The death of the physical body and the later casting off of the astral and mental bodies (*kama-manasic* vestures) are represented by the reaping and subsequent dissolution of root and straw. The winnowing of the grain from the enclosing membrane or chaff corresponds to the withdrawal of the Ego, with its developed powers, from the last vestiges of the disintegrating personality. This occurs at the conclusion of the intermediate period between two Earth lives which follows the separation of the Ego from the lower, mortal principles, which then disintegrate.[1] This is called *Devachan* (Sk.), meaning literally " home of the gods ", and referring also to a state of consciousness in which the fruits of good deeds performed during the preceding Earth life are fully enjoyed. Thereafter a new cycle opens for both Macrocosm and microcosm, since a new physical incarnation also begins for the Monad-Ego

Thus the time period of Joseph's dream corresponds to that of ripened corn and harvesting, or the closing phases of a life cycle. This also implies the near approach of the opening of its successor. In Biblical terms the Israel cycle is closing and the Joseph cycle is about to begin, the Logos of that cycle being represented by Joseph. The powers harvested from the past and preserved, as are seeds in a granary, are depicted by the sheaf of Joseph, each grain of which might be thought of as a Monad of the Macrocosm and a potential power in the microcosm.

Clearly the Logos of a new System is young only in relation to that System, itself new-born. Actually " He " is the most highly evolved Being of the preceding System—its first fruits. In the dream, therefore, though Joseph is the youngest of the brethren his sheaf remains upright, whilst those of his older brothers make obeisance to it; for the brothers, in the Macrocosmic sense, are the assistant *Cosmocratores* or the *Dhyan Chohans*, the Sephirothal manifestation of powers and attributes of the Solar Logos Itself.

The dream of Joseph is thus a symbolical dramatisation of universal processes and procedures. It also portrays the Logos-to-be absorbed in contemplation of the numerical principles and laws by which He first " dreams ", or mentally conceives, the future Universe which He will later project as an external expression in time and space. A hint of this occurs in Lewis Carrol's book, *Alice Through the Looking-Glass*—a highly, if unconsciously, allegorical work. The reader is referred to the incident of the finding of the dreaming and snoring Red King by Alice, Tweedledum and Tweedledee. Thus interpreted, Alice would represent the Ego and the twins the Higher and Lower Mind with whom she dances, debates, and visits the Red King. In the King's presence she is told by them that she, like themselves, is not real but " only a thing in his dream ". This is a parallel to the Eastern (Vedantic) doctrine of *Maya*, in which only the

---

[1] For a fuller exposition of this process see *Through the Gateway of Death*, Geoffrey Hodson.

changeless and eternal Principle is Real. All that changes, meaning the manifested Universe and its contents, is from this point of view *Maya*—an illusion or dream. The divine Dreamer—the Red King in the book—is also thought of as the Logos rapt in contemplation—the *Maha-Yogi* Whose creative ideas are the Archetypes according to which all forms are moulded, in this sense being but dreams.

If, at this point, it be asked why the oldest son or brother does not become the Logos of the new cycle, since presumably he would personify the most highly developed product, or son, it is to be remembered that in a Solar System there are many Offices as well as many *Dhyan Chohanic* fruits. The line of succession to each Office is carefully preserved, each being occupied by a member of the Sephiroth according to predominant attributes. These differing Offices and functions in the externalisation of divine Thought, or production of an objective Universe, are well presented and explained in the Kabbalistic Tree of Life with its Ten Sephiras, each an Agent for the outpoured divine life.[1]

Joseph-like, the chosen Logos is then " born " or deeply incarnated, in one sense imprisoned (lowered into the pit) within the matter of the Solar System, this being the divine Immanence. Thus clothed, He is a new creation. His manifestation is symbolised by a Nativity and He portrayed as a little child. In one sense He has surrendered His full spiritual freedom by that voluntary " birth ". Even whilst in His highest consciousness and being, His Transcendence, He is still free, nevertheless in His material manifestation within the limits of His Solar System He is bound. Similarly the Monad-Ego of man is transcendent in relation to its mortal personality, whilst during incarnation it is partially bound within the imprisonment of the physical body.

The *Dhyan Chohans*, however, are not all similarly restricted. The Offices held by the majority of Them are fulfilled at lofty spiritual levels alone, where life and consciousness, though circumscribed, are not wholly limited as is the case at the physical level. These Officials are not, therefore, " born ". All this is brilliantly shown in Joseph's dream of his upright sheaf to which those of his older brothers make obeisance. Again, in order that these profound truths may be veiled from the profane, the purely human attribute of capacity for jealousy and hatred is drawn as a cover or blind over the revelation.[2]

> *Gen.* 37: 9. *And he dreamed yet another dream, and told it to his brethren, and said, Behold, I have dreamed a dream more; and, behold, the sun and the moon and the eleven stars made obeisance to me.*

---

[1] See Appendix—" The Sephirothal Tree ".

[2] cf. Loki, Hagen, Typhon-Set, the Titans, King Kamsa and Devadatta.

10. *And he told it to his father, and to his brethren: and his father rebuked him, and said unto him, What is this dream that thou hast dreamed? Shall I and thy mother and thy brethren indeed come to bow down ourselves to thee to the earth?*

11. *And his brethren envied him; but his father observed the saying.*

JOSEPH'S DREAM OF CELESTIAL BODIES

Here the Macrocosmic principles of "Creation" are deliberately indicated. Human beings are eliminated from the allegory, the brothers being represented by the sun, moon and eleven stars. The sun is the Logos, the moon is the matter of the Universe, and the eleven stars are Zodiacal Powers and Intelligences, twelve in all when conjoined with the sun.

In the microcosmic interpretation the sun is the individual *Atma*, the Monad in manifestation both as an Ego and as a personality. The moon is the individual *Prakriti*, the Monad-illumined and thus specialised substance of all the vehicles, and particularly of those of the mortal man in any one incarnation; for the moon is the planet of generation, death and disintegration. This substance of which the superphysical and physical bodies are built corresponds universally to the matter of the planes of Nature and to the sheaths of differing degree of density in which the one life is clothed.

The stars correspond to the intelligent life-essence of each of the bodies or Principles of man. However, it was not the physical celestial bodies which made obeisance in the dream but rather their informing Intelligences, whose collaboration was obtained. The life-essence of each of man's bodies is vibrationally attuned to the informing Spirit or *Dhyan Chohan* of one of the stars. These vibrate in unison, interaction continually occurring.

Normally the interior, Zodiacal qualities in man and the external influences of the twelve Signs are beyond human control. When the later stages of evolution are entered upon, however, the Monad assumes increasing control of Planetary, stellar and Zodiacal attributes and influences on the one hand, and of their effects upon his various vehicles on the other. Ultimately he completely masters them, and it is this state which is mirrored in the two dreams of Joseph.

This Chapter of *Genesis* and these verses may, I suggest, be regarded as typical examples of the revelation and yet concealment of potentially power-bestowing knowledge. As above interpreted, the dream refers to the kabbalistic doctrine that—as stated in the opening pages of this Volume—the whole Universe with all its parts, from the highest plane down to physical Nature, is regarded as being interlocked, interwoven, to make a single whole—one body, one organism, one power, one life, one consciousness, all cyclically evolving under one law.   The " organs " or parts of the Macrocosm, though apparently separated in space and plane of manifestation, are in fact harmoniously inter-related, inter-communicative, and continually interactive.   *The human being who discovers this truth could enter the power aspect of the Universe and tap any one of these forces. He would then become endowed with almost irresistible influence over both Nature and his fellow men.*   A similar example of the use of the Sacred Language is given in the story of Joshua making the sun and the moon stand still.[1]

Returning to the Thirty-seventh Chapter of *Genesis*, Joseph personifies the forthgoing Ray of the Monad (*Ātma*) nearing Adeptship, and therefore capable of controlling the manifestation in him of the solar and lunar forces.   This achieved, the mind of the Initiate is both perpetually illumined (it is always day) and able to overcome all adverse attributes (enemies) hitherto present in his human nature.

In the story of Joseph the whole incident happens in a dream, thus implying a supramundane state of awareness.   Acting consciously in his immortal Selfhood Joseph, type of all Initiates, brings his vehicles, their powers and their attributes under the direction of his will.   These are represented by his brothers who, correctly in one sense, resent the idea of being placed in a subordinate position.   The father, however, or Monad, comprehends or observes " the saying ".

Gen. 37: 12. *And his brethren went to feed their father's flock in Shechem.*

13. *And Israel said unto Joseph, Do not thy brethren feed the flock in Shechem? come, and I will send thee unto them.   And he said to him, Here am I.*

14. *And he said to him, Go, I pray thee, see whether it be well with thy brethren; and well with the flocks; and bring me word again.   So he sent him out of the vale of Hebron, and he came to Shechem.*

15. *And a certain man found him, and, behold, he was wandering in the field; and the man asked him, saying, What seekest thou?*

16. *And he said, I seek my brethren; tell me, I pray thee, where they feed their flocks.*

17. *And the man said, They are departed hence; for I heard them say, Let us go to Dothan.   And Joseph went after his brethren, and found them in Dothan.*

18. *And when they saw him afar off, even before he came near unto them, they conspired against him to slay him.*

19. *And they said one to another, Behold, this dreamer cometh.*

---

[1] *Joshua* 10: 12–14.

20. *Come now therefore, and let us slay him, and cast him into some pit, and we will say, Some evil beast hath devoured him: and we shall see what will become of his dreams.*

21. *And Reuben heard it, and he delivered him out of their hands; and said, Let us not kill him.*

22. *And Reuben said unto them, Shed no blood, but cast him into this pit that is in the wilderness, and lay no hand upon him; that he might rid him out of their hands, to deliver him to his father again.*

23. *And it came to pass, when Joseph was come unto his brethren, that they stript Joseph out of his coat, his coat of many colours that was on him;*

24. *And they took him, and cast him into a pit: and the pit was empty, there was no water in it.*

25. *And they sat down to eat bread: and they lifted up their eyes and looked, and, behold, a company of Ishmeelites came from Gilead with their camels bearing spicery and balm and myrrh, going to carry it down to Egypt.*

26. *And Judah said unto his brethren, What profit is it if we slay our brother, and conceal his blood?*

27. *Come, and let us sell him to the Ishmeelites, and let not our hand be upon him; for he is our brother and our flesh. And his brethren were content.*

28. *Then there passed by Midianites merchantmen; and they drew and lifted up Joseph out of the pit, and sold Joseph to the Ishmeelites for twenty pieces of silver: and they brought Joseph into Egypt.*

29. *And Reuben returned unto the pit; and, behold, Joseph was not in the pit; and he rent his clothes.*

30. *And he returned unto his brethren, and said, The child is not; and I, whither shall I go?*

31. *And they took Joseph's coat, and killed a kid of the goats, and dipped the coat in the blood;*

32. *And they sent the coat of many colours, and they brought it to their father; and said, This have we found: know now whether it be thy son's coat or no.*

33. *And he knew it, and said, It is my son's coat; an evil beast hath devoured him; Joseph is without doubt rent in pieces.*

34. *And Jacob rent his clothes, and put sackcloth upon his loins, and mourned for his son many days.*

35. *And all his sons and all his daughters rose up to comfort him; but he refused to be comforted; and he said, For I will go down*

into the grave unto my son mourning.. Thus his father wept for him.

36. *And the Midianites sold him into Egypt unto Potiphar, an officer of Pharaoh's, and captain of the guard.*

The reader is here referred to the passage on Cosmogenesis at the beginning of part three of this Volume. A study of the life of Joseph as an allegorical description of the emanation of creative and formative power, life and Intelligence (Logos), and of the shaping of Universes with all which they produce, is here offered. As Joseph is lowered into a pit deep in the earth, so these Logoic attributes become embodied, " lowered ", " imprisoned ", " buried " in densest matter. This descent is followed by an ascent out of the depths towards the spiritual heights, a procedure which is also symbolically portrayed in the life story of Joseph by his liberation from the pit and transportation to Egypt. All this Wisdom of the Ages concerning the " creation " and perfecting of Universes is, I suggest, perceptible in these closing Chapters of the *Book of Genesis.*

The first " Being " to emerge from infinity to finiteness is the supreme Emanator, personified in this allegory by Israel in conscious unity with the Lord God.[1] From this concentration of the irresistible, outpoured, creative power there further emerges a more individual manifestation thereof. This " Being " is to perform the function of an active Logos throughout the life-period (*Manvantara*) of the Universe-to-be. Personified by Joseph, who was sent out by his father into the field, the Logos— Joseph-like—goes out into the " field "—the area of Self-manifestation and evolution.

The hostility of the brothers then met with is a cleverly constructed and very effective blind for the collaboration between the Logos and His " Hosts ", the Archangel and angel Hierarchies associated with the whole vast enterprise of the emanation, fashioning and evolution of a Universe. These are jealous, hostile and actively destructive only in the sense that their task is to " allure ", " induct ", " imprison " and " enchain " (allegorically) the Logoic life and its Source.[2] All that is described in the above verses of Chapter Thirty-seven is susceptible of interpretation in these terms.

The reader may here be reminded that one of the methods used by writers of the Sacred Language is to conceal and yet reveal a profound and normally secret, because power-bestowing, knowledge by describing it in reverse. In such a case the characters in the stories will be made to act in enmity to the hero, to be directly hostile and to plot—and even

---

[1] *Gen.* 28: 13–15.

[2] q.v. *The Kingdom of the Gods,* Pt. Three, Ch. V, " The Inverse Sephiras and the Problem of Evil ".

achieve in some measure—his downfall even if, as in Joseph's case, this proved to be only temporary. The fact, be it remembered, is that they personify agencies active in the formation of Universes and planets and in the generative processes in the organic kingdoms of physical Nature. Thus, though made to appear evil, these Agencies (*Elohim* [1]) are actually beneficent. The murderous intentions of Joseph's brethren towards him, for example, and the way in which these intentions were actively expressed, constitute an allegory of the very opposite relationship between the Logos and the cosmic genetic Agencies. This relationship is, of course, entirely collaborative. Such a method of writing is to be discerned in many of the Myths and Scriptures of ancient peoples, in which great material Powers are made to be at war with whichever character in the story is personifying the Logos. This hostility is only apparent, and the way in which it is described is a cover or blind for the *real* revelation.

If it be objected that such a method is unnecessary, it is repeated that Powers and procedures are being revealed whereby a developed will can control human minds for better or for worse. The need for secrecy thus becomes apparent, particularly in descriptions of emanative and formative processes. Another reason for the original secrecy was that this deeply occult knowledge was in ancient times imparted under a vow of silence to Initiated Members of the Temples of the Greater Mysteries. Times change, however, and the esotericism of one age becomes the exoteric knowledge of a successor. Hence it is permissible nowadays openly to refer to certain, but not all, ideas which originally were wrapped in the profoundest secrecy. The real revelation, however, is not of ideas stated in words, but rather consists of the direct experience itself—in this case actually to see the *Elohim* at work.

JOSEPH—PERSONIFICATION OF THE ETERNAL WISDOM

A further possible interpretation of the great allegories must not be overlooked. It is founded upon the application of the first of the four keys, namely that all the recorded, supposedly external, historical events also occur interiorly. All happens within every individual, each event being descriptive of a subjective experience of man, whether advancing by the normal evolutionary method or achieving hastened unfoldment by treading the Way of Holiness. The latter choice is made after the spiritual Self has begun to illumine the mortal man, who in eventual response seeks and finds spiritual wisdom and a Temple of the Mysteries wherein successive Initiations are conferred. Such a possible interpretation of the life of Joseph is now considered.

---

[1] *Elohim*—see Glossary.

Patriarchs and heroes are thus regarded as personifications of the Eternal Wisdom, the *Gnosis* itself. Their adventures, trials and triumphs portray the process of bringing illumination to the human mind, collective and individual. From this point of view Joseph typifies the Eternal Wisdom. His birth portrays its first perception by recipient human minds, and his coat of many colours the effect upon it of analysis, *ahamkara*,[1] modification and limitation.

The hatred and jealousy of Joseph's brothers allegorically describe the resistance of the mind, the emotions, and the general attitude of the personality, to the reception of spiritual illumination and the implications of its application to life—notably to established habits, many of which must go. The mortal man or lower self at first tends to resent the implied ascendancy which the Higher Self will gradually assume. The ultimate and inevitable complete domination of the outer by the inner Self is instinctively foreseen and resisted. Eventually the personal will must be surrendered. The natural, selfish, worldly outlook (the brothers)—now on its deathbed—calls into action a self-saving instinct to prevent, or at any rate to stave off, the day of triumph. The brothers plot the death of Joseph (the influence of spiritual wisdom in worldly life), as did King Kamsa that of Shri Krishna and King Herod that of Jesus. They seek to destroy the influence of the dawning idealism, to bury truth deep in the " matter " of mind, brain and material pursuits. Symbolically, Joseph is forcibly lowered into the pit.

Failing in their impious design, the brothers commercialise occult wisdom. Joseph is sold into slavery, as spiritual knowledge is so constantly sold for material gain. Nevertheless the power of the awakening spiritual Self proves to be irresistible. The Eternal Wisdom inevitably triumphs, as did Jesus in driving the moneychangers out of the Temple.[2] The slavery and imprisonment are, however, but temporary (Joseph is raised from the pit). Governorship over the whole nature of man (Egypt) is attained and the nations (the human Race) and the family (the individual vehicles of the Initiate) are fed from an abundance which exists amidst the famine-stricken condition (unillumined state) of the rest of mankind.

Moreover, the divine Power and Light are handed on, as the story later reveals. Benjamin receives, hidden in his cornsack, a silver cup[3]— symbol of the Higher Mind receptive of the hidden Truth. Each Adept who passes beyond humanity hands on his wisdom to a chosen but natural successor amongst men, training and aiding him to the rapid fulfilment of human destiny in the attainment of perfected manhood. Benjamin is

[1] *Ahamkara* (Sk.)—see Glossary.
[2] *Matt.* 21: 12.
[3] *Gen.* 44: 2.

a permutation of the beloved disciple, Ananda or John, upon whom the Teacher bestows especial love.

JOSEPH AS INITIATE IN THE GREATER MYSTERIES

As a description of the Mysteries, the life story of Joseph allegorically portrays the progress of the Candidate through the Degrees of a Sacred Rite. Birth represents passage through the first Great Initiation. The mother personifies the Mysteries themselves, whilst the father represents the Hierophant. The elder brothers are the Officiants and other members of the Temple. The two dreams describe the effects upon consciousness of the Initiations into the Second and Third Degrees. The bowing of the brothers' sheaves to that of Joseph signifies that development and attainment by the Candidate as a result of which spiritual and occult progress is both won and acclaimed. The existence of the sheaves themselves indicates that it was harvest time, which in its turn refers to the gathering into a synthesis of all the developed powers and fruits of preceding incarnations. In the symbolism of the Mysteries corn represents both richness of attainment and the achievement of the required standard of a particular Degree.

Similarly the sun, the moon and the stars which in the second dream make obeisance to the dreamer represent the solar, planetary and Zodiacal attainments[1] required for admittance into the Third Degree. Whilst the sheaves of the earlier dream indicate for the most part the harvested fruits of successive lives as mortal man, the heavenly bodies of the later one refer to the newly awakened cosmic powers of the Higher Self. Their obeisance indicates that they have been mastered and that their powers are now consciously wielded by the inner Will of the Candidate's (Joseph's) essential Self, the true dreamer of the wondrous dream.

[1] See Glossary—The Law of Correspondences.

CHAPTER III

JOSEPH IN EGYPT

SINCE the Thirty-eighth Chapter of the *Book of Genesis* does not contain direct occult allusions and offers little or no instruction to the student, and since it breaks the narrative of the life of Joseph, interpretations are continued from the beginning of Chapter Thirty-nine.

> *Gen.* 39:   *Joseph, advanced in Potiphar's house, resisteth his mistress's temptation: he is falsely accused, and cast into prison: God is with him there.*

Although Egyptian monuments, literature and history give little support for the incidents narrated in this and the following Chapters of *Genesis*, their historical probability is not here denied. The story of Joseph is, however, so conceived and related, and includes so much supernatural intervention, that it offers a fruitful field for the student of symbology.

In general Joseph himself may clearly be perceived as a personification of both the Macrocosmic and microcosmic Spirit, life and consciousness indwelling in Universe and in man. His story closely portrays the cyclic processes of forthgoing and return—the descent or emanation of the divine life from its spiritual Source into the deepest densities of matter (the pit), its tribulations therein, its emancipation and its ultimate return to the Source. It is indeed a great parable enunciating the law of cycles, as also does the Parable of the Prodigal Son.[1]

The Chapter of *Genesis* under consideration allegorically describes the beginning of entry upon the pathway of return and the varied resistances to the ascent of Spirit offered by matter. In the human interpretation Joseph as the inner Self in a new physical body grows up towards adolescence, as the action of Potiphar's wife—introducing the sex motif—indicates. Nevertheless, the imprisonment which follows portrays the still potent influence of matter over Spirit and of the physical body over the Soul of man. The subsequent release from prison and the rise to power refer to later stages of the great journey, whilst the wise and beneficent actions—and especially the death in honour—refer to the triumphant return of life to its Source towards the end of *Manvantara*.

---

[1] q.v. Vol. I of this work, Pt. Four.

As will later be shown, the entry of the Israelites into Egypt, their bondage to the Egyptians and their subsequent deliverance, all portray the same processes in Nature, as do so many other Scriptural and Mythological narratives.

THE NARROW WAY

The possibility that a man may forestall Nature, may hasten deliverance from the bondage of the flesh and attain in advance of his Race to liberation or Salvation, is also indicated in the story of Joseph. In this case, as is not unusual, the meanings of certain symbols are reversed. Egypt, for example, was at that time a centre of the spiritual life, and its Temples, their Sanctuaries and their Halls of Initiation into the Lesser and the Greater Mysteries offered the necessary assistance.

Joseph's successful resistance of the temptations associated with sex desire (Potiphar's wife), his undeserved imprisonment, his deliverance as a result of the exercise of an occult power (interpretation of dreams) and his subsequent rise to the chief position in the Kingdom, all allegorically portray passage through the Initiatory tests and Rites and the attainment of the accompanying expansions of consciousness. These culminate in the attainment of Adeptship, generally portrayed by a figurative death and resurrection, meaning the transcendence of all limitations imposed by matter during evolution through the human kingdom of Nature.

Then follows entry into the superhuman kingdom, with conscious absorption into the life and Spirit of the Universe, though mysteriously without the total loss of identity. This is the Salvation of Christianity, *Moksha* or Liberation of Hinduism and *Nirvana* of Buddhism. When this state is attained during the present period of human occupation of the planet, enforced self-spiritualisation is implied. This process is referred to by Jesus as entering in at the strait gate and treading the narrow way.[1] Isaiah refers to the pathway of hastened attainment as "The way of holiness".[2]

As has been noted earlier, this relatively secret or occult life has from the earliest period of man's occupation of the Earth been followed by a small number of spiritually awakening and awakened human beings. Guidance by a Master upon this secret pathway, descriptions of experiences through which the Soul passes, the tests, ordeals and triumphs of the candidate—all these run like a silver thread, now hidden, now revealed, which is woven into the "tapestry" of the Scriptures and Mythologies of ancient peoples. The great figures—heroes, prophets, Apostles and Saviours—all

[1] *Matt.* 7: 13, 14.
[2] *Is.* 35: 8.

represent successful followers of the Ancient Way who have arrived at various stages of attainment. The story of their lives is extremely instructive for those who can pierce the veil of allegory and symbol beneath which the secrets of occult science, Discipleship and Initiation are concealed.[1]

> Gen. 39: 1.   *And Joseph was brought down to Egypt: and Potiphar an officer of Pharaoh, captain of the guard, an Egyptian, bought him of the hands of the Ishmeelites, which had brought him down thither.*

The first verse of Chapter Thirty-nine of the *Book of Genesis* tells of the capture of Joseph, his journey to Egypt and his purchase by Potiphar, an Officer of Pharaoh and Captain of the Guard.   Here the story of the early stages of the ascent of life from the mineral kingdom may be allegorically referred to, since Potiphar's name means " gift of the risen one ".   This is supported by the statement that Joseph, though still a captive and a slave, is granted a measure of freedom, being brought and placed in the service of Potiphar, a wise and discerning man.

> Gen. 39: 2.   *And the LORD was with Joseph, and he was a prosperous man; and he was in the house of his master the Egyptian.*

JOSEPH FINDS GRACE IN HIS MASTER'S EYES

The statement that " the Lord was with Joseph " does not so much indicate that the Logos of the Solar System had singled him out for personal favours as that the Lord within him, his own divine Self, was beginning increasingly to direct his motives and life and inwardly to enlighten him. The *dramatis personae* each represent a part and a power of the constitution of man.   In such a reading of the story the Lord is the divine Monad, itself a Ray of the Supreme Deity, the one eternal Light.   Potiphar stands for the mind and his wife for the emotions, whilst their house refers to awareness in the physical body.

Joseph, when helpless in the pit into which his brothers had lowered him and so shut out from the light of day, portrays that stage of human evolution at which there is no spiritual awareness during waking consciousness.   His inner Self had not yet begun to endow him with the degree of illumination which later enabled him to interpret dreams and wisely to foresee and prepare against a famine.   Nevertheless his earlier history, and especially his own dreams, indicate that Egoically he was unusually advanced, being of considerable evolutionary stature.   Thus for him Egypt does not represent bondage to sensual and material existence, this being its usual interpretation— as in the case of the Israelite nation as a whole, for

---

[1] For a fuller exposition of this subject see Vol. I of this work, Pt. Six.

example. Rather it was for Joseph a centre of the Ancient Mysteries where the Great Initiations were conferred.

Every Candidate for Initiation proves himself by passing successfully through certain temptations, and through tests of preparedness and capacity. These also are described in allegory in Joseph's experiences in Egypt, and will be considered in their due place.

> Gen. 39: 3. *And his master saw that the LORD was with him, and that the LORD made all that he did to prosper in his hand.*
>
> 4. *And Joseph found grace in his sight, and he served him; and he made him overseer over his house, and all that he had he put into his hand.*

In the various aspects of human nature, personified by the characters in inspired allegories, Joseph represents the highly evolved, illumined Ego, the unfolding, immortal Being. Throughout his whole nature, mental, emotional and physical, this Dweller in the Innermost displays wisdom and self-command. Symbolically, Joseph finds favour in the eyes of Potiphar and is recognised as being divinely inspired.

> Gen. 39: 5. *And it came to pass from the time that he had made him overseer in his house, and over all that he had, that the LORD blessed the Egyptian's house for Joseph's sake; and the blessing of the LORD was upon all that he had in the house, and in the field.*

Joseph's overseership of the house and affairs of Potiphar indicates domination of the more earthly part of human nature by the indwelling spiritual Self. As noted above Joseph, the Ego, had become sufficiently evolved to be in charge of his outer nature—his mind, emotion and body (Potiphar's house and fields).

> Gen. 39: 6. *And he left all that he had in Joseph's hand: and he knew not ought he had, save the bread which he did eat. And Joseph was a goodly person, and well favoured.*

Potiphar's trust in Joseph, and the fact that he left the whole management of his affairs in Joseph's hands, describes that state at which the physical nature has, in its turn, been surrendered to idealism and direction by the inner Self. This surrender, implying detachment, dispassion and personal disinterestedness, is one of the marks of the highly evolved person and a sure sign that they are approaching readiness for Initiation and the expansions of consciousness which this will produce.

Acceptance of a Candidate by those who are already initiated, and passage through a Ceremony of Consecration, can occur only as a recognition of spiritual unfoldment. The immortal Self is visible to the Hierophant and his Officers, and is seen to display those powers and qualities which characterise man at the required evolutionary stage of development. The essential, therefore, is not passage through a Rite and receipt of a Degree, important though these are, but rather the achievement of a certain stage of unfoldment.   In this the aspirant is not entirely alone, however.   Assistance in the development of wisdom, comprehension and faculties is always available, whilst in addition guidance in bringing the fruits of such progress to bear upon and be expressed through the outer mortal man in his waking hours is both needed and received.   The Initiatory Rite, with its descent of power, definitely assists in this procedure.   The touch of the wand of power—the thyrsus in the hand of the Hierophant—upon the crown of the head of the Candidate opens up the channels of communication between the inner and the outer Selves of the Initiate.   These consist of whirling funnels of force in the etheric and superphysical bodies, and of organs in the physical brain, which become intensely vivified by the descent of the Hierophantic power.   Thereafter the Initiate has access to his own living Self, which in its turn can also illumine and inspire him in his daily life.   The narrative indicates that Joseph, " a goodly person, and well favoured ", was approaching readiness for the receipt of this spiritual and occult assistance.

> Gen. 39: 7.   *And it came to pass after these things, that his master's wife cast her eyes upon Joseph; and she said, Lie with me.*

THE ATTEMPTED SEDUCTION OF JOSEPH

Every Candidate for Initiation must have reached a sufficient degree of self-command to enable him to resist desire and the temptations of the flesh. This attainment has been gradual, but is frequently represented in allegories of Initiation by a single incident descriptive of resistance to temptation to indulge, sometimes illicitly, in the pleasures of sense and sex.   Potiphar's wife is made to play the role of temptress.

In other allegorical versions of this theme the would - be seducer is male, and even a deity.   Thus Apollo pursued Daphne, and Zeus had intercourse with various nymphs and young women.   The story of the attempted seduction of Joseph by Potiphar's wife is not only an incident which may actually have occurred; it is also a symbolical description both of victory by man over desire and of an actual test of readiness for Initiation.[1]

> Gen. 39: 8.   *But he refused, and said unto his master's wife, Behold, my master wotteth not what is with me in the house, and he hath committed all that he hath to my hand;*
>
> 9.   *There is none greater in this house than I; neither hath he kept back anything from me but thee, because thou art his wife; how then can I do this great wickedness, and sin against God?*

The major part of the key to the mystery of sex transmutation is given in Joseph's reply.   This consisted of the application of the reason, the powers

---

[1] q.v. *The Idyll of the White Lotus*, Ch. VIII, M.C.

of the mind, to the dangerous situation. In his case reason was stronger than either temptation or desire, if indeed he was conscious of the latter. The responsibilities of Office and the call of duty were advanced as reasons for refusal to respond to the invitation.

> *Gen.* 39:10. *And it came to pass, as she spake to Joseph day by day, that he hearkened not unto her, to lie by her, or to be with her.*

In preparation for Initiation the ordeal is made to continue, the temptation being repeated until victory is attained. In Joseph's case only sternness of will, an appeal to reason and complete devotion to duty—the threefold secret of success—were evoked.

> *Gen.* 39:11. *And it came to pass about this time, that Joseph went into the house to do his business; and there was none of the men of the house there within.*
>
> 12. *And she caught him by his garment, saying, Lie with me: and he left his garment in her hand, and fled, and got him out.*

Whilst in the literal reading of the account of the incident the woman's retention of the garment of Joseph may seem natural under the circumstances, the language of symbols is also employed; for a garment is used in that language to represent a vehicle of consciousness, as also a covering, and even an encrustation affecting the mind. Nakedness, on the other hand, implies freedom from such limitations, the faithful exposure of intellect to Spirit, and an unclouded expression of the spiritual through the human nature of the subject of a narrative. All occurs within one person, and in this case Joseph rose above the distracting and distorting influences brought to bear upon him. Symbolically, a garment was left behind.

> *Gen.* 39:13. *And it came to pass, when she saw that he had left his garment in her hand, and was fled forth,*
>
> 14. *That she called unto the men of her house, and spake unto them, saying, See, he hath brought in an Hebrew unto us to mock us; he came in unto me to lie with me, and I cried with a loud voice;*
>
> 15. *And it came to pass, when he heard that I lifted up my voice and cried, that he left his garment with me, and fled, and got him out.*
>
> 16. *And she laid up his garment by her, until his lord came home.*
>
> 17. *And she spake unto him according to these words, saying, The Hebrew servant, which thou hast brought unto us, came in unto me to mock me:*
>
> 18. *And it came to pass, as I lifted up my voice and cried, that he left his garment with me, and fled out.*

A lying accusation, apparently supported by evidence, is brought by Potiphar's wife against Joseph. The treacherous nature of certain aspects of man's human emotions is here portrayed. An apparently inescapable

14

experience, source of suffering and test, must necessarily be passed through by Joseph, as also by every Candidate for Initiation, especially those who during the time of their trial remain in the outer world of men.   Even in ordinary life unsatisfied desire, envy, jealousy, hatred, and fear that position and power may be lost, can evoke in certain people the worst of human attributes.   Those susceptible to their influence turn against and betray friends, teachers and leaders.   For example, Peter denied the Christ; Judas betrayed Him.

> Gen. 39: 19.   *And it came to pass, when his master heard the words of his wife, which she spake unto him, saying, After this manner did thy servant to me; that his wrath was kindled.*
>
> 20.   *And Joseph's master took him and put him into the prison, a place where the king's prisoners were bound; and he was there in the prison.*

THE IMPRISONMENT OF JOSEPH

As the mind can and frequently does inhibit the illuminating functions of the intuition, thereby imprisoning consciousness, so Potiphar—representing the mind when a victim of delusion born of deceit—temporarily imprisoned Joseph, the illumined spiritual Self.   All allegorical dramas, it must be remembered, are enacted within one person, namely man as a person and as a Race.   The various characters personify attributes of that person—qualities, powers, weaknesses and vehicles of consciousness, whether habitual or just beginning to appear.

Joseph, the foster-father of Jesus, is portrayed as a wise and mature person, indicating a highly developed mind possessed by a highly evolved man.   Potiphar also represents the mind, but at a lower level of evolution. He, in consequence, fell a prey to the treacherous and untrue accusations of his wife (desire), and imprisoned his hitherto trusted Officer, Joseph (the illumined mind).

The narrative is thus carried beyond the realm of mere crude emotion into that of the mind, the limitations of which are displayed.   The psychological revelations are thus quite profound, as in so many Scriptural narratives in which the language of symbols is employed.

> Gen. 39: 21.   *But the LORD was with Joseph, and shewed him mercy, and gave him favour in the sight of the keeper of the prison.*

Joseph himself, however, is too highly evolved to be seriously incommoded by the imprisonment, his intuitive powers and gift of interpretation in no wise affected.

> Gen. 39: 22.   *And the keeper of the prison committed to Joseph's hand all the prisoners that were in the prison; and whatsoever they did there, he was the doer of it.*

23. *The keeper of the prison looked not to any thing that was under his hand; because the LORD was with him, and that which he did, the LORD made it to prosper.*

The prison thus represents both the substance of man's mental body—mind-stuff—and those attributes of the mind which, misused, prevent its illumination by direct perception or intuition. Prisoners themselves personify those people who have become thus restricted, whilst the whole prison, together with its keepers and its inmates, aptly portrays the temporarily limiting effects—particularly on those people of a wholly materialistic and individualistic mentality—produced upon human consciousness by incarnation in a mortal personality. Joseph, said to be favoured by the Lord God, is the illumined spiritual Self of a highly evolved man, and therefore is never entirely subject to the above-mentioned hindrances. The last two verses of the Chapter indicate that this degree of evolutionary stature had been attained by Joseph. The statement that all that was accomplished in the prison was done by him may be interpreted as meaning that his inner Self was in complete command of the outer man. The keeper's apparent neglect of his Office, and the relegation of his duties to Joseph, would seem to support these interpretations.

It is worthy of note that although Potiphar's wife, by a false accusation, was the cause of Joseph's imprisonment, she is nevertheless not mentioned again in the narrative. The Initiated inner Self can neither be successfully lured nor in any way affected by desire. The last verse of the Chapter indicates that the innermost Self, the Monad (the Lord), could and did empower and inspire the immortal Soul (Joseph).

CHAPTER IV

JOSEPH INTERPRETS HIS FELLOW PRISONERS' DREAMS

Gen. 40: *The butler and baker of Pharaoh are imprisoned; Joseph hath charge of them; he interpreteth their dreams. The ingratitude of the butler.*

Gen. 40:
1. *And it came to pass after these things, that the butler of the king of Egypt and his baker had offended their lord the king of Egypt.*

2. *And Pharaoh was wroth against two of his officers, against the chief of the butlers, and against the chief of the bakers.*

3. *And he put them in ward in the house of the captain of the guard, into the prison, the place where Joseph was bound.*

4. *And the captain of the guard charged Joseph with them, and he served them; and they continued a season in ward.*

5. *And they dreamed a dream both of them, each man his dream in one night, each man according to the interpretation of his dream, the butler and the baker of the king of Egypt, which were bound in the prison.*

6. *And Joseph came in unto them in the morning, and looked upon them, and, behold, they were sad.*

7. *And he asked Pharaoh's officers that were with him in the ward of his lord's house, saying, Wherefore look ye so sadly to day?*

8. *And they said unto him, We have dreamed a dream, and there is no interpreter of it. And Joseph said unto them, Do not interpretations belong to God? tell me them, I pray you.*

9. *And the chief butler told his dream to Joseph, and said to him, In my dream, behold, a vine was before me;*

10. *And in the vine were three branches; and it was as though it budded, and her blossoms shot forth; and the clusters thereof brought forth ripe grapes:*

11. *And Pharaoh's cup was in my hand; and I took the grapes, and pressed them into Pharaoh's cup, and I gave the cup into Pharaoh's hand.*

12. *And Joseph said unto him, This is the interpretation of it; The three branches are three days:*

13. *Yet within three days shall Pharaoh lift up thine head, and restore thee unto thy place; and thou shalt deliver Pharaoh's cup into his hand, after the former manner when thou wast his butler.*

The purely secular interpretation of the butler's dream given to him by Joseph by no means exhausts the spiritual possibilities. Whether these were in the authors' minds cannot be determined. The symbology is, however, so significant and the allegory so coherent as to suggest veiled instruction concerning profound truths.

THE VINE

The vine with three branches, for example, may be regarded as a symbol of the vital energy by which the Universe is sustained, and of the power or thrust of Spirit which is responsible for the evolution of life and form. This is the mysterious, inexhaustible power ceaselessly at work within a Universe from the first momemt of its emanation from the Absolute, throughout its objective existence, and up to its final withdrawal back into its Source. It is, in fact, that invisible and intangible quality which is called " life ". The tree of life in the Garden of Eden, the Sephirothal Tree of Kabbalism and the vine, as indeed all fruit-bearing trees, are used as symbols of this hidden force in Nature. Thus, apart from the divinatory interpretation given by Joseph to the butler, the dream was also a revelation of deep universal significance. The spiritual life-force, or " Great Breath ", is actively expressed in three ways or as three currents of power. In the dream symbolism these are represented by the three branches of the vine, and in World Religions by the three Persons of the Blessed Trinity. This latter has lead to grossly anthropomorphic concepts of the threefold divine manifestation.

In the dream the vine budded and brought forth blossoms, followed by ripened grapes. Here are portrayed in symbol the unfolding and evolutionary processes inherent throughout all Nature, and this is the spiritual interpretation of the dream—namely that nothing throughout the Universe is static (the vine budded), that innate powers unfold from within (fruit was produced), and that forms improve their capacity to express those powers as a result of the evolutionary process (the fruit ripened).

The Initiates of the Sanctuaries of the Mysteries of old were taught the fact of evolution, even though this was not discovered by Western science until modern times. In reality it was a re-discovery. Although Darwin limited his conception of evolution to the development of forms, since they alone were able to be observed by him, nevertheless he partially revealed[1]

[1] q.v. *Origin of Species* (1859), C. R. Darwin.

a profound truth—the parallel unfoldment of life and development of form. The choice of fruit-bearing trees and phases of their life as symbols of evolution is exceedingly apt, for fruit trees display in their forms and natural processes a deep spiritual verity.[1]

PHARAOH'S CUP

In addition to the interpretation of the butler's dream given by Joseph, the symbol of the cup may also refer to a localisation of a universal principle, such as the material form of a Solar System, and also to the vehicle or body in which the inner Spirit of man abides, the Vesture of Light, the " Robe of Glory ",[2] the Causal Body. The Pharaoh's or King's cup, filled with grape juice and placed in Pharaoh's hand by the dreamer, symbolises that state of evolution and illumination in which the individual has become aware of the universal. The Initiate whose experiences are being described by means of allegory, as I have suggested, has come to know completely that divine Spirit and life which is his true Self, and also that it is identical with the Spirit and life of the Universe as a whole—Pharaoh's cup is full of wine. The same interpretation may be applied to all cups and chalices used as symbols in the Sacred Language.

Since the free life principle of the Universe (the vine and its products) is the subject of the dream, and service to the Pharaoh constitutes the culminating action of the dreamer, the attainment of freedom is implied. Liberation has been gained from the shackles of desire and from all bodily limitations, symbolised as they are by the prison and its head keeper. The illusion of self-separateness (a prison indeed) has also been transcended. Thus the butler's dream proves to be susceptible of interpretation as a description of the expansion of consciousness which the Initiate has attained, the familiar symbols of grape, wine and drinking cup being employed.

Since the facts of the unfoldment of Monads, whether pertaining to Universe or man, and of the development of forms were in those days part of the secret teachings of Initiation, it may well be that the two dreams recorded in this Chapter of *Genesis* are veiled references to experiences passed through by Joseph during his own Initiation.[3] All the incidents leading to Joseph's imprisonment, his remarkable freedom and prestige whilst there, his fellow prisoners' dreams, their interpretation and his subsequent liberation, may well be regarded as, in fact, having happened to one person. Although this may well have been a Hebrew Initiate, perhaps Joseph himself, the events when interpreted may also refer to every Initiate, since all who win admission

---

[1] see also Vol. II of this work, Pt. Two, Ch. II and Pt. Three, Ch. V.
[2] Gnostic term for the Causal Body. See Glossary—Causal Body.
[3] *Mk*. 4: 11.

to the Greater Mysteries pass through similar experiences and receive similar revelations.   This view is to some extent supported in verse thirteen of the Fortieth Chapter of *Genesis* by the mention of the three days which were to elapse before the butler was to be freed and restored to his Office. In olden days the period required for the expansions of consciousness produced by Initiation was three days and three nights, during which time the body lay entranced, sometimes supine upon a cross and sometimes in a tomb.

The spiritual Soul, the immortal part of man, was thus freed from the heavy limitations of bodily encasement and elevated for three days and nights into spiritual awareness, after which it returned to the body.   Possibly with similar intention, Jonah was made to spend three days and three nights in the interior of a large fish, and Jesus was buried for the same period of time, after having informed His disciples that He would pass through a comparable experience to that of Jonah.[1]   Conscious absorption into the all-pervading life principle of the Universe, with realisation of complete identity with that life, formed part of the mystic effect of the Rite of Initiation, knowledge of certain fundamental laws and facts of Nature, divine and human, being also bestowed.   After awakening, the Candidate was instructed physically and verbally in such secret knowledge as pertained to the Degree to which he had attained.[2]

If such an illumined man ever took to writing, whether voluntarily or under instructions, he would perforce include in whatever he wrote only veiled references to his experiences and knowledge.   Instructed in the Sacred Language invented and used by his predecessors, he would be able to record—perhaps as historical metaphor—much of what he had passed through and learned.   As Hebrew Kabbalists affirm,[3] the authors of the *Pentateuch* may be presumed to have followed this practice, using Jewish history as a basis for their revelations.

Studied from this point of view, the butler's dream is an excellent example of an allegory which reveals in symbol the universal process of evolution.

Gen. 40: 14. *But think on me when it shall be well with thee, and shew kindness,*
I pray thee, unto me, and make mention of me unto Pharaoh,
and bring me out of this house;

These words of Joseph to the butler hardly ring true.   They may perhaps be regarded as a deliberate inconsistency.   It does not seem reasonable that Joseph, the acting keeper of the prison, who enjoyed superior prestige and was, moreover, a seer who was consulted, should seek favours from one of the other prisoners who was only a domestic servant.   It is distinctly

---

[1] *Matt.* 12: 40.

[2] q.v. Vol. I of this work, Pt. Six, Ch. I.

[3] q.v. *Zohar* III, 152 a, and many other Kabbalistic works, some of which are referred to in the Bibliography in Vol. II of this work.

stated that " the Lord was with Joseph ",[1] and he would therefore have no need to ask a butler to ingratiate him with the Pharaoh. The reader thus receives a suggestion that an undermeaning should be sought, not only to the particular occasion recounted, but also to the whole narrative.

A key to the interpretation of the imprisonment of Joseph and all that befell him consists of the fact that the seven Principles of man are introduced into the story under the guise of people and powers. The chief baker represents the vital or nutrifying principle[2] in the physical body, and even the physical body itself. The butler personifies the emotional nature with its access to the intuitive faculty, as evidenced by his remarakable dream of the life processes in Nature. The mind is portrayed by the keeper of the prison, whose power is delegated to Joseph in the sense that the illumined Ego inspires the otherwise materialistic mind. The prison itself is the material world and the prisoners the mortal personality of man, composed of the three main vehicles—physical, emotional and mental. Joseph is the Initiated spiritual Self attaining to freedom of the limitations of the outer man, particularly those of the mind (is released from prison). Joseph frees himself, be it noted, not by either subterfuge or force, but solely by virtue of his own character and the exercise of his special capacities. Indeed, he submits almost passively on the outer plane, whilst at the same time bringing to bear upon the problem the intuitive and interpretative powers of the Higher Self, thereby winning both freedom and honour.

The intuition is not personified, but portrayed as a power to interpret dreams. This means not only dreams as visions by night, but—far more— the dream which is material life itself, including the illusion of self-separate existence distinct from all other selves. To the illumined inner man physical life is as a dream, spiritual awareness being the true waking state. Joseph, having evolved to the stage where he knew this, is correctly portrayed as a seer and an interpreter of dreams. The Lord God Who inspired Joseph is his own purely spiritual Self, the Dweller in the Innermost, the Monad-*Ātma*, the true Father in Heaven.

THE SEVEN PRINCIPLES OF MAN AS PORTRAYED DURING THE IMPRISONMENT OF JOSEPH

(1) The Physical Body	... ...	the Prison.
(2) The Etheric Double	... ...	the Baker.
(3) The Emotional Nature	... ...	the Butler.
(4) The Mental Body (Manas II)	...	the Keeper of the Prison.

---

[1] *Gen.* 39: 21.

[2] The Etheric Double. q.v. *Lecture Notes of the School of the Wisdom*, Vol. I (Rev. Ed.), Ch. III, Geoffrey Hodson.

(5) The Ego in the Causal Body (Manas I) Joseph.

(6) The Intuitional Body (*Buddhi*) ... Joseph as Interpreter.

(7) The Spiritual Body (Monad-*Ātma*) ... The Lord God.

Joseph's plea to the butler for him to intercede on his behalf for the good graces of Pharaoh indicates the necessity for the establishment of harmonious relationships between the inner, immortal and the outer, mortal self. This, therefore, is sought rather than demanded or obtained by force. It is not an inconsistency, but a reference to the best method of obtaining cooperation between the various parts of human nature. Resistances are overcome by a process of harmonisation rather than by the exercise of power in their suppression. Transmutation, and not repression, is the ideal way of changing such " enemies " into " friends " from the point of view of subduing undesired attributes. Similarly Jason, leader of the Argonauts, subdued the two serpents guarding the Golden Fleece not by the aid of the might of Hercules, but through the mediation of Orpheus and the charm of his music.

Gen. 40: 15. *For indeed I was stolen away out of the land of the Hebrews; and here also have I done nothing that they should put me into the dungeon.*

If Joseph's words be lifted out of time, especially immediate time, then he is describing the descent of the Monad into matter, as is also indicated by his being lowered into the pit. The enforced imprisonment of the divine in man within a physical body is similarly if allegorically portrayed, together with the resultant hardships and limitations experienced, particularly on the downward arc and at the turning point of the cycle.[1]

Gen. 40: 16. *When the chief baker saw that the interpretation was good, he said unto Joseph, I also was in my dream, and, behold, I had three white baskets on my head;*

17. *And in the uppermost basket there was of all manner of bakemeats for Pharaoh; and the birds did eat them out of the basket upon my head.*

THE BAKER'S DREAM INTERPRETED

The dreams of the butler and the baker have in common the number three. They differ, however, in the nature of the substance specified, in Joseph's interpretations of the dreams, and in their outcome. In the butler's case the triple substance was a fruitful vine, a natural, growing, living plant and, moreover, a source of sustenance. Divination apart, this represents the triune Deity in Nature and in man, the power, life and consciousness of Macrocosm and microcosm. As earlier suggested, the vine is a symbol of

---

[1] see Charts between pages 42 and 43,

the vitalising and sustaining life-force. The ripened grape and its juice typify that life coming to fruition, reaching maturity in both Universe and illumined man. To dream, then, of a vine with three branches which brought forth ripe grapes was to know by direct experience the triple spiritual powers within Nature and man, and particularly in the dreamer himself.

In the baker's dream the substance (bakemeats) was not a natural but an artificially prepared food. Baskets are also the products of the hand of man, even though woven from the dried stems of plants. The suggestion is therefore less of living than of dead material, and Joseph accordingly interpreted the dream as a prophecy of death. The baker, he said, would be killed in three days.

Whilst not wishing to read more into the symbols of the cup and the baskets than is reasonably permissible, and remembering the adjurations of such learned Hebrew Kabbalists as Rabbi Simeon Ben Joachai, who is reputed to have written or compiled the *Book of Splendour* or *Zohar*,[1] nevertheless the distinction between the substances from which the cup and baskets had been constructed may indicate a difference in both state of consciousness and position in evolution. A cup, being formed of solid matter, has permanence and does not permit the escape of its contents through the sides. A basket, on the other hand, is not long lasting and is not a closed container. The bakemeats are lost, however, having been taken by the birds of the air.

The three baskets and their contents, prepared by man, may refer to his three mortal bodies of mind, emotion and flesh. These can neither comprehend divine power and wisdom in their purest state nor, being subject to time and change, can they—basket-like—retain them. Joseph's divinatory interpretation was consonant with this idea, in that to him the three baskets meant three days (v. 18), at the end of which death would come to the baker, as proved to be true.

> *Gen.* 40: 18. *And Joseph answered and said, This is the interpretation thereof; the three baskets are three days:*
>
> 19. *Yet within three days shall Pharaoh lift up thy head from off thee, and shall hang thee on a tree; and the birds shall eat thy flesh from off thee.*
>
> 20. *And it came to pass the third day, which was Pharaoh's birthday, that he made a feast unto all his servants; and he lifted up the head of the chief butler and of the chief baker among his servants.*

---

[1] *Zohar* III, 152 a, in which it is stated: ". . . the Torah, in all its words, holds supernal truths and sublime secrets."

21. *And he restored the chief butler unto his butlership again; and he gave the cup into Pharaoh's hand;*

22. *But he hanged the chief baker; as Joseph had interpreted to them.*

The two dreams may also be deemed significant as allegorical portrayals of the principle of the reflection of the triple Deity in both the matter of the Universe and the make-up of man. The cup represents the containing vehicle for the higher triplicity, and the baskets the receptacles for the lower, or the reflection of the same. In philosophic thought the former is regarded as the " Real "[1] and the latter as the unreal.[2]

To dream of a cup (the immortal Self) portrays freedom; to dream of a basket (the mortal man) indicates imprisonment. It should always be remembered that all the people in such metaphorical narratives personify parts of the constitution and qualities of the character of one person, and that the events allegorically describe experiences through which that person passes.[3] Thus the butler, like the other persons in the story, personifies an attribute of Joseph's own mind.

Gen. 40:23. *Yet did not the chief butler remember Joseph, but forgat him.*

A characteristic quality of human nature is here portrayed. If the butler be regarded as portraying certain undesirable attributes, notably those of self-seeking and selfishness, then—so far as personal service is concerned—the tendency to neglect or even forget a benefactor would be in character. His dream had been interpreted, his mind had been put at rest about it, and he had regained both his freedom and his Office. Apparently he thereafter ceased to trouble himself about the fellow prisoner who had asked him to intercede with Pharaoh on his behalf. According to the story, however, the butler went free and Joseph remained in prison. Nevertheless, as the next Chapter of *Genesis* shows, the imprisonment was not to last much longer. The forgetfulness and perfidy of the butler could not cause Joseph to be imprisoned for a greater period than his destiny and his capacities permitted.

An Eastern saying states that " The mind is the great slayer of the real ".[4] Joseph, though he had advanced along the Way of Holiness and had passed through the Gateway of Initiation, had not quite outgrown those mental tendencies which are portrayed by the action of the butler in failing to respond to Joseph's request to " make mention of me to Pharaoh, and bring me out of this house." In this part of the narrative of

---

[1] Real: That which is eternal and unchanging. *e.g.*, The Infinite.

[2] Unreal: That which is transitory and changing. *e.g.*, The finite.

[3] see Pt. One, Ch. II—The Second Key.

[4] q.v. *The Voice of the Silence* Fragment I, from *The Book of the Golden Precepts*, translated and annotated by H. P. Blavatsky.

Joseph's life guidance is offered, not only in the moral but also in the occult sense; for, although it is man's essential means of gaining information, nevertheless the mind remains the great enemy, even up to the threshold of " Salvation " or Adeptship. The concrete or " lower " mentality is not only the slayer of the Real, but is also the potential prison of the higher, interpretative intellect and of the intuition and its fruits. The individualistic as well as the over-critical and argumentative tendencies of the human mind must eventually be outgrown or superseded, it thereafter ceasing to be a limitation, having been changed into an illumined instrument in the service of the liberated inner Self.

CHAPTER V

THE DREAMS OF PHARAOH

Gen. 41:   *Pharaoh's two dreams: Joseph interpreteth them: he giveth Pharaoh counsel. Joseph is advanced: he begetteth Manasseh and Ephraim. The famine beginneth.*

Gen. 41: 1. *And it came to pass at the end of two full years, that Pharaoh dreamed: and, behold, he stood by the river.*

       2. *And, behold, there came up out of the river seven well favoured kine and fatfleshed; and they fed in a meadow.*

       3. *And, behold, seven other kine came up after them out of the river, ill favoured and leanfleshed; and stood by the other kine upon the brink of the river.*

       4. *And the ill favoured and leanfleshed kine did eat up the seven well favoured and fat kine. So Pharaoh awoke.*

       5. *And he slept and dreamed the second time: and, behold, seven ears of corn came up upon one stalk, rank and good.*

       6. *And, behold, seven thin ears and blasted with the east wind sprung up after them.*

       7. *And the seven thin ears devoured the seven rank and full ears. And Pharaoh awoke, and, behold, it was a dream.*

Several well-known symbols are employed in these verses. Among them are a dreaming King and his dreams, a river and its meadows, kine and corn, fatness and leanness, and the predatory devouring of the fat kine by the lean ones and of the full ears of corn by the thin ones. Moreover, by the description of events which could not possibly have occurred, the attention of the reader is drawn to an undermeaning. Kine, whether fat or lean, do not eat each other, being herbivorous. Similarly cornstalks do not feed upon each other, but upon their natural food. If it be answered that these things happened in a dream, in which all things can seem possible, then it should be remembered that many of the events in dreams are themselves symbolic and therefore worthy of serious consideration.

The setting of the three dreams—those of the butler, of the baker and of Pharaoh—and the effect of their interpretations upon Joseph, should also be noted. His occult perceptions enabled him to make these interpretations, if only from one point of view—the divinatory or physically prophetic. The result was his liberation from prison and his advancement under Pharaoh to the highest position in the land.   Strangely enough it was not as Ruler of Egypt, but as an interpreter of dreams, that Joseph won his freedom and his elevation to so high a rank.

If the whole story of Joseph be given a mystical meaning then, as has already been suggested, his going forth into the field and his enforced descent into the pit describes the path of forthgoing from a purely spiritual into a densely material condition.   This refers to both the outpouring of the divine life into a Universe and the descent of the spiritual Self of man into physical birth.   Similarly the raising of Joseph from the pit, his liberation from prison and his appointment as " ruler over all the land of Egypt ",[1] portray the returning arc of the great journey of life and the progress of the spiritual Self to deliverance, perfection, " the measure of the stature of the fulness of Christ."[2]

" ENTERING THE STREAM "

The introduction of accounts of the supernatural and the impossible (as in Pharaoh's dream where kine eat kine), and of divine intervention, not only suggest a deeply symbolical meaning but also describe the path of hastened unfoldment and the experiences of those who tread that path. From this point of view the dreams are revelations of the spiritual wisdom attained by mystics and of the expansions of consciousness produced by passage through the great Initiations.

This view is supported by the introduction of the symbol of the river into the first verse of Chapter Forty-one of *Genesis*.   A reference to the river or ever-flowing stream of the outpoured life of the Logos may here be discerned, as also to direct experience of unity with that life, referred to in occult terminology as " entering the stream ".   Pharaoh, however, did not himself go into the river but remained standing upon its bank.   He was on the verge, as it were, of embarking upon a further evolutionary phase, but had not yet done so.   One of the various functions of the preparations for Initiation, and of the Rite itself, is to bring this about.   The touch of the thyrsus upon the head of the Candidate opens up and sets in operation the channels of communication between the Ego and the physical brain.   Before this can happen, however, both the inner Self and the outer man must have attained to a certain level of evolution.   The description of the dream begins, therefore, with the statement that Pharaoh stood by the river, meaning that he was almost ready for Initiation or " to enter the stream ".

As has so often occurred, occult knowledge reaching those unable to understand its hidden significance can become degraded into superstition.

---

[1] *Gen.* 41: 40–44.
[2] *Eph.* 4: 13.

In India, for example, very large numbers of people bathe in sacred rivers and other waters under the impression that a purification, a blessing and ultimate salvation will be the results. Admittedly, strong faith, even when founded on a misinterpretation of the effects of ceremonial, can produce potent results. Some benefit may therefore accrue to those who in all sincerity perform sacred Rites. Belief that the continuance of indulgences and evil practices are permissible so long as bathing is continued is, however, one of the harmful aspects of such blind faith. Theological dogmas affirming the possibility of escape from the educative operation of the law of cause and effect, and the forgiveness of sins without due restitution and proper resolve not to sin again, are regarded in occult philosophy as being potentially harmful. No intermediary, such as a divine Saviour, and no action of bathing in sacred waters, can possibly preserve a wilful culprit from the effects, interior and external, of deliberate wickedness. Nevertheless, when a man becomes a Candidate for Initiation and stands upon the brink of " the stream " ready to enter it, then almost incalculable blessings may be received. These, however, are not to be regarded as unearned spiritual riches or " grace ", since all of them have been previously won either earlier in the same life or in preceding incarnations.

THE SYMBOLISM OF KINE

These blessings may be symbolised by the kine in Pharaoh's dream, which are made to emerge from the river. In many World Scriptures kine are used as symbols for divine fertility, reproductive capacity and boundless supply. Oxen add the quality of service, whilst bulls accentuate that of masculine virility and creative capacity. Both are seen as manifestations of those God-like attributes in both Nature and man. The uninitiated, ignorant of these inner meanings, worship the outer form—an all too common example of the degeneration of sublime truth into crude superstition. The wise, on the other hand, recognising the aptness of the symbology, reverence the divine power which it represents and see in such living creatures manifestations of that power.

Whilst it is undesirable at all times to carry the interpretative process too far, the introduction into the dream of the number seven suggests a numerical significance. Macrocosmically, this is a ruling number referring to the levels of density of matter of which the Universe consists—the so-called planes of Nature—and also to the divine consciousness, Presence and Orders of Intelligences associated with each of such planes.[1] Similarly, in man the microcosm, his seven vehicles of action and awareness at those levels, his evolutionary progression and his accompanying experiences are all indicated

[1] see Appendix—The Sephirothal Tree.

by this number.   It also denotes a major change in both universal and racial history and in the affairs of men.   A sevenfold cycle has been completed and its successor is about to open.

Corn has from time immemorial been used as a symbol for the fertility of Nature in its aspect of all-provider.   Ears of corn were introduced into the Eleusinian Rites of Initiation, for example, and are depicted on the third card (the Empress) of the Trumps Major of the *Tarot*.[1]   They are also referred to in modern Freemasonry, where they are given the same significance.   The general and more exoteric meaning attributed to ears of corn is that of abundance, whilst esoterically the all pervading, divine life-force and its complete availability to Universe and man are indicated. The masses are unaware of the esoteric meaning, but the Initiate learns it by direct experience of unity with that life.   Joseph perceived and related the not dissimilar temporal meaning of the symbology and of the number seven.   Famine was imminent, supplies were going to be greatly reduced, and it was essential to prepare for the emergency.

Gen. 41: 8. *And it came to pass in the morning that his spirit was troubled; and he sent and called for all the magicians of Egypt, and all the wise men thereof: and Pharaoh told them his dream: but there was none that could interpret them unto Pharaoh.*

    9. *Then spake the chief butler unto Pharaoh, saying, I do remember my faults this day :*

    10. *Pharaoh was wroth with his servants, and put me in ward in the captain of the guard's house, both me and the chief baker :*

    11. *And we dreamed a dream in one night, I and he; we dreamed each man according to the interpretation of his dream.*

    12. *And there was there with us a young man, an Hebrew, servant to the captain of the guard; and we told him, and he interpreted*

---

[1] The *Tarot*: A pack of seventy two cards, for a long time in the possession of the Gipsy people.   Much altered in modern versions, they are exoterically regarded as of relatively recent, though unknown, origin.   An exoteric view of them is that they represent an extremely ancient pictorial and symbolic presentation of the deepest occult and spiritual mysteries concerning God, man, the Universe, and the relationship between them. According to this view they are a symbolic and pictorial text-book of the Ageless Wisdom —a veritable Bible.   Their origin is variously traced to Egypt, India, Tibet and China. The religious art of the ancient peoples of each of those countries displays examples of the cards in a modified form.   The meaning of the word *Tarot* is not decisively known, it having been associated with the Egyptian Deity *Ptah* and with the word *Ta* (Path) *Ro* (Royal), meaning the royal path of life.   The ancient hieroglyphic Egyptian word *tara* (to require an answer or to consult) is also considered as a possible origin of the word. In another view, the word *Taro* is associated with the divinity *Ashtaroth*, in its turn supposedly derived from the Indo-Tartar *tan-tara*, the *Tarot*, the Zodiac.   q.v. *The Tarot*, Paul Foster Case, and other works.

> to us our dreams; to each man according to his dream he did interpret.
>
> 13. And it came to pass, as he interpreted to us, so it was; me he restored unto mine office, and him he hanged.

Two states of consciousness are here indicated—passage through mystical experiences (dreams) and enquiry for enlightenment. These aptly portray the condition of the inner Self of a Candidate for Initiation. At this stage he or she is already illumined and has begun to convey spiritual light to the outer personality (Pharaoh). Thus the search has begun, the quest for truth has been embarked upon. As is not unusual, the needed guidance can come from apparently lowly persons, such as a butler or even a supposed criminal in prison. In the choice of possible sources of spiritual knowledge, truth and light, the truly enquiring mind is unaffected either by convention or by worldly station. This is exemplified in the story of St. Christopher. Before he was canonised he saw an old woman of lowly degree waiting to cross a river—symbolical, doubtless, of "the stream" said to be entered by successful Candidates for Initiation. Taking her upon his shoulders, he found that "she" was in reality the Christ-child Himself (pure wisdom) in disguise. Together they cross the river (Initiation) and reach the "further shore" (Adeptship). The Nativity of the Christ similarly occurred in the humble surroundings of a stable. Returning to the Biblical verses, Pharaoh's readiness for the direct receipt of truth as an interior experience is affirmed by the fact that in the first dream he was standing on the banks of a river. He awoke, slept again and had a second dream. On awakening, after the magicians and wise men of Egypt had failed to interpret his dreams, he sought for and found the needed guidance from Joseph, who was still a prisoner. Man's age-old and continuing search for truth is thus allegorically described, as also is the non-discriminatory direction of that search.

> Gen. 41: 14. Then Pharaoh sent and called Joseph, and they brought him hastily out of the dungeon: and he shaved himself, and changed his raiment, and came in unto Pharaoh.
>
> 15. And Pharaoh said unto Joseph, I have dreamed a dream, and there is none that can interpret it: and I have heard say of thee, that thou canst understand a dream to interpret it.
>
> 16. And Joseph answered Pharaoh, saying, It is not in me: God shall give Pharaoh an answer of peace.

The fact that Pharaoh successfully turned to so lowly a being as a prisoner in a dungeon after his official wise men had failed him, may also be regarded as a reference to the limitations of orthodox religion. As already indicated, a lowly man was turned to as a source of inspiration and guidance. Where spirituality and discernment are concerned, rank and station in the realm are without significance. Reality is a great leveller, as Diogenes demonstrated to Alexander in Greece, and Joseph to Pharaoh in

Egypt.   True spirituality is no respecter of persons, and in Joseph Pharaoh found not only an interpreter but one who recognised and affirmed that his interpretations were the result not of any special mental capacities as a mortal man, but of the activity of the divine within him.   Thus, even in the historical sense, the account is full of deep meaning.

Mystically interpreted, Pharaoh—the ruling mental power and life of the outer man—turns to the immortal Self, the divine Spirit (Joseph) in search of light and truth, knowing that Spirit alone to be the source of true illumination.   The whole man is thus allegorically described as having reached such a stature that he could no longer be kept in prison.   Neither mind nor body could any more inhibit the powers of the immortal Self, for which now they are vehicle rather than prison.   The fact that the King himself orders the liberation of Joseph, and eventually elevates him to the highest position in the land, indicates not only recognition of this inner power but also complete surrender to it—the all-important factor.

Gen. 41: 17.   *And Pharaoh said unto Joseph, In my dream, behold, I stood upon the bank of the river:*

18.   *And, behold, there came up out of the river seven kine, fatfleshed and well favoured; and they fed in a meadow:*

19.   *And, behold, seven other kine came up after them, poor and very ill favoured and leanfleshed, such as I never saw in all the land of Egypt for badness:*

20.   *And the lean and the ill favoured kine did eat up the first seven fat kine;*

21.   *And when they had eaten them up, it could not be known that they had eaten them; but they were still ill favoured, as at the beginning.   So I awoke.*

22.   *And I saw in my dream, and, behold, seven ears came up in one stalk, full and good;*

23.   *And, behold, seven ears, withered, thin, and blasted with the east wind, sprung up after them;*

24.   *And the thin ears devoured the seven good ears; and I told this unto the magicians; but there was none that could declare it to me.*

As these verses merely repeat the account of Pharaoh's dreams, no further comment is here needed.

Gen. 41: 25.   *And Joseph said unto Pharaoh, The dream of Pharaoh is one; God hath shewed Pharaoh what he is about to do.*

26.   *The seven good kine are seven year; and the seven good ears are seven years; the dream is one.*

Joseph immediately perceives—and so informs Pharaoh—that the number seven and the two main symbols, kine and corn, have the same meaning in each case.   They both represent time, each single symbol passing for one year.

Gen. 41: 27. *And the seven thin and ill favoured kine that came up after them are seven years; and the seven empty ears blasted with the east wind shall be seven years of famine.*

Joseph here reveals himself not only as an interpreter, but also as a prophet. He foresees the future, interprets the lean kine and the empty ears of corn as representing famine, and warns Pharaoh in good time so that he may prepare against the disaster.

Gen. 41: 28. *This is the thing which I have spoken unto Pharaoh; What God is about to do he sheweth unto Pharaoh.*

29. *Behold, there come seven years of great plenty throughout all the land in Egypt;*

30. *And there shall arise after them seven years of famine; and all the plenty shall be forgotten in the land of Egypt; and the famine shall consume the land;*

31. *And the plenty shall not be known in the land by reason of that famine following; for it shall be very grievous.*

32. *And for that the dream was doubled unto Pharaoh twice; it is because the thing is established by God, and God will shortly bring it to pass.*

Joseph offers an explanation of what he calls the " doubling " of the dream, namely two different symbols being used to refer to the same condition of the land of Egypt. Each of the two was in its turn doubled, in that there were fat and lean kine and good and withered corn. It must be admitted, however, that in the literal sense the divinatory interpretation is somewhat far-fetched, and it is not surprising that Pharaoh's wise men and magicians failed to suggest even a worldly interpretation of the two dreams—that they foretold oncoming periods of both abundance and famine. This failure of Pharaoh's soothsayers might be thought somewhat unusual, since the annual inundations of the land by the River Nile, upon which prosperity depended, were carefully noted and measured, records having been kept throughout a considerable number of years. The absence of any historical reference to seven years of famine in Egypt also suggests that the authors intended the whole narrative to be regarded as an allegory with mystical significance. Such a view would be in harmony with ideas expressed by ancient Rabbinical writers that "....the Torah,[1] in all of its words, holds supernal truths and sublime secrets ".

The interpretation of the dreams as revelations of successive septenary cycles has greater probability than if they were regarded purely as history, particularly as this revelation was part of the then concealed knowledge revealed to Initiates in the Sanctuary. Even though today the more exoteric portions of the doctrine of the sevenfold manifestation of Deity, and of

---

[1] *Torah*— " law ", meaning the *Pentateuch*.

septenary cycles in the life of Universes, Races and individuals, are publicly taught in philosophic literature, they are still far from being generally known, accepted and understood.   The esoteric significance of the number seven and its ramifications has not yet been wholly divulged nor, one may presume, is it likely to be completely revealed before the Race's entry upon the intuitive age.[1]   Individuals, however, may discern the hidden truth, whilst Initiates like Joseph have progressively received it in the Sanctuary.

The dreams of Pharaoh, it must be remembered, are the mental experiences of one person.   Joseph, who interprets them, represents the spiritually illumined inner Self of that same person, whilst all the other characters in the story of Joseph's life in Egypt are symbolic portrayals of various parts of the sevenfold make-up of man at different stages of evolution and undergoing different experiences.   The complexity of man, especially his sevenfold nature, was well known by the ancient writers, who had been instructed concerning it in the Mystery Schools of their days.   Forbidden under vows of silence to reveal it directly, yet desirous of preserving such valuable knowledge, they made it available to mankind in allegorical form in the Scriptures of the world.   This method of the bestowal upon humanity of profound and potentially power-bestowing knowledge was also used by the Sages of old.   When deciding to make these revelations they personified occult forces and procedures in both Cosmos and man in terms of gods, goddesses and human beings, and the interactions of these forces as intercourse between them.   Many of the gods and goddesses of ancient peoples are thus represented in the microcosm as the more spiritual parts of man, derived as they are from the one Source, referred to as the Father of the gods.   All characteristics and all actions attributed to the gods allegorically describe the qualities, the faculties and the mutual interplay of the seven Principles of man, and especially the varied powers appropriate to each of them.   The supposed intercourse of the gods—Zeus, for example—with human beings typifies the relationships between the divine and the human parts of man's nature.   This is an all-important key to the interpretation of the Scriptures and Mythologies of ancient peoples.

The same is true of the Macrocosm, where the existence, presence and activities of the divine and archetypal realms of being and their associated Intelligences are similarly described as attributes and actions of various gods.   The mortals who are admitted to intercourse of various kinds with the gods and goddesses Macrocosmically represent the divine Mind in Nature and its electrical energy, vitality and generative and regenerative forces.   All these are personified as the immortals, their mortal associates, and the demi-gods who are the children of their unions.

---

[1] See Glossary—Chain.

Gen. 41: 33. *Now therefore let Pharaoh look out a man discreet and wise, and set him over the land of Egypt.*

34. *Let Pharaoh do this, and let him appoint officers over the land, and take up the fifth part of the land of Egypt in the seven plenteous years.*

35. *And let them gather all the food of those good years that come, and lay up corn under the hand of Pharaoh, and let them keep food in the cities.*

36. *And that food shall be for store to the land against the seven years of famine, which shall be in the land of Egypt; that the land perish not through the famine.*

37. *And the thing was good in the eyes of Pharaoh, and in the eyes of all his servants.*

38. *And Pharaoh said unto his servants, Can we find such a one as this is, a man in whom the Spirit of God is ;*

39. *And Pharaoh said unto Joseph, Forasmuch as God hath shewed thee all this, there is none so discreet and wise as thou art ;*

40. *Thou shalt be over my house, and according unto thy word shall all my people be ruled; only in the throne will I be greater than thou.*

41. *And Pharaoh said unto Joseph, See, I have set thee over all the land of Egypt.*

JOSEPH'S RISE TO POWER

In the literal reading of these verses Joseph, having displayed wisdom and foresight, gains the confidence of Pharaoh, who appoints him as his Prime Minister. Esoterically, however, the outer man in all his parts (Pharaoh and his kingdom) surrenders to the immortal, inner Self (Joseph). Thereafter, in both senses, all things work out as Joseph had prophesied and advised. The essential qualities of caution and forethought, and the recognition of variability in the affairs of both ordinary and Initiated men, are also indicated in the wise advice which Joseph gave and Pharaoh accepted.

Gen. 41: 42. *And Pharaoh took off his ring from his hand, and put it upon Joseph's hand, and arrayed him in vestures of fine linen, and put a gold chain about his neck;*

The culmination and the harvested fruits of completed cycles (the ring) are here referred to. Macrocosmically, a septenary[1] cycle (Chain, Round Globe and Race[2]) closes and its successor is about to open (Joseph's new

[1] see *Gen.* 41: 18–30.
[2] see Glossary— Chain.

position in the realm). In the microcosmic application of the symbols employed the human Race attains to one of its successive culminations, and spiritualised man achieves a level of awareness in which realisation of oneness and of the law of cycles so changes and rejuvenates the mortal personality that it is renewed.

Pharaoh's ring placed upon the hand of Joseph indicates the capacity to put interior expansions of consciousness and the knowledge gained from them into active operation in the management of life. The ring symbolises both eternity and eternal cyclic progression. When these are realised the enlightened one becomes empowered and, as it were, enthroned. The vestures of fine linen represent the illumined aura, and the gold chain the symbol of the authority of the inner Self over the outer man, with which authority the Initiate is vested. In this more esoteric rendering these gifts are not received from without as benefices from a King, but are self-achieved and symbolise the natural results of spiritual and occult development. It will be recalled that a similar symbology is used in describing the return home of the Prodigal Son.[1]

> *Gen.* 41 : 43. *And he made him to ride in the second chariot which he had; and they cried before him, Bow the knee; and he made him ruler over all the land of Egypt.*

The language used in describing the triumph of Joseph somewhat suggests passages from Rituals of Initiation, and enthronement as Ruler for a certain period of time in a Chair of Office in the Temple of the Mysteries. Response to the words " Bow the knee " would indicate recognition of authority and the readiness of the other Initiates of the Temple to obey. The chariot as a whole is a symbol of both victory and a victorious man. The details of the component symbolism may be readily interpreted. The horse, for example, being a quadruped, represents the fourfold personal nature. The body of the chariot refers to the vesture of light, the Causal Body, whilst the rider within typifies the immortal Self after having attained to complete command of all vehicles of consciousness and activity. The wheels, being circular and so without end, suggest both the deathlessness achieved by the high Initiate, and the Eternal Principle. A whip, when used, would refer to the stimulating and onward-driving impulses which the Higher Self (the rider) conveys to the outer man (horses). The fact that Joseph was given the second chariot indicates that he was not yet an Adept, but was within measurable reach of that exalted state.

> *Gen.* 41 : 44. *And Pharaoh said unto Joseph, I am Pharaoh, and without thee shall no man lift up his hand or foot in all the land of Egypt.*
>
> 45. *And Pharaoh called Joseph's name Zaphnath-pa-a-neah; and he gave him to wife Asenath the daughter of Poti-pherah priest of On. And Joseph went over all the land of Egypt.*

[1] q.v. Volume I of this work, Pt. Four.

In these verses the natural actions of a grateful King arise from and are blended with the almost supernatural powers displayed by Joseph after illumination had been attained.   The events narrated concerning Joseph's imprisonment, liberation and installation in a high Office may well have happened, even though no references to any of them have thus far been discovered in Egyptian historical records.   Nevertheless the introduction into the story of Joseph's supernormal powers of perception as the basis and cause of the King's actions, and the use of the symbols which are interpreted above, do point to a possible revelation of supra-mundane ideas, laws and truths.

The contrast between Joseph's immediately preceding status as prisoner and his subsequent condition is here most marked.   In a brief space of time he is transported from a dungeon into the highest Office in the land under Pharaoh, given an official name and a wife, and is sent on an apparently official journey throughout Egypt.   Each successive phase of illumination, each new expansion of consciousness attained by a devotee or Initiate, can indeed seem to him to resemble a passage from darkness to light.   This progression continues until the last great secret is discovered and the Initiate moves on to the highest possible human development—the attainment of the stature of perfected manhood, an ascended Adept.   The symbol of the chariot, a vehicle of travel, may refer to Joseph's rapid progression in consciousness and his near approach to that exalted state.

The bestowal upon a person of a name other than that of his family may refer to changes in his inner nature, his phase of development and his degree of attainment.   Changes of name not infrequently occur in the *Pentateuch*, and in other occult works.   Jesus, for example, followed the custom of Adept Teachers in giving newly accepted disciples a mystic name symbolic of their attainment of an intimate relationship with Him.[1]   Marriage, which changes a woman's name, indicates in the symbolical language less a physical union than a conscious blending of the mortal with the immortal parts of man's nature, sometimes called " the heavenly marriage ". This mystical reading is somewhat underscored by the statement that Asenath was the daughter of a priest, who is associated with the Mysteries of religion.

Gen. 41 : 46. And Joseph was thirty years old when he stood before Pharaoh king of Egypt.   And Joseph went out from the presence of Pharaoh, and went throughout all the land of Egypt.

THE NUMBERS SEVEN AND THIRTY

As the number seven connotes the completion of a major cycle of both human and divine manifestation, so the number three indicates a completed

[1] *Mk.* 3: 17.

minor cycle which is a component of the larger cyclic fulfilment. In one of its many meanings seven is a number connoting completed self-expression of indwelling consciousness and life in a field of evolution. Three, on the other hand, represents rather an interior condition of readiness and ability to embark upon such self-expression. The triad is an essential of self-manifestation, whether human or divine. Mentally, for example, it represents the knower, that which is known and the act of cognition. In a more deeply interior significance it indicates the Self, the not-self and the inter-active relationship between them.

The number one alone is unavoidably inoperative. A pair provides the possibility of extension, and a triad is the product of the active relationship of the pair. The addition of naughts to numbers contained in allegories may be either a blind or a suggestion of the level or degree of power. Thus Joseph was thirty when his liberation from the dungeon and his exaltation to high Office in Egypt occurred, and Jesus was said to be thirty years old, or nearly so, when His full ministry began. This may be because the tenth triad of years is about to open—an age at which the divine triplicity in man finds conditions favourable to bestowal of mystic illumination upon the personality, whereupon a high calling is embarked upon. The inner, threefold Self, the true immortal man, is able to convey to the mind-brain that degree of spiritual power and enlightenment which bestows the impulse and capacity for the beginning of both new interior experiences and more effective outer action. Even in normal human life the period of change from the twenties into the thirties can be a time when the highest idealism and the deepest understanding influence both motive and conduct. Maturity follows, deepening experience and adding wisdom to decisions and to the resultant actions.

In the familiar symbol of Solomon's Seal,[1] the upward-pointing equilateral triangle symbolises the threefold manifestation of Deity. The down-ward pointing equilateral triangle of the same size interlaced with it represents the reflection and expression of the higher Triad in matter of three degrees of density—the mental, emotional and physical planes. The diagram completes a geometrical portrayal of both the divine Triplicity and the human spiritual Triad in any field of manifestation. The circle drawn around the figure refers in part to the necessary enclosure of the field of expression and activity, the boundary of awareness, the " Ring-pass-not ".[2]

These and other applications of the symbols of numbers are referred to in the statement in this verse of *Genesis* that Joseph was thirty years old when he passed through the mystical experiences which led to his highest attainments. It is of interest that another wise and mature Joseph, also the son

[1] see diagram facing p. 99.
[2] Ring-pass-not—see Glossary.

of a Jacob,[1] appears as one of the members of a family triad in the New Testament, namely the foster father of Jesus Who, as already said, entered upon His mission at about the age of thirty.

Gen. 41 : 47. *And in the seven plenteous years the earth brought forth by handfuls.*

48. *And he gathered up all the food of the seven years, which were in the land of Egypt, and laid up the food in the cities; the food of the field, which was round about every city, laid he up in the same.*

49. *And Joseph gathered corn as the sand of the sea, very much, until he left numbering; for it was without number.*

Three symbols are here employed—the number seven, corn and abundance of supply. The number seven has already been interpreted, chiefly as referring to a completed cycle, whether in the Macrocosm or in the microcosm, and a summing up and carrying over of the fruits which had been harvested into the succeeding cycle. Thus for seven years Joseph gathered up and preserved the ripened corn of Egypt, storing it against future need. In this case that need is referred to as a famine, an acute shortage of food. Harvested corn is a symbol of the powers and capacities attained at the close of a cycle, whilst abundance refers to the fact that these are most plenteous, being the ultimate fruitage gained from the almost infinite potentialities locked up in the Immortal Germ of both Universe and man from the beginning of the cycle.

In a mystical interpretation corn and bread refer to spiritual and mental food, which consists of food for the mind—knowledge and understanding of divine truth. Joseph, typifying the Initiate, had become richly endowed with occult and mystic wisdom. The abundance which Egypt enjoyed during the first period of Joseph's Office also typifies this rich endowment, or entry into the fullness of knowledge.

Gen. 41 : 50. *And unto Joseph were born two sons before the years of famine came, which Asenath the daughter of Poti-pherah priest of On bare unto him.*

51. *And Joseph called the name of the firstborn Manasseh; For God, said he, hath made me forget all my toil, and all my father's house.*

52. *And the name of the second called he Ephraim; For God hath caused me to be fruitful in the land of my affliction.*

Forgetfulness of past sorrows and gratitude for fruitfulness and prosperity are suggested by the fact that Joseph is said to have had two children. His marriage to Asenath, the birth of two sons and their naming, may portray the transference of acquired wisdom through the mind to the emotional and physical parts (the two sons) of the outer, mortal personality. Interior

---

[1] *Matt.* 1; 16.

illumination is first experienced by the true Self of man, the Spirit indwelling in the immortal vesture of light. The transference of the effects of such exaltations of consciousness to the body and the bodily life must be systematically brought about by all Initiates of the Sanctuaries who, in obedience to the laws governing such attainment (Yoga), deliberately harmonise the mortal nature of man with the higher, immortal Self.

The seven Principles and vehicles which, with the indwelling Spirit, constitute the total human being are sometimes described in inspired allegories as members of a family. The parents generally represent the more spiritual aspects of man's nature, whilst the offspring indicate the mortal vehicles.[1] The processes of naming, of the bestowal of gifts, and of the later handing on of such Offices as those of Patriarch, Prophet or Judge to the children, may refer to the handing on of power both from one cycle to the next and from one incarnation of a human Ego to its successor.

Should it appear necessary, pardon is here asked for the frequent references in this work to the procedure of the transference of spiritual power from the Logos of one Universe to that of its successor, from one incarnation of a Monad-Ego to the next, and also from the Hierophant of a Temple of the Mysteries to His successor in Office. This repetition is deliberate, being due to the conviction that the idea involved is of great importance. Throughout the years of my study of the Bible and my attempts to interpret it as an exposition of the One Wisdom Religion, I have arrived at the conclusion that such a fundamental procedure concerning the manifestation of spiritual power, wisdom and intelligence occurs in obedience to a system of unbroken and ordered progression. The law is somewhat fully commented on in Chapter XI of Part Six of Volume II of this work, in which Macrocosmic and microcosmic transmissions of power and authority receive consideration. The subject is indeed of great significance, if only because it provides assurance of both the eternal existence of the Spirit-Essence of manifested Universes and the unfailing, and so utterly to be trusted, preservation and sequence of incarnation and development of the human Monad. When accepted, the affirmation that in the reality of his existence man is immune from death can provide a spiritual and philosophic Rock of Ages upon which confidence in the assured safety and imperishability of the spiritual Self may be unshakeably established. This is affirmed in many World Scriptures. In the *Bhagavad-Gita*, as translated by Sir Edwin Arnold in his peerless poem, *The Song Celestial*, it is stated as follows :

" I say to thee weapons reach not the Life;
Flame burns it not, waters cannot o'erwhelm,
Nor dry winds wither it. Impenetrable,
Unentered, unassailed, unharmed, untouched,

---

[1] see Glossary—Soul.

> Immortal, all-arriving, stable, sure,
> Invisible, ineffable, by word
> And thought uncompassed, ever all itself,
> Thus is the Soul declared ! "

Thus the essential human being is affirmed to be immortal and everlasting—a truth which it is important that man should possess, particularly during an age of transition like the present, characterised as it is by so much destruction and death.

> Gen. 41 : 53. And the seven years of plenteousness, that was in the land of Egypt, were ended.
>
> 54. And the seven years of dearth began to come, according as Joseph had said; and the dearth was in all lands; but in all the land of Egypt there was bread.
>
> 55. And when all the land of Egypt was famished, the people cried to Pharaoh for bread: and Pharaoh said unto all the Egyptians, Go unto Joseph; what he saith to you, do.
>
> 56. And the famine was over all the face of the earth; and Joseph opened all the storehouses, and sold unto the Egyptians; and the famine waxed sore in the land of Egypt.
>
> 57. And all countries came into Egypt to Joseph for to buy corn; because that the famine was so sore in all lands.

Revelation by means of numbers is included in the narrative of the life of Joseph. The Lord God, the Centre and the Source of all existence, is represented by the number one; plenty and famine by a pair; the triad by the age of Joseph; whilst the dreams introduce the number seven. This portion of the *Pentateuch* may thus be regarded as a revelation of spiritual and metaphysical truths by means of numbers, symbols and allegories.

Periods of plenty can refer symbolically to ages or epochs of the full manifestation of the divine power, life and consciousness in a Universe or any of its components, and this can apply to Solar System, Race or nation. The withdrawal of the hitherto outpoured life, on the other hand, is symbolised by famine. Activity and rest, expression and cessation, and other similar pairs of opposites, are described in the Sacred Language as alternations of plenty and of famine respectively.

Plenty, mystically interpreted and applied to civilisations, nations and smaller groups as well as to persons, also typifies fullness of spiritual experience insofar as evolutionary attainment permits. Famine, from this point of view, is used to imply limitation—even absence—of interior illumination. Within the major cycles of a nation's inception, rise, attainment of greatest height and gradual decline, minor cycles which repeat those phases can also occur. A study of the history of nations throughout a sufficient period of time leads to the discovery that they have passed through such major and minor cycles. Culture, philosophy and religion can reach their height (plenty) during a minor period, later to be followed by gross superstition, materialism and concentration upon physical existence and enjoyment (famine).   Similarly, during his lifetime man can also experience times of upliftment and aspiration which alternate with conditions of spiritual deadness and of concentration, sometimes enforced, upon the concerns of physical life.   Even the greatest mystics who have described their spiritual enlightenment refer to this alternation of periods of interior illumination and mental darkness.   As we have seen, plenty and famine are used in the Sacred Language as symbols for these two opposing and alternating conditions.

Fields, gardens and vineyards on the one hand, and wildernesses and deserts on the other, are also used to typify these two states.   Even Jesus was conscious of temptation during His forty days in the wilderness.[1]   The statement in verse fifty-six that there was a famine " over all the face of the earth " cannot be accepted as historically true, even though Egypt and surrounding countries may on occasion have suffered a decline of prosperity and shortages of food.   Similarly, whilst accounts of a great flood—which are to be found in the Scriptures of the Hindus, the Babylonians, the Hebrews and the Mayans, as also in Greek mythologies—indicate that the rising of the waters was very widespread, no authentic historical or geological records of a total world inundation exist.[2]   Neither such Egyptian records as are available nor the writings of contemporary and later historians in other Mediterranean countries tell of such a disaster.   It is therefore reasonable to assume that, consonant with the method of allegorical writers, psychological and mental states of nations and individuals are here being described.

The highly developed man, particularly the Initiate, is forewarned of the possibility of such alternations and taught how to preserve equanimity during periods of exaltation and depression.   In consequence, he is able to establish himself so firmly in a spiritual state (plenty) that the onset of less spiritual conditions of the mind (famine) can neither cause him wholly to lose his upliftment nor plunge him into despair.   Joseph, personifying such an informed and trained mystic, was so well supplied with corn that he could feed both his Egyptian subjects and the people of surrounding countries even whilst, allegorically, famine raged all about him.

---

[1] *Matt.* 4: 1–11.

[2] q.v. Ch. III of Part Two of Vol. II of this work and *Lecture Notes of the School of the Wisdom*, Vol. I (Rev. Ed.), Ch. XIV, Sec. 3, p. 361 *et seq.*

CHAPTER VI

JACOB SENDS HIS SONS TO EGYPT

JACOB sendeth his ten sons to buy corn in Egypt: they are imprisoned by Joseph for spies: their remorse for Joseph: their return: their relation to Jacob.

> *Gen.* 42: 1. *Now when Jacob saw that there was corn in Egypt, Jacob said unto his sons, Why do ye look one upon another*
>
> 2. *And he said, Behold, I have heard that there is corn in Egypt: get you down thither, and buy for us from thence; that we may live, and not die.*

" THERE IS CORN IN EGYPT "

The scene now changes from Joseph's home in Egypt to the country of his birth. He and his associates are temporarily replaced in the narrative by his father and his brothers. Evidently at that time there was famine in the land of Canaan, and the Patriarch took steps to replenish the local supplies. The phrase, " there is corn in Egypt ", has come down to modern days as a saying descriptive of a state of plenty existing amid a surrounding state of want. The step which Jacob took of sending his sons to an available source of food, their journey to Egypt and its favourable results, may be interpreted in the same way as have the alternating conditions of plenty and famine in Egypt, and Joseph's foresight and his storage of corn during the good years.

If the narrative of supposed physical events be regarded as also applicable to mental and spiritual levels of consciousness, then the action of Jacob may be interpreted as referring to steps to be taken for the recovery of lost or diminishing spiritual awareness. The land of Canaan, in this reading, typifies mankind in a condition of partial or complete loss of spirituality. The proper course to be pursued is allegorically indicated, namely to send sons (thoughts) to a source of supply. This source is man's own spiritual nature which is always in a state of abundance, being composed of divine powers and attributes. Since the Lesser and Greater Mysteries were still operative in Egypt at that time, the two statements that there was corn in Egypt and that Jacob sent his sons there for food may be regarded as symbolically appropriate.

Gen. 42 : 3. *And Joseph's ten brethren went down to buy corn in Egypt.*

4. *But Benjamin, Joseph's brother, Jacob sent not with his brethren; for he said, Lest peradventure mischief befall him.*

BENJAMIN IS RETAINED AT HOME

Whilst Jacob's action in keeping Benjamin at home may in a literal reading be regarded as a simple precaution, it is also descriptive of a quality in human nature which finds expression both in the ordinary affairs of life and in the fulfilment of the conditions necessary for illumination.   In his secular and his spiritual motives and actions, man is prone to offer only an incomplete self-giving and self-surrender.   He tends to hold something back.   Symbolically, Benjamin is not sent to Egypt.   In religious matters especially, and even on the Path of Discipleship, man is inclined— not unnaturally—to cling to some specially valued quality or habit.   If the narrative be thus read then Joseph, the spiritual Self, sees through the subterfuge and the withholding.   He first accuses the brothers of being spies, and then demands that Benjamin also be brought into Egypt as proof of their innocence (Chapter Forty-two of *Genesis*, verses Fourteen to Sixteen).

Gen. 42 : 5. *And the sons of Israel came to buy corn among those that came: for the famine was in the land of Canaan.*

6. *And Joseph was the governor over the land, and he it was that sold to all the people of the land: and Joseph's brethren came, and bowed down themselves before him with their faces to the earth.*

7. *And Joseph saw his brethren, and he knew them, but made himself strange unto them, and spake roughly unto them; and he said unto them, Whence come ye? And they said, From the land of Canaan to buy food.*

8. *And Joseph knew his brethren, but they knew not him.*

The preceding interpretation is somewhat supported by the statement that Joseph knew his brethren, but they failed to recognise him.   Similarly the inner Self of man, as personified by Jacob in the first place, knows its vehicles of self-expression and their Zodiacal qualities, these being personified by his family (twelve sons).   The outer, mortal man does not normally know of the existence of his own spiritual Self even though, experiencing a divine discontent (famine) and the inexpressible longing of the inner man for the Infinite (need for spiritual food), he feels drawn towards it after a certain phase of evolution has been entered (seeks and finds the Path).

This also applies to Joseph and the visiting brethren.   These were ten in number, Benjamin remaining at home.   The inner Self is whole, integrated, illumined, whilst the outer Self, composed of many qualities and faculties, is divided and can even be at war within itself.   Under such conditions man in his brain-mind is not perceptive enough to be aware of his own divine nature, even though it is always present (" And Joseph knew his brethren, but they knew not him. ").   Otherwise expressed, in the narrative the ten brothers were sent by their father to Egypt and came into Joseph's presence. This may be read as a description of that stage of the development of man at which, conscious of the emptiness of life (famine) and yet without a philosophic and spiritual understanding, the search for truth (Egypt and stocks of food) begins.

Gen. 42: 9. *And Joseph remembered the dreams which he dreamed of them, and said unto them, Ye are spies; to see the nakedness of the land ye are come.*

10. *And they said unto him, Nay, my lord, but to buy food are thy servants come.*

11. *We are all one man's sons; we are true men, thy servants are no spies.*

12. *And he said unto them, Nay, but to see the nakedness of the land ye are come.*

13. *And they said, Thy servants are twelve brethren, the sons of one man in the land of Canaan; and, behold, the youngest is this day with our father, and one is not.*

14. *And Joseph said unto them, That is it that I spake unto you, saying, Ye are spies;*

15. *Hereby ye shall be proved; By the life of Pharaoh ye shall not go forth hence, except your youngest brother come hither.*

16. *Send one of you, and let him fetch your brother, and ye shall be kept in prison, that your words may be proved, whether there be any truth in you; or else by the life of Pharaoh surely ye are spies.*

17. *And he put them all together into ward three days.*

When at last the inner Self of man becomes strong enough to dominate the outer self, it will brook no denial.   All must be surrendered.   Allegorically, the unillumined sons of Jacob must be brought into the presence of their illumined brother, Joseph.

A spiritual law is here enunciated,[1] human attempts to evade its full provisions being described in metaphor.   Such evasion, being contrary to the law of self-surrender which governs unyieldingly the procedure of hastened illumination, cannot be permitted and eventually the full surrender of the human to the divine is made.   This demand and its eventual complete response are well described in Francis Thompson's poem, *The Hound of Heaven*, particularly in the following line:

" Naked I wait Thy love's uplifted stroke ! "

---

[1] see Pt. One, Ch. I, under cross - heading: " Selfless Giving Brings Spiritual Enrichment ".

If at this point it be asked why the text should not be regarded as simple history alone, it may be answered that of course each reader of the Bible is quite free to make his own interpretation.   Indications of undermeanings are not generally to be found so much in historical records as in the manner of their telling.   Impossibilities, incredibilities, divine interventions, and the systematic use of allegories and symbols point to an intention on the part of the authors to impart timeless and sometimes power-bestowing truths by means of narration of events in time.[1]   The truths revealed and guidance given to man in both his material and his spiritual life are of such great value as to justify in those so moved a diligent and faithful attempt to draw back the veil of allegory and symbol.

The time-period of the arrest—three days—recorded in verse seventeen may be regarded as an example of this appeal, when reading the Scriptures, to employ the intuition and apply the keys of interpretation.   Symbolical meanings of the number three have already been suggested.   One of them is that it refers to the triple nature of both the immortal and the mortal parts of man.   Immortal man is threefold, being a reproduction and an expression of the triple Godhead, whilst his mortal nature is composed of his mind, his emotions and his physical body.   The ten brothers,[2] in their turn, represent attributes of the latter, and their imprisonment for three days indicates that the whole of the threefold nature of the mortal man is involved. Mind, emotion and body must each make a complete surrender, especially of their most valued attribute, which is so often kept back—as indicated by the absence of the youngest son, Benjamin.

> Gen. 42: 18. And Joseph said unto them the third day, This do, and live; for I fear God;
>
> 19. If ye be true men, let one of your brethren be bound in the house of your prison: go ye, carry corn for the famine of your houses :
>
> 20. But bring your youngest brother unto me; so shall your words be verified, and ye shall not die.   And they did so.
>
> 21. And they said one to another, We are verily guilty concerning our brother, in that we saw the anguish of his soul, when he besought us, and we would not hear; therefore is this distress come upon us.

---

[1] see Pt. One, Ch. I, Cross-heading: " The Veil of Allegory " and " Time as Mirror of Eternity ", and Ch. II from Cross-heading: " Incongruities as Clues to Deeper Meanings ", to end of Ch.

[2] The same applies to the twelve sons of Jacob, the twelve Tribes of Israel and the twelve disciples of Jesus, all of whom personify characteristics of human beings at different phases of their development. The story of Hercules performing his twelve labours may be similarly interpreted.

The foregoing interpretation is somewhat supported by the admission recorded in verse twenty-one that the brethren felt a sense of guilt and were therefore ready to make amends.

Gen. 42: 22. *And Reuben answered them, saying, Spake I not unto you, saying, Do not sin against the child; and ye would not hear? therefore, behold, also his blood is required.*

23. *And they knew not that Joseph understood them; for he spake unto them by an interpreter.*

24. *And he turned himself about from them, and wept; and returned to them again, and communed with them, and took from them Simeon, and bound him before their eyes.*

Simeon is forcibly taken as a hostage until the brothers return with Benjamin. Even so human nature, still clinging to some treasured possession or indulgence, offers an alternative, something less precious, being as yet unready for full surrender. If this interpretation be accepted, a deep psychological insight is displayed by the writers of the story of Joseph in Egypt. This particularly concerns the attitude of mind of Candidates for spiritual progress through the Grades of the Mysteries, especially when confronted with the difficulties, psychological and physical, inseparable from passage through those Grades. In this, the Initiatory reading, the term "famine" may be interpreted as a symbolic description of a certain poverty of spiritual wisdom in contrast to full spiritual awareness as typified by plenty.

Gen. 42: 25. *Then Joseph commanded to fill their sacks with corn, and to restore every man's money into his sack, and to give them provision for the way: and thus did he unto them.*

26. *And they laded their asses with the corn, and departed thence.*

JOSEPH AS PERSONIFICATION OF A HIEROPHANT OF THE MYSTERIES

Spiritual wisdom and knowledge (symbolised by sacks of corn) are received by the outer man in his brain-mind from the spiritual Self (personified by Joseph). The immediate need of the aspirant seeking both occult progress and interior illumination is thus met, and from sources in Egypt, which at that time was one of the world's great Centres of the Ancient Mysteries. It may well be here repeated that the story of Joseph is the story of the Spirit, the Soul and the body of every man. In the episodes referred to in these Chapters, the progress of the spiritual Soul of man upon the pathway of swift attainment would also seem to be described; for the incidents are indeed susceptible of interpretation as allegories of interior experiences, limitations of development, and consequent difficulties encountered by aspirants seeking to tread that Path. It should also be

16

remembered that all the main characters in such an allegory represent vehicles of consciousness, powers, attributes and weaknesses of one person, who is man himself.

Joseph, for example, personifies the spiritual Soul at an advanced stage of evolution towards Adeptship. He is therefore able to provide the awakened and seeking personal nature, represented by the brothers who visit him, with needed wisdom (food). As an Officiant in a Temple of the Greater Mysteries Joseph personifies the Hierophant.[1] In an Initiatory interpretation, the complete episode may be regarded as an allegorical description of preparation for, and the conferring of, an Initiation.

The experience of Simeon, who is held as a hostage and is bound in prison, aptly portrays the limiting effects of incarnation in a physical body (imprisonment) and its unresponsiveness to the inner Self (famine). Benjamin, the youngest son, who is most generously treated by Joseph, personifies the dawning intuitive faculty, the " little child " state of mind, whilst the father Jacob, who remains at home, may be looked upon as representing the Monad, the Dweller in the Innermost. Israel, as a country suffering famine, represents the material state of the man bereft of Egoic and Monadic " riches ", and Egypt the Causal Body in which the Ego (Joseph) abides, which contains the stored up riches (faculties and capacities) resulting from former lives.

The story itself may be interpreted as an account of the drawing together of the Monad-Ego or spiritual part of evolved man on the one hand and the personal vehicles on the other, in order that the whole man, immortal and mortal, may participate in the attainment of hastened evolutionary progress. The fruits are additional powers of will, wisdom, realised unity with all that lives, and comprehension of the laws and processes under which the abstract Divinity becomes manifest in the concrete forms of Nature (corn, money and a silver cup).

> *Gen.* 42: 27. *And as one of them opened his sack to give his ass provender in the inn, he espied his money; for, behold, it was in his sack's mouth.*
>
> 28. *And he said unto his brethren, My money is restored; and, lo, it is even in my sack: and their heart failed them, and they were afraid, saying one to another, What is this that God hath done unto us ?*

---

[1] This view is somewhat supported by the statement that Joseph has symbolic dreams (*Gen.* 37), resists Potiphar's wife (*Gen.* 39) and is able to interpret the dreams of Pharaoh's servants (*Gen.* 40), and later of Pharaoh himself (*Gen.* 41: 25 *et seq.*), and correctly predict the famine. Occult tradition draws attention to the fact that the name of the father both of the Joseph of this narrative and of Joseph the husband of the Virgin Mary was Jacob (*Matt.* 1: 16), suggesting possible similar identity, as of reincarnations of the same spiritual Soul.

JOSEPH'S BRETHREN—PERSONIFICATIONS OF SPIRITUALLY AWAKENED MAN

The spiritual need (famine) had been recognised and acknowledged (journey to Egypt for food). As always occurs when the acknowledgement is genuine, when the cry for wisdom is sincere, a response had been received. Under such conditions the life processes can prove prodigally generous. The Hierophant of the Temple (Joseph) holds naught back, not only giving to each aspirant the needed supply of " corn " but also returning his own expenses, as it were. This unlooked-for benefit can produce wonder and amazement in the mind of the recipient. Rich stores, not only of wisdom and knowledge but sometimes even of wealth, can flow unexpectedly into the possession of the sincere, ardent and selfless aspirant.

Gen. 42: 29. *And they come unto Jacob their father unto the land of Canaan, and told him all that befell unto them; saying,*

30. *The man, who is the lord of the land, spake roughly to us, and took us for spies of the country.*

31. *And we said unto him, We are true men; we are no spies:*

32. *We be twelve brethren, sons of our father; one is not, and the youngest is this day with our father in the land of Canaan.*

33. *And the man, the lord of the country, said unto us, Hereby shall I know that ye are true men; leave one of your brethren here with me, and take food for the famine of your households, and be gone;*

34. *And bring your youngest brother unto me: then shall I know that ye are no spies, but that ye are true men: so will I deliver you your brother, and ye shall traffick in the land.*

35. *And it came to pass as they emptied their sacks, that, behold, every man's bundle of money was in his sack: and when both they and their father saw the bundles of money, they were afraid.*

These verses reveal again that the brothers did not recognise Joseph as one of their number, a member of their own family. Changed from the time when they lowered him into the pit, fully grown up and robed in both power and the vestments of power, he was unknown to them. Failure to recognise, followed by recognition, is not infrequently used in the writings of the Sacred Language. Mary Magdalene does not at first recognise her Master when she meets Him in the garden after His Resurrection. When he mentions her name, however, she recognises Him and at once addresses Him by the title descriptive of His relationship with her—" Rabboni; which is to say, Master. "[1] Similarly, Joseph's brethren did not for some time recognise him in his new and exalted position.

[1] Jn. 20: 16.

Mystically interpreted, a phase in the development of spiritual awareness is here represented. For some time after the quest for light has begun the aspirant is unaware of the source of the inspiration by which he was inwardly moved. Even when conscious that such a source exists, its real nature is not at first recognised. The interior impulse is sufficiently strong, however, to bring illumination and understanding (corn and money) and to bestow upon the devotee the will to continue the search for light. The two conditions of famine and plenty, it may be repeated, refer to mental states—the absence and the presence of spiritual understanding and intuitiveness. In due course the cry for light is answered abundantly. Famine is then replaced by plenty. The grief of Mary Magdalene gives way to happiness on discovery that the Master still lives. The veil falls away from the eyes of the disciples at Emmaus. The " hoodwink " of materialism and mental blindness is removed after Initiation.

The two mystical states of failure to recognise and subsequent recognition are also presented by allegories of the arrival of a hero or Saviour who withholds his name—indeed may even forbid attempts to discover it, as in the case of Lohengrin. In such cases a warning is given against undue particularisation of a universal principle, such as forcing abstract Truth to subscribe to the limitations of personal outlook. Allegorically, a name is sought but for a time withheld. Should the warning be disregarded the illumination may be lost. Symbolically, by her insistence upon knowing his name Elsa (the concrete mind) loses Lohengrin (the intuition and the wisdom it reveals). Ultimately, however, every idea so revealed becomes justified at the bar of the intellect.

> Gen. 42: 36. *And Jacob their father said unto them, Me have ye bereaved*
> *of my children: Joseph is not, and Simeon is not, and ye will*
> *take Benjamin away: all these things are against me.*
>
> 37. *And Reuben spake unto his father, saying, Slay my two sons,*
> *if I bring him not to thee: deliver him into my hand, and I will*
> *bring him to thee again.*
>
> 38. *And he said, My son shall not go down with you; for his brother*
> *is dead, and he is left alone: if mischief befall him by the way*
> *in the which ye go, then shall ye bring down my grey hairs with*
> *sorrow to the grave.*

Resistance to the law of complete surrender by which alone full enlightenment may be gained, and a certain mental if not unnatural perversity, are here portrayed. This condition is descriptive of a difficult phase through which every mystic must pass. A certain obstinacy, combined with possessive desire, can persist as an attribute and this for a time may hold up the progress of the Soul towards light and truth. The necessity for the sacrifice of what is held most dear causes the Soul to shrink from so great a loss. Eventually, however, as earlier in the case of Abraham and

Isaac, mental readiness is attained and the surrender made. This is followed by the discovery that when the mind has liberated itself from possessiveness, the surrender is not demanded. Instead of a great and dreaded loss, a wondrous gain is experienced. There is always a ram in the thicket.[1]

This principle operates not only in the spiritual life in general, and particularly in the attainment of pure wisdom, but also in the affairs of daily life. Undue possessiveness, jealousy and suspicion always come between those who suffer from them and the happiness which they seek. In these verses Jacob in his old age is made to reveal these limitations and also the operation of this law.

[1] *Gen.* 22: 13.

CHAPTER VII

JOSEPH IS REUNITED WITH HIS BRETHREN

Gen. 43: *Jacob is hardly persuaded to send Benjamin. Joseph entertaineth his brethren; their fears; he maketh them a feast.*

Gen. 43: 1. *And the famine was sore in the land.*

2. *And it came to pass, when they had eaten up the corn which they had brought out of Egypt, their father said unto them, Go again, buy us a little food.*

3. *And Judah spake unto him, saying, The man did solemnly protest unto us, saying, Ye shall not see my face, except your brother be with you.*

4. *If thou wilt send our brother with us, we will go down and buy the food:*

5. *But if thou wilt not send him, we will not go down: for the man said unto us, Ye shall not see my face, except your brother be with you.*

6. *And Israel said, Wherefore dealt ye so ill with me, as to tell the man whether ye had yet a brother?*

7. *And they said, The man asked us straitly of our state, and of our kindred, saying, Is your father yet alive? have ye another brother? and we told him according to the tenor of these words: could we certainly know that he would say, Bring your brother down?*

8. *And Judah said unto Israel his father, Send the lad with me, and we will arise and go; that we may live, and not die, both we, and thou, and also our little ones.*

9. *I will be surety for him; of my hand shalt thou require him: if I bring him not unto thee, and set him before thee, then let me bear the blame for ever:*

10. *For except we had lingered, surely now we had returned this second time.*

11. *And their father Israel said unto them, If it must be so now, do this; take of the best fruits in the land in your vessels, and carry down the man a present, a little balm, and a little honey, spices and myrrh, nuts, and almonds:*

12. *And take double money in your hand; and the money that was brought again in the mouth of your sacks, carry it again in your hand; peradventure it was an oversight;*

13. *Take also your brother, and arise, go again unto the man :*

Judah her epersonifies the very Spirit which inspires an aspirant to seek the inner light. He represents also that intuitive perception which has reached the mind-brain of the outer man, and eventually enabled him to override and outgrow the limitations of a former, narrower outlook. The phase of unfoldment has at last been reached at which those limitations are transcended and, despite a still remaining sense of loss, the full surrender is made. Israel surrenders Benjamin, his youngest and most beloved son.

Gen. 43: 14. *And God Almighty give you mercy before the man, that he may send away your other brother, and Benjamin. If I be bereaved of my children, I am bereaved.*

The surrender is not made without difficulty, but it *is* made. Thereafter, symbolically, famine will be replaced by plenty, separation from loved ones will lead to joyous reunion.

Gen. 43: 15. *And the men took that present, and they took double money in their hand, and Benjamin; and rose up, and went down to Egypt, and stood before Joseph.*

16. *And when Joseph saw Benjamin with them, he said to the ruler of his house, Bring these men home, and slay, and make ready; for these men shall dine with me at noon.*

17. *And the man did as Joseph bade; and the man brought the men into Joseph's house.*

THE NOONDAY FEAST OF REUNION

Feasts in the Sacred Language are descriptive of the interior sense of spiritual replenishment, the fulfilled state and the serene ease which are experienced when mystical unions are achieved. These unions are of varying degree and are entered into progressively as phases of unfoldment are passed through.

The primary union is between the mind-brain of the outer, mortal man and the consciousness of the Inner Ruler Immortal, the spiritual Soul. This is followed by the fusion of the higher intellect with the intuitive Principle, in its turn leading to entry into the state of being in which abides the inmost Self of man, the Dweller in the Innermost. Each of these experiences is gradual and may appear as if attained through successive minor unifications, bringing great intellectual clarification and illumination—a condition of consciousness often symbolised by feasting.[1] Both of these lead to the

[1] q.v. Vol. I of this work, pp. 195–8 Adyar Ed., and pp. 189–192 Quest Book Series, see *Luke* 15: 23,

greatest of all realisations of unity—that of the Spirit of man with the Spirit
of the Cosmos.   Although man-Spirit and God–Spirit have always been
one, their unity has not hitherto been realised.   All preceding discoveries
of oneness and their accompanying expansions of consciousness are included
in this great attainment of freedom from the illusion of being a self-separate
individuality.   Such an experience is referred to symbolically as a union,
reunion, or marriage between actors in the allegorical dramas of which the
Sacred Language is built.

The hour of noon at which Joseph decides that the feast must occur
may be regarded as a hint of the presence of an underlying occult allusion.
The sun represents the highest Principle in man, the innermost Self, the
Monad, whilst the solar ray of power (*Ātma*) is the very core of human
existence.   Just as night, sleep, blindness and darkness sometimes symbolise
conditions of temporary mental darkness and weakness, so day describes
their opposites—the illumined and empowered state.   The hour of high
noon is the period and condition of consciousness in which the realisation
of the Self as divine reaches its greatest height.   This is an apt analogy,
since the sun exercises its maximum power each day at its zenith.   It is
at that moment, therefore, that in inspired allegories important events are
made to happen.   In certain occult rituals Initiatory Rites are said to occur
when the sun is at its meridian.   Joshua, it will be remembered, forced
the sun to stand still in the midst of the heavens,[1] thereby supposedly
prolonging the period of daylight.   The complete physical impossibility
of such a feat and of such a result does not necessarily indicate ignorance of
the heliocentric system, but rather does it point to the presence in the text
of a spiritual revelation.[2]   The Initiate brings his highest spiritual power
(the sun) to a position of complete command over his whole being, and
especially the mind, which is thereafter maintained in a state of full illumination (day).   In consequence the proclivities of the outer nature are all
subdued (the enemy[3] is defeated).   Similarly, in the verses under consideration Joseph is made to order the feast celebrating the family reunion for
the hour of noon.

Gen. 43: 18. *And the men were afraid, because they were brought into Joseph's
house; and they said, Because of the money that was returned in
our sacks at the first time are we brought in; that he may seek
occasion against us, and fell upon us, and take us for bondmen,
and our asses.*

19. *And they came near to the steward of Joseph's house, and they
communed with him at the door of the house,*

[1] *Joshua* 10: 12–14.
[2] see Pt. One of this Vol., Ch. II, (f).
[3] The Gibeonites in the story of Joshua (*Joshua* 10).

20. *And said, O sir, we came indeed down at the first time to buy food;*

21. *And it came to pass, when we came to the inn, that we opened our sacks, and, behold, every man's money was in the mouth of his sack, our money in full weight: and we have brought it again in our hand.*

22. *And other money have we brought down in our hands to buy food: we cannot tell who put our money in our sacks.*

23. *And he said, Peace be to you, fear not: your God, and the God of your father, hath given you treasure in your sacks: I had your money.   And he brought Simeon out unto them.*

24. *And the man brought the men into Joseph's house, and gave them water, and they washed their feet; and he gave their asses provender.*

The tortuous nature of these incidents, the alarm experienced by the brethren, their attempts to clear themselves before the steward, his explanation and the reappearance of Simeon as the assurance of their security—all these describe typical activities of the mind, for the mind of unillumined man is tortuous, indirect, fearful, seeing hostile plots where none exist and constantly desiring self-justification.   Illumination is, however, about to be attained.   The inner Self (Joseph), robed in light, is about to reveal itself to the outer, mortal man (his brethren) with its many qualities and limitations (each brother).   The steward serves as link between the two, as bridge between the abstract, prophetic intellect and the more factual, concrete mind, thereby preparing for their blending.

Mental clarification is essential to the attainment of mystic union. When the mind is in doubt, and in addition is afraid, there can be neither clear vision nor profound interior enlightenment.   This would seem to be recognised by the authors of these passages in *Genesis*, who introduce the steward as a character in the drama and cause him, as a trusted servant of Joseph, to remove the apprehension of his brethren and so prepare them for the acceptance of Joseph's generosity.

All these procedures, it must be remembered, describe changes of consciousness occurring within one man—every man, indeed—who is on the threshold of illumination.[1]   Understanding of truth, serenity of mind and quietness of heart are essential precursors to illumination and Initiation.

Biblical references to the washing of feet—in which Joseph's brethren engaged—indicate both the purification of the whole nature and the " cleansing " of the mind of all impurities or obstructions to the receipt of spiritual illumination.   In some cases descriptions of actions involving the feet may be regarded as references (if an apparent pun may be forgiven) to under-

---

[1] see Pt. One of this Volume, Ch. II—some Keys of Interpretation.

standing, and also to the general conduct of life.[1]   The fact that the asses, normally stubborn quadrupeds, were given provender may be taken to indicate that the fourfold mortal man was mentally satisfied, content, serene.

> *Gen.* 43 : 25. *And they made ready the present against Joseph came at noon: for they heard that they should eat bread there.*
>
> 26. *And when Joseph came home, they brought him the present which was in their hand into the house, and bowed themselves to him to the earth.*

EVERY SYMBOL SCINTILLATES WITH MEANING[2]

Again, deeply interior states of mind immediately preceding spiritual upliftment are allegorically described.   To give presents to an exalted person implies that mental self-surrender which is essential to entry into the mystical state, just as bowing typifies selflessness and humility before one who is immeasurably greater.   Pride, it is thus shown, is completely banished, as also are fear and distrust.

If all these preliminaries merely recount minor actions on the part of the characters in the story, they are hardly worth recording.   If, on the other hand, essential conditions for true expansion of consciousness and union with the spiritual Self are being described, then each action, however apparently slight, is full of significance.   The whole story becomes a manual or text book of guidance upon the Pathway to the Inner Light.   The symbols used, the arrangement of the actions and the order of events as related are so precisely appropriate as descriptions of states of consciousness passed through by neophytes that a mystical interpretation may permissibly be justified.

> *Gen.* 43 : 27. *And he asked them of their welfare, and said, Is your father well, the old man of whom ye spake?   Is he yet alive?*
>
> 28. *And they answered, Thy servant our father is in good health, he is yet alive.   And they bowed down their heads and made obeisance.*

The narrative continues, the more intimate relationship between the immortal and the mortal selves of man being thus allegorically described. Question and answer in the Sacred Language, as also in occult Rituals, indicate the close approach and mutual *rapport* between the two protagonists, particularly when the interchanges are harmonious.

> *Gen.* 43 : 29. *And he lifted up his eyes, and saw his brother Benjamin, his mother's son, and said, Is this your younger brother, of whom ye spake unto me?   And he said, God be gracious unto thee, my son.*

---

[1] *Gen.* 18:4; 24:32; 43:24; 1 *Sam.* 25:41; *Luke* 7:38 and 44; *Jn.* 13:5–14; I *Tim.* 5: 10.
[2] Kabbalism,

30. *And Joseph made haste; for his bowels did yearn upon his brother: and he sought where to weep; and he entered into his chamber, and wept there.*

31. *And he washed his face, and went out, and refrained himself, and said, Set on bread.*

32. *And they set on for him by himself, and for them by themselves, and for the Egyptians, which did eat with him, by themselves; because the Egyptians might not eat bread with the Hebrews; for that is an abomination unto the Egyptians.*

33. *And they sat before him, the firstborn according to his birthright, and the youngest according to his youth; and the men marvelled one at another.*

34. *And he took and sent messes unto them from before him; but Benjamin's mess was five times so much as any of their's. And they drank, and were merry with him.*

Interpretations of the symbology of tears and of feasts have already been suggested. Mystically these verses indicate that full spiritual awareness, full realisation of the divine Self, though imminent, had not yet been achieved. The existence of some barriers is made apparent, since Joseph neither ate at the same table with his brothers nor revealed their true relationship.

THE MYSTICAL IDENTITY

The processes of the discovery of the Self, of knowing as a direct interior experience one's true identity, and of attaining unbroken realisation of unity, are preceded by many years—and even many lives—of gradual preparation and unfoldment. These are marked by increasing manifestations of the powers of the inner Self in the physical body. Genius, leadership and many special faculties indicate approach to the great discovery. Quite often, however, these developments are unconscious and unexplained manifestations of the light and power of the spiritual Self of evolved man. The genius rarely knows the true source of his powers. The divine *afflatus* does descend upon him, but he knows not whence. When at last the true Self reveals itself to the brain-mind, as Joseph later reveals himself to his brethren, fully conscious illumination is attained. The light and fire within are then recognised as divine in origin and that origin is known as his own true Self, the Father-in-God within the bodily man.

BENJAMIN—DAWNING SPIRITUAL INTUITIVENESS

Benjamin, absent at the first meeting between Joseph and some of his brethren, is now present and may be taken to represent the dawning intuitive sense which is already beginning to illumine the formal mind. From the point of view of the inner Self (Joseph) this is the most valuable part of the outer personality, even though the intuitive faculty is as yet potential rather than actual (Benjamin is the youngest son). The fact that Benjamin is born of the same mother as Joseph supports such an interpretation. The two are closely akin and the intuitive faculty is one of the attributes of the immortal Self of man. Benjamin therefore receives more than do his brothers, the number five possibly being a hint that spiritual intuitiveness is an attribute of the fifth Principle of man—that of divine Wisdom manifest in the inner self. The other four, beginning with the densest, are the physical, the emotional, the purely mental and that of the abstract intellect, the Causal Body. The sixth and seventh Principles consist of vehicles for the spiritual will and the true Dweller in the Innermost, which is the Monad. This, however, is but one of many classifications of the seven parts of which every human being consists, and the reference here to the number five may or may not have an occult significance.

ALL IS WITHIN

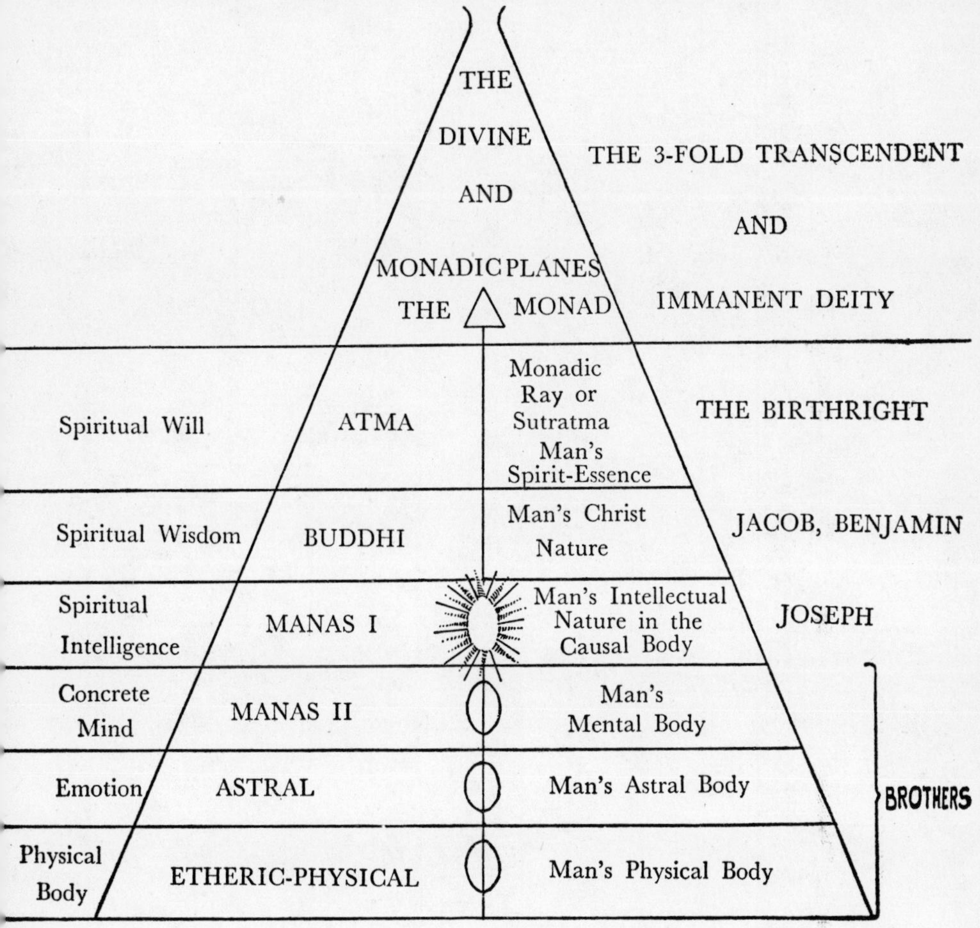

THE
DIVINE
AND
MONADIC PLANES
THE MONAD
THE 3-FOLD TRANSCENDENT
AND
IMMANENT DEITY
Spiritual Will
ATMA
Monadic Ray or Sutratma Man's Spirit-Essence
THE BIRTHRIGHT
Spiritual Wisdom
BUDDHI
Man's Christ Nature
JACOB, BENJAMIN
Spiritual Intelligence
MANAS I
Man's Intellectual Nature in the Causal Body
JOSEPH
Concrete Mind
MANAS II
Man's Mental Body
Emotion
ASTRAL
Man's Astral Body
BROTHERS
Physical Body
ETHERIC-PHYSICAL
Man's Physical Body

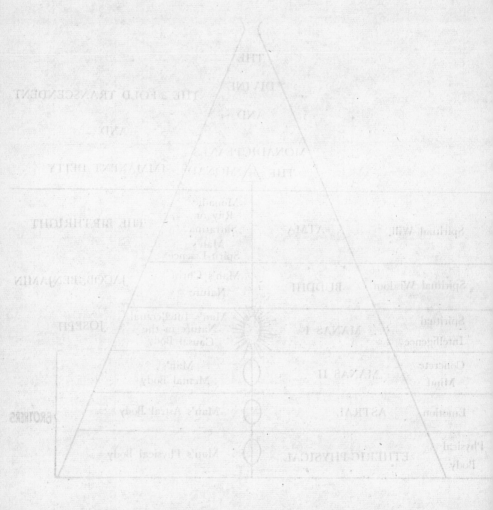

CHAPTER VIII

THE GIFT OF A SILVER CUP

Gen. 44: *Joseph's policy to stay Benjamin. Judah's humble supplication to Joseph.*

Gen. 44: 1. *And he commanded the steward of his house, saying, Fill the men's sacks with food, as much as they can carry, and put every man's money in his sack's mouth.*

2. *And put my cup, the silver cup, in the sack's mouth of the youngest, and his corn money. And he did according to the word that Joseph had spoken.*

Admittedly this Forty-fourth Chapter of the *Book of Genesis* may be read literally as an account of the generosity born of family love and of happiness at reunion, these two experiences causing Joseph to provide for his brothers. So many strange actions are, however, ascribed to Joseph that the Chapter may also be read as possessing underlying meanings.

A mystical interpretation applicable to every devotee would indicate a reference to the riches received by the mortal personality (the brethren) when consciously united with the inner, immortal, spiritual Soul (Joseph). Benjamin's sack would then represent both the enclosing aura and, more particularly, the mental body which is the receptacle of spiritual power, life and consciousness. This spiritually nutrifying life-force is symbolised by the corn, which is received according to maximum capacity, each brother's sack being filled. Joseph, in such a reading, represents the conjoined Spirit-Essence and the abstract intellect within the vesture of light[1] (Joseph's palace in the city of Egypt where the reunion is made to occur).

If, however, a Rite of Initiation performed in a temple of the Greater Mysteries is being described by means of allegory and symbol, then Joseph represents the Hierophant, his servants the other Officiants in the Ceremony, and the corn the transferred hierophantic power, wisdom and knowledge. The value of such illumination, and the great necessity for it experienced by the Candidate, are indicated by the famine in the country in which the brethren lived. Symbolically, an unillumined mind and heart are always in a state of " famine ", whether aware of it or not. Candidates for Initi-

---

[1] The Causal Body—see Glossary.

ation, being spiritually awakened and intellectually seeking men and women, experience so pressing a need that their pre-Initiation state is comparable to and aptly exemplified by famine. When the condition of a whole nation, or of one of its groups, is thus being referred to allegorically, the actual experience is always that of each and every person, of one man—notably the Initiate himself.

The youngest son, in this case Benjamin, generally personifies less a person than the awakening intuitive faculty, the emerging but as yet under-developed Christ-nature. Especial attention is always given to this new-born, child-like faculty, as is portrayed in Nativity and post-Nativity narratives in which the babe is said to be visited by angels, shepherds and Magi who offer their gifts. The aid given to these " little ones " may take the form of white spiritual power which descends into the Candidate's aura at the Rite of Consecration. This added and special gift is here aptly symbolised by a silver cup. Silver, being a white metal, corresponds vibrationally[1] to the Spirit-Essence (*Ātma*) of Universe and man. The gift is appropriately cup-shaped to indicate the Eucharistic ministrations to mankind of every Initiate, as allegorically portrayed by the priestly dis-pensation of the wine within the chalice at Holy Communion. The symbolism of the Holy Grail offers a further variant of this experience through which every illumined human being passes.

Benjamin thus personifies the dawning Christ-principle, whilst the filling of his sack with corn and the added gift of the silver cup imply the special assistance given to those who in their gradual evolution have reached the state of readiness for Initiation.

Gen. 44: 3. *As soon as the morning was light, the men were sent away, they and their asses.*

In the Sacred Language morning and light indicate the attainment of spiritual awareness. Whether referring to *Manvantara*, national life, or passage through an Initiation on the pathway to Adeptship, light in the above sense has been attained and a new phase entered upon.

Gen. 44: 4. *And when they were gone out of the city, and not yet far off, Joseph said unto his steward, Up, follow after the men; and when thou dost overtake them, say unto them, Wherefore have ye rewarded evil for good?*

5. *Is not this it in which my lord drinketh, and whereby indeed he divineth? ye have done evil in so doing.*

6. *And he overtook them, and he spake unto them these same words.*

7. *And they said unto him, Wherefore saith my lord these words? God forbid that thy servants should do according to this thing:*

---

[1] q.v. Chart of Correspondences preceding Pt. Five of Vol. II of this work (Adyar Ed.) and Glossary—The Law of Correspondences.

8. *Behold, the money, which we found in our sacks' mouths, we brought again unto thee out of the land of Canaan; how then should we steal out of thy lord's house silver or gold?*

9. *With whomsoever of thy servants it be found, both let him die, and we also will be my lord's bondmen.*

10. *And he said, Now also let it be according unto your words? he with whom it is found shall be my servant; and ye shall be blameless.*

11. *Then they speedily took down every man his sack to the ground, and opened every man his sack.*

12. *And he searched, and began at the eldest, and left at the youngest: and the cup was found in Benjamin's sack.*

13. *Then they rent their clothes, and laded every man his ass, and returned to the city.*

14. *And Judah and his brethren came to Joseph's house; for he was yet there: and they fell before him on the ground.*

15. *And Joseph said unto them, What deed is this that ye have done? wot ye not that such a man as I can certainly divine?*

16. *And Judah said, What shall we say unto my lord? what shall we speak? or how shall we clear ourselves? God hath found out the iniquity of thy servants: behold, we are my lord's servants, both we, and he also with whom the cup is found.*

17. *And he said, God forbid that I should do so: but the man in whose hand the cup is found, he shall be my servant; and as for you, get you up in peace unto your father.*

18. *Then Judah came near unto him, and said, Oh my lord, let thy servant, I pray thee, speak a word in my lord's ears, and let not thine anger burn against thy servant: for thou art even as Pharaoh.*

19. *My lord asked his servants, saying, Have ye a father, or a brother?*

20. *And we said unto my lord, We have a father, an old man, and a child of his old age, a little one; and his brother is dead, and he alone is left of his mother, and his father loveth him.*

21. *And thou saidst unto thy servants, Bring him down unto me, that I may set mine eyes upon him.*

22. *And we said unto my lord, The lad cannot leave his father: for if he should leave his father, his father would die.*

23. *And thou saidst unto thy servants, Except your youngest brother come down with you, ye shall see my face no more.*

24. *And it came to pass when we came up unto thy servant my father, we told him the words of my lord.*

25. *And our father said, Go again, and buy us a little food.*

26. *And we said, We cannot go down; if our youngest brother be with us, then will we go down: for we may not see the man's face, except our youngest brother be with us.*

27. *And thy servant my father said unto us, Ye know that my wife bare me two sons:*

28. *And the one went out from me, and I said, Surely he is torn in pieces; and I saw him not since:*

29. *And if ye take this also from me, and mischief befall him, ye shall bring down my gray hairs with sorrow to the grave.*

30. *Now therefore when I come to thy servant my father, and the lad be not with us; seeing that his life is bound up in the lad's life:*

31. *It shall come to pass, when he seeth that the lad is not with us, that he will die: and thy servants shall bring down the gray hairs of thy servant our father with sorrow to the grave.*

32. *For thy servant became surety for the lad unto my father, saying, If I bring him not unto thee, then I shall bear the blame to my father for ever.*

33. *Now therefore, I pray thee, let thy servant abide instead of the lad a bondman to my lord: and let the lad go up with his brethren.*

34. *For how shall I go up to my father, and the lad be not with me? lest peradventure I see the evil that shall come on my father.*

As in the interpretation of all allegories, each character personifies an aspect of one human being, and all the events and the experiences described occur within the consciousness of that single person. Briefly, Joseph is the higher Self, the brethren as a group personify the outer man, and Benjamin the nascent intuitive faculty. The events narrated describe interior changes and psychological reactions of each and every human being at certain phases of their evolution. The wrongful accusations which followed Joseph's beneficence are all descriptive of those changes of mind, such as doubt, to which every one is submitted who has decided to hasten his progress and has been especially assisted to do so. The circumstances of life, precipitations of *karma* and other experiences—all these can cause a devotee or an Initiate temporarily to doubt the reality of his mystical experiences. This is sometimes described as being in a wilderness or desert.

The illogical, unjust and very unkind conduct of Joseph towards his quite innocent brothers is unacceptable to the reasoning mind. Furthermore, it is contrary to the character of Joseph, whether the passage is read literally or interpreted metaphorically. If an affront to the intellect is thus encountered when reading the Scriptural and mythological allegories of ancient peoples, a search for a possible hidden meaning is always advisable and is generally indicated by the affront itself. The unaccountable and dishonest behaviour of Joseph towards his brethren narrated in this Chapter of *Genesis* may perhaps be read as a description of those temporary lapses from the spiritual ideal to which even the most promising aspirants are subject. Both guidance concerning and warning against the possibility may be gained from a perusal of the verses under consideration from this point of view.

Not only is bodily life subject to a strange law of alternations and cycles, not only is a certain repetitiveness discernible in personal and racial events, but also the psychological and intellectual experiences of man are likewise subject to such phenomena. Even Jesus, the Christ, experienced the states of consciousness symbolised by a wilderness and by the darkness in Gethsemane. He, prototype of every successful aspirant and Initiate, shrank from accepting the oncoming sorrow which He so clearly foresaw. Nevertheless He persisted and so succeeded where many others have failed.

The pathway of discipleship and Initiation is " strewn with the remains" of those who having travelled it—perhaps to the limit of their power—were thus unsuccessful. This defeat is temporary, however, since it is only the mortal personality which is involved. It was the immortal Self of man which set forth upon the great quest and inspired its bodily personality to do the same. For this reason the failure is not final, and is applicable only to the particular incarnation in which it occurs. Indeed, a recovery may be made later in that same life, but if this does not happen the great endeavour will most surely be undertaken in a later incarnation.

The strange withdrawal of the awakening power, life and light of the inner Self occurs for various reasons, amongst them the operation of the law of cycles referred to above. Astrological progressions month by month and year by year—and even day by day—distinctly portray the fluctuations, under the law, in the relationship between the inner and the outer man. The position of the sun relevant to the moon, together with the aspects assumed by other planets as shown in the progressed horoscope, provides an example of these fluctuations and this information can also be useful in its assurance that the changes are but temporary.

Experiences being passed through in the deeper depths of a human being may be thus regarded, and their effects upon the outer man evaluated accordingly. The above interpretation of the remaining verses of this Chapter may, in consequence, be useful to spiritually awakening aspirants, as also may other accounts of such adverse changes in the lives of heroes and of Saviours as recorded in the Mythologies and Scriptures of ancient peoples. Just as the ebb and flow of ocean tides are characterised by wave-like motions, so until Adeptship or " the further shore " is reached the life of the spiritual neophyte must also be subject to wavelike alternations of lofty exaltations (crests) and of withdrawals of spiritual inspiration (troughs). This must be so, since the undulatory life processes are totally

17

impersonal.   Only when a human being has wholly realised his identity
with the inherent life of the Solar System, as at Adeptship or near approach
thereto, does this alternation cease so far as consciousness is concerned.

If a moral may be drawn from the account of the strange conduct of
Joseph as recorded in this Chapter of *Genesis*, and from other not dissimilar
actions by the central figures in allegorical dramas, then such moral would
be that all aspirants to hastened unfoldment should always hold steadfastly
to the ideal and continue on the pathway however dark the heavens may
appear to be, however dry the surrounding countryside, and however the
whole enterprise may seem to have lost its appeal.   These times of spiritual
aridity, moreover, are the periods in the life of every human being rising
towards greatness when certain capacities are developed which otherwise
would remain dormant.   To keep on despite every obstacle, whether arising
from difficult circumstances in the outer life or from interior conflicts, is no
doubt the message of such stories as the one under consideration.[1]

---

[1] *cf. Matt.* 4: 1–11; *Matt.* 26: 42.

CHAPTER IX

JOSEPH RESTORES UNITY WITHIN HIS FAMILY

Gen. 45:   *Joseph maketh himself known to his brethren, and comforteth them in God's providence. He sendeth for his father. The spirit of Jacob is revived.*

Since this Chapter, with its dramatic reversal of Joseph's conduct towards his brethren and his self-revelation to them, is susceptible of a deeply spiritual interpretation, the commentaries already offered may perhaps here be permissibly brought together and restated. The apparently sudden change from an official to a fraternal relationship may be interpreted as part of an allegory descriptive of a profound spiritual experience.

As if under an inner compulsion, the spiritual Self (Joseph) reveals itself to the mortal man (the brethren as a multiple symbol) whilst he is wide awake and fully aware of himself and his surroundings (Joseph's house in Egypt). Since unillumined man would gain but little from descriptions of such spiritual expansions and their physical realisation, they are revealed by the authors of *Genesis* by means of an allegory of the union of those who have for a long time been apart (Joseph's absence in Egypt). This method of teaching is frequently used in World Mythologies and Scriptures. Hero and heroine meet and are united, for example. Members of families or tribes who have long been separated are brought together. Travellers, voyagers and adventurers come home at last. Ulysses returns to Ithaca and Penelope, and Persephone is restored by Hermes to her mother's arms. The Israelites reach the Promised Land,[1] and the Prodigal Son is reunited with his family.[2] Generally prizes are won, presents are given and feasts are partaken of by the various characters in the great allegorical dramas. Such narratives may either be regarded as history blended with fable, or as parables descriptive of mystical attainments and experiences which reveal hidden laws and processes of Nature, and the innate powers and destiny of man.

If the latter approach be used, then the self-revelation of Joseph to his brethren as described in this Chapter of *Genesis* may be regarded as an alle-

---

[1] *Joshua* 3:17; 5:6.
[2] *Lk.* 15:11–32.

gory of regained mystical experience, and of entry into the inner realms of Nature and into the state of consciousness in which the spiritual Self of man abides.   When such self-revelations and reunions occur in the Sacred Language after accounts of stress and demands for great effort, then they are illustrative of the process of " taking the Kingdom of Heaven by storm ".

The obstacles which temporarily prevent return, such as hesitation, delays and subterfuges sometimes included in such allegories, are all descriptive of difficulties in the attainment of Self-discovery following full surrender to the Divine.   Thus in conformity with this method of writing, Joseph is described as delaying the revelation of himself to his brethren. Similarly Ulysses, who has encountered many grave difficulties throughout his long voyage, enters his home in disguise and overpowers enemies within the home (the suitors) before disclosing his true identity.   His wife Penelope, who has been embarrassed by the suitors and troubled by the absence and delayed return of her husband, in her turn resorts to the subterfuge of weaving a tapestry by day and undoing it by night, its completion being a condition under which alone she will make her choice.

The *Book of Exodus,* to be considered in a later Volume of this work, similarly uses as allegories such incidents as the hardening of Pharaoh's heart and his breaking of his promises to let the Israelites depart.   These are less historical narratives,[1] than descriptions of mystical states of consciousness and the difficulties met with in the process of attaining them.   As recorded in the New Testament, the exceedingly painful journey of Jesus from the Judgment Hall to Golgotha, His scourging, His forcible crowning with thorns and the Crucifixion itself, are susceptible of similar interpretation. All these may be regarded as symbolic of the mystical "wounds"—mental, psychical and physical—which every aspirant suffers as he treads " The way of holiness" [2]—the Way of the Cross—meaning the pathway of illumination and Initiation.[3]

The incidents of this Chapter of the *Book of Genesis* are also susceptible of interpretation as being descriptive of psycho-spiritual experiences and changes which precede the mystic's full realisation of his true identity.   In the life of every mystic—as also of every occultist who is fortunate enough to receive the assistance made available in the instructions and Ceremonies of the Greater Mysteries—a time comes when the great interior illumination

---

[1] Despite the practice of the Ancient Egyptians of making historical records of events, no references have as yet been found to the presence in Egypt of either Joseph or Moses. Nor, so far as is at present known, are such unforgettably dramatic events as the ten plagues by which the freedom of the Israelites from bondage in Egypt is supposed to have been won, and the parting of the waters of the Red Sea, included in Egyptian history.

[2] *Is.* 35: 8.

[3] This subject is further considered in Vol. I of this work, particularly in Pt. Five, Ch. II.

is attained. This is in the main twofold. First, he knows himself to be completely distinct from his body, his emotions and his mind, these being mortal whilst he himself is immortal, immune from death. The second revelation is that the Spirit in him is a Ray of the Godhead and forever inseparably united with its Source. These two discoveries are later followed by a third, in which duality vanishes. The Spark then knows itself one with the Flame, the dew-drop one with the ocean of life, the Monad being identical with the one eternal Principle.

> *Gen.* 45: 1. *Then Joseph could not refrain himself before all them that stood by him; and he cried, Cause every man to go out from me. And there stood no man with him, while Joseph made himself known unto his brethren.*
>
> 2. *And he wept aloud; and the Egyptians and the house of Pharaoh heard.*
>
> 3. *And Joseph said unto his brethren, I am Joseph: doth my father yet live? And his brethren could not answer him: for they were troubled at his presence.*

Eventually the time of the great revealing arrives. The attraction of the Spirit is experienced by the material Principles of man, evoking a yearning for the mystic union. Allegorically, Joseph reveals himself to his brethren. Whilst, according to the literal sense of the first verse, it is but natural that Joseph would desire privacy for the occasion, it is also true that self-elevation and illumination, being deeply interior, are best entered into in solitude; therefore Joseph causes every man to go out from him. The audible weeping and the shedding of tears may be taken to be descriptive of the final stress and strain which precede full spiritual attainment. In addition, there are evidences of joy as that consummation draws near. Then both feeling and thought are given free expression.

When, at last, Joseph does reveal his identity to his brethren, saying " I am Joseph ", his brothers are troubled. The mystic, even though long prepared by both premonitory experiences and knowledge derived from the writings of others, can suffer some personal stress before finally breaking through into realisation of his own divine nature and its unity with God.

> *Gen.* 45: 4. *And Joseph said unto his bretheren, Come near to me, I pray you. And they came near. And he said, I am Joseph your brother, whom ye sold into Egypt.*

The limitations imposed upon the reincarnating human Ego (Joseph) by incarnation in the material vehicles of mind, emotion, vitality and flesh are great indeed. Birth into them is not inaptly described as the lowering into a pit, the deepest and darkest part of which would correspond to the physical body itself. Even advanced spiritual Souls experience a grave loss of power and means of self-expression when physically embodied during waking hours. Indeed, the conditions of earthly life are so foreign to those

of the level of the abstract intelligence at which the inner Self abides that
they might well be symbolised by residence in an alien land.   Enforced
rebirth may similarly be regarded as exile.   The story of Joseph's brethren
who lowered him into the pit, and later sold him to the merchants, has
already been interpreted.   The Intelligences concerned with all processes,
Macrocosmic and microcosmic, of the descent of consciousness into dense,
material encasement and its later liberation, are personified by the brethren
and the merchants respectively.

In this later phase of Joseph's story in which the accent is upon self-
freeing from the limitations of dense matter and its attributes, Joseph
typifies an Initiate on the threshold of final liberation.   At this stage, an
integration of the whole nature of man occurs, the differentiation between
the inner and the outer—the immortal and the mortal—parts virtually
disappearing.   Allegorically, Joseph reveals himself to his brethren and
begs them to draw very near to him, an intimate family reunion then
occurring.

> Gen. 45: 5. *Now therefore be not grieved, nor angry with yourselves, that
> ye sold me hither: for God did send me before you to preserve
> life.*

Those who are able to assent to an allegorical reading such as is indicated above may find in this verse one of the keys to the interpretation of
accounts of outgoing and returning journeys, and of advances from lowliness
to loftiness.   The story of Joseph reveals a sublime purpose, even though
giving it only a material significance, namely to supply food in years of
famine.   The actual purpose of all such cyclic movements is the germination
and development of those seed-like powers which have been present, though
latent, in the inner Self of man from the time of his emergence from the
divine Consciousness.

Famine represents the absence of spiritual impulses, guidance, light,
during the earlier phases of human development whilst in incarnation
in a physical body.   Evolution dispels this, bestowing upon advanced man
deepening realisation of spiritual power and increasing facility in its exercise
at all levels of self-expression—spiritual, intellectual, cultural and physical.
This is symbolised by feeding those who are hungry, giving drink to those
who are thirsty, and a change from a condition of famine to that of plenty.
Thus Joseph in no way reproaches his brothers, and moreover tells them not
to reproach themselves since a sublime purpose was being fulfilled throughout.   Ethical precepts are also presented, namely that one should both
forgive one's enemies and not give way unduly to remorse for past
mistakes.

> Gen. 45: 6. *For these two years hath the famine been in the land: and yet
> there are five years, in which there shall neither be earing nor
> harvest.*

7. *And God sent me before you to preserve you a posterity in the earth, and to save your lives by a great deliverance.*

8. *So now it was not you that sent me hither, but God: and he hath made me a father to Pharaoh, and lord of all his house, and a ruler throughout all the land of Egypt.*

Allegorically, the brothers performed no evil when they lowered Joseph deep into the earth and sold him;[1] for only so might he come to the fulfilment of his life and be as a father to a great King of a great land.

Gen. 45: 9. *Haste ye, and go up to my father, and say unto him, Thus saith thy son Joseph, God hath made me lord of all Egypt: come down unto me, tarry not;*

10. *And thou shalt dwell in the land of Goshen, and thou shalt be near unto me, thou, and thy children, and thy children's children, and thy flocks, and thy herds, and all that thou hast:*

11. *And there will I nourish thee; for yet there are five years of famine; lest thou, and thy household, and all that thou hast, come to poverty.*

12. *And, behold, your eyes see, and the eyes of my brother Benjamin, that it is my mouth that speaketh unto you.*

13. *And ye shall tell my father of all my glory in Egypt, and of all that ye have seen; and ye shall haste and bring down my father hither.*

Complete integration or unification of the whole nature of illumined man is brought about when once the true Self is revealed. Mutual recognition by the inner Self (Joseph) and the outer personality (the brethren) indicates a complete harmonisation of all the aspects of human nature—spiritual, intellectual and physical. Mystical experience of oneness with the Divine brings about an interior harmonisation, so that the illumined mystic knows himself to be a whole individual composed of the inner, spiritual will (the Lord), the evolving immortal Self (Joseph), and the mind, emotions and physical body (the brethren).

The past and the present are also combined. The fruitage of former lives on Earth, and even the memory of those lives, become consciously available to highly evolved man. As the past is the parent of the present, so his earlier existences in forms together constitute the " father " of his present self. Jacob, the father of Joseph, represents that past and those existences, the products of which must be brought into full consciousness and be made fully available to the present personality. This may be the inner significance of Joseph's insistence that his father be brought to Egypt to live near him and under his protection.

---

[1] q.v. Vol. II of this work, Pt. Two, Ch. II.

Gen. 45: 14. *And he fell upon his brother Benjamin's neck, and wept; and Benjamin wept upon his neck.*

15. *Moreover he kissed all his brethren, and wept upon them: and after that his brethren talked with him.*

16. *And the fame thereof was heard in Pharaoh's house, saying, Joseph's brethren are come: and it pleased Pharaoh well, and his servants.*

17. *And Pharaoh said unto Joseph, Say unto thy brethren, This do ye; lade your beasts, and go, get you unto the land of Canaan;*

18. *And take your father and your households, and come unto me: and I will give you the good of the land of Egypt, and ye shall eat the fat of the land.*

19. *Now thou art commanded, this do ye; take you wagons out of the land of Egypt for your little ones, and for your wives, and bring your father, and come.*

20. *Also regard not your stuff; for the good of all the land of Egypt is yours.*

The intimate unification or fusion of all the parts of man are here described, the symbolism having been earlier interpreted. The total powers of the present human being and all the products of his past have now become both inter-harmonised and actively available. Metaphorically, amidst prevalent famine there will be safety, and even plenty. Historical probability is not, however, denied. A generous King might well thus wish to reward a Prime Minister who, by an act of foresight, had saved him and his people from famine. Here again a moral as well as a mystical meaning may legitimately be discerned.

THE REJECTED STONE BECOMES THE CHIEF CORNER-STONE

In addition to the interpretations of the Joseph allegory already given, a further revelation is made. This concerns a fundamental law governing the spiritual way of life. Under that law the aspirant passes through the apparently unavoidable experience of temporary rejection, and even betrayal. This is, however, followed by a universal, and sometimes triumphant, acceptance and acclaim. The person who is first unwanted eventually becomes recognised as worthy of the highest honour whilst his contribution, though hitherto considered undesirable—and perhaps scorned—proves to be essential to the further progress of the nation, or of humanity as a whole. Jesus, Himself a memorable example of the operation of this law,[1] proclaimed

---

[1] *Is.* 53: 3–5; *Matt.* 67: 68; *Acts.* 4: 11,

that "...The stone which the builders rejected, the same is become the head of the corner. "[1]

A further example is presented in the story of Joseph, who was betrayed, lowered into a pit, then sold, and later was delivered, re-established amongst men and became a citizen of the first rank. Thus, those who are destined to become great because of the qualities of character inherent within them evidently must first experience faithlessness and repudiation by others. The principle of the ultimate acceptance of the previously unacceptable is indeed exemplified in full in the recorded account of the life of Joseph; for in truth the rejected stone became the chief corner-stone, Joseph proving to be the saviour of the Kingdom and, in consequence, being honoured and trusted by the King.

The fact that the marked change from imprisonment and distrust to freedom and the confidence of the Pharaoh was brought about by supernormal means—dreams—strongly suggests the presence of a mystical under-meaning. Joseph was freed and achieved advancement, not by any physical prowess or the defeat of any enemies, but by virtue of his own inherent wisdom from which he derived the capacity convincingly to interpret dreams and correctly to prophecy the future. This unusual, and even unlikely, element in the story, together with the fact that Egyptian historical records make no reference to him and his exploits, supports a study of the saga of Joseph less from the historical and more from the mystical point of view. The wholehearted adoption of Joseph's family by Pharaoh, and the extreme generosity indicated in verses seventeen to twenty, may also be regarded as giving weight to this view.

> *Gen.* 45: 21. *And the children of Israel did so; and Joseph gave them wagons, according to the commandment of Pharaoh, and gave them provision for the way.*
>
> 22. *To all of them he gave each man changes of raiment; but to Benjamin he gave three hundred pieces of silver, and five changes of raiment.*

Thus interpreted, the journey to the famine-stricken native land in order to bring the father back to the adoptive land where the brother reigns in power, and where food is assured, indicates both a movement in consciousness and an evolutionary progression. The whole nature of the mortal man is now guided and illumined by the inner self. As we have already seen, under that influence complete unification of all aspects of human nature—in modern terms, psychological integration—is sought and eventually achieved. A new cycle in the life of the person who passes through this experience is then entered upon. Spiritual and intellectual " famine " is replaced by sufficiency. Joseph, the long absent brother, is restored to the family and bestows upon it both protection and riches.

[1] *Matt.* 21: 42.

THE SYMBOLISM OF NUMBERS, METALS AND CHANGE OF RAIMENT

The two gifts to Benjamin—silver and raiment—are here numbered and each of these numbers conveys certain meanings. Indications are found in ancient literature of a development which gave to numbers their real significance, and employed them in a system of symbolism which referred to something more than enumeration alone.

Numbers can be used as symbols, because the Universe is established upon a co-ordinated plan in which quantitative relations are repeated through different states and planes. Number is common to all planes of Nature, and thus unites them. By the study of numbers, therefore, one may learn the fundamental laws of the creation, constitution and progressive events in the lives of both Universes and men; for man is a modification of cosmic elements, a concentration of cosmic forces.

Every number has a certain power which is not expressed by the figure or symbol employed to denote quantity only. This power rests in an occult connection existing between the relations of things and the Principles in Nature of which they are the expressions.[1]

Three hundred pieces of silver suggest, for example, that the gifts refer to the higher Triad in man, the threefold spiritual Self, whilst the metal silver indicates the awakened spiritual will. A law of correspondences exists under which metals are in mutual resonance or vibratory sympathy with certain parts of the Universe and of the make-up of man.

Iron corresponds to the emotional nature of man, the planet Mars and the Sign Scorpio; gold to the vital energy, the Sun and Leo; mercury to spiritual wisdom, the planet Mercury and Virgo; lead to the concrete mind, Saturn and Capricorn; tin to the Auric Envelope, Jupiter and Sagittarius; copper to the abstract intellect, Venus and Libra; silver to the spiritual will, Uranus and Aquarius.[2]

Thus Joseph's gift of silver to Benjamin indicates not only a transference of a material substance from one person to another, but also that by hierophantic power Benjamin's inner will had become strengthened and more active within the immortal Self which, being threefold, is designated by the number three (three hundred).

Changes of raiment indicate expansions of consciousness, new outlooks upon life, newly attained levels of spiritual awareness.[3] The fact that Benjamin was given five changes may indicate either that the Fifth Grade

[1] Vol. I this work, Part Tthree, Ch. III.—" The Symbolism of Numbers ".

[2] For a fuller exposition see Sec. 5, Ch. XIII, and accompanying Chart, of Vol. I (Rev. Ed.) of Lecture Notes, The School of the Wisdom, Geoffrey Hodson. See also the Chart on p. 233 of Vol. II of this work (Adyar Ed.).

[3] For a fuller interpretation see Vol, I of this work, Pt. Four, Ch. III—" The Pathway of Return ".

in the Mysteries had been passed through, or that the fifth or the intuitive Principle in man had been awakened into increased activity—or possibly both. In Christian terminology the interior Christ-consciousness has been " born " and unfolded, the Christ or " Anointed " state has been entered. The words of Angelus Silesius come to one's mind, for he wrote :

" Though Christ a thousand times in Bethelehem be born
 And not within thyself, thy self will be forlorn.
The cross on Golgotha thou lookest to in vain
 Unless, within thyself, it be set up again. "

Benjamin personifies the Christ Power and Presence in man, and this is why he was favoured above his brothers.

> Gea. 45: 23. *And to his father he sent after this manner; ten asses laden with the good things of Egypt, and ten she asses laden with corn and bread and meat for his father by the way.*
>
> 24. *So he sent his brethren away, and they departed: and he said unto them, See that ye fall not out by the way.*

The father, Jacob, who has not so far participated in the family journeyings and reunion, represents in this phase of Joseph's story the innermost Source (*Ātma*) and the totality in unity of every human being. This abstract Principle in man is sometimes personified by the Deity and sometimes by a Patriarch as head of a tribe or a family. As Patriarchs occupy their Office for limited periods, at the end of which they pass away and a new leader replaces them, so a succession of manifestations (physical incarnations) of the Spirit in man marks his progress to perfection.

The Dweller in-the-Innermost remains the same, namely the Monad itself. Evolutionary progression brings out additional powers or newly expressed spiritual faculties, so that the very nature of the man *seems* to be changed. When this phase of development has reached a certain degree it closes, the father dying and being succeeded by one of his sons.

The number ten—twice used as the number of asses and she-asses laden with corn sent by Joseph to his father—indicates the fulfilment of a period of activity, the completion of a cycle; for ten is the number of totality, a synthesis of all the preceding numbers, a rounding off, as it were, of a particular cycle.

The journey made by Jacob in Canaan under the orders of Joseph and Pharaoh, with instructions that he be brought to Egypt, may be regarded as descriptive of the close of one cycle of cosmic, human and Initiatory activity (Jacob later dies) and entry upon its successor.

> Gen. 45: 25. *And they went up out of Egypt, and came into the land of Canaan unto Jacob their father,*
>
> 26. *And told him, saying, Joseph is yet alive, and he is governor over all the land of Egypt. And Jacob's heart fainted, for he believed them not.*

27. *And they told him all the words of Joseph, which he had said unto them: and when he saw the wagons which Joseph had sent to carry him, the spirit of Jacob their father revived;*

28. *And Israel said, It is enough: Joseph my son is yet alive: I will go and see him before I die.*

HISTORY OR ALLEGORY

Although no historical reference to these events has as yet been found, it is not entirely impossible that they might have occurred. Doubt of this arises, however, from the Biblical statements concerning the important part which Joseph played in the direction, under Pharaoh, of the nation's economy, agriculture, and self-protection against famine. All of these functions would have been sufficiently significant to have been recorded in the contemporary history of Egypt. An allegorical reading is supported not only by their exclusion from the records, but also by the inclusion in the Scriptural narrative of so much that is supernatural. Joseph claimed, for example, that the Lord God actually sent him to Egypt.[1] It is also recorded that Joseph possessed and exercised mystical powers such as the interpretation of dreams and the capacity to foresee, and so guard against, an oncoming famine. His father Jacob, in his turn, is said to have been directly instructed by the Lord God.[2]

The numbers and other symbols employed, the eagerness of Joseph, the revivification of Jacob, his father, and Jacob's divinely inspired journey into Egypt—all these also suggest a possible revelation of spiritual and occult truths, laws and procedures. This is achieved by means of the personification, as members of a family, of the various bodies and powers of man, and an allegorical description of the expansions of consciousness achieved by advanced humanity. If the narrative be thus read, one profound truth amongst many others is indeed discernible. This is that when the aspiring thoughts of spiritually awakened man are turned sincerely and meaningfully toward the Godhead within him, that divine Presence becomes more and more readily accessible to, and sheds spiritual grace upon, the outer man. The inner Ego, the spiritual Soul, Joseph, then becomes united in full consciousness with the Supreme Deity—Jacob, his father, visits him in Egypt.

---

[1] *Gen.* 45: 5, 7, 8 and 9.
[2] *Gen.* 46: 2, 3 and 4,

CHAPTER X

JOSEPH'S FATHER JOURNEYS INTO EGYPT

Gen. 46:   *Jacob is comforted by God at Beer-sheba: he goeth into Egypt: the number of his family: Joseph meeteth him.*

Gen. 46: 1. *And Israel took his journey with all that he had, and came to Beer-sheba, and offered sacrifices unto the God of his father Isaac.*

2. *And God spake unto Israel in the vision of the night, and said, Jacob, Jacob. And he said, Here am I.*

3. *And he said, I am God, the God of thy father: fear not to go down into Egypt: for I will there make of thee a great nation.*

4. *I will go down with thee into Egypt; and I will also surely bring thee up again: and Joseph shall put his hand upon thine eyes.*

The possibility of a mystical interpretation is here again supported by the further inclusion in the narrative of a description of an action of the Supreme Deity. Unless a secret wisdom concerning the relationship between the Deity in Universe and man is being revealed, the affirmation that the Logos of a Universe should thus personally direct the travels of the ruling family of an obscure tribe is, at the very least, somewhat unlikely. A mystical interpretation certainly lends greater probability to the story. The divine Principle (the Monad referred to as " the Lord God ") in spiritually awakened man empowers the innermost Self to enter into intimate unity with the immortal Self or unfolding spiritual Soul (Joseph), and through that with the mortal personality and all its attributes (the brethren). The ultimate unification of all the elements and characteristics of human nature is in reality here being described.

The record set out in verses five to twenty-six of this Chapter of the *Book of Genesis* is no doubt of great importance to the Hebrew people, but not necessarily to the general reader. The descendants of Israel, their wives and their offspring, from whom the nation developed, are all named and numbered. Again the passages may well be regarded as historical, though an interpretation of the names and numbers by the kabbalistic system strongly suggests the presence of occult allusions. In this sense a tribe and a family together constitute a microcosm which humanly represents the Macrocosm. Thus viewed, the leader and his family are used to symbolise creative Intelligences, *Elohim*,[1] who assist in the fashioning of a Universe. The names given, male and female, in both their soniferous[2] and numerical significances point to this revelation. Such a reading is supported by the initial statement referring to the beginning of the journey. This would seem to be upheld by the further statement that the Lord God visited Israel in a dream, and that He advised the journey to Egypt and promised national greatness. As in the emanation of a new Universe, the action is divinely initiated, so divine intervention in human affairs is also affirmed.

From this proffered general interpretation a return is now made to a verse by verse consideration of the remaining portion of Chapter Forty-six.

> Gen. 46: 27. *And the sons of Joseph, which were born him in Egypt, were two souls: all the souls of the house of Jacob, which came into Egypt, were threescore and ten.*
>
> 28. *And he sent Judah before him unto Joseph, to direct his face unto Goshen: and they came into the land of Goshen.*
>
> 29. *And Joseph made ready his chariot, and went up to meet Israel his father, to Goshen, and presented himself unto him; and he fell on his neck, and wept on his neck a good while.*
>
> 30. *And Israel said unto Joseph, Now let me die, since I have seen thy face, because thou art yet alive.*
>
> 31. *And Joseph said unto his brethren, and unto his father's house, I will go up, and shew Pharaoh, and say unto him, My brethren, and my father's house, which were in the land of Canaan, are come unto me;*
>
> 32. *And the men are shepherds, for their trade hath been to feed cattle; and they have brought their flocks, and their herds, and all that they have.*
>
> 33. *And it shall come to pass, when Pharaoh shall call you, and shall say, What is your occupation?*
>
> 34. *That ye shall say, Thy servants' trade hath been about cattle from our youth even until now, both we, and also our fathers: that ye may dwell in the land of Goshen; for every shepherd is an abomination unto the Egyptians.*

The descent or approach of the inward Spirit of illumined man having been allegorically described, the quest carried out by the aspirant and its

---

[1] *Elohim*—see Glossary.

[2] Soniferous. In occult philosophy certain words, when sounded in a particular way, are said to be capable of exerting both physical and superphysical influences. These can produce either beneficial or adverse effects upon the person who pronounces them with knowledge, and upon those to whom the sounds become audible. In the Sanskrit language such words, and sentences composed of them, are said to be *mantric*, meaning sacred speech as an instrument of thought-power, from the root *man*—to think.

fulfilment are then referred to. The tender reunion and Joseph's tears upon his father's neck appropriately portray the intimacy and depth of such interior and mystical union.

THE SYMBOL OF DECEIT

The resort to deceit (although shepherds in reality, they were to describe themselves as herdsmen) advised by Joseph and followed by Jacob and his sons, who were presumably under divine guidance, is significant. Abraham deliberately committed the same error in declaring his wife Sarai to be his sister, so that she became the mistress of Pharaoh, who granted favours to Abraham in consequence. Yet he, like Jacob, is said to have been under the protection of the Lord. These passages, if read literally, indicate that the Bible cannot be regarded as the inspired word of God from beginning to end; for the mind is revolted at the trickery advised and which was practised upon their hosts by trusted leaders who were, moreover, said to be inspired men under divine direction. Since shepherds were an abomination unto the Egyptians of the time, Joseph instructed his brethren not to reveal the truth concerning their occupation, but to pretend instead that they were dealers in cattle. Later on, however, they told the truth.

The reader of the *Book of Genesis* is faced with two possibilities. Either the founders of the Hebrew nation practised deceit for personal gain, were common tricksters, or else a mystical revelation is intended. The latter, surely the more acceptable, is indeed indicated by the inclusion of many accounts of supernatural intervention, by the use of various symbols, and by repeated affirmations that the Patriarchs and their families were under divine guidance and protection.

The *Pentateuch* bears the mark of many hands, the style and substance of the narratives showing considerable variance. This is especially apparent to the student of symbolism, who finds that on the one hand deeply occult revelations are being made and universally used symbols employed for the purpose, whilst on the other hand certain passages appear to be purely or largely literal and historical. The concluding Chapters of *Genesis* display such variations. One might almost assume that if and when historians wrote the records Initiates among the Hebrews read them through and interpolated passages or words in order to bestow upon the documents that deeper significance which is characteristic of occult writings.

Gen. 47:   *Joseph presenteth five of his brethren, and his father, before Pharaoh; he giveth them habitation and maintenance. He getteth all the Egyptians' property to Pharaoh. The priests' land not bought, etc.*

Gen. 47: 1. *Then Joseph came and told Pharaoh, and said, My father and my brethren, and their flocks, and their herds, and all that they have, are come out of the land of Canaan; and, behold, they are in the land of Goshen.*

2. *And he took some of his brethren, even five men, and presented them unto Pharaoh.*

3. *And Pharaoh said unto his brethren, What is your occupation? And they said unto Pharaoh, Thy servants are shepherds, both we, and also our fathers.*

4. *They said moreover unto Pharaoh, For to sojourn in the land are we come; for thy servants have no pasture for their flocks; for the famine is sore in the land of Canaan: now therefore, we pray thee, let thy servants dwell in the land of Goshen.*

5. *And Pharaoh spake unto Joseph, saying, Thy father and thy brethren are come unto thee:*

6. *The land of Egypt is before thee; in the best of the land make thy father and brethren to dwell; in the land of Goshen let them dwell: and if thou knowest any men of activity among them, then make them rulers over my cattle.*

7. *And Joseph brought in Jacob his father, and set him before Pharaoh: and Jacob blessed Pharaoh.*

JACOB AND HIS SONS WELCOMED IN EGYPT

Joseph now stands in the presence of five of the male members of his family. His father, Jacob, and these, his brothers, are with him in Egypt. They have been presented to Pharaoh, welcomed by him, and granted their place and their position in the land.

The complete silence of all Egyptian records of this period of the country's history so far as Joseph and his family are concerned may be due to the disturbances caused by the domination of the Hyksos. The greater probability, however, is that a parable has been deliberately created by the inspired Authors of the *Pentateuch*. If the narrative be thus viewed, then a certain appropriateness may be discerned; for an Initiate, as personified by Joseph, achieves a complete harmonisation of all the parts of his nature— spiritual, intellectual and physical—and their unification into one instrument of awareness and action in the service of the Monad. Jacob and his sons typify those various parts. Jacob is the spiritual Ray (*Ātma*), representative of the Monad. Joseph is the immortal, spiritual Self approaching Adeptship through the portals of the great Initiations. The brothers, in their turn, personify various characteristics of the four component bodies[1] of the mortal man.

---

[1] q.v. Vol. I of this work, p. 64 Adyar Ed., and p. 63 Quest Book, U.S.A.

THE TWELVE SONS OF JACOB PERSONIFY ZODIACAL QUALITIES

The various powers represented by the twelve Signs of the Zodiac and their planetary " Rulers ", and all the developed faculties and natural attributes of a high Initiate are brought together under the direction of the will, to which they are utterly subservient. Although the powers represented by the Zodiac and by each of Joseph's brethren appear earlier in this Volume, they are here repeated as being appropriate to the passage under consideration. Thus the Mystery teachings of the Chaldean, and sometimes the Egyptian, Sanctuaries concerning both the Macrocosm and the microcosm are all revealed in these pseudo-histories of the Jewish Patriarchs and of the founding of the Hebrew nation. The symbology employed is largely astrological. The attributions of the Signs of the Zodiac to the twelve sons of Jacob and Tribes of Israel are as follows:

Aquarius	...	Reuben (" unstable as water ").
Gemini	...	Simeon and Levi (a strong fraternal association).
Leo	...	Judah (the strong lion of his tribe, "a lion's whelp").
Pisces	...	Zebulun (he " shall dwell at the haven of the sea ").
Taurus	...	Issachar (" a strong ass couching down ", and therefore associated with stables, byres, etc.).
Virgo-Scorpio	...	Dan (" a serpent by the way, an adder in the path, that biteth the horse heels ").
Capricorn	...	Naphtali (" a hind let loose ").
Cancer	...	Benjamin (ravenous).
Libra	...	Asher (" Out of Asher his bread shall be fat ").
Sagittarius	...	Joseph (" his bow abode in strength ").
Aries	...	Gad (" a troop shall overcome him; but he shall overcome at the last. ").
Virgo	...	Dinah, the only daughter of Jacob.

Tradition shows the alleged Tribes carrying the twelve Signs on their banners. The above correspondences are deduced from the words addressed by the dying Jacob to his sons, and in his definitions of the future of each Tribe.[1]

The famine which afflicted the land of Canaan, and therefore Jacob and his sons who were living there, allegorically portrays the condition of human consciousness which precedes embarkation upon the search for wisdom. The symbols usually employed are famine and hunger, the necessity for physical food being related to a pressing need for philosophic understanding and spiritual " food ". A state of hunger not inaptly describes the condition of man's vehicles of consciousness before they are unified, vivified and

---

[1] *Gen.* 49.

18

empowered by the presence, the action and the wisdom of the awakened spiritual Self. Once gathered together and unified, all the parts of man share in the realisation of the indwelling Presence of the Divine, which is the true man. Allegorically, famine then ceases and is replaced by both plenty and honour. Thus Jacob and his family were afflicted by famine. In order to relieve it they went to Egypt, a topographical symbol in one interpretation for a place where Temples of the Mysteries existed. Arriving there they were supplied with an abundance of food and given their due place in the land. Bondage within Egypt, on the other hand, implies subservience to the flesh.

This method of revelation by means of allegory is also employed, as has been hitherto suggested, in the story of the life of Joseph. Once delivered from the pit and taken to Egypt, his rise had been rapid. He arrived in Egypt virtually a slave, was caught in an intrigue and falsely accused, condemned and imprisoned. He displayed occult powers in interpreting dreams and was thereafter liberated, eventually to become Grand Vizier of Egypt. In that Office he served both the Egyptian peoples and his own family, saving them from famine.

Thus is allegorically portrayed, in the form of a story of adventure, the hastened progress of the Soul of man towards perfection and the experiences and attainments through which it passes on the upward way.

Gen. 47: 8. *And Pharaoh said unto Jacob, How old art thou ?*
9. *And Jacob said unto Pharaoh, The days of the years of my pilgrimage are an hundred and thirty years: few and evil have the days of the years of my life been, and have not attained unto the days of the years of the life of my fathers in the days of their pilgrimage.*

As elsewhere suggested, up to the time of writing no record of the episodes narrated in the closing Chapters of *the Book of Genesis* have been discovered, although Semitic types of heads are to be seen amongst carvings illustrating Egyptian history at or about this period. Neither Joseph nor his family figure in Egyptian history relating to the period during which Joseph is reported to have saved the land from famine. Furthermore, the events described in the *Book of Exodus* are not recorded, despite the profoundly dramatic nature of the visitation of the plagues upon Egypt and the departure therefrom of the Israelites under the leadership of Moses.

Whilst the absence of such records up to the present time does not prove that such events did not occur, nevertheless grounds do exist for an occult and mystical interpretation of these portions of the *Torah*. Examination of them from these points of view leads to knowledge concerning the emanation and formation of Universes, the normal evolutionary pathway trodden by mankind, and the laws and processes which apply to the deliberate hastening of man's spiritual and intellectual development. This has ever been aided by passage through the Grades of the Lesser and Greater Mysteries[1] of which Egypt was at that time, and still is, an acknowledged Centre.[2]

The land of Egypt, largely because of the presence there of Joseph, proved to be of at least dual significance for the Israelites.   On the one hand relief from famine, welcome, and settlement in the country were granted unto Jacob and his family.   On the other hand, however, during the later period as recorded in the *Book of Exodus*, Egypt became for the Hebrew people a land of cruel bondage, even slavery.

As already indicated, these mutually opposed experiences offer opportunity for their interpretation from the purely mystical and spiritual points of view.   With the exception of Joseph, Jacob's family may be regarded as personifications of the mortal aspects of every human being, whilst Joseph symbolises man's immortal Soul.   The family's need represents recognition of lack of knowledge and understanding, whilst the journey is symbolic of the consequent search for spiritual light and truth.

Light dawned upon them and truth was discovered by them, as indicated by their receipt of corn, money, a silver cup, security, a country and a home.   Mystically interpreted, these imply the attainment of wisdom and knowledge and the intellectual security so provided.   As has been seen, the language employed and the recognisable symbols which are included all support this reading, whilst the total absence of historical records both casts doubt upon the historicity of the record of the events and encourages its study from the symbolic point of view.   If this be accepted, then the whole story of the entry into Egypt and the exodus therefrom by the Israelites may be read as an example of a remarkable allegory of occult, mystical and spiritual unfoldment on the pathway to hastened attainment of human perfection, or Adeptship.

Thus viewed, the land of Egypt itself may be regarded as a topographical symbol for a state of consciousness in which illumination is attained.   The existence of the Egyptian Mysteries, their Hierophants and other Officiants, lends weight to this approach.   These beneficent Institutions were themselves designed to bring about such spiritual realisations and experiences as would fulfil the intellectual need for understanding of the meaning and purpose of human life.

Gen. 47: 10. *And Jacob blessed Pharaoh, and went out from before Pharaoh.*

The search for spiritual light and truth nears its end.   The mortal man in whom the " inexpressible longing for the Infinite " now dominates the whole conduct of his life has not only himself found an acceptable source of knowledge, but in addition his highly evolved mental principle (Jacob) has itself become illumined (is in Egypt).

[1] The Mysteries—see Glossary.

[2] q.v. *Lecture Notes of the School of the Wisdom*, Vol. I (Rev. Ed.), p. 481, Geoffrey Hodson.

Gen. 47: 11. *And Joseph placed his father and his brethren, and gave them a possession in the land of Egypt, in the best of the land, in the land of Rameses, as Pharaoh had commanded.*

All tests have been successfully passed, all difficulties overcome, and the aspirant is established in truth (settled in Egypt) and accepted as a member of the spiritual community (" the best of the land ").

Gen. 47: 12. *And Joseph nourished his father, and his brethren, and all his father's household, with bread, according to their families.*

The interpretation earlier offered for the symbol of corn may here also be applied to bread, with the added suggestion that by means of contemplation (yeast) knowledge had become both spiritual power and occult wisdom.   Truth had not only been received, but was so fully assimilated as to bestow spiritual and intellectual faculties born of understanding (eating bread).

Gen. 47: 13. *And there was no bread in all the land; for the famine was very sore, so that the land of Egypt and all the land of Canaan fainted by reason of the famine.*

14. *And Joseph gathered up all the money that was found in the land of Egypt, and in the land of Canaan, for the corn which they bought: and Joseph brought the money into Pharaoh's house.*

15. *And when money failed in the land of Egypt, and in the land of Canaan, all the Egyptians came unto Joseph, and said, Give us bread: for why should we die in thy presence ? for the money faileth.*

16. *And Joseph said, Give your cattle; and I will give you for your cattle, if money fail.*

The symbol of famine has already been interpreted from both the Macrocosmic and the microcosmic points of view.   In the latter, the resultant hunger indicates recognition—to the degree of suffering—of the total absence of understanding of the plan, purposes and objectives of human existence.   Every human being who has ever embarked upon a determined search for knowledge has experienced this intellectual " famine ", the " hunger " which it causes, and the resultant determination to find out truth for himself.   Joseph, having succeeded in this quest, was a fully illumined and highly developed teacher, and was in consequence able effectively to assist those who followed after him (his family) on the pathway to truth.

Gen. 47: 17. *And they brought their cattle unto Joseph: and Joseph gave them bread in exchange for horses, and for the flocks, and for the cattle of the herds, and for the asses: and he fed them with bread for all their cattle for that year.*

18. *When that year was ended, they came unto him the second year, and said unto him, We will not hide it from my lord, how that*

our money is spent; my lord also hath our herds of cattle; there is not ought left in the sight of my lord, but our bodies, and our lands;

19. *Wherefore shall we die before thine eyes, both we and our land? buy us and our land for bread, and we and our land will be servants unto Pharaoh; and give us seed, that we may live, and not die, that the land be not desolate.*

If the allegorical approach be accepted, then the deeper aspects of the search for knowledge—as also of knowledge itself—are indicated in these verses. Famine continues externally even though bread is supplied. The symbol of seed is now introduced into the story, and this may be interpreted as implying that the great quest is not for knowledge alone, but for the very source of knowledge. This is divine Truth itself as contained in the vastnesses of the Universal Mind[1] wherein all Truth perpetually abides, but less as concrete and conceptual ideas than as abstract varieties.

Gen. 47: 20. *And Joseph bought all the land of Egypt for Pharaoh; for the Egyptians sold every man his field, because the famine prevailed over them; so the land became Pharaoh's.*

21. *And as for the people, he removed them to cities from one end of the borders of Egypt even to the other end thereof.*

22. *Only the land of the priests bought he not; for the priests had a portion assigned them of Pharaoh, and did eat their portion which Pharaoh gave them: wherefore they sold not their lands.*

23. *Then Joseph said unto the people, Behold, I have bought you this day and your land for Pharaoh: lo, here is seed for you, and ye shall sow the land.*

The totality of the hunger and the determination to satisfy it are here referred to by means of an allegory of national famine. Joseph, as the possessor of both bread and seed, personifies interiorly the power (his Office) and the beneficence (generosity) innate in the spiritual aspects of the constitution of man—divine Will and divine Wisdom. Interpreted as a description of the passage of a Candidate through the Grades of the Mysteries, the narrative shows Joseph as the reigning Hierophant who confers successive Initiations (bread and seed).

Gen. 47: 24. *And it shall come to pass in the increase, that ye shall give the fifth part unto Pharaoh, and four parts shall be your own, for seed of the field, and for your food, and for them of your households, and for food for your little ones.*

25. *And they said, Thou hast saved our lives: let us find grace in the sight of my lord, and we will be Pharaoh's servants.*

---

[1] *Mahat* (Sk.).   The first principle of Universal Intelligence and Consciousness.

Surrender of self-desire, of egotism and of pride of possession is here allegorically portrayed as a natural result of the elevation of Spirit which these two verses describe.

Gen. 47: 26. *And Joseph made it a law over the land of Egypt unto this day, that Pharaoh should have the fifth part; except the land of the priests only, which became not Pharaoh's.*

27. *And Israel dwelt in the land of Egypt, in the country of Goshen; and they had possessions therein, and grew, and multiplied exceedingly.*

28. *And Jacob lived in the land of Egypt seventeen years: so the whole age of Jacob was an hundred forty and seven years.*

29. *And the time drew nigh that Israel must die: and he called his son Joseph, and said unto him, If now I have found grace in thy sight, put, I pray thee, thy hand under my thigh, and deal kindly and truly with me; bury me not, I pray thee, in Egypt:*

30. *But I will lie with my fathers, and thou shalt carry me out of Egypt, and bury me in their burying place. And he said, I will do as thou hast said.*

31. *And he said, Swear unto me. And he sware unto him. And Israel bowed himself upon the bed's head.*

All cycles eventually reach their close, all quests their goal, and all seekers for truth and perfection their greatest fulfilment. Strangely, this is not an extension of personal reign and capacity, but the very opposite. Once the stature of high Initiate and Adept has been attained by the traveller on the ancient pathway to the discovery of truth, all limitations—particularly those based upon the delusion of self-separate existence—are outgrown. This transcendence of self, portrayed in world allegories either as decapitation or premature death, is descriptive of the final stages of human evolution. In many cases this is followed by a supernatural resurrection, implying complete transcendence of the " prison " or " tomb " of self-centredness. Both the death of Jacob and the return of his phycial body to the home of his fathers indicate this attainment; for the death of heroes and Saviours is indeed but figurative or symbolical, being descriptive only of the death of self and self-interest.

CHAPTER XI

THE CLOSING YEARS OF JACOB'S LIFE

Gen. 48:   *Joseph with his sons visiteth his sick father. Jacob repeateth God's promise, and taketh Ephraim and Manasseh as his own; he blesseth Joseph's sons.*

THE TRANSFERENCE OF POWER FROM OFFICIANT TO IMMEDIATE SUCCESSOR

If the events related in this Chapter are anything more than family history, then procedures involved in the transmission of power and authority from the presiding Official of one period to that of its successor are here being described.[1] Jacob's choice of the younger son to be greater than the older brothers indicates that such succession is not necessarily dependent upon seniority alone. In the Sacred Language younger sons are sometimes specially favoured, since they personify the latest in time, and therefore the greatest attainment and degree of interior unfoldment. In allegories of the present historical epoch, which is characterised by man's development of his dual mental powers and their vehicles—the abstract, prophetic intelligence and the concrete, analytical mentality—youngest sons generally refer to the supra-mental, intuitive faculty.

The symbology of earlier Chapters of *Genesis* describing Joseph's relationship with his brothers supports this reading; for it employs the same device of the choice of the youngest for special favours. Benjamin thus receives the gift of a silver cup in his sack of corn.[2] In this Chapter Ephraim is set before Manasseh, and Jacob prophecies that the younger will become greater than Manasseh and that " his seed shall become a multitude of nations."[3]

Acts of laying on of hands in blessing refer not only to the transmission of spiritual power and authority, but also to a transference of actual physical influence and magnetism which is brought about by direct contact. This is very important, because it ensures that the whole being of the recipient—

---

[1] q.v. Vol. II of this work, Pt. Six, Ch. XI.
[2] *Gen.* 44: 12.
[3] *Gen.* 48: 19.

spiritual, intellectual and physical—shall receive the transmitted power, life-force and magnetism of the predecessor before the latter's retirement or death.

Gen. 48: 1. *And it came to pass after these things, that one told Joseph, Behold, thy father is sick: and he took with him his two sons, Manasseh and Ephraim.*

2. *And one told Jacob, and said, Behold, thy son Joseph cometh unto thee: and Israel strengthened himself, and sat upon the bed.*

3. *And Jacob said unto Joseph, God Almighty appeared unto me at Luz in the land of Canaan, and blessed me,*

4. *And said unto me, Behold, I will make thee fruitful, and multiply thee, and I will make of thee a multitude of people; and will give this land to thy seed after thee for an everlasting possession.*

5. *And now thy two sons, Ephraim and Manasseh, which were born unto thee in the land of Egypt before I came unto thee into Egypt, are mine; as Reuben and Simeon, they shall be mine.*

The prophecies by the Lord God to the Hebrew Patriarchs, that their nation would greatly increase in numbers and populate much of the Earth, must of necessity, in the light of history, be regarded as of spiritual rather than of material and purely human and racial significance. This view gains support when the *Torah* is regarded as being far less an account of the creation of the world and of an early period in the history of the Hebrews than an allegorical description of both Cosmogenesis and the whole of humanity upon the planet Earth. All nations are involved in the great story, as also is each individual man—whether primitive, advanced, Initiate or Adept.

The succession of Races, the appearance of their leaders, and the formal transference of power from one Patriarch to his successor, are described in conformity with such a view. This reading, it is also suggested, shows the *Torah* as transcending the limitations of time to include the events of a whole world period; for the great story tells not only of the past, but also of the present and the future of the whole human Race, such being part of the value of the Hebrew *Torah* or Law.

In terms of human history none of the prophecies of the future greatness and leading world role of the Hebrew peoples have, as yet, been fulfilled. Spiritually, however, and applied to the evolution of the consciousness of mankind, their fulfilment is assured, since the domination and illumination of the lower mortal man by his divine Self are inevitable.

THE MESSIANIC AGE

The prophecy of the Lord to Jacob at Luz must therefore be read as being founded upon this truth and as a provision of that time on Earth when man's purely spiritual powers and qualities shall govern all relationships between individual persons, and also between the nations of the world. This, it is suggested, will be the true Messianic Age, international rather than national and the product of the evolutionary progress of mankind.

Gen. 48: 6. *And thy issue, which thou begettest after them, shall be thine, and shall be called after the name of their brethren in their inheritance.*

7. *And as for me, when I came from Padan, Rachel died by me in the land of Canaan in the way, when yet there was but a little way to come unto Ephrath: and I buried her there in the way of Ephrath; the same is Bethlehem.*

Interpreted in the above light, the supposedly historical people in the great story are also personifications of aspects of human nature. Man's powers, qualities and tendencies towards certain forms of conduct, typical of one or other of the seven parts of the constitution of man, are also portrayed by the seven stems of the Menorah.[1]

The story is thus universal, although containing elements of the early history of the Israelites which are used as a basis for the allegory. Even certain of the places said to have been visited by the Patriarchs and their families have, in their turn, their occult and symbolical significance, each being descriptive of an attribute of human nature and of a phase of human evolution. Thus Jacob, when reviewing his own past and telling of the death and burial of his wife Rachel, is also revealing truths of profound significance—universal, planetary, racial, and concerning the unfoldment of the innate powers in each and every human being.

Gen. 48: 8. *And Israel beheld Joseph's sons, and said, Who are these?*

9. *And Joseph said unto his father, They are my sons, whom God hath given me in this place. And he said, Bring them, I pray thee, unto me, and I will bless them.*

The bodily awareness of the retiring Patriarch evidently had begun to grow dim; for he failed to recognise his grandsons. In consequence, he must transfer his ordained power to his successor, as explained in the introductory remarks at the commencement of this Chapter.

Gen. 48: 10. *Now the eyes of Israel were dim for age, so that he could not see. And he brought them near unto him; and he kissed them and embraced them.*

11. *And Israel said unto Joseph, I had not thought to see thy face: and, lo, God hath shewed me also thy seed.*

12. *And Joseph brought them out from between his knees, and he bowed himself with his face to the earth.*

[1] Menorah—see Glossary.

13. *And Joseph took them both, Ephraim in his right hand toward Israel's left hand, and Manasseh in his left hand toward Israel's right hand, and brought them near unto him.*

14. *And Israel stretched out his right hand, and laid it upon Ephraim's head, who was the younger, and his left hand upon Manasseh's head, guiding his hands wittingly; for Manasseh was the firstborn.*

15. *And he blessed Joseph, and said, God, before whom my fathers Abraham and Isaac did walk, the God which fed me all my life long unto this day.*

The intimacy of this procedure of the transference of power is revealed more particularly in the thirteenth verse, in which the action becomes almost ceremonial, whilst the contact between the hands is indicative of the component polarities—negative or left and positive or right—of the transmitted power.

Gen. 48: 16. *The Angel which redeemed me from all evil, bless the lads; and let my name be named on them, and the name of my fathers Abraham and Isaac; and let them grow into a multitude in the midst of the earth.*

17. *And when Joseph saw that his father laid his right hand upon the head of Ephraim, it displeased him: and he held up his father's hand, to remove it from Ephraim's head unto Manasseh's head.*

18. *And Joseph said unto his father, Not so, my father: for this is the firstborn; put thy right hand upon his head.*

19. *And his father refused, and said, I know it, my son, I know it: he also shall become a people, and he also shall be great: but truly his younger brother shall be greater than he, and his seed shall become a multitude of nations.*

Israel, as the reigning Official, knew well of these polarities, whilst his son, Joseph, is made to appear completely ignorant of them. His father is insistent, however, and eventually blesses the sons of Joseph, as well as Joseph himself, in the manner which he knew to be the correct one considering the influences and forces involved.

The reference in the sixteenth verse to the Angel may possibly refer to the Archangel Head of that Hierarchy of the *Elohim*[1] which watched over and evolved side by side not only with the young Hebrew nation, but also with the whole human Race upon the planet Earth; for, be it remembered, the *Torah* is a history of humanity as a whole, being related however in the form of an epic story of the Hebrew people.

---

[1] *Elohim*—see Appendix to this Volume and Glossary.

The Ageless Wisdom, upon which I believe the authors of the *Torah* to have been drawing, tells also that each nation is placed in the charge of an exalted Member of the Angelic Hierarchy, and it is not impossible that Jacob was indeed aware of the existence of the National Angel of the Hebrew Race.[1]

Gen. 48: 20. *And he blessed them that day, saying, In thee shall Israel bless, saying, God make thee as Ephraim and as Manasseh: and he set Ephraim before Manasseh.*

21. *And Israel said unto Joseph, Behold, I die: but God shall be with you, and bring you again unto the land of your fathers.*

22. *Moreover I have given to thee one portion above thy brethren, which I took out of the hand of the Amorite with my sword and with my bow.*

The immediate transference of power from Jacob to Joseph is here described, a reference also being made to the destiny of the Hebrews under Joseph's care. Not only one small group of people, dislodged from its tribal home, but also the whole of humanity is involved, and its history and destiny are included in these closing verses of this Forty-eighth Chapter of the *Book of Genesis.*

A spiritual identity exists, be it ever remembered, between each individual person, his nation, and the human Race as a whole. The *Torah* is so related that this identity, this intimacy, oneness and mutuality of the manifesting divine Spirit in all that exists, is allegorically revealed therein. In consequence, the experiences of one person reflect those of the Universe as a whole. The evolutionary progress throughout the ages of that one person is an inseparable and interactive part of the total evolution of the Universe. Indeed, Macrocosm and microcosm—whatever the dimensions given to these twin existences—are one, as both the most ancient and the more modern seers have with one voice proclaimed.

[1] q.v. *The Kingdom of the Gods*, Geoffrey Hodson.

CHAPTER XII

THE DEATH AND BURIAL OF JACOB

Gen. 49 : *Jacob calleth his sons together: he pronounceth curses on Reuben,*
and on Simeon and Levi; a blessing on Judah, etc. He charges
them concerning his burial; his death.

The inclusion of the oration made by the dying Jacob to his sons makes
this one of the most remarkable Chapters in the Bible, particularly from the
occult point of view; for in it the unity of the Macrocosm and the
microcosm is affirmed.[1]

The process of dying at a great age, surrounded by offspring and
possessed of wealth, symbolises the fulfilment of human existence, the completion of the human pilgrimage, the attainment of perfected manhood or
Adeptship. This implies freedom from enforced physical rebirth, a last
death as man, the end of an epoch.

Completed interior unfoldment and victory over all human weaknesses
are indicated by the security, honour and good position of the family in
Goshen. External well-being and wealth are customarily used in the
Sacred Language to connote interior well-being and spiritual fulfilment.
Poverty, on the other hand, denotes the absence of developed powers, though
sometimes it refers only to the absence of personal awareness of them. A
man may have material wealth, and even great mental skill and ability, and
yet be pitifully poor because of the lack—which can be almost total—of
spiritual idealism, wisdom and understanding. Physical poverty, then, is a
symbol for an impoverished psycho-spiritual state, and material well-being
is used to denote its opposite.

MACROCOSM AND MICROCOSM UNITED IN THE ADEPT

The Macrocosm in the occult sense is the totality of Cosmos, all existence—physical, superphysical and spiritual. The microcosm, which is man,
is a profound and—except to the highest seers—unfathomable mystery;
for in terms of inexhaustible power, indwelling life-force and directive
intelligence—conceived in terms of force rather than substance—the whole

---

[1] Law of Correspondences—see Glossary.

of Cosmos is mysteriously present within the Monad of man. The Zodiac, its component stars and their Archangelic Regents, Who are highly evolved Intelligences associated with them (*Dhyan Chohans*),[1] Solar Logoi, suns and planets are not only within man—he is actually composed of them. Indeed, they form the very fabric of his being.

The evolution of the Monad of man partly consists of the emergence of these inherent Macrocosmic Presences and powers from the germinal to the active state. The more developed a human being is, the greater the degree in which the potencies and the Intelligences associated with the sun and the twelve Zodiacal Signs are expressed through his seven vehicles.[2] The perfected man is one in whom this process has advanced to such a stage that he is no longer human, but superhuman; no longer man, but Adept. The Macrocosm has then become manifested to such a remarkable degree in the microcosm that in the liberated consciousness of the Adept the two are realised as one.

THE ZODIACAL POWERS IN MAN—THEIR USE AND MISUSE

In this interpretation Jacob dying—to human limitations—typifies the Adept degree of attainment. His sons are his powers and—if symbolically and sometimes adversely, in order to conceal a vital truth and the power which possession of it bestows—he describes each of them in terms of Zodiacal qualities. These attributes are given elsewhere in this Volume. When translated into theurgical action, unlimited power resides in this knowledge. Discordant elements of society might prematurely discover a part of it and, not having developed the stability of mind and the moral sense which would ensure its constructive use, they could misuse it, thus bringing injury to themselves and to all those who come within their influence. This information—in both its speculative (as in this book) and its operative senses—is only taught directly, and always in secret, during the Great Initiations. In fact, one of the reasons for the invention and use of the Symbolical Language was to record this wisdom, preserve it, and yet make it available to mankind in allegorical and symbolical form.

Pursuant to this method of writing the twelve sons of Jacob and their offspring—the twelve Tribes of Israel—are less physical people than personifications of divine Presences and powers in the Cosmos. The acceptance of Scripture as history alone has led to errors of interpretation, and has thus deprived humanity of valuable knowledge. When Jacob is described as having been gathered unto his people[3] and his body is said to be buried with

---

[1] *Dhyan Chohan*—see Glossary.
[2] see Glossary—Monad-Ego.
[3] *Gen.* 49: 29.

those of his predecessors, a revelation by means of allegory is being made concerning both the Path of Forthgoing and Return[1] and the conscious blending of the Macrocosm with the microcosm in perfected man.

Jacob journeys into Egypt, which was then an active Centre of both the Greater and the Lesser Mysteries. In an Initiatory reading he there receives the benediction of Initiation, develops his inborn powers to full maturity, and reaches Adeptship or " the measure of the stature of the fulness of Christ ".[2]   Thereafter he " dies ", meaning to the limitations of the human kingdom of Nature, and so enters into the freedom of the Universe which every liberated man achieves.   The authors of the *Pentateuch* here employ the allegory of Jacob's journey to Egypt, and of his death and burial, in order to describe this mystical experience.

> Gen. 49: 1. *And Jacob called unto his sons, and said, Gather yourselves together, that I may tell you that which shall befall you in the last days.*
>
> 2. *Gather yourselves together, and hear, ye sons of Jacob; and hearken unto Israel your father.*

A major cycle is closing and its fruits—the innate powers and qualities unfolded upto that time—are described in the verses which follow.   Indications concerning the succeeding cycle are also given.   The authors of the *Book of Genesis* make use of the necessary recording of an historical event to convey profoundly significant philosophic knowledge drawn from the Ancient Wisdom.   This knowledge concerns the numerical classifications into which all orders of creation—kingdoms of Nature and human beings, for example—naturally fall.   In addition the doctrine of the inter-relationships, and so perpetual interactions, between man and Universe and planet and Cosmos is revealed.

ZODIACAL SYMBOLOGY

The number twelve is applied to these classifications, representing—as it does by addition—the number three, thus referring to the triple nature of the active, creative Logos.   History here takes second place, whether it be concerned with tribes, offspring or disciples; for the characteristics of the supposedly historical and physical human beings in the narrative are portrayed in such a manner as to reveal the twelvefold Zodiacal correlations between man and Universe.

In Chapter Forty-nine of the *Book of Genesis* the story of a family and a tribe is thus lifted completely beyond the limitations of a purely historical record and thereby given a cosmic significance.   In this procedure we

---

[1] q.v. Volume I of this work, Pt. Four.
[2] *Eph.* 4: 13.

discern the intention of the authors to record supposed history metaphorically, thus constructing a vehicle for the revelation of ideas which completely
transcend a narrative of events in time and place.

Although Jacob's attribution of various qualities to his sons is somewhat
indirect in certain cases,[1] the whole subject-matter is nevertheless worthy
of examination from this point of view. A revelation is then discovered of
such deeply occult knowledge as the intimate relationships and correlations
between Archangelic Regents of Constellations and Stars and their corresponding manifestations and expressions both here on this planet and within
every human being.[2] In this connection it is interesting to note that vast
distances in space neither prevent nor reduce the functional interaction between the apparently far distant and remote on the one hand and the natural
phenomena and inhabitants of this planet on the other.

Thus unity is presented as the underlying truth, whilst distance in space
according to the limited perceptions of man is an illusion. To his eyes
the Cosmos consists of differing objects with varying degrees of materiality,
whilst to Adept and Archangel all are the products of one ever-active Power
throughout the field of divine manifestation. Although this field may
be physically spatial, the energy itself is one and the same wherever
expressed

Gen. 49: 3. *Reuben, thou art my firstborn, my might, and the beginning
of my strength, the excellency of dignity, and the excellency of
power:*

4. *Unstable as water, thou shalt not excel; because thou wentest
up to thy father's bed; then defiledst thou it: he went up to my
couch.*

JACOB DESCRIBES HIS SONS IN ASTROLOGICAL TERMS

These two verses which are descriptive of the character of Jacob's
firstborn son, Reuben, may well be regarded as mutually contradictory
according to a literal reading alone. Evidently Reuben failed to live up
to the ideal in his father's mind as " my might, and the beginning of my
strength, the excellency of dignity, and the excellency of power ". Despite
these great qualities, their expression through Reuben as he grew up was
greatly reduced, if not rendered impossible, by the characteristic of instabi-
lity; for Reuben is described as being " unstable as water ". The Zodiacal
Sign of Aquarius is thus indicated, however indirectly, and a correspondence
with that Sign applied to the eldest son.

[1] *Gen.* 49: 3, 4.
[2] For an exposition of this subject see Ch. XIII of Vol. I (Rev. Ed.) of *Lecture Notes
of the School of the Wisdom*, Geoffrey Hodson, and Glossary to this Vol.—" Law of
Correspondences ".

Gen. 49: 5. *Simeon and Levi are brethren; instruments of cruelty are in their habitations.*

6. *O my soul, come not thou into their secret; unto their assembly, mine honour, be not thou united: for in their anger they slew a man, and in their selfwill they digged down a wall.*

7. *Cursed be their anger, for it was fierce; and their wrath, for it was cruel: I will divide them in Jacob, and scatter them in Israel.*

The intimate association in their father's mind of Simeon and Levi suggests a reference to the Zodiacal Sign of Gemini, in which two aspects of one power, generally called twins, are brought together and yet shown in diversity. The evolutionary procedure in Nature, as well as the task of the Geminian personality in man, is to eliminate this tendency to divide because of opposite characteristics, and thereby to harmonise into unity of both motive and conduct the duality so evident in all Geminian manifestations. A person born under the Sign of Gemini finds himself capable of a twofold self-expression, and in the early phases of evolution as indicated by the characteristics of Simeon and Levi these can be antagonistic, and so lead to difficulties until a harmonisation has been achieved. This is not an easy task since the ideal on the one hand, represented by one half or part of the Geminian nature in man, and the actual on the other hand, may be at enmity. Possibly the authors intended to draw attention to this antagonism, and even hostility, by describing the brethren as having exhibited anger and expressed it as murderers.

Gen. 49: 8. *Judah, thou art he whom thy brethren shall praise: thy hand shall be in the neck of thine enemies; thy father's children shall bow down before thee.*

9. *Judah is a lion's whelp: from the prey, my son, thou art gone up: he stooped down, he couched as a lion, and as an old lion; who shall rouse him up?*

10. *The sceptre shall not depart from Judah, nor a lawgiver from between his feet, until Shiloh come; and unto him shall the gathering of the people be.*

11. *Binding his foal unto the vine, and his ass's colt unto the choice vine; he washed his garments in wine, and his clothes in the blood of grapes:*

12. *His eyes shall be red with wine, and his teeth white with milk.*

The Zodiacal attribution of the Sign Leo to Judah is apparent, since the power of rulership and the Office of kingship—both leonine—are appropriately described. If wine be taken as a symbol of wisdom distilled from knowledge (grapes), then evolutionary advancement and the later stages of the development of innate powers are being symbolically described. The intimate association of conduct and appearance with the vine, grapes and wine, even affecting the washing of Judah's clothes and the appearance of his eyes and teeth, may all be interpreted as indicating an attainment of such wisdom that the whole nature is " wine-like ", or expressive of wisdom in every undertaking.

Gen. 49: 13. *Zebulun shall dwell at the haven of the sea; and he shall be for an haven of ships; and his border shall be unto Sidon.*

A habitation beside the sea—the ancient port of Sidon—may be read as a personification by Zebulun of the Sign Pisces. A dweller by the sea, he must thereby have been in intimate association with fishes. Zebulun, therefore, may be taken to be representative of the type of products of Nature, and the characteristics of man, attributed to the Sign Pisces.

Gen. 49: 14. *Issachar is a strong ass couching down between two burdens:*

15. *And he saw that rest was good, and the land that it was pleasant; and bowed his shoulder to bear, and became a servant unto tribute.*

Whilst procreative power is especially attributed to the bull—hence the Sign Taurus—nevertheless the bull is a member of the *genus* ox, which animal was widely used as a beast of burden in ancient times. Since asses, however, were also thus employed, astrologers have presumably considered the association of these two families of beasts of burden to be so similar as to be interchangeable. In consequence Issachar, whom his father Jacob described as " a strong ass couching down between two burdens ", has become associated with the ox, and so with the Sign Taurus.

Gen. 49: 16. *Dan shall judge his people, as one of the tribes of Israel.*

17. *Dan shall be a serpent by the way, an adder in the path, that biteth the horse heels, so that his rider shall fall backward.*

18. *I have waited for thy salvation, O LORD.*

The correspondence between the serpent and the scorpion gives rise to the possibility of the association of Dan with the Zodiacal Sign Scorpio. The serpent, however, has in the language of symbols been given at least two beneficent meanings. One of these is comprehension, including wise judgment and spiritual intuitiveness—not inapt attributions of the lawgiver and judge. Thus it seems appropriate that Jacob should begin his description of Dan by referring to his future Office of Judge of the people of Israel.

A deeper and more occult interpretation would, however, seem to be permissible, especially since it is hinted at in the eighteenth verse where, in his father's mind, Dan is associated with salvation by the Power of the Lord. A reference may here be discerned to the second meaning given to the symbol of the serpent, namely the divine, creative power present in the body of man, sometimes called " the Serpent Fire " and in Sanskrit *Kundalini*.[1]

---

[1] *Kundalini*—see Glossary.

19

When this normally sleeping force is aroused into supernormal activity the limitations of bodily encasement can be overridden and the man, thus freed, becomes aware of his own divine and eternal nature.   In this aspect he is immortal, deathless, and assured of the full expression of his spiritual powers.   Perchance it was to this meaning of the serpent symbol that Jacob referred in the eighteenth verse.

> *Gen.* 49: 19. *Gad, a troop shall overcome him: but he shall overcome at the last.*
>
> 20. *Out of Asher his bread shall be fat, and he shall yield royal dainties.*

The Zodiacal correspondence given by astrologers to Gad is with the Sign Aries, ruled as it is by the planet Mars.   In early phases of human evolution combativeness, whether personal or national, can lead to destruction.   In the evolved person, however, it makes victory over the lower nature of man possible.   Refinement then follows, producing the characteristics of gentleness and of readiness to direct Arietic qualities and martial tendencies to an exploration of the hitherto unknown aspects of human nature, and to victory over all that would delay hastened progress towards this goal.

> *Gen.* 49: 21. *Naphtali is a hind let loose: he giveth goodly words.*

A correspondence with the goat family, and so with the Zodiacal Sign Capricorn, may here be regarded as reasonably acceptable.

> *Gen.* 49: 22. *Joseph is a fruitful bough, even a fruitful bough by a well; whose branches run over the wall:*
>
> 23. *The archers have sorely grieved him, and shot at him, and hated him:*
>
> 24. *But his bow abode in strength, and the arms of his hands were made strong by the hands of the mighty God of Jacob; (from thence is the shepherd, the stone of Israel:)*
>
> 25. *Even by the God of thy father, who shall help thee; and by the Almighty, who shall bless thee with blessings of heaven above, blessings of the deep that lieth under, blessings of the breasts, and of the womb:*
>
> 26. *The blessings of thy father have prevailed above the blessings of my progenitors unto the utmost bound of the everlasting hills: they shall be on the head of Joseph, and on the crown of the head of him that was separate from his brethren.*

References to archers, to Joseph's bow, and to archery in general, however symbolical, would associate Joseph with the Sign Sagittarius.   In view of his later contributions to the welfare of his family, the somewhat symbolical descriptions by Jacob of his son Joseph are quite apt from both the material and the spiritual points of view.

Gen. 49: 27. *Benjamin shall ravin as a wolf: in the morning he shall devour the prey, and at night he shall divide the spoil.*

The description of Benjamin as a ravening wolf devouring its prey suggests both the Sign Cancer and the parasitical disease of the same name. Although Jacob's daughter, Dinah, is not here mentioned, her maidenhood may justify her choice by astrologers to represent the Sign Virgo.[1]

Gen. 49: 28. *All these are the twelve tribes of Israel: and this is it that their father spake unto them, and blessed them; every one according to his blessing he blessed them.*

29. *And he charged them, and said unto them, I am to be gathered unto my people: bury me with my fathers in the cave that is in the field of Ephron the Hittite,*

30. *In the cave that is in the field of Machpelah, which is before Mamre, in the land of Canaan, which Abraham bought with the field of Ephron the Hittite for a possession of a burying place.*

31. *There they buried Abraham and Sarah his wife; there they buried Isaac and Rebekah his wife; and there I buried Leah.*

32. *The purchase of the field and of the cave that is therein was from the children of Heth.*

33. *And when Jacob had made an end of commanding his sons, he gathered up his feet into the bed, and yielded up the ghost, and was gathered unto his people.*

THE FIELD OF MACHPELAH

These closing verses of the Forty-ninth Chapter of the *Book of Genesis,* with their description of the death and burial of Abraham, Sarah and certain members of their family, culminating in the death of Jacob himself, are susceptible of interpretation as revealing some knowledge concerning the final stages of universal, racial and individual human evolution.

If this approach be acceptable, then the preceding descriptions of the characters of the sons of Jacob and of the corresponding tribes of Israel refer to phases of the gradual development, and also to the eventual attainment, of full expression of the twelve inherent or Zodiacal powers locked up in the spiritual " seed " or Monad[2] of man. This " Dweller in the Innermost " of each human being who is evolving through the present period of manifestation (*Manvantara*) of our Solar System contains germinally within itself these twelve capacities. The words of Jacob to his sons in these closing verses may be read as veiled revelations of the ultimate stages of development

---

[1] The reader is referred to the table of astrological associations appearing earlier in this Volume.

[2] Monad—see Glossary.

to be reached by the end of the era, in its turn symbolised by Jacob's death and burial.

A hint of this achievement may possibly be found in verse thirty, where the name of the field in which the burial cave existed is given as " Machpelah ". This word, especially in its first syllable, resembles a word uttered at low breath by certain Officers during an important Rite in Freemasonry. If this interpretation be permissible, supported as it is by the inclusion of the word " Machpelah " in a description of the close of a tribal dispensation, then a reference may be discerned to procedures followed in the Temples of the Greater Mysteries of old, of which modern Freemasonry is considered to be a representative.

THE PATHWAY TO PERFECTION

Occult philosophy includes the idea of the existence of a path of hastened progress, a way of self-quickening, treading which the goal of human evolution or twelvefold development is achieved ahead of the normal time, and therefore in advance of the rest of humanity. In this largely secret way of life, which includes victory over adverse attributes and the unfoldment from within of occult, theurgic and spiritual powers, a record of each phase of development is kept by an Official in the Hierarchy of the Adepts of this planet. The title of this Adept Keeper of the Records is *Maha-Chohan*, a Sanskrit word meaning " Great Lord ".

The activities of the Great White Brotherhood all of which are directed towards the fulfilment of Nature's grand design—including the attainment of Masterhood by those who pass through trials, tests and successive Initiations leading to the final goal—are entirely secret. References in the Sacred Language to such actitivities are, in consequence, heavily concealed behind a veil of allegory and symbol. Such a veil may be employed in these closing Chapters of *Genesis*, most of the events described in them being without either historical or anthropological support. As previously stated even the existence of Jacob himself, his twelve sons and the tribes named after them is in doubt, as also are the events related about their journey to Egypt, their meeting with Joseph, and his beneficent treatment of them under agreement with the reigning Pharaoh.

Certain other words appearing in the closing verses of this Chapter may be similarly regarded. Two of these are " cave " and " field ". As already mentioned, the Ceremonies of the Greater Mysteries were always performed in complete secrecy, and in some cases in a crypt or other underground part of a Temple.[1] The word " cave " also suggests a deep recess,

---

[1] Partial descriptions found in ancient literature—as of the Eleusinia, for example—are always of the Lesser Mysteries alone.

and is used allegorically to refer to the innermost depths of the make-up of man wherein abides the Monad, or unit of pure Spirit-Essence. The word " field " may in its turn refer to a Universe or a planet, and microcosmically to the Auric Envelope[1] of individual man; for these three are the " fields " in which cosmic and human evolution take place, the Monad or divine " seed " having, according to an agricultural simile, been " planted " therein.

Whilst neither Chapter nor verse divisions are clearly indicated in the original writings of the *Torah*, the episodes described in the last two Chapters of *Genesis*, and the language in which they are written, would seem to be susceptible of such interpretations as are here offered.

CHAPTER XIII

THE JOSEPH CYCLE

Gen. 50:   *The mourning for Jacob: his funeral.   Joseph prophesieth
to his brethren of their return to Canaan: his age, and death.*

JOSEPH PERSONIFIES THE INITIATE WHO BECOMES AN ADEPT

The interpretation given of the narrative of the life of Jacob, particularly in the preceding Chapter of this book, may also be applied to the account of the life of his son Joseph; for he, like his father, is united with his family and its descendants and with them journeys to the land of his birth where his father is to be buried.

Minor cycles overlap and the Patriarch of one period of Office generally participates in the closing years of Office of his predecessor.   After assuming leadership he continues the process of administration until he completes the cycle of his activities, and in his turn dies and is buried.   A similar procedure is followed by Hierophants in the Lesser and the Greater Mysteries.

The restatement of the enmity and perfidy of his brothers towards Joseph as described in this Chapter of *Genesis* is worthy of note, particularly from the point of view of occult psychology.   They are still afraid of him after Jacob's death, but he forgives them and cares compassionately for them and all their people.   The numerous energies, qualities of character, motives and tendencies which the brethren personify, and which form part of the complexity of the nature of a human being, can indeed be the causes of war both between men and within each man.   The very matter of his bodies, or rather the three *gunas*[1] or attributes of that matter, can become unequally expressed, particularly during this present age when humanity is passing through highly individualistic phases of development.   Indeed at this time strife is evident within him—the true Armageddon, interior and mystical.   When, however, the later phases of man's evolution are entered upon, his nature becomes more harmonious and its diverse elements increas-

---

[1] *Gunas* (Sk.)—see Glossary.

ingly under the control of the inner Self. In the language of symbols families are reunited, countries are subdued and harmony reigns, as was finally the case between Joseph and his brethren.

Adverse experiences of a single life, including especially those of childhood and adolescence, can establish areas of distress and dis-equilibrium in the human *psyche*. The tendency to these disabilities, and the *karma* of suffering from them, have both been brought over from a preceding life. Moreover, unless harmonised and healed some of them can be carried forward into succeeding incarnations. Before the higher Initiations can be conferred these warring and pain-producing factors must be reconciled. This is largely achieved by the reincarnating Ego which, Joseph-like, has become wise and powerful enough to bring about a restoration of health and interior harmony.

The very substance of which the mental, emotional, etheric and physical bodies are composed itself resists the spiritualising and harmonising process; for the elemental consciousness inhabiting that substance is travelling on the downward arc towards coarser emotional experiences and denser embodiment in physical matter.[1] This involving consciousness of the matter of his bodies is part of the subjective Devil or evil in man, and is sometimes personified either by Satan or by the dark angels who are said to be at war with the angels of light.[2] The spiritual Self of man which inhabits these four bodies has, on the other hand, long ago embarked upon the Pathway of Return.[3] Its objective is liberation from the imprisoning and coarsening influences of life in the physical and emotional bodies. An interior conflict is thus inevitable and continuous and this, as we have seen, is one possible microcosmic interpretation of Armageddon or *Kurukshetra*.[4]

Jacob and Joseph, as Initiates approaching Adeptship or the completion of the human cycle, both achieved victory in this interior warfare, even though they suffered mystical wounds in the process.[5] Their physical well-being and security, and the assembling in the closing years of their lives of all the members of their families, partly describe this psycho-spiritual attainment. The highest honours having been achieved, Joseph leaves his body at the age of one hundred and ten years and is, in his turn, buried with his forefathers.

These general observations are intended as an introduction to the study of this Fiftieth Chapter of *Genesis*, and they are now followed by a more detailed examination of it verse by verse.

---

[1] q.v. Vol. I of this work, Pt. Four.

[2] q.v. *The Kingdom of the Gods*, Pt. Three, Ch. V, Geoffrey Hodson.

[3] q.v. Vol. I of this work, Pt. Four.

[4] *Kurukshetra*: The Hindu Armageddon described in the *Mahabharata*; the scene of the Divine Discourses of *The Bhagavad Gita*.

[5] q.v. Vol. I of this work, p. 43 Adyar Ed., and p. 42 Quest Book, U.S.A.

Gen. 50:1. And Joseph fell upon his father's face, and wept upon him, and kissed him.

2. And Joseph commanded his servants the physicians to embalm his father: and the physicians embalmed Israel.

3. And forty days were fulfilled for him; for so are fulfilled the days of those which are embalmed: and the Egyptians mourned for him three-score and ten days.

4. And when the days of his mourning were past, Joseph spake unto the house of Pharaoh, saying, If now I have found grace in your eyes, speak, I pray you, in the ears of Pharaoh, saying,

5. My father made me swear, saying, Lo, I die: in my grave which I have digged for me in the land of Canaan, there shalt thou bury me. Now therefore let me go up, I pray thee, and bury my father, and I will come again.

6. And Pharaoh said, Go up, and bury thy father, according as he made thee swear.

THE JACOB CYCLE CLOSES

Joseph's grief at the death of his father, Jacob, the embalming of the body, the request to Pharaoh for permission to take it to Canaan for burial and Pharaoh's consent, are all susceptible of interpretation as descriptions of the ends of cycles. If this rendering be further developed in terms of occult philosophy, then these closures of cycles would include the following: the consummation of *Manvantara* leading to the onset of the night of *Pralaya*, whether of a Solar System as a whole (*Maha-Pralaya*) or of component Schemes, Chains, Rounds, Globes, Races and civilisations;[1] the death and disappearance of the bodies of all organisms; the completion of a cycle of human existence; and the subsequent entry of the Monad into the Super-human kingdom of Nature, entering which the perfected human Ego is conscious of oneness with its Source—a state of awareness symbolised by entry into the land of Canaan.

If the analogy be permitted, then the tears of Joseph shed upon his father's body not only tell of the grief of a bereaved son, but are also a possible reference to the so-called " Waters of Space " into which, at their dissolution, all material objects disappear.

The laborious—but in actuality entirely unnecessary—plans for taking the body of Jacob all the way back to Canaan, and their fulfilment, also refer to a return of the essence and the substance of each completed cycle, of whatever dimensions, to the Source, which is pre-cosmic Spirit-matter in a conjoined and relatively passive relationship.

[1] see Glossary—Chain.

As has been earlier remarked, this change from activity to passivity, of form to formlessness, and of active life to peaceful rest, is a fundamental, unchanging procedure of Nature. It is one of the secret teachings of the Mysteries of old, revealed direct to Initiates but to the outside world by the use of metaphor and allegory alone. Thus the death of a central figure refers to the end of a cycle, the choice of a specially chosen place for the tomb implies return to the Source, whilst the burial itself implies the resumption of that darkness which brooded over " the face of the deep "[1] (*Pralaya*), to be replaced by light when the new cycle dawns (*Manvantara*).

Doubtless the numbers given in the third verse are also significant and susceptible of interpretation according to the above-mentioned terms of allegorical method and terminology. Particularly does the number seventy, reducible to seven, indicate the completion of a minor cycle, the end of an age.

Gen. 50: 7. *And Joseph went up to bury his father: and with him went all the servants of Pharaoh, the elders of his house, and all the elders of the land of Egypt,*

8. *And all the house of Joseph, and his brethren, and his father's house: only their little ones, and their flocks, and their herds, they left in the land of Goshen.*

9. *And there went up with him both chariots and horsemen: and it was a very great company.*

10. *And they came to the threshing floor of Atad, which is beyond Jordan, and there they mourned with a great and very sore lamentation: and he made a mourning for his father seven days.*

11. *And when the inhabitants of the land, the Canaanites, saw the mourning in the floor of Atad, they said, This is a grievous mourning to the Egyptians: wherefore the name of it was called Abelmizraim, which is beyond Jordan.*

12. *And his sons did unto him according as he commanded them:*

The affirmation that on his journey to Canaan Joseph was accompanied by " all the servants of Pharaoh, the elders of his house, and all the elders of the land of Egypt ", can hardly be taken literally. In consequence it must surely be regarded as either a monstrous exaggeration to show the importance of Joseph's position in Egypt, or as an indication that in the cosmic sense the totality of objective, manifested existences is withdrawn into the quiescent state. Since the latter view harmonises with the interpretation offered of the first six verses of the Fiftieth Chapter, it may safely be thus regarded. The reference in the tenth verse to the crossing of the River Jordan may also be taken as descriptive of passage from one state of existence to a successor, the River Jordan thus being employed as a topographical symbol for

[1] *Gen.* 1: 2.

an episode or condition of fundamental change—in this case from activity to rest.

> *Gen.* 50: 13. *For his sons carried him into the land of Canaan, and buried him in the cave of the field of Machpelah, which Abraham bought with the field for a possession of a burying place of Ephron the Hittite, before Mamre.*

The reference to the field of Machpelah wherein both Abraham and his wife, Sarah, were buried accentuates the idea that the close of every cycle (the death of Jacob) brings about a return to the identical condition into which the products of the earlier cycle had " descended ", namely passive, pre-cosmic Space. The word " Machpelah " has already been considered, and readers are referred to the commentary on the burial of Ciparah as described in the Twenty-third Chapter of *Genesis* for suggested interpretations.

> *Gen.* 50: 14. *And Joseph returned into Egypt, he, and his brethren, and all that went up with him to bury his father, after he had buried his father.*
>
> 15. *And when Joseph's brethren saw that their father was dead, they said, Joseph will peradventure hate us, and will certainly requite us all the evil which we did unto him.*
>
> 16. *And they sent a messenger unto Joseph, saying, Thy father did command before he died, saying,*
>
> 17. *So shall ye say unto Joseph, Forgive, I pray thee now, the trespass of thy brethren, and their sin; for they did unto thee evil: and now, we pray thee, forgive the trespass of the servants of the God of thy father. And Joseph wept when they spake unto him.*
>
> 18. *And his brethren also went and fell down before his face; and they said, Behold, we be thy servants.*
>
> 19. *And Joseph said unto them, Fear not: for am I in the place of God?*
>
> 20. *But as for you, ye thought evil against me; but God meant it unto good, to bring to pass, as it is this day, to save much people alive.*
>
> 21. *Now therefore fear ye not: I will nourish you, and your little ones. And he comforted them, and spake kindly unto them.*

THE JOSEPH CYCLE OPENS

In the small compass of these verses a new era begins. Since it was new only for the brethren, and the personification of power (Joseph) remains the same, it may be assumed that merely the closing sub-cycle of a major cycle is involved.

Of interest, more particularly in the human sense, is the account of the further reconciliation between Joseph and his brethren, their confession and request for pardon, and his complete and very generous forgiveness. Although related as applying to persons, the impersonal law of cause and effect is doubtless being revealed, together with the state of complete reharmonisation achieved at the closing of the cyclic sequence of action and reaction. Whilst this is of Macrocosmic significance, the approach to Adeptship is also being referred to, since this state cannot be attained until every action has been followed by an appropriate reaction, every debt paid to both Nature and man, and a surplus acquired in favour of the actor. Then, and then only, can the human kingdom be transcended and the Monad continue its evolution as occult Sage, Rishi, Adept.

The superabundance of favour earned by many lives and many acts of selfless service to humanity (Joseph's beneficence) is a characteristic of the closing phases of evolution through the human kingdom and entry into a higher state. This is indicated—if the account be read symbolically—by Joseph's ready forgiveness of the injury, even to the extent of murder,[1] which his brothers had planned and attempted to execute against him when he came into the field. Not vengeance but pardon, not imprisonment or execution but forgiving love, were shown by Joseph to his erring brethren. Similarly the Christ upon the Cross prayed for those who crucified Him, saying, " Father, forgive them; for they know not what they do. "[2]

If these approaches be acceptable, then the closing Chapters of the *Book of Genesis* may be regarded as being deliberately written in the language of allegory in order to bestow upon the Hebrew people—and through them and their sacred books, to all humanity—a profound wisdom concerning the inception and the conclusion of Macrocosmic and microcosmic manifestations of the Divine. To this is added knowledge of the experiences met with and passed through by men as they become superhuman beings.

Gen. 50: 22. *And Joseph dwelt in Egypt, he, and his father's house: and Joseph lived an hundred and ten years.*

23. *And Joseph saw Ephraim's children of the third generation: the children also of Machir the son of Manasseh were brought up upon Joseph's knees.*

24. *And Joseph said unto his brethren, I die: and God will surely visit you, and bring you out of this land unto the land which he sware to Abraham, to Isaac, and to Jacob.*

25. *And Joseph took an oath of the children of Israel, saying, God will surely visit you, and ye shall carry up my bones from hence.*

26. *So Joseph died, being an hundred and ten years old: and they embalmed him, and he was put in a coffin in Egypt.*

[1] *Gen.* 37: 24.
[2] *Luke* 23: 34.

JOSEPH'S DEATH AND BURIAL

In the Sacred Language the death of a man, in the sense in which it is used in the *Book of Genesis*,[1] means both the death of an age and the end of the passage of the Monad through the human kingdom of Nature. Thus in these concluding verses Joseph dies, is put in a coffin, and is buried in the land of Egypt.

Although a limited number of cycles, their presiding Logoi, and the processes of involution, evolution and withdrawal into the source are actually referred to in the Old Testament, nevertheless the wisdom revealed beneath the veil of allegory refers to all cycles, of whatever dimensions, that have ever existed and will ever exist. The underlying principles, laws and procedures are ever the same, and so will ever remain, and this is part of the greatness of the revelation deeply hidden beneath a supposed historical record of the history of the Hebrew nation which is found in the *Book of Genesis*, as also in the rest of the *Pentateuch* and in much of the *Torah* as a whole.

The seeker for wisdom must, however, be prepared to delve deeply, to discover, and to interpret according to the classical keys, the numberless treasures of spiritual and occult wisdom and law which lie beneath the surface of all allegorical writings, littered with debris though that surface may appear to be.

*   *   *   *   *

So ends the great *Book of Genesis*—a marvellous cup filled with the "wine" of the esoteric knowledge of the Sanctuaries of ancient days. Temples of the Ageless Wisdom exist to-day, even if less easily discoverable, and in them are to be found the selfsame teachings, laws, successions, Initiations and radiations of the light of Truth. World changes are not reflected in the Mysteries, which are repositories and conveyors of eternal and unchanging Ideas. A sack of corn containing a silver cup awaits every Benjamin who finds himself called by a Hierophant (Joseph) from the " famine-stricken " outer world to the " storehouse " from which an elder brother (a Master) Who has already attained will, in prodigal abundance, supply a gift of the golden grain of eternal verities.

---

[1] In the New Testament death may be regarded as a symbol for that condition of the mind in which it is totally unresponsive, or dead, to the influence of the spiritual Self. The active presence of the awakened Christ-nature, personified by Jesus, restores the dead person to life, namely to responsiveness to conscience and Egoic inspiration. Thus Jesus raises from the dead the daughter of Jairus and Lazarus, the brother of Martha and Mary.

THE SEPHIROTHAL TREE
ACCORDING TO THE KABBALAH

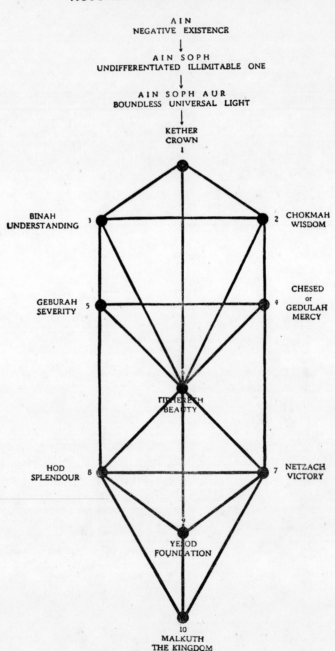

AIN
NEGATIVE EXISTENCR

AIN SOPH
UNDIFFERENTIATED ILLIMITABLE ONE

AIN SOPH AUR
BOUNDLESS UNIVERSAL LIGHT

KETHER
CROWN
1

BINAH
UNDERSTANDING 3

CHOKMAH
WISDOM 2

GEBURAH
SEVERITY 5

CHESED
or
GEDULAH
MERCY 4

TIPHERETH
BEAUTY

HOD
SPLENDOUR 8

NETZACH
VICTORY 7

YESOD
FOUNDATION

10
MALKUTH
THE KINGDOM

APPENDIX

THE SEPHIROTHAL TREE

APPENDIX

THE SEPHIROTHAL TREE

THE *Kabbalah* has been variously described as an unwritten or oral tradition, as the esoteric doctrine of the Jewish religion and as the hidden wisdom or theosophy of the Hebrew Rabbis of the Middle Ages, who are said to have obtained it from older secret doctrines. The Hebrew word is derived from the root QBL, " to receive ". Included in the meaning of the word, therefore, is the practice of transmitting esoteric knowledge by word of mouth.

On examination, the *Kabbalah* proves to be a system of theosophy which claims to be of celestial origin and to have reached the early Hebrew Patriarchs through the ministry of the angels. King David and King Solomon are said to have been initiated into the *Kabbalah*, and a legend exists that Rabbi Simeon Ben Jochai took the step of writing a portion of the teachings down at the time of the destruction of the second Temple. His son, Rabbi Eleazar, his secretary and his disciples gathered together his treatises and from them composed the *Zohar*, meaning " Splendour ", which is the literary source of Kabbalism. The author of the main part of the *Zohar* is, however, recognised by modern kabbalistic scholars[1] to have been Rabbi Moses de Leon, a Kabbalist of Thirteenth Century Spain.

THE TEN ORDERS OF ANGELS

The Angelic Hosts occupy an important place in the cosmogonical scheme of the *Kabbalah*, in which the Sephiroth are described as the potencies and modes of action (*shaktis*)[2] of the living God, the ten archetypal numbers (from *safar*— to count) taken as the fundamental powers of all being. This notion of feminine potencies in God, which attain their fullest expression in the tenth and last Sephirah, seems utterly incongruous in exoteric Jewish thinking, which is strictly monotheistic and masculine.

THE LOGOS DOCTRINE

The fashioning of the Universe by the power of sound or " speech " is also basic to Kabbalism. The names of the ten Sephiroth are regarded

---

[1] q.v. *On the Kabbalah and Its Symbolism*, Gershom G. Scholem, trans. by Ralph Manheim (Routledge and Kegan Paul, London), and other modern works.

[2] *Shakti*—see Glossary.

as the creative names which God gave to Himself. The action and development of the mysterious force which is the seed of all creation is none other than speech or "speech-force" expressive of archetypal thought. The process of the manifestation of divine life is construed as the unfolding of the elements of speech. This is indeed one of the *Zohar's* favourite symbols. The world of divine emanation is one in which the human faculty of speech is anticipated in God. According to the *Zohar*, the successive phases of emanation include the abysmal[1] will, formative thought, inner and inaudible word, audible voice, and ultimately man's utterance of words.

Kabbalists thus regard the Sephiroth as ten spheres of divine manifestation in which God emerges from His hidden abode, and as forming the "unified universe" of God's life. They are also referred to as "mystical crowns of the holy King", "the ten names of God", and "the King's faces", meaning his varying aspects. The Sephiroth also possess other implications, four of which are the mystical Face of God, the ten stages of the inner world through which He descends from the inmost recesses, the garments of Divinity, and the beams of light which radiate from the Godhead.

Ten Orders of manifested Beings are associated with the ten Sephiras, which constitute the kabbalistic Tree of Life. They are regarded as Emanations of Deity, each Sephira representing a number, a group of exalted ideas, titles and attributes, and a Hierarchy of spiritual Beings outside of humanity. Each Sephira has a fourfold nature in correspondence with the four worlds of the Kabbalist. These are: Atziluth—the Archetypal World, or World of Emanations, the Divine World; Briah—the World of Creation, also called *Khorsis*, the World of Thrones; Yetzirah—the World of Formation and of Angels; Assiah—the World of Action, the World of Matter.

In Atziluth the Sephiras manifest through ten different aspects, represented by the ten holy Names of God in the Hebrew Scriptures. In Briah they are expressed through the ten Archangels, and in Yetzirah through the Choirs or Hosts of the Angels. In Assiah, and especially on the physical plane, they are associated with the physical planets and the subtile elements of which these are said to be composed. They are also regarded as being in mutual resonance with the *chakras* in the mental, emotional and etheric bodies of man and their related glandular and nerve centres.[2]

The Sephiras are depicted as both numbers and circles, an idea presumably echoed by Proclus who wrote :—" Before the mathematical numbers, there are the *self-moving* numbers; before the figures apparent, the vital figures, and before producing the material worlds *which move in a circle*,

---

[1] Abysmal—concerning primal chaos; the fathomless, pre-cosmic depths.
[2] q.v. *Lecture Notes of the School of the Wisdom*, Vol. I (Rev. Ed.), Geoffrey Hodson.

the Creative Power produced the invisible circles."[1]   At the head of each
Hierarchy of spiritual Intelligences is a named Archangel, under Whom are
gradations of angels who perform significant functions in the emanation,
formation, preservation and transformation of a Universe.

THE ANGELS IN CHRISTIANITY

The Christian religion, which contains much kabbalistic thought,
teaches that there are nine Orders of Angels, severally called Angels,
Archangels, Thrones, Dominations, Principalities, Virtues, Powers, Cherubim and Seraphim, certain qualities and activities being assigned to each
of these Orders.   Angels and Archangels are sent as messengers in matters
of high importance, as were Gabriel and Raphael.   Thrones contemplate
the glory and equity of the divine judgments and influence men to rule
with justice.   Dominations are supposed to regulate the activities and duties
of the Angels, whilst Principalities preside over peoples and provinces and
serve as Angelic Rulers (National Angels) of the nations of the world.
Virtues have the gift of working miracles.   Powers are a check on evil
spirits.   Cherubim excel in the splendour of knowledge and so enlighten
mankind with wisdom and the Seraphim, being most ardent in divine love,
inspire mankind with that quality.   In nearly all the Biblical accounts of
men's visions of God, He is described as transcendent in glory and surrounded
by countless multitudes of His Angels.[2]

Kabbalism, whilst naming them differently, gives to these Beings their
due place and certain additional functions.   In common with other cosmogonies, it postulates the existence of an Absolute as the basis of everything.
This is regarded as Negative Existence, AIN or " No-thing " and has
been described as an illimitable abyss of Glory.   It has three veils which
are called AIN, meaning the negatively existent, AIN SOPH, the limitless
without form, being or likeness with anything else, and AIN SOPH AUR,
the limitless light, which concentrates into the first and highest Sephira of
the Sephirothal Tree called Kether, the Crown.

These successive veils, concealing even whilst providing vehicles for the
illimitable Source, appear to have been given a number of symbolic meanings—Macrocosmic and microcosmic—in World Scriptures and Mythologies.   They may possibly be referred to in the Twenty-fourth Chapter of
Genesis, verse sixty-five, as the veil which Rebecca (virgin space) placed
over her face on the approach of Isaac (the Spirit of God); in the Thirty-
fourth Chapter of *Exodus*, verses thirty-three and thirty-four, when Moses
removed his veil as he went in before the LORD to speak with Him, having

---

[1] Quoted in *The Secret Doctrine*, Vol. IV, p. 122 (Adyar Ed.), H. P. Blavatsky.
[2] A fuller exposition is to be found in *The Kingdom of the Gods*, Geoffrey Hodson.

20

placed it upon his face before addressing the people; and in the Twenty-seventh Chapter of *Matthew*, verse fifty-one, where the veil of the Temple is stated to have been " rent in twain from the top to the bottom " when Jesus " yielded up the ghost " upon the Cross.   As indicated above and, with regard to Rebecca, on pages 402 and 403 of Volume II of this work, the symbol of the veil—Paroketh in Kabbalism—is susceptible of interpretation in both the   Macrocosmic sense, as above, and microcosmically as the veil between the immortal Self of man and the mind of his mortal personality.

The nine[1] letters AIN SOPH AUR are said to shadow forth the nine Sephiras as hidden ideas or seed-thoughts which, when manifestation begins, are represented by archangelic Beings or " Gods " (*Elohim*).   In the description of this process, as stated above, the Limitless Ocean of Light is said to concentrate a centre, which is the first Sephira, the Crown, which in turn gives birth to the nine others, the last or tenth being called Malkuth, the Kingdom, meaning " all Nature manifested ".   Together, the ten Sephiras represent the emanation and development of the powers and attributes of Deity.   Each number is an outward symbol for inner creative forces and processes and their personifications as Archangels or Builders of the Universe. Some of these are male and some female, or rather of positive and negative potencies, Deity having conformed Itself thus in order that It could create— or, more correctly, emanate—the Universe.   Man, being made in the image of Deity, is physically male and female also.

KETHER

The first Sephira is Number One, the Monad of Pythagoras.   As already mentioned, this Sephira is called Kether Elyon, the " Supreme Crown " of God, and also the Ancient of the Ancient Ones, the Ancient of Days, the Primordial Point, the White Head, the Inscrutable Height and the Vast Countenance or Macroposopus.   The following passage from *The Book of Daniel* would seem to refer to this Sephira: " I beheld till the thrones were cast down, and the Ancient of days did sit, whose garment was white as snow, and the hair of his head like the pure wool : his throne was like the fiery flame, and his wheels as burning fire.   (Apparently the Logos of a Solar System, Chain or Round, the 'White Head' of Kabbalism).   A fiery stream issued and came forth from before him: thousand thousands ministered unto him (the Angelic Hosts), and ten thousand times ten thousand stood before him (the Monads of His Scheme, Chain, Round or Planet).... I saw in the night visions, and, behold, one like the Son of man came with the clouds of heaven, and came to the Ancient of Days, and they brought

---

[1] PH (as in SOPH)—P in the Hebrew alphabet.

him near before him (the Sanat Kumāra[1]). And there was given him dominion, and glory, and a kingdom, that all people, nations, and languages, should serve him; his dominion is an everlasting dominion, which shall not pass away, and his kingdom that which shall not be destroyed....But the saints of the most High (the Adepts) shall take the kingdom, and possess the kingdom for ever, even for ever and ever...."[2]

In its highest and abstract aspect Kether is in association with Adam Kadmon (the Heavenly Man), a synthesis of the whole Sephirothal Tree, the Archetype of all Creation and all humanity and, in one possible reading, the first Adam of *Genesis*. Kether is also called *Seir Anpin*, " Son of the Concealed Father ", and so in this highest aspect must be regarded as the Logos, the *Christos* of the Fourth Gospel.

Since one cannot create alone, Kether is said to vibrate across the field of manifestation or to reflect itself in matter to produce a feminine or dyad, from which in turn all beings and all things emanate, having been hitherto contained within Kether. The Archangel Head of the associated Hierarchy of Angels is severally named Metatron or " beside (or beyond) the Throne ", Prince of Faces, Angel of the Presence, World Prince, El Shaddai—the Omnipotent and Almighty One—the Messenger, and Shekinah, this last being associated with the cloud of glory which rested on the Mercy Seat upon the Ark of the Covenant within the Holy of Holies.[3] Shekinah is also regarded as identical with AIN SOPH AUR, the veil of AIN SOPH, pre-cosmic substance or virgin space, *Mulaprakriti*, or the *Parabrahmic* root, of Hinduism.

The Order of Angels in Kether is the Chaioth Ha-Qadesh, " Holy Living Creatures ". They are associated with the Kerubim[4] and regarded as governors of the four elements in their highest sublimation. They would seem to correspond to the *Lipika*,[5] the Celestial Recorders or " Scribes ", the Agents of *karma* in Hinduism. This Hierarchy is concerned with the initiation of the whirling motions by means of which primordial atoms or " holes in space "[6] are formed, presumably using the force which in Tibetan is called *Fohat*, the essence of cosmic electricity, the ever-present electrical energy and ceaseless formative and destructive power in the Universe, the

---

[1] *Kumaras* (Sk.). The four great Beings in the Occult Hierarchy of Adepts Who help on the evolution of humanity; also applied to the Ever-Virgin Youth and His disciples, Who are said in occult philosophy to have founded the Adept Hierarchy on this planet. *Sanat Kumāra* is the name given to this Head or Chief of Earth's Adepts.

[2] *Dan.* 7.

[3] *Ex.* 40: 35.

[4] Usually spelt in Kabbalism with a " K " rather than " Ch " and so pronounced. *Ez.* 1: 5 *et seq.*

[5] *Lipika*—see Glossary.

[6] From an Occult Catechism quoted in *The Secret Doctrine*, Vol. I (Adyar Ed.), p. 203, H. P. Blavatsky.

universal propelling, vital force, the *primum mobile*, whose symbol is the *svastika*. In Kether are thus said to be " the beginnings of the whirls ", the first stirrings of the divine creative Essence. Evidently Ezekiel in his exalted vision in some degree beheld this process, for he says: " And I looked, and, behold, a whirlwind came out of the north, a great cloud...."[1] One of the chief duties of the members of this Angelic Hierarchy is to receive this Essence in Kether and carry it to the succeeding Hierarchy of the Auphanim or " Wheels ", associated with the second Sephira.

CHOKMAH

Kether produces the other nine Sephiras, the second being Chokmah, " Wisdom " or primordial idea of God, a masculine, active potency or Father reflected from Kether. Chokmah is the second Adam, from whom is produced Eve, and is associated with Microposopus, " the Lesser Countenance ". The Archangel Head of the Angelic Hierarchy is Ratziel, " the Herald of Deity ", " the Delight of God ". The Order of Angels is the Auphanim or " Wheels ", so-called in reference to the vortex, whirlwind or whirlpool-producing action of the *primum mobile*. From this Order are said to be drawn the Angels of the Planets, who are described in the First Chapter of *Ezekiel*. The planetary correspondence is with the Zodiac as a whole, and in some systems with Uranus.[2]

BINAH

The third Sephira is a feminine, passive potency called Binah, " Intelligence " of God, the Understanding, co-equal and contemporaneous with Chokmah, to whom She is as Eve, the Mother Supernal. Binah is also called Ama (Mother), combined with Ab (Father) for the maintenance of order in the Universe. She is sometimes referred to as the Great Sea, and kabbalistically these two Powers weave the web of the Universe.[3] The Archangel Head is Tzaphqiel, " He who beholds God ", or " Contemplation of God ". The Order of Angels is the Arelim, " the Mighty Ones ", the Thrones of Christian angelology. The number Two, as a principle, is like two straight lines which can never enclose a space and is therefore powerless until number Three forms a primary triangle. Binah performs that function and makes evident the supernal, but not the material, active Trinity. This upper Triad remains in the Archetypal world, whilst the

---

[1] *Ez.* 1: 4.

[2] The Kabbalistic Correspondences do not always agree with those given in *The Secret Doctrine* by H. P. Blavatsky.

[3] q.v. *The Secret Doctrine*, Vol. I (Adyar Ed.), p. 148, H. P. Blavatsky.

seven Sephiras which follow create, sustain and transform the manifested material world. In Kabbalism the planet associated with Binah is Saturn.

The union of Chokmah and Binah, " Wisdom " and " Intelligence ", produces Supernal Knowledge, called Daath in Kabbalism. Daath itself is not regarded as a Sephira, but is included in some diagrams of the Sephirothal Tree, in which it is placed between Chokmah and Binah.

CHESED

An active dyad now exists in Chokmah and Binah. Their union produced Chesed, a masculine or active potency. Chesed is " Love " or " Mercy " of God and is also called Gedulah, " Greatness " or " Magnificence ". The Archangel Head is Tzadqiel, " Justice of God ", " Righteousness of God ". The Order of Angels is the Chasmalim, " Scintillating Flames ", " Brilliant Ones ". They are the Dominations of Christian angelology and are regarded as Angels of Light. The associated planet is Jupiter.

GEBURAH

From Four or Chesed emanated the feminine, passive, fifth potency, Geburah, the " Power " of God, " Severity ", " Strength ", " Fortitude ", " Justice " chiefly manifested as the power of stern judgment and punishment. This Sephira is also named Pachad, " Fear ". The Archangel Head is Kahamael, " the Right Hand of God ", and is sometimes called the Punishing Angel. The Order of Angels is the Seraphim, known in Christian angelology as Powers. They are thus described in Isaiah 6: 1-3:

"....I saw also the Lord sitting upon a throne, high and lifted up, and his train filled the temple.

" Above it stood the Seraphims: each one had six wings; with twain he covered his face, and with twain he covered his feet, and with twain he did fly.

" And one cried unto another, and said, Holy, holy, holy, is the LORD of hosts: the whole earth is full of his glory. "

The Hebrew name of the Seraphim is translated " Serpents ", and as this is related to the verbal root ShRP, " to burn up ", it may be assumed that these are the fiery Serpents associated with the creative fire[1] and processes in both Nature and man. The planet is Mars.

---

[1] Kundalini—see Glossary.

TIPHERETH

From Chesed (masculine) and Geburah (feminine) emanated the sixth and uniting Sephira, Tiphereth, " Beauty " or " Mildness ", the heart and centre of the Sephirothal Tree. This Sephera is also named Rahamin, the " Compassion " of God. This is said to be the place allotted by the Israelites to the Messiah and by the early Christians to the Christ. The Archangel Head is Michael, " who is like unto God ". The Order of Angels is the Malachim, meaning " Kings " and known in Christianity as Virtues. Another system places Raphael here, and Michael in the eighth Sephira. The Sun is associated with Tiphereth.

In terms of planes of Nature and levels of normal human consciousness, Tiphereth marks both a boundary and a place of union between the Divine and the human, the Macrocosm and the microcosm, the abstract and the concrete. Here symbolically is said to exist Paroketh, the so-called veil of the " temple " of both seven-planed Nature and seven-principled man. This veil must be pierced by those who would ascend in consciousness the middle pillar of the kabbalistic Tree of Life, liberate themselves from the purely human delusion of separated selfhood, which must be " crucified ", and enter into realisation of unity with the One Great Self of All. Thereafter the spiritual forces of the abstract or formless worlds and their angelic directors may be invoked both to quicken human evolution by arousing the hidden powers in the *chakras*[1] in the personal nature and bodies of man, and to assist in various kinds of occult work.

By the union of Geburah or " Justice " with Chesed or " Mercy ", Beauty, Harmony and Clemency are produced and the second Sephirothal Trinity is then complete. This sixth Sephira, Tiphereth, with the fourth, fifth, seventh, eighth and ninth, is spoken of as the Microposopus or Lesser Countenance, the microcosm, the reflection into manifestation of Macroposopus, the Macrocosm, and also its antithesis.

NETZACH

The seventh Sephira is Netzach, the " Lasting Endurance " of God, " Firmness ", " Victory ". The Archangelic Head is called Hamiel, " the Grace of God ", and the Order of Angels is the *Elohim*, " the Gods ", also called Tsarshisim, " Brilliant Ones ", and known as Principalities in Christianity. In the Tenth Chapter of *The Book of Daniel*, verses five and six, Hamiel is described thus:

" Then I lifted up mine eyes, and looked, and behold a certain man clothed in linen, whose loins were girded with fine gold of Uphāz:

' His body also was like the beryl, and his face as the appearance of lightning, and his eyes as lamps of fire, and his arms and his feet

[1] *Chakras*—see Glossary.

like in colour to polished brass, and the voice of his words like the voice of a multitude. "

The planet associated with this Sephira is Venus.

HOD

From Netzach proceeded the feminine, passive potency, Hod, the eighth Sephira, the " Majesty " of God, " Splendour ", the God of Armies. The Archangel Head is Raphael, " Divine Physician ", the Angel of Healing, intermediary between man and God, who is assisted by a Hierarchy of ministering Angels known in one interpretation as the *Beni Elohim*, " the Sons of God ", and as Archangels in Christianity. The planet is Mercury.

YESOD

Hod and Netzach together produced the ninth Sephira, Yesod, the " Basis ", the Foundation of all actual forces in God, " the Mighty Living One ". The Archangel Head is Gabriel, " the Mighty One of God ". The Order of Angels is the Kerubim, " the Holy Living Creatures ", the Angels of Christianity. Evidently an intimate connection exists between the Kerubim of the first Sephira in the supernal worlds and those of Yesod in the etheric counterpart of the outer, material Universe. They are sometimes called Aishim or " the Flames ", and are also referred to as the four Angels of the subtle elements of earth, fire, water and air.

The Kerubim are associated with the constellations of Taurus, Leo, Scorpio and Acquarius, or the Bull, the Lion, the Eagle and the Man. Part of their duty is said to be to gather the forces of Nature on the astral plane, pour them into the kingdom of Earth, Malkuth, and control them in all their complex manifestations. They are also regarded as Agents of the *Lipika* or Recorders, the Lords of *Karma* and Regents of the four quarters of the Universe. The planet is the Moon. Netzach, Hod and Yesod together complete the third Trinity in the Sephirothal Tree.

MALKUTH

From the ninth Sephira came the tenth and last, completing the decad of the numbers. It is called Malkuth, the kingdom of Earth, all Nature, and also the Queen, Matrona, the Inferior Mother. Shekinah is another name for Malkuth, which would therefore seem to represent the veil of both primordial matter and physical Nature.

Two Archangels are associated with Malkuth. They are the Metatron of Kether and His brother and co-worker, Sandalphon, the kabbalistic

Prince of Angels. Sandalphon, the Dark Angel, may be regarded as the densely material *shakti* or manifested power of Metatron, the Bright Angel. Since the planet Earth is the place of the outworking of man's physical *karma*, Sandalphon is sometimes regarded as an Angel of personal *karma*. Metatron, on the other hand, is associated with the Celestial Agents of *karma* Who are concerned with the self-created destiny of the human race as a whole, doubtless not only on Earth but also throughout the Solar System. The Archangel of our Earth in particular is said to be Auriel, " the Light of God ". The Order of Angels is the Ishim or " Fires ". No single planet, unless it be the Earth, is allotted to Malkuth, which Sephira apparently includes the whole of physical Nature and is concerned with the four subtle and material elements and their use in the building and transformation of the " kingdom " of the visible Universe.

Such, briefly described, is the Sephirothal Tree, " the ten spheres of divine manifestation in which God emerges from His hidden abode. Together they form the 'unified universe' of God's life, the 'world of union', both the ensemble and the particulars of which the Zohar attempts to interpret in an unending variety of speculation....

" The Sefiroth are called 'mystical crowns of the Holy King' notwithstanding the fact that 'He is they, and they are He'. They are the ten names most common to God, and in their entirety they also form His one great Name. They are 'the King's faces', in other words His varying aspects, and they are also called the inner, intrinsic or mystical Face of God. They are the ten stages of the inner world, through which God descends from the inmost recesses down to His revelation in the Shekhinah. They are the garments of the Divinity, but also the beams of light which it sends out . . . "

" The ten Sefiroth constitute the mystical Tree of God or tree of divine power, each representing a branch whose common root is unknown and unknowable. But *En-Sof* is not only the hidden Root of all Roots, it is also the sap of the tree; every branch, representing an attribute, exists not by itself but by virtue of *En-Sof*, the hidden God. And this tree of God is also, as it were, the skeleton of the universe; it grows throughout the whole of creation and spreads its branches through all its ramifications. All mundane and created things exist only because something of the power of the Sefiroth lives and acts in them. "[1]

KABBALISTIC INTERPRETATIONS OF SCRIPTURE

The *Kabbalah* includes three methods of Scriptural interpretation called *Gematria*, *Notariqon* and *Temura*.

[1] q.v. *Major Trends in Jewish Mysticism*, Gershom G. Scholem.

Gematria is based on the relative numerical values of words, those of similar numerical values being considered to be explanatory of each other, and this theory is also extended to phrases. Thus in the word *Shin*, Sh[1] is 300 and is equivalent to the number obtained by adding up the numerical values of the letters of the words RVCh ALHIM, *Ruach Elohim*, the Spirit of the *Elohim*. Sh is therefore a symbol of the Spirit of the *Elohim*.

Notariqon is derived from the Latin word *notarius*, a shorthand writer. There are two forms of *Notariqon*. In the first form every letter of a word is taken for the initial or abbreviation of another word, so that from the letters of a word a sentence may be formed. Thus every letter of the word BRAShITh, *Berashith*, the first word in *Genesis*, is made the initial of a word, and we obtain BRAShITh RAH ALIM ShIQBLV IShRAL ThVRH, *Berashith Rahi Elohim Sheyequebelo Israel Torah*: " In the beginning the *Elohim* saw that Israel would accept the law. "

The second form of *Notariqon* is the exact reverse of the first. By this the initials or finals, or both, or the medials, of a sentence are taken to form a word or words. Thus the *Kabbalah* is called ChKMh NSThRH, *Chokhmah Nesethrah*, " the secret wisdom ".

Temura is permutation. According to certain rules one letter is substituted for the letter preceding or following it in the alphabet, and thus from one word another word of totally different orthography may be formed. (Based on *The Kabbalah Unveiled*, S. L. MacGregor Mathers).

This exposition in outline of the more exoteric elements of Kabbalism has been synthesised from a number of works on the subject, to the authors of which acknowledgement is here gratefully made. Amongst others are the *Zohar* (original and excerpts under that title by *Gershom G. Scholem*); *The Kabalah, Its Doctrines, Developments and Literature*, Christian D. Ginsburg, LL.D.; *The Kabbalah Unveiled*, S. L. MacGregor Mathers; *The Secret Wisdom of the Qabalah*, J. F. C. Fuller; *The Secret Doctrine in Israel*, A. E. Waite; *Isis Unveiled* and *The Secret Doctrine*, H. P. Blavatsky.

[1] SH, a single consonant—S.

GLOSSARY

Absolute, The: The impersonal, supreme and incognisable Principle of the Universe. See Parabrahman.

Adept (Latin). *Adeptus*, " He who has obtained ". An Initiate of the Fifth Degree in the Greater Mysteries, a Master in the science of esoteric philosophy, a perfected man, an exalted Being who has attained complete mastery over his purely human nature and possesses knowledge and power commensurate with lofty evolutionary stature. A fully initiated Being who watches over and guides the progress of humanity.

Adi (Sk.): " The first, the primeval ". The Foundation Plane, the first field of manifestation, " the foundation of a Universe, its support and the fount of its life." For an exposition of the seven planes of Nature see *Through the Gateway of Death*, Geoffrey Hodson.

Adonai (Heb.): Substitute for " Lord " or Jehovah, JHWH.

Ahamkara (Sk.): The first tendency towards definiteness, regarded as the origin of all manifestation. In man the conception of " I ", self-consciousness or self-identity, the illusion of self as a self-separate existence in contradistinction to the reality of the universal One Self. Awareness of this universality is expressed in the words of the Christ: " I and my Father are one." (*Jn.* 10:30) The illusion of separateness, the " Great Heresy ", is regarded as the source of human sorrow and suffering. Self-emancipation from this delusion is the sure way to happiness and peace.

Akasa (Sk.): " The subtle, supersensuous, spiritual essence which pervades all space. The primordial substance erroneously identified with ether. But it is to ether what spirit is to matter. . . . It is, in fact, the Eternal Space in which lies inherent the Ideation of the Universe in its ever-changing aspects on the planes of matter and objectivity, and from which radiates the *First Logos* or expressed thought. This is why it is stated in the *Puranas* that *Akasa* has but one attribute, namely sound, for sound is but the translated symbol for *Logos*— ' Speech ' in its mystic sense." q.v. *The Theosophical Glossary*, H. P. Blavatsky.

Amshashpends (Pers.): The Seven Planetary *Logoi*, as well as the creative Hosts who carry out their will. The six Angels or divine Forces, personified as gods, who attend upon *Ahura Mazda* (the personified Deity, the Principle of Universal Divine Light of the Parsees), of which He is the synthesis and the seventh.

Analogeticists: The Neo-Platonic School, founded in 191 A.D. by Ammonius Saccus, included Alexandrian philosophers who sought to interpret the Bible according to a system of allegory, analogy and symbol and were, in consequence, named Analogeticists.

Anupadaka (Sk.): " Parentless ", self-existing, born without progenitors, applied to both a plane of Nature—the second from above—and to those Great Beings who are in this sense parentless or " self-born of the Divine Essence ".

Archetype (Gr.): " First-moulded " or stamped. The ideal, abstract or essential " idea ". The divine conceiving from which arises the divine " idea " of the whole Universe in time and space; the governing Power in creation. " When God first looked out of eternity (if one may say that he ever *first* looked out), he saw everything as it would happen and at the same time he saw when and how we would create each thing." (From *Meister Eckhart*, by Raymond Blankey, Harper and Row).

Arhat (Sk.): " The worthy ". Exoterically, " one worthy of divine honours ". Esoterically, an Initiate of the Fourth Degree who has entered the highest Path and is thus emancipated from both self-separateness and enforced rebirth.

Astral: The region of the expression of all feelings and desires of the human soul. See also *Kama*.

Atma (Sk.): " The Self". The Universal Spirit, the seventh principle in the septenary constitution of man, the Supreme Soul. The Spirit-Essence of the Universe. (Paramatman—" the Self Beyond ").

Atomic: In occult science this word is used for the foundation-bricks of the Universe and in the strict etymological sense, meaning that it " cannot be cut or divided " (Gr.). One of the fundamentals of occultism is that the elements of Nature are atoms on the material side and Monads on the energy side, both being indivisible. The Greek philosophers Democritus, Leucippus, Epicurus, Ennius and Lucretius advanced the view that matter was composed of atoms, and these scholars came to be known as " atomists " in consequence. q.v. *First Principles of Theosophy*, Ch. X, C. Jinarajadasa.

Augoeides (Gr.): " The self-radiant divine fragment ", the Robe of Glory of the Gnostics and the *Karana Sharira*, " Causal Body ", of Hinduism.

Aura (Gr. and Lat.): A subtle, invisible essence or fluid that emanates from human, animal, and even inanimate, bodies. A psychic effluvium, superphysical and physical, including the electro-vital emanations from the physical body in the case of man. It is usually oviform or egg-shaped and is the seat of the Monadic, spiritual, intellectual, mental, passional and vital energies, faculties and potentialities of the whole sevenfold man.

Auric Envelope: The whole aura, with reference to both the edge or extreme range of the auric radiations (envelope) and the presence of germinal powers, particularly those retained in the immortal vesture of the triple Self known as the Causal Body. This vehicle is more especially symbolised by the arks of the Flood legends of the Scriptures of ancient peoples, and by boats introduced into other allegorical narratives such as those of the ships built by Argus and Deucalion (Greek mythology), that built for Vaivasvata (*Mahabharata,* the *Puranas* and the *Brahmanas*), and that upon which Christ performed the miracle of the stilling of the tempest (*Matt.* 8: 23-26). The edge and sum total of the substance of the seven human bodies, physical and superphysical, and their subtle radiations.

Avatar (Sk.): The doctrine of Divine incarnation or " descent ".

Avatara (Sk.): " Descent ". The incarnation of a Deity, especially Vishnu, the Second Aspect of the Hindu *Trimurti.*

Brahma Vidya (Sk.): " The wisdom of Brahma ", the Supreme Deity.

Brahman (Sk.): The impersonal, supreme and incognisable Principle of the Universe, from the Essence of which all emanates and into which all returns. Extracted from *The Theosophical Glossary,* H. P. Blavatsky, and other sources.

Brahma's Day: " A period of 2,160,000,000 (Earth) years during which Brahma having emerged out of his golden egg (*Hiranyagarbha*), creates and fashions the material world (being simply the fertilizing and creative force in Nature). After this period, the worlds being destroyed in turn by fire and water, he vanishes with objective nature, and then comes Brahma's Night." q.v. *The Theosophical Glossary,* H. P. Blavatsky.

Brahma's Night: " A period of equal duration, during which Brahma is said to be asleep. Upon awakening he recommences the process, and this goes on for an AGE of Brahma composed of alternate ' Days ', and ' Nights ', and lasting 100 years [of 2,160,000,000 (Earth) years each]. It requires fifteen figures to express the duration of such an age; after the expiration of which the *Mahapralaya* or the Great Dissolution sets in, and lasts in its turn for the same space of fifteen figures." q.v. *The Theosophical Glossary,* H. P. Blavatsky.

Buddhi (Sk.): The sixth principle of man, that of intuitive wisdom, vehicle of the seventh, *Atma,* the supreme Soul in man. Universal Soul. The faculty which manifests as spiritual intuitiveness. The bliss Aspect of the Trinity.

Causal Body: The immortal body of the reincarnating Ego of man, built
of matter of the " higher " levels of the mental world. It is called
Causal because it gathers up within it the results of all experiences,
and these act as causes moulding future lives and influencing future
conduct.

Chain: In occult philosophy a Solar System is said to consist of ten Planetary Schemes. Each Scheme, generally named according to its
physically visible representative, is composed of seven Chains of
Globes. In terms of time a Chain consists of the passage of the life-
wave seven times around its seven Globes. Each such passage is
called a Round, the completion of the seventh ending the life of the
Chain. The Globes of a Round are both superphysical and physical
and are arranged in a cyclic pattern, three being on a descending
arc, three on an ascending arc and the middle, the fourth Globe,
being the densest of all and the turning point. The active period of
each of these units, from Solar System to Globe, called *Manvantara*,
is succeeded by a passive period of equal duration, called *Pralaya*.
The completion of the activity of the seventh Globe of the seventh
Round of the seventh Chain brings to an end the activity of a Planetary Scheme. Our Earth Scheme is now in its fourth Round of its
fourth Chain, and the life-wave is half-way through its period of
activity on the fourth Globe, the physical Earth. Thus, the densest
possible condition of substance is now occupied by Spirit and so by
the Monads or Spirits of men. The resistance of matter is at its
greatest in this epoch, and this offers an explanation of the difficulties
of human life at this period. The occupation of a physical planet by
man consists of seven racial epochs and phases of evolutionary development. Throughout this work these are referred to as Root Races.
According to that portion of occult philosophy which is concerned
with the evolution of both the Immortal Soul and the mortal personality of man, an orderly progression is revealed. The basic rule
is stated to be that the indwelling, conscious life in the mineral, plant,
animal and human kingdoms of Nature advances to the kingdom
above during a period of one Chain. Since each Chain is composed
of seven Rounds, each Round is expected to be characterised by
progress through subsidiary stages of the ultimate attainment for the
Chain as a whole. Applied to man, the Monad has evolved Chain
by Chain through mineral (first Chain), plant (second Chain) and
animal (third Chain) into the individualised, self-conscious state
characteristic of a human being of the fourth Chain. This is man's
present position, and by the end of each of the remaining Rounds of
this fourth Chain a certain degree of development will be attained.
These stages chiefly concern the unfoldment of capacity for awareness

and effective action—spiritual, intellectual, cultural and physical. Thus occult anthropology presents an orderly and systematic scheme of development for the life of all kingdoms of Nature.

At the end of the Seventh Root Race of this Fourth Round on Earth the mass of humanity will have achieved the level now known as Initiateship or spiritual regeneration, characterised by Christ-consciousness, which includes both realisation of the unity of life and compassion for all living beings. At the end of the seventh Round the human race now evolving on Earth is expected to achieve the stature of Adeptship or perfected manhood, " the measure of the stature of the fulness of Christ." (Eph. 4: 13). q.v. *The Solar System*, A. E. Powell, and *Lecture Notes of the School of the Wisdom*, Vol. I, Geoffrey Hodson.

Chakra (Sk.): A " wheel " or " disc ". A spinning, vortical, funnel-shaped force-centre with its opening on the surfaces of the etheric and subtler bodies of man and its stem leading to the superphysical counterparts of the spinal cord and of nerve centres or glands. There are seven main *chakras* associated severally with the sacrum, the spleen, the solar plexus, the heart, the throat and the pituitary and pineal glands. *Chakras* are both organs of superphysical consciousness and conveyors of the life-force between the superphysical and physical bodies. q.v. *The Chakras*, C. W. Leadbeater.

Chaos: The term " Chaos " is used in its more philosophic meaning throughout this work to connote, not utter confusion but the following various significations:—the " Abyss ", the " Great Deep ", the pri-mordial, pre-atomic condition in which matter existed before the first atoms and planes of Nature were " created "; primordial space; an infinite, formless void; the root of matter in its first remove from the unknown Absolute; the impenetrable veil between what can be seen by the cognisable eye and the invisible actuality of the first active Logos; the primeval " waters " of life; the Virgin Mother of Cosmos; the divine substance which alone exists throughout all eternity, bound-less and absolute. q.v. *The Theosophical Glossary*, H. P. Blavatsky.

Correspondences: See Law of Correspondences, The.

Cosmocratores (Gr.): " Builders of the Universe ", the " World Architects " or the creative Forces personified.

Creation: The emergence and subsequent development of a Universe and its contents is regarded in occult philosophy as being less the result of an act of creation, followed by natural evolution, than a process of emanation guided by intelligent Forces under immutable Law. The creation or emergence of Universes from nothing is not an accept-able concept, the Cosmos being regarded as emanating from an all-containing, sourceless Source, the Absolute.

Demiurgos (Gr.): The Demiurge or Artificer, the Supernal Power which built the Universe. Freemasons derive from this word their phrase " Supreme Architect ". With the occultist it is the third manifested Logos, or Plato's second God, the second Logos being represented by him as the " Father ", the only Deity that he, as an Initiate of the Mysteries, dare mention. The demiurgic Mind is the same as the Universal Mind, named *Mahat* (Sk.), the first " product " of Brahma.

Devas (Sk.): " Shining ones ", spiritual Beings, Planetary Logoi, and Hierarchies of Archangels and angels. The main stages of *devic* development have each their own name. Nature spirits, like animals and birds, are actuated by a group consciousness shared with others of the same genus. Gods, Sephiras, *devas* and angels have evolved out of group consciousness into separate individuality, as has man. Archangels, especially, have transcended the limitations of individuality and have entered into universal or cosmic consciousness, as has the Superman or Adept.

Dhyan Chohans (Sk.): The " Lords of Contemplation ", the divine Intelligences charged with the supervision of Cosmos.

Dhyani (Sk.): " Expert in Yoga ". Also a generic name for spiritual Beings, Planetary Logoi, and Hierarchies of Archangels and angels. The term *Dhyana* signifies a state of profound contemplation during which the *Dhyanin* becomes united with the highest parts of his own constitution and communes therewith. *Dhyan-Chohans*, " Lords of Contemplation ", are members of the Host of Spiritual Beings Who live in this exalted state and supervise the cyclic evolution of life and form in a Solar System. Monadically, man is an embryo *Dhyan-Chohan*, and at the close of the Planetary Age will himself have become a fully developed " Lord of Contemplation ".

Ego: The threefold, immortal, unfolding spiritual Self of man in its vesture of light, the " Robe of Glory " of the Gnostics and the *Karana Sharira* or Causal Body of Hindu philosophy. This higher Triad evolves to Adeptship by virtue of successive lives on Earth, all linked together because they are reincarnations of the same spiritual Self. Thus the Ego is an individualised manifestation of the Monad, which is the eternal Self of man, the Dweller in the Innermost, a unit of the Spirit-Essence of the Universe. The term is used throughout this work to denote the unfolding spiritual Self of man in which the attribute of individuality inheres. The adjective " Egoic " refers to the Ego in this sense.

Elemental Kingdoms: Three pre-mineral kingdoms are passed through on the involutionary or descending arc which is followed by the radiated monadic Ray. Arrival at the mineral kingdom marks the stage of

deepest descent into matter. Thereafter the upward or evolutionary
arc is entered upon, the plant kingdom being the next embodiment
of the ascending monadic life. This phase is in due course followed
by entry into and passage through the animal, human and superhuman kingdoms. q.v. *Man: Whence, How and Whither*, A. Besant
and C. W. Leadbeater.

Elohim (Heb.): "Gods". A sevenfold power of Godhead, the male-
female Hierarchies of creative Intelligences or Potencies through
which the Divine produces the manifested Universe; the unity of the
powers, the attributes and the creative activities of the Supreme
Being. "Elohim" is a plural name, the singular form of the word
being "Eloha", *i.e.*, a "god". "Elohim", therefore, literally
means "gods", personifications of divine attributes or the forces at
work in Nature. Admittedly the "Elohim" are also conceived as
a Unity in the sense that They all work together as One, expressing
One Will, One Purpose, One Harmony. Thus Their activities are
regarded as the manifestation of the Eternal One, the Absolute.
"Elohim" might therefore be explained as "the Unity of gods" or
"the Activities of the Eternal One", namely God omnipresent and
revealing Himself outwardly in creative activity. Partly paraphrased
from *The Unknown God*, P. J. Mayers.

Fohat (Tib.): "Divine Energy". The constructive force of cosmic electricity, polarised into the positive and negative currents of terrestrial
electricity; the ever-present electrical energy; the universal, propellant,
vital force.

Gnosis (Gr.): Lit. "knowledge". The technical term used by the schools
of religious philosophy, both before and during the first centuries of
so-called Christianity, to denote the object of their enquiry. This
spiritual and sacred knowledge, the *Gupta Vidya* of the Hindus, could
only be obtained by Initiation into Spiritual Mysteries, of which the
ceremonial "Mysteries" were a type.

Gnostics (Gr.): The philosophers who formulated and taught the *Gnosis*
or Knowledge. They flourished in the first three centuries of the
Christian era. The following were eminent: Valentinus, Basilides,
Marcion, Simon Magus, etc.

God: In occult philosophy the term "God" in its highest meaning refers
to a Supreme, Eternal and Indefinable Reality. This Absolute is
inconceivable, ineffable and unknowable. Its revealed existence is
postulated in three terms: an absolute Existence, an absolute Consciousness, and an absolute Bliss. Infinite Consciousness is regarded
as inherent in the Supreme Being as a dynamic Force that manifests
the potentialities held in its own infinitude, and calls into being forms
out of its own formless depths. See also pp. 118 *et seq.*

21

Group Soul: The pre-individualised manifestation of the human Monads when evolving through the mineral, the plant and the animal kingdoms of Nature.   q.v. *A Study in Consciousness*, A. Besant.

Gunas (Sk.): "A string or cord". The three qualities or attributes inherent in matter: *Rajas*, activity, desire; *Sattva*, harmony, rhythm; *Tamas*, inertia, stagnation. These correspond to the three Aspects of the Trinity—Father, Son and Holy Ghost—or Brahma, Vishnu and Shiva respectively.

Hierophant (Gr.): "One who explains sacred things". The discloser of sacred learning and the Chief of the Initiates. A title belonging to the highest Adepts in the temples of antiquity, who were teachers and expounders of the Mysteries and the Initiators into the final great Mysteries.   q.v. *The Theosophical Glossary*, H. P. Blavatsky; *Eleusis and the Eleusinian Mysteries*, George E. Mylanos—refer to Index; *The Eleusinian Mysteries and Rites*, Dundley Wright; *The Mysteries of Eleusis*, Georges Meautis.

Initiate: From the Latin *Initiatus*. The designation of anyone who was received into and had revealed to him the mysteries and secrets of occult philosophy.   q.v. Part VI of Volume I of this work.

Initiation: A profound spiritual and psychological regeneration, as a result of which a new " birth " a new beginning and a new life are entered upon. The word itself, from the Latin *Initia*, also implies the basic or first principles of any science, suggesting that Initiates are consciously united with their own First Principle, the Monad from which they emerged. Both the Lesser and the Greater Mysteries, ancient and modern, confer Initiations of various Degrees upon successful Candidates.

Kabbalah (Heb.): From QBLH, "an unwritten or oral tradition". The hidden wisdom of the Hebrew Rabbis derived from the secret doctrine of the early Hebrew peoples.   q.v. *The Kingdom of the Gods*, Pt. III, Ch. IV, Geoffrey Hodson, and Appendix to this Volume.

Kama (Sk.): "Desire", feeling, emotion. See Astral.

Karma (Sk.): "Action", connoting both the law of action and re-action, cause and effect, and the results of its operation upon nations and individuals.   q.v. *Reincarnation, Fact or Fallacy?*, Geoffrey Hodson.

Kether (Heb.): "The Crown", the first Sephira of the Kabbalistic Sephirothal Tree, which "gives birth to" the nine others, the last or tenth being called Malkuth, the Kingdom, meaning all Nature manifested. Together the ten Sephiras represent the emanation and development of the powers and attributes of Deity. Each Number is an outward symbol for inner creative forces and processes, and their personifications as Archangels or Builders of the Universe.

Kumaras (Sk.): " Beings of original spiritual purity ". The four great Beings in the Occult Hierarchy of Adepts Who help on the evolution of humanity; also applied to the Ever-Virgin Youth and His disciples, Who are said in occult philosophy to have founded the Adept Hierarchy on this planet. *Sanat Kumara* is the name given to this deeply revered Head or Chief of Earth's Adepts. q.v. *Lecture Notes of the School of the Wisdom,* Vol. I (Rev. Ed.), Ch. XVI, Sec. 4, Geoffrey Hodson.

Kundalini (Sk.): " The coiled up, universal Life Principle ". A sevenfold, superphysical, occult power in Universe and man, functioning in the latter by means of a spiral or coiling action, mainly in the spinal cord but also throughout the nervous systems. It is represented in Greek symbology by the Caduceus. When supernormally aroused this fiery force ascends into the brain by a serpentine path, hence its other name, the " Serpent Fire ". q.v. *The Hidden Wisdom in the Holy Bible,* Vol. I, Pt. III, Ch. I under " Serpents "; *Lecture Notes of the School of the Wisdom,* Vol. II, Ch. I, Sec. III, Geoffrey Hodson; *The Serpent Power,* Arthur Avalon (Sir John Woodroffe).

Kundalini Shakti (Sk.): The power of life; one of the forces of Nature. The occult electricity intimately associated with Azoth of the Alchemists, the creative principle in Nature, and *Akasa* (Sk.), the subtle, supersensuous, spiritual essence which pervades all space. The seven-layered power in the base of the spine of man, composed of three currents which flow along three canals in the spinal cord, named *Ida* (negative), *Pingala* (positive) and *Sushumna* (neutral). These names are sometimes also applied—erroneously—to the currents of force which flow in these canals. q.v. *The Kingdom of the Gods,* Geoffrey Hodson.

Law of Correspondence, The: The harmonious co-ordination or mutual resonance between the many apparently separate parts of the Universe and corresponding parts of the constitution of man. Occult philosophy teaches that all components of both Macrocosm and microcosm are interwoven and interactive according to a universal system of vibrational interchange. In his spiritual, intellectual, psychical and physical make-up man is regarded as a miniature replica or epitome of the whole Order of created beings and things, a model of the totality of Nature. He is said to contain within himself the collective aggregate of all that has ever existed, does at any time exist and will ever exist throughout the eternity of eternities. The Chinese philosopher Lao Tzu expressed this in his words: " The Universe is a man on a large scale." Eliphas Levi quotes from the *Kabbalah*: " The mystery of the earthly and mortal man is after the mystery of the supernal and immortal one." This view is indeed basic to

Kabbalism, which affirms that man may be regarded as a symbolic transparency through which the secrets of the Cosmos may be discerned. In the Bible one reads: ". . . God said, Let us make man in our image, after our likeness. . . ." (*Gen.* 1: 26) Inspired allegories may, therefore, and indeed should, be equally understood in both the Macrocosmic and the microcosmic senses.

Light: To be regarded as the divine Intelligence, the first Emanation of the Supreme, that light which according to the Gospel of St. John is the life of men. Not to be confused with the light of the sun, which is a focus or lens by which the rays of the primordial light become materialised and concentrated upon our Solar System and produce all the correlations of forces. The criticism that light appeared three days before the sun is thus disposed of.

Lingam (Sk.): Physically, the phallus. A symbol of abstract creation and of the divine, masculine, procreative force.

Lipikas (Sk.): The Celestial Recorders, the Agents of *karma*. Exoterically four and esoterically seven great " Scribes ". The Lords of Karma Who, as far as man is concerned, adjust beneficence and adversity resulting from former deeds.

Logos (Gr.): " The Word ", " A divine, spiritual Entity ". The manifested Deity, the outward expression or effect of the ever-concealed Cause. Thus speech is the *Logos* of thought, and *Logos* is correctly translated into Latin as *Verbum* and into English as " Word " in the metaphysical sense. See *Vach*.

Logos Doctrine: The Universe is first conceived in divine Thought, which is the governing power in creation. The creative " Word " expressive of the idea is then " spoken " and the hitherto quiescent seeds of living things germinate and appear from within the ocean of Space, the Great Deep. q.v. *Lecture Notes of the School of the Wisdom*, Vol. II, Pt. 2, Sec. 2, Geoffrey Hodson.

Macrocosm (Gr.): Literally " Great Universe " or Cosmos.

Maha-Chohan (Sk.): " Great Lord "; also descriptive of a Grade of Adeptship, that of the Seventh Initiation. q.v. *Lecture Notes of the School of the Wisdom*, Vol. I (Rev. Ed.), Ch. XVI, Secs. 3 and 5, Geoffrey Hodson.

Maha-Manvantara (Sk.): " Great interlude between the *Manus* or Creative *Logoi*." The major, total period of universal activity which includes numberless inner cycles, finite and conditioned or minor periods called *Manvantaras*. A day of Brahma lasts 100 " years ", each of which occupies a period of 2,160,000,000 (Earth) years, according to Hindu cosmogonical chronology. It requires fifteen figures to express the duration of such an age. q.v. *The Theosophical Glossary*, H. P. Blavatsky.

Manas (Sk.): " Mind ". Generally used in reference to the planes of Nature built of mind-stuff, and to the mental faculties of man.

Mantras (Sk.): Verses from the *Vedas* rhythmically arranged so that, when sounded, certain vibrations are generated, producing desired effects upon the physical and superphysical bodies of *Mantra* Yogis and the atmosphere surrounding them.

Manu (Sk.): " Thought ". A generic term applied to Creators, Preservers and Fashioners. *Manvantara* means, literally, the period presided over by a *Manu*. According to their function and Office they are called Race, Seed, Round and Chain *Manus*, and so on up to the Solar Logos Himself. *Pralaya*, on the other hand, is a period of obscuration or repose, whether planetary or universal—the opposite of *Manvantara*—and is symbolised in *Genesis* and in all flood legends by their deluges.

Manvantara (Sk.): " Period between *Manus* ". Epoch of creative activity. A period of manifestation, as opposed to *Pralaya* (see preceding reference to *Manu* and also under Chain).

Medium: One who acts as a channel of transmission. A person whose Etheric Double is less closely knitted to the dense physical body than is the case with non-mediums. Such a condition renders the medium susceptible to the withdrawal of the substance of the Etheric Double and its use in producing physical phenomena. The procedure is aided by the voluntary submission of the medium's mind and will to such invisible entities as may be producing the occurrences. This extreme passivity also tends to lead to various degrees of unconsciousness in the medium, ranging from partial to complete trance. In these conditions the medium loses all control of both mind and body and is generally but not always, depending upon the degree of trance, unaware of what may be taking place. As a method of self-spiritualisation, of attaining self-mastery and of discovering truth, the surrender of oneself to an invisible entity is not recommended by occultists. Some disadvantages are: the serious weakening, up to complete loss, of the control of the personality by the Immortal Self; the likelihood of self-delusion; and the danger of becoming obsessed, and even driven insane, as the result of psychic invasion by undesirable, lower astral entities.

Mercavah or *Mercaba* (Heb.): " chariot ". According to Kabbalists the Supreme Lord, after He had established the Ten Sephiroth, used Them as a chariot or throne of glory on which to descend upon the souls of men. Also a hidden doctrine delivered only as a mystery orally, " face to face and mouth to ear ". q.v. *Appendix, The Sephirothal Tree.*

Microcosm (Gr.): "Little Universe". The reflection in miniature of the Macrocosm. Thus the atom may be spoken of as the " microcosm " of the Solar System, its electrons moving under the same laws; and man may be termed the " microcosm " of the Universe, since he has wi hin himself all the elements of that Universe.

Moksha (Sk.): " To release ". The state attained when a man becomes a *Dhyan-Chohan*. One who is thus released is called a *Jivanmukta* (Sk.), " freed " spirit. Liberation from the delusion of self-separateness (Hinduism).

Monad (Gr.): " Alone ". The divine Spirit in man, the " Dweller in the Innermost ", which is said to evolve through the sub-human kingdoms of Nature into the human and thence to the stature of the Adept, beyond which extend unlimited evolutionary heights. The description of the destiny of man given by the Lord Christ supports this concept, for He said: " Be ye (Ye shall be—R. V.) therefore perfect, even as your Father which is in heaven is perfect." (*Matt.* 5: 48—A. V.).

Monad-Ego: A dual term used in this work to connote the individualised manifestation of the human Monad as triple Spirit, the Higher Triad, in a vesture of light or " Robe of Glory ", the Causal Body. The Divine Spark or Dweller in the Innermost (Monad) which in the course of evolution has attained to self-conscious individuality as man (Ego) and during life on Earth is embodied in vehicles of mind, emotion and flesh.

Mulaprakriti (Sk.): " Root matter ", " undifferentiated substance ". The abstract, deific, feminine principle, the *Parabrahmic* root. *Prakriti* (Sk.). Nature or matter as opposed to Spirit, the two primeval aspects of the One Unknown Deity.

Mysteries, The: From Muo (Gr.), " to close the mouth ", *Teletai* (Gr.), " Celebrations of Initiation ". The Sacred Mysteries were enacted in the ancient Temples by the initiated Hierophants for the benefit and instruction of the Candidates. A series of secret dramatic performances, in which the mysteries of cosmogony and Nature were personified by the priests and neophytes. These were explained in their hidden meaning to the Candidates for Initiation. q.v. *Eleusis and the Eleusinian Mysteries*, George E. Mylonas; *The Eleusinian and Bacchic Mysteries*, Thomas Taylor; *The Mysteries of Eleusis*, Georges Méautis, Professor at the University of Neuchatel.

Nirvana (Sk.): " Having life extinguished ". Conscious absorption in the One Life of the Cosmos, or absolute consciousness (Buddhism).

No-thing: From the point of view of finite intelligence, the Kabbalistic *Ain Soph*, " No-thing ", the Absolute.

Occultist: A student of the " hidden " powers, forces and intelligences in Nature. Whilst necromancy may—very undesirably—be resorted to by such a student, the practice is frowned upon by all teachers of white or wholly altruistic occultism. These point out that the discovery of truth demands increasing self-control, and that any surrender of one's will to another leads to self-delusion and untruth.

All researches motived by the twin ideals of attaining knowledge and so of becoming more helpful to mankind are, in consequence, carried out whilst in command of mind and will. The power to produce occult phenomena is developed by self-training, but these are always the result of the will and thought of the operator employed in that full consciousness and complete self-command which are essential to success.

Occult Science: " The science of the secrets of nature—physical and psychic, mental and spiritual; called Hermetic and Esoteric Sciences. In the West, the Kabbalah may be named; in the East, mysticism, magic, and Yoga philosophy, which latter is often referred to by the Chelas in India as the *seventh* ' Darshana ' (school of philosophy), there being only *six Darshanas* in India known to the world of the profane. These sciences are, and have been for ages, hidden from the vulgar for the very good reason that they would never be appreciated by the selfish educated classes, nor understood by the uneducated; which the former might misuse them for their own profit, and thus turn the divine science into *black magic*. . . ." q.v. *The Theosophical Glossary*, H. P. Blavatsky.

Where subjects dealt with in the text pertain more to philosophy than to science, the term " occult philosophy " is used. In general, however, the two terms may be regarded as synonymous. The words " according to my limited understanding and interpretation of their teachings " are to be regarded as implicit in all references to these two aspects of the Secret Doctrine wherever they occur throughout this work. Chief sources drawn upon: the literature of I Ching, Taoism and Confucianism; the *Vedas*, the *Upanishads*, the *Puranas*, the *Vedanta* and other philosophical systems of Hinduism; Zoroastrian, Egyptian, Greek and Roman religions and philosophies; Celtic and Nordic Mythologies; the *Kabbalah*; Hebrew Scriptures and Commentaries; *The Secret Doctrine* and other books by H. P. Blavatsky; additional works as indicated in the Bibliography.

Om or *Aum* (Sk.): The name of the triple Deity. A syllable of affirmation, invocation and divine benediction.

One Life, The: " It is the ONE LIFE, eternal, invisible, yet omnipresent, without beginning or end, yet periodical in its regular manifestations —between which periods reigns the dark mystery of Non-Being;

unconscious, yet absolute Consciousness, unrealisable, yet the one self-existing Reality; truly ' A Chaos to the sense, a Kosmos to the reason.' " q.v. *The Secret Doctrine*, Vol. I, (Adyar Ed.), p. 70, H. P. Blavatsky.

Parabrahm (Sk.): " Beyond Brahma ". The Supreme, Infinite Brahma, the " Absolute ", attributeless, secondless Reality, the impersonal, nameless, universal and Eternal Principle. Brahman (Sk.). The impersonal, supreme and incognisable Principle of the Universe, from the Essence of which all emanates and into which all returns. q.v. *The Theosophical Glossary*, H. P. Blavatsky, and other sources.

Pentateuch: *Penta* (Gr.): " five " and *teukhos*, " books ". The first five books of the Old Testament.

Pitris (Sk.): " Forefathers ", " progenitors ". Highly evolved, incorporeal, spiritual beings, products of preceding evolutionary epochs, who build for the Monad the mental, emotional, etheric and physical vehicles whereby it is brought into touch with the external worlds at these levels and is enabled to act and evolve in them. Three of the ten main classes of *Pitris* referred to in Hindu philosophy (*Vishnu Purana*) are the *Asuras* who build the mental bodies, the *Agnishvattas* who build the emotional bodies and the *Barhishads* who build the etheric and physical bodies. Other classes are named *Kumaras* and *Manasaputras*. The *Pitris* are also referred to as the Fathers who set the types for mankind at the beginning of the various great periods of solar and planetary evolution.

Plenty and Famine: Periods of plenty can refer symbolically to ages or epochs of the full manifestation of the divine power, life and consciousness in a Universe or any of its components, and this can apply to Solar System, Race or nation. The withdrawal of the hitherto outpoured life, on the other hand, symbolises famine. Activity and rest, expression and cessation, and other similar pairs of opposites are described in the Sacred Language as alternations of plenty and famine respectively. Plenty, mystically interpreted and applied to civilisations, nations and smaller groups as well as to persons, also typifies fullness of spiritual experience insofar as evolutionary attainment permits. Famine, from this point of view, is used to imply limitation—and even absence—of interior illumination. Within the major cycles of a nation's inception, rise, attainment of greatest height and gradual decline, minor cycles which repeat those phases can also occur. A study of the history of nations throughout a sufficient period of time leads to the discovery that they have passed through such major and minor cycles. Culture, philosophy and religion can reach their height (plenty) during a minor period, later to be followed by gross superstition, materialism and concentration upon physical existence and enjoyment (famine). Similarly, during his lifetime a man can also experience times of upliftment and aspiration which alternate with conditions of spiritual deadness and cf concentration, sometimes enforced, upon the concerns of physical life. Even the greatest mystics who have described their spiritual enlightenment refer to this alternation of periods of interior illumination and mental darkness. As we have seen, plenty and famine are used in the Sacred Language as symbols for these two opposing and alternating conditions.

Prakriti (Sk.): Primary original substance; the productive element from and out of which all material manifestations or appearances are evolved; Nature in general as the " producer " of beings and things, with Spirit (*Purusha*) as the ever-active Creator; the veil of *Purusha*, the two in reality being one.

Pralaya: " Epoch of quiescence ". A period of obscuration or repose, whether planetary or universal. There are said to be four kinds of *Pralayas* or such states of changelessness: cosmic *Pralaya*, when the totality of manifested Universes is dissolved; partial *Pralaya*, referring to any component which is dissolved during *Maha-Manvantara*; human *Pralaya*, when man has identified himself with the One Absolute or entered *Nirvana*; and physical *Pralaya*, as in a state of profound and dreamless sleep. *Pralaya*, then, refers to the period when the life of a Globe, Round, Chain or Solar System is partially or completely indrawn, activity or manifestation ceasing in part or in whole. A *Pralaya* of a single Planet—corresponding somewhat to Winter—is a minor *Pralaya*, that of a Solar System a *Maha-Pralaya*, and a general dissolution of the whole Cosmic System a *Prakritika-Pralaya*. During a minor *Pralaya* " the Planets remain intact, though dead, just as a huge animal, caught and embedded in polar ice, remains the same for ages." Readers unaccustomed to the idea that our Solar System is but one in both a number and a succession of such may find strange the affirmation in occult philosophy that the present Solar System was preceded by an unknown number cf precursors, and in its turn will be followed by an infinite number of successors. As in the past, each of these will in the future progress along an evolutionary spiral towards ever greater degrees of the development of its indwelling life and consciousness, and its individual intelligences. q.v. *The Secret Doctrine*, p. 146 (Original Edition).

Pre-Initiate: The psycho-spiritual transformation known as Initiation, at which realisation of the oneness of all life is attained, is accompanied by ceremonial admission to the Greater Mysteries and marks a definite evolutionary stage. The term " pre-Initiate man " used throughout this work designates those who have not yet reached that stature.

Purusha (Sk.): " Man " as " The Heavenly Man " or Adam Kadmon of Kabbalism; " The Great Breath "; the masculine creative potency in Cosmogenesis (*Prakriti*—matter—being the feminine potency); an interchangeable term with *Brahma*, the " Creator ", the everlasting, divine, spiritual Self, the Monad, whether of a Universe, a Solar System or an individual entity such as man.

Ring-pass-not: The outermost edge or limits marked out by the Logos within Which His System is to appear.   Macrocosmically, the presumed boundary within which is contained the consciousness of all beings evolving within the circumscribed field or area of Space. Microcosmically, the Auric Envelope.   Applied solely to states of consciousness, this term signifies the circles or frontiers, great or small, to which realisation and awareness are limited.   In the course of evolution each entity reaches successive stages of unfoldment, out of which its consciousness cannot pass to the conditions attained at later or higher phases of development.   This applies to beings at all degrees of growth, from animal to Solar Deity, each having a limit to its range of awareness, this being appropriate to its evolutionary stature.   For animals the Ring-Pass-Not is Self-consciousness, which they lack.   For man it concerns full spiritual Self-awareness and ability to realise dimensions of space beyond the normal three.   These limitations may also be regarded as portals or " points of transmission " leading from one plane of existence to another.

Round: See Chain.

Ruach (Heb.): " Breath, spirit, wind, expansion, spiritualisation."

Salvation: Exoterically, redemption or the state of being saved; esoterically, realisation of oneness with God (Christianity).

Sanat Kumara: See Kumaras.

Sephira (Heb.): An emanation of Deity.   See Appendix, *The Sephirothal Tree*.

Serpent Fire: See *Kundalini* and *Kundalini Shakti*.

Seven Rays, The: A term used in occult philosophy for the seven main classes of Monads and the powers, qualities and weaknesses by which they are expressed in the seven differing types of human beings.   q.v. *The Seven Rays*, Ernest Wood, and *The Seven Human Temperaments*, Geoffrey Hodson.

Shakti (Sk.): " Ability ", " power ", capability, faculty, strength.   The outgoing energy of a god is spoken of as his wife or *shakti*.   Thus, although a Deity or a central personage and his consort or wife are presented as two separate people, the latter (wife) actually personifies attributes or powers of the former (husband).   In consequence, the supposed pair in reality represent one being.

Siddhis (Sk.): " Occult powers developed by *Yoga*."

Skandhas (Sk.): " Groups of innate attributes " of the finite which endure between macrocosmic manifestations and microcosmic incarnations, uniting and re-appearing as inherent qualities at the dawn of *Manvantaras* and at each human birth.

Soul: When spelt with a capital " S " this word refers to the unfolding, immortal, spiritual Self of man, the true individuality behind the bodily veil. When spelt with a small " s " it is used for the *psyche* or mental, emotional, vital and solid physical parts of the mortal man. Heb. *Nephesh Chaiah*, " souls of life " or " living soul ". (*Gen.* 2: 7).

Spirit: Not an entity but that which belongs directly to Universal Consciousness. The most tenuous, formless and immaterial spiritual substance, the divine Essence.

Squaring the Circle: The circle represents the boundless ALL and the square the limited, temporary form. To square the circle is to resolve the elements of individuality back into their universal freedom, to liberate the centre of divine consciousness or spiritual awareness, which is man, from its particular to its universal existence.

Sun: In occult philosophy the physical sun is regarded as the densest of the seven vehicles of the Solar Logos, the mighty Being in Whom and by Whom the Solar System exists. The other six vehicles are said to be constructed of superphysical matter of decreasing degrees of density, and to be sheaths and centres for the radiation of the power, life and consciousness of the Solar Logos.

Sutratma (Sk.): " Thread-self ". A current of spiritual life-force, a golden thread of continuous life upon which the seed atoms or nuclei of the seven bodies of man are " strung ". q.v. *A Study in Consciousness*, A. Besant.

Tarot, The: A pack of seventy-two cards, for a long time in the possession of the Gipsy people. Much altered in modern versions, they are exoterically regarded as of relatively recent, though unknown, origin. An esoteric view of them is that they represent an extremely ancient pictorial and symbolic presentation of the deepest occult and spiritual mysteries concerning God, man, the Universe, and the relationship between them. According to this view they are a symbolic and pictorial text book of the Ageless Wisdom—a veritable Bible. Their origin is variously traced to Egypt, India, Tibet and China. The religious art of the ancient peoples of each of those countries displays examples of the cards in a modified form. The meaning of the word *Tarot* is not decisively known, it having been associated with the Egyptian Deity *Ptah* and with the word *Ta* (Path) *Ro* (Royal), meaning the royal path of life. The ancient hieroglyphic Egyptian word *Tara* (to require an answer or to consult) is also considered as a possible origin of the word. In another view the word *Taro* is associated with the divinity *Ashtaroth*, in its turn supposedly derived from the Indo-Tartar *tan-tara*, the *Tarot*, the Zodiac. q.v. *The Tarot*, Paul Foster Case, and other works.

Tattva (Sk.): " The abstract principle of substance ", physical and super-physical. The subtle elements. The essential nature of things. " That-ness " or " quiddity ". *Mahatattva*, the first differentiation of pre-cosmic space.

Torah (Heb.): " Law ". The *Pentateuch* or Law of Moses.

Vach: The mystic personification of speech. The female Logos, one with *Brahma*, Who created " Her " out of one half of " His " body. Also called " the Female Creator ". Esoterically the subjective force emanating from the creative Deity.

Waste: The arena of purely material life.

Yuga (Sk.): An age of the world. The *Kali* or dark *Yuga* is the turning or balancing point of materiality in a series of seven cycles or racial epochs, each with its four ages. According to Hindu philosophy as expounded in the *Puranas, Kali Yuga* began in the year 3,102 B.C., at the moment of Shri Krishna's death. Each *Yuga* is preceded by an epoch called in the *Puranas Sandhya*, " twilight " or " transition " period, and is followed by another age of like duration called *Sandhyansa*, " portion of twilight ". Each of these is equal to one-tenth of the *Yuga* and in consequence, in accordance with this ancient system of chronology, the Earth is now in the " portion of twilight " of *Kali Yuga*, the dark or iron age. Hence, presumably, the difficulties to which the human Race has been and is still subject.

Zohar: " The Book of Splendour ", the basic work of Jewish Mysticism, the greatest exposition of the *Kabbalah*.

BIBLIOGRAPHY

Book of Dead: Budge, E. A. Wallis.
Collected Poems: Stephens, James. (Macmillan & Co., London, 1931).
First Principles of Theosophy: Jinarajadasa, C.
Gloria in Excelsis, The
Hidden Wisdom in the Holy Bible, The: Vols. I and II, Hodson, Geoffrey.
Idyll of the White Lotus: Collins, Mabel.
Idylls of the King: Tennyson, A.
Isis Unveiled: Blavatsky, H. P.
Jewish Encyclopaedia, The
Kingdom of the Gods, The: Hodson, Geoffrey.
Lecture Notes of the School of the Wisdom: Vols. I & II, Hodson, Geoffrey.
Mahatma Letters, The: Sinnett, A. P.
Major Trends in Jewish Mysticism: Scholem, Gershom, G.
Man Visible and Invisible: Leadbeater, C. W.
Message of the Scrolls, The: Yodin, Yigall (Gussett & Dunlop, N.Y.).
Occult Powers in Nature and in Man: Hodson, Geoffrey.
Origin of Species: Darwin, C. A.
Pistis Sophia: Mead, G. R. S.
Reincarnation, Fact or Fallacy?: Hodson, Geoffrey.
Secret Doctrine, The: (Adyar Ed.) Blavatsky, H. P. (Theosophical Publishing
    House, Adyar, Madras, India).
Seven Human Temperaments, The: Hodson, Geoffrey.
Symbolism of Numbers.
Tarot, The: Case, Paul Foster.
Theosophical Glossary, The: Blavatsky, H. P.
Through the Gateway of Death: Hodson, Geoffrey.
Voice of the Silence, The: Blavatsky, H. P.
Zohar: (Various Translations): Scholem, Gershom, G.

BIBLIOGRAPHY

Book of Dead, Budge, E. A. Wallis.

Collected Poems, Stephens, James, Macmillan & Co., London, 1927.

First Principles of Theosophy, Jinarajadasa, C

Gita in Outline, The.

Hidden Treasures in the Holy Bible, The, Vols. 1 and 11, Hodson, Geoffrey.

Indus of the Divine Name, Collins, Mabel.

Hymns of the Rigveda, Griffith, A.

Idyll of the White Lotus, H. P.

Jacob's Descending, The.

Kingdom of the Gods, The, Hodson, Geoffrey.

Lecture Notes of the School of the Wisdom, Vols. 1 & 11, Hodson, Geoffrey.

Mahabharata Story, The, Sastri, A. P.

Moon Teachings, Jacob's Wandering, Solution, Geoffrey, C.

New Truths and Realities, Leadbeater, C. W.

Meaning of the Sounds, The, Veda, Sigall Canon & Dunlop, A. ?

Occult Poetry in Shakespeare (?), Mead, Hodson, Geoffrey.

Origin of Species, Darwin, C. A.

Petra Sophia, Mead, G. R. S.

Reincarnation, Fact or Fallacy?, Hodson, Geoffrey.

Secret Doctrine, The, Adyar Ed., Blavatsky, H. P., Theosophical Publishing House, Adyar, Madras, India.

Seven Human Temperaments, The, Hodson, Geoffrey.

Symbolism of Vowels.

Tertium Quid, Case, Paul Foster.

Theosophical Glossary, The, Blavatsky, H. P.

Through the Gateway of Death, Hodson, Geoffrey.

Voice of the Silence, The, Blavatsky, H. P.

Vishnu, various Translations; Scholtie, Geoffrey, C.

INDEX

A

AB, 308
Abelmizraim, 297
Abimelech, 62, 66, 67
Abraham, 41, 80, 109, 244-5, 298, 299; death and burial, 56; God (of), 67, 81, 129, 132, 140, 282; and Sarah, 291
Abram, 84
Absolute, 54, 82, 85, 100, 213
Absolute Deity, 186
Abstract intellect, 266
Achilles, 59, 150
Acquarius, 311
Adept (see also Initiate, Master), 49, 82 88, 105, 138, 146, 164, 285, 299; attainments, 29, 146; Brotherhood, 146-7, 292
Adeptship, 46, 48, 64, 153, 187, 220, 225, 257, 275, 299
Adi plane, 94
Adi-tattva, 58
Adonais, 44, 192
Agape, 35, 133
Ahab, 74
Ahamkara, 202
Ahuzzath, 67
Ani, 54; Nothing, or, 305
Ain-Soph, 100; limitless without form, 305, 307
Ain-Soph Aur—limitless light, 305, 306, 307
Air, 93
Aishim, 311
Akasa, 93, 96
Akasa-tattva, 96
Alexander, 255
Alice Through the Looking-Glass, 195
All, 54
Allegory, 23; teachers used language of, 4; veil of, xi, 4, 21, 87, 110, 153, 157, 213, 240, 292, 300; of arisings from pits and sepulchres, 74-5; of Butler's dream, 215; of Cosmogenesis, 91, 98, 155; of creative process, 154; of cycles 74, 78, 89; of deaths and burials, 74; of descents into pits, 74; of emasculations, 164; of entombments 74; of Esau, 60, 65; of feeding five thousand, 35; of evolution, 25; of femmes fatales, 74; of flood, 30; freedom from bondage, 74; of Isaac and Esau's deception, 40, 71-2, 78; of Isaac's life and old age, 70-1; of Jacob wrestles a " man ", 149; of Jacob's journey into Padanaram, 116; Jacob's marriages, 86, 102, 107, 111; of Joseph into pit, 183;

of Story of Joseph, 45, 183, 187, 241; of Joseph's brothers hatred, 193; of Joseph's coat of many colours, 191; of Laban's pursuit of Jacob, 123, 125; of Logos doctrine, 90-1; of marriages, 85; of Nativities of (world) Saviours, 49; of Prodigal son (parable), 178; of Rebekah and Jacob, 40, 71-2; of revelations of occult truths by, 18; of speech, 173; of spirit and matter, 74; of succession to power, 75-6; of successions through heirs, 74; of surrender of possession, 278; of Torah, 145; of trickery and deception, 71-2, 124, 167
Allon-bachuth, 172
Ama, 308
Amorite, 283
Angelus Silesius, 267
Angel(s), 146, 282; in Christianity, 305-6, 311; National, 305; Orders of, 303, 305
Angelic, Heirarchy, 78, 200, 283
Annunciation, 21, 153, 164
Angelic, 57
Apas, 119
Apocryphal New Testament, The, M. R. James, 34
Apollo, 208
Aquarius, 266, 273, 287
Arbah, 176
Archangels, 146, 282, 305, 306, 311 Orders of, 287
Archetype(al) idea, 145
Arelim, 308
Argonauts, 25, 217
Aries, 273, 290
Ark, 30, 93
Ark of the Covenant, 307
Armageddon, 294
Arnold, Edwin (Sir), 234
Arupa, 112
Aryan Race, 111
Ascension, 23, 187
Asenath, 184, 230
Asher, 105
Assiah, 304
Astrology, science of, 105, 111
Atad, 297
Atma, 60, 61, 76, 78, 97, 197, 198, 254
Atmic, consciousness, 151 fire, 114, 142; power, 77; ray, 65
Atziluth, 304
Auckland Star, The, 12
Augoeides, 18, 186, 190
Aum, xiv, 147

T